The Community Performance Reader

The Community Performance Reader brings together core writings and critical approaches to community performance work, presenting practices in the United Kingdom, the United States, Australia and beyond. This volume offers a complex and comprehensive anthology of key writings in the vibrant field of community performance, spanning dance, theatre and visual practices.

The *Reader* uniquely combines classic writings from major theorists and practitioners such as Augusto Boal, Paolo Freire, Dwight Conquergood and Jan Cohen-Cruz, with newly commissioned essays that bring the anthology right up to date with current practice.

This book can be used as a stand-alone text or, together with its companion volume, *Community Performance: An Introduction*, to offer an accessible and classroom-friendly introduction to the field of community performance.

Petra Kuppers is a community artist, a disability culture activist and Associate Professor of English, Theatre and Women's Studies, University of Michigan. She is the author of *Disability and Contemporary Performance: Bodies on Edge* (2003), *The Scar of Visibility: Medical Performance and Contemporary Art* (2007) and *Community Performance: An Introduction* (2007).

Gwen Robertson is Associate Professor of Art History at Humboldt State University specializing in twentieth-century and contemporary art.

The
Community
Performance
Reader

■ Edited by

Petra Kuppers
and
Gwen Robertson

Routledge
Taylor & Francis Group

LONDON AND NEW YORK

First published 2007
by Routledge
2 Park Square, Milton Park, Abingdon, Oxon OX14 4RN

Simultaneously published in the USA and Canada
by Routledge
270 Madison Ave, New York, NY 10016

Reprinted 2008

Routledge is an imprint of the Taylor & Francis Group, an informa business

Typeset in Perpetua and Helvetica by
Florence Production Ltd, Stoodleigh, Devon

British Library Cataloguing in Publication Data
A catalogue record for this book is available from the British Library

Library of Congress Cataloging in Publication Data
The community performance reader/edited by Petra Kuppers and
Gwen Robertson.
    p. cm.
  Includes bibliographical references and index.
  1. Performing arts – Social aspects.   I. Kuppers, Petra.
  II. Robertson, Gwen.
  PN1590.S6C66   2007
  792.02′2—dc22   2006027283

ISBN10: 0–415–39230–6 (hbk)
ISBN10: 0–415–39231–4 (pbk)

ISBN13: 978–0–415–39230–3 (hbk)
ISBN13: 978–0–415–39231–0 (pbk)

Contents

Illustrations

Planting. Workshop in the Catlins, Southland Region, New Zealand.

Photo: Petra Kuppers.

Contributors

Diane Amans is a dance artist and director of Freedom in Dance, a UK company specialising in work with older people and intergenerational groups. Her career has included working in education, managing dance projects in health and community settings, choreographing work for community groups and contributing to continuing professional development of staff in the arts, health, social care and industry. Diane has carried out research into community dance practice in England and produces training materials and resource packs for artists working in participatory dance contexts.

Jessica Berson is a Lecturer in Drama at the University of Exeter, and previously taught at Wesleyan University and Grinnell College. A Certified Laban Movement Analyst, she received her Ph.D. from the University of Wisconsin-Madison, where she studied with Sally Banes. Jessica is also a dance artist who has focused on youth and intergenerational performance, and is interested in exploring the intersections of artistic and social concerns in community performance.

Marcia Blumberg teaches Theatre at York University in Toronto, Canada. She has published many articles and is the co-editor with Dennis Walder of *South African Theatre As/And Intervention* (1999).

Augusto Boal is a Brazilian theatre director, writer and politician, and his publishing credits include the influential *Theatre of the Oppressed* (1971), *Games for Actors and Non-Actors* (1992), *The Rainbow of Desire* (1995), and *Legislative Theatre* (1998). A major influence on community theatre developments and beyond, Boal continues to teach internationally.

Nicolas Bourriaud is a French curator and art critic. His major publications include *Postproduction* (2005) and *Relational Aesthetics* (1998). He rose to international prominence through the 1995 exhibition 'Traffic' (shown at the CAPC in Bordeaux) where he first outlined his idea of 'relational aesthetics'. Throughout his work, Bourriaud has shown a strong interest in artists whose work is committed to interpersonal relations and social exchange rather than representation alone.

Rebecca Caines is a performance maker and new researcher, currently completing her Ph.D. at the School of Media, Film and Theatre, at the University of NSW in Sydney, Australia. Her background is in facilitating, writing and producing for multi-media young people's performance in regional Australia; and in research and publication in the field of Australian and Canadian site-specific, community-based 'guerrilla' performance.

Jan Cohen-Cruz is Associate Professor at New York University Tisch School of the Arts, coordinating the Drama Department's Minor in Applied Theatre. He wrote *Local Acts: Community-Based Performance in the United States* (2005), edited *Radical Street Performance* and, with Mady Schutzman, co-edited *Playing Boal: Theatre, Therapy, Activism* and *A Boal Companion: Dialogues on Art and Cultural Politics*.

Dwight Conquergood was a distinguished scholar, educator, film-maker and community activist, and chair of the Northwestern University, Department of Performance Studies; and he was to serve as Director of the Center for Interdisciplinary Research in the Arts. As an ethnographer, he worked extensively in international refugee camps and in immigrant neighborhoods in Chicago.

Glenda Dickerson is Director of Center for World Performance Studies, and Professor of Theatre at the University of Michigan. She has more than twenty years' experience as a professional director and writer.

Gerard Delanty is Professor of Sociology at the University of Liverpool. His books include *Community* (2003), *Challenging Knowledge: The University in the Knowledge Society* (2001) and *Citizenship in the Global Age: Culture, Society and Politics* (2000). Delanty also serves as chief editor of the *European Journal of Social Theory*.

Eugene van Erven lives in the Netherlands and is an expert in Asian political theatre and international community theatre. He is the author of *Community Theatre: Global Perspectives* and *Radical People's Theatre*.

Ana Flores is a sculptor, environmentalist and community arts advocate who lives in southern Rhode Island and Nova Scotia, Canada. She is Artist in Residence at the Kettle Pond Visitor Center in Charlestown RI, the Rhode Island headquarters for the US Fish & Wildlife Service. Her work has been shown throughout the United States, New Zealand and Canada, and she is represented by the Alva Gallery in New London.

Paulo Freire was a Brazilian educator whose theories and practices of empowerment have influenced pedagogues and others around the world. His *Pedagogy of the Oppressed* (1973), one of many books written by him, remains a core text for understanding the dynamics of political voice and literacy.

Terry Galloway is a deaf, queer writer and performer who writes and performs. She has been a visiting artist at the California Institute of the Arts and the University of Texas in Austin and has received grants in both writing and performance from the NEA, Texas Institute of Letters, PEW Charitable Trusts, the Able Trust, the Texas Institute of Letters and the Florida and Texas Divisions of Cultural Affairs. At the moment, she is, like many other disabled artists in the USA without institutional affiliations, broke and *sans* health insurance.

Anita Gonzalez is an Associate Professor at the State University of New York – New Paltz (Ph.D. University of Wisconsin, 1997). She has written book reviews and articles about multicultural and international performance for *Modern Drama, Journal of Dramatic Theory and Criticism* and *Dance Research Journal*. She is the author of *Jarocho's Soul: Cultural Identity and Afro-Mexican Dance* (Rowan and Littlefield). Gonzalez has been an artist in residence at Rockefeller's Bellagio Center and has won multiple awards for theatre production and research, including three Fulbright Senior Scholar Awards.

Deborah Hay is an independent dance artist. She does not work in community performance contexts, but her ways of thinking about movement have influenced practitioners in many countries. Her publications include *Moving Through the Universe in Bare Feet* (1975), *Tasting the Blaze* (1985), *Lamb at the Altar: The Story of a Dance* (1994), and *My Body, the Buddhist* (2000).

Baz Kershaw is Professor of Drama at the University of Bristol, and his publications include *Politics of Performance* (2005) and *Radical in Performance: Between Brecht and Baudrillard* (1999). He also served as contributing co-editor for *Cambridge History of British Theatre*, vol. 3 (2004) and *Engineers of the Imagination: The Welfare State Handbook* (1983).

Petra Kuppers is Associate Professor in the Department of English Literature and Language at the University of Michigan, Ann Arbor, where she teaches in performance and disability studies. She is the author of *Disability Contemporary Performance: Bodies on Edge* (Routledge, 2003), and *The Scar of Visibility: Medical Performances and Contemporary Arts* (University of Minnesota Press, 2007), and she works as a community performance leader.

Christine Lomas is a Senior Teaching Fellow, School of Performance and Cultural Industries, University of Leeds. She works on interventionist and celebratory approaches to dance-making, and her writings on working collaboratively with developmentally disabled people has influenced many practitioners.

Theresa J. May is Assistant Professor of Theatre at the University of Oregon. She was previously at Humboldt State University, where she was Associate Artistic Director of Earth Matters On Stage: Ecodrama Playwrights Festival. She co-authored *Greening Up Our Houses: A Guide to a More Ecologically Sound Theatre*, with Larry K. Fried (Drama Book Publishers, 1994), and her current book project is *Earth Matters On Stage: Implications of Ecology in American Theater*.

Ubong Samuel Nda is Lecturer in Theatre at the University of Uyo, Nigeria. He gained his Ph.D. with the thesis 'Theatre and Environmental Conservation' from the University of Calabar, and he has worked on issues of environmentalism, rural media and drama.

Devora Neumark is co-director of Engrenage Noir's LEVIER Programs promoting and advocating creative connections between artists and community groups. She is also a faculty member in the MFA/Interdisciplinary Art program at Goddard College, a progressive student self-directed, low-residence program in Plainfield, Vermont. A direct dialogic process, an emphasis on active listening, and the willingness to risk vulnerability as strength are all integral to her interdisciplinary art practice, teaching, and community organizing.

Cedar Lorca Nordbye's BA thesis exhibition at Hampshire College in Massachusetts was entitled 'Prints and Drawings to Save the World'. He received his MFA from the University of Iowa. He has written for *Afterimage*, *Sculpture Magazine* and was a regular contributor for the *Kalamazoo Gazette*, but primarily engages in various forms of social sculpture (playing the part of Professor at the University of Memphis being the predominant and ongoing sculpture).

Cynthia Novak, also known as Cynthia Jean Cohen Bull, was a respected dance writer, anthropologist and dance artist who taught at Wesleyan College. She published *Sharing the Dance: Contact Improvisation and American Culture* (1990).

Donna Marie Nudd is an Associate Professor of Performance Studies in the Department of Communication at Florida State University. Her major areas include feminist criticism, pedagogy, radical performance, and adaptation for film and theatre. In 1987, Donna Marie Nudd co-founded the Mickee Faust Club with Terry Galloway.

Graham Pitts is an Australian writer who has worked on many community arts and public arts projects. He teaches in community cultural development at the Victoria College of the Arts, writes extensively on community arts, and produces plays and large-scale community performance productions.

Helen Poynor is Senior Lecturer in Theatre and Performance at the University of Plymouth. She is co-author with Libby Worth of the monograph, *Anna Halprin* (2004), published in Routledge's Performance Practitioner series, and has co-edited *Dancers and Communities*, a collection of writings about community dance in Australia.

Gwen Robertson received her Ph.D. in Art History from the University of Iowa and is currently an Associate Professor of Art History at Humboldt State University, specializing in twentieth-century and contemporary art. Her research and teaching interests center on rethinking how the arts contribute to contemporary life.

Carrie Sandahl is an Associate Professor in the School of Theatre at Florida State University. Her research and creative activity focus on disability and gender identities in live performance, including theatre, dance, and performance art. She is co-editor, with Philip Auslander, of *Bodies in Commotion: Disability and Performance* (University of Michigan Press, 2005), an interdisciplinary, international collection of essays in disability performance studies.

Becky Shaw is an artist who employs humorous and critical methods to explore the relationship between the individual and society. She currently lectures in Drawing at Camberwell College, University of the Arts, London, and is a researcher in the Centre for Death, Dying and Society, University of Bath, UK. She was co-director of Static Gallery, Liverpool, 2000–6, and continues to develop projects with director, architect Paul Sullivan.

Libby Worth is Lecturer in Theatre Practice at Royal Holloway College, University of London, and has trained at the Tamalpa Institute with Anna Halprin. She co-wrote the monograph, *Anna Halprin* (2004), with Helen Poynor for Routledge's Performance Practitioner series. She is a movement practitioner specializing in the interweaving of dance and theatre, and in site-specific performance.

Permissions

Blumberg, Marcia. 'Puppets Doing Time in the Age of AIDS.' Originally published in *Performing Democracy: International Perspectives on Urban Community-Based Performance*, edited by Susan Haedicke and Tobin Nellhaus (Ann Arbor, MI: University of Michigan Press, 2001). © 2001. Reprinted by permission of University of Michigan Press.

Boal, Augusto. *Theatre of the Oppressed*. Excerpt from Chapter 4, pp. 142–55. Translation copyright © 1974 by Charles A. and Maria-Odilia Leal McBride. Originally published in Spanish as *Teatro de Oprimido* in 1974, copyright © by Augusto Boal and in English by Urizen Books in 1979. Published by Theatre Communications Group. Used by permission of Theatre Communications Group.

Bourriaud, Nicolas. *Relational Aesthetics*. © 1998. Excerpt from pp. 11–24. Reprinted by permission of Les Presses du Réel.

Cohen-Cruz, Jan. *Local Acts: Community-based Performance in the United States*. © 2005 by Jan Cohen-Cruz. Excerpt from Chapter 7, pp. 173–80. Reprinted by permission of Rutgers University Press.

Conquergood, Dwight. 'Performing a Moral Act: Ethical Dimensions of the Ethnography of Performance.' Originally published and reprinted by permission of *Text and Performance Quarterly*, vol. 5 (1985), 1–13. www.tandf.co.uk

Delanty, Gerard. *Community*. © 2002. Excerpt from pp. 113–20. Reprinted by permission of Routledge.

Dickerson, Glenda. 'Festivals and Jubilations on the Graves of the Dead: Sanctifying Sullied Space.' Excerpt from pp. 117–26. Originally published in *Performance and Cultural Politics*, Elin Diamond, editor. © 1996. Reprinted by permission of Routledge.

Acknowledgments

Assembling Readers is a long and gratifying task: you can read much, find new voices, and assemble multiple pathways through fields you care deeply about. We both enjoyed our journey.

Thanks are in order to many different people and institutions. First of all, we wish to thank all those practitioners and teachers at many conferences and workshops who filled out questionnaires about the materials they use for teaching community dance, theatre and art classes: these questionnaires provided the basis for this collection. Secondly, we want to thank the participants in the Community Performance conference, and we wish to acknowledge the generous support of Bryant University, the Rhode Island Foundation and ACN (Art Culture Nature).

Petra's other thanks are in the accompanying book to this Reader, *Community Performance: An Introduction*.

Gwen must begin with Petra. Without her incredible energy, friendship, vision, commitment, passion, talent, knowledge, writings, and good humor, there would be no project. Gwen is awed by and grateful for Petra's capacity to understand people and ideas, art and community. There could not have been a better partner and friend to work with to create this book. She would also like to thank the many artists and scholars who have shared their practices, explained their ideas, and tirelessly rewritten manuscripts to fill the pages of this Reader. Special thanks to Cedar Nordbye who introduced Gwen to community performance art in the first place, compelled her to join the Community Performance conference, and who constantly reminds her that the glass is half-full. Ruth Ben-Tovim and Trish O'Shea showed Gwen that art history might have something to say about community performance and generously gave of their time and work to make the connection a reality. Becky Shaw made the critical work fun and, throughout the course of the project, helped Gwen keep her perspective. Lastly, Gwen's deepest gratitude to Eric and Tess for, well, everything else.

Finally, Petra wants to thank Gwen: this Reader would not have happened without her encouragement, support and valuable critical skills. It's been a deep pleasure working with such a loyal, smart and generous co-editor and friend.

Scene from *Confrontar el Dragon!*, Breast Cancer Health Project, Fortuna, California, 2006, a play performed after Mass for a dominantly Spanish-speaking audience.

Photo: Petra Kuppers.

General introduction

■ Petra Kuppers and Gwen Robertson

A SENTENCE THAT STARTS 'Community performance is . . .' should, arguably, begin this book. Trying to finish that sentence, however, is no easy matter. What *is* a field that draws from so many different disciplines and traditions, and yet is bound by none? Community performance has theatrical elements, but it is not theatre. Community performance can be led by visual artists, but it does not need to stay in the museum or other familiar art establishments (though it can *make use of* these spaces). Community performance is enriched by the discipline of dance, but it need not include choreography. In fact, community performance *is not* bound by the arts as it crosses into other, less conventionally artistic practices, such as economic development, human rights politics, disability culture, community redevelopment, capacity building (i.e. building the ability of a community to help itself and to survive). Instead, community performance moves with and through wider contemporary art practices, creating links between different realms, spaces, stories and bodies.

A brief scan of the table of contents may help. If, as we are willing to argue, these scholars and practitioners represent a snapshot of the field, community performance *is* inherently interdisciplinary. These writers are an eclectic group who defy the impulse to read only what one already knows, and this may be the most refreshing part of community performance – it asks for an audience that is open to change and interested in rethinking relationships between ideas.

A Reader, by definition, operates to define a field, providing parameters, offering examples and creating a history for an idea or practice. This Reader, together with its companion, *Community Performance: An Introduction*, is no exception. At its heart, the goal of this volume is to provide as complex and comprehensive a sense of community performance practices as possible. But what, again, *is* community performance?

Perhaps we might argue that community performance involves a set of attitudes or precepts more than anything else. The diverse practices in this book share the belief that artistic practices can have an effect on the social world. None of the contributors of this book believe that the artist, the intellectual or the community worker should be sequestered from society. Quite the contrary. In every case, there is a commitment to dialogue, interaction, and a fundamental belief that the audience – the community – has something to offer; and that the very notion of artist/product/audience needs to be rethought. Artists lose their specialist status, and become companions in a collaborative search for an expressive relation to the world that celebrates and critiques *both* difference and cohesion.

Consequently, this book addresses community performance as a mode of work that nourishes itself from avant-garde and contemporary art practices. Even though many community performance practitioners 'apply' models and methods garnered elsewhere to community situations (hence formulations such as 'applied theatre'), many more practitioners question and challenge existing methods, and develop new ways of working in response to social, cultural and aesthetic pressures. This collection tries to pay attention to the breadth of work out there: community performance as an enriching aspect of social life, community performance as radical politics, and community performance as aesthetic experimentation.

This book, then, aspires to draw together diverse practices and diverse people in order to illustrate that a community of thinkers already exists – a reminder particularly helpful in a field where many struggle alone, and where isolation and lack of professional development opportunities are common. For the student, possibly new to the field, it provides much needed theoretical and practical foundations with writers and artists such as Boal and Freire, paired with the exciting work of many other contemporary practitioners, and critics writing about community performance. For the accomplished community performance artist, this Reader brings confirmation that engaged, community-based work occurs throughout the globe and represents not a few, unusually dedicated, individuals, but rather a gathering field that shares an unusual commitment to community thinking.

Many of the voices in this book offer an insight into the personal journeys of artists who work to extend creative processes beyond themselves to people who might not conventionally see themselves as artists. To keep their practice attentive to the hydraulics of power, community performance artists often work through intense self-reflexive processes. And thus, most of the work discussed in these pages is created collaboratively, challenging conventional ideas of the artist as core creator or specialist. Additionally, in most of the writings included, the choreographer/director/leader/facilitator/initiator and her or his political consciousness are still very much in evidence. This book asks whether this blending of creative process into the potentially political concerns of community is contradictory. Or does it constitute a necessary re-definition of notions of empowerment, individuality, society, and even of art? These are the kinds of questions that scholars of community performance need to address as the field develops.

In a range of art fields, community performance practices grow out of strong hopes and desires. Susan Chandler Haedicke writes on community-based devised performance: '[It is] an activist form of dramaturgy which aims to influence and alter the actual world, not just reflect it. It provides an avenue to individual empowerment and community development as it moves the audience into a new role: an artist, a maker of culture who can create a community' (1998: 132). To alter the world – and to see it being altered – to experience its alteration in the behaviors, words, bodies and eyes of a group of people – that is the head (and full-body) rush that community performance can offer. Indeed, Jan Cohen-Cruz writes, 'Given the field's capacity to respond to various arenas of human endeavor it is not surprising that every practitioner I have talked with considers community-based performance not a career but a way of life' (2005: 6). Some of this hope and this fervor shine through the readings we have assembled here. We took care to balance academic accounts with genres chosen by the practitioners we've invited to participate in this collection, and in this multiplicity of voices and ways of speaking, the power of community performance as a transformative personal and communal journey becomes experiential.

We think that the stakes of this kind of practice are particularly compelling in this historic moment. Based on the idea of social interaction, private and public space, and transgression of all kinds, the resonances of these ideas and potentials are extremely necessary in a world where individual freedoms are being questioned and powers of expression feared. The idea for this collection emerged from a conference called Community/Performance, which took place at Bryant University in the US in June 2004. This international conference happened in the shadow of warfare (and its attendant issues of problematic border-crossings, visa work and a necessarily deep awareness of issues of privilege and exclusion), and not long after the conference at least two of the countries of which many of the contributors in this book are citizens (the UK and the US), waged war. This warfare, which still continues (in both literal and figural ways), sharpens how we think about community performance and its place in the world.

During the conference, we all addressed these questions:

• What is the efficacy of arts interventions in building communities?
• What are the present and future roles of the arts in our social projects?
• Are there separate aesthetics of community arts?
• What are the relations between performance theory and practice?
• What communities are being served/serve themselves?
• What factors hinder or further collaboration, dissemination, organization and sharing?
• What are the relationships between activism and action, between performance and the performative, between the artistic and art?
• What are the practices of transformation and transgression in our contemporary cultural scene?
• What are the shapes, the smells, the scenes, the people and the places of politics?

We believe that these questions, and many others like them, provide a basis for thinking about the practices and potential of community performance to develop.

In this collection, contributors find ways to address these questions, and discuss the kaleidoscope of issues that arise from the two core terms, community and performance. Both of these terms are open-ended, and neither describes a specific political project. Notions of 'community' can be deeply exclusionary and reactionary as well as core concepts in empowerment struggles, and 'performance' can refer to repressive, liberatory, destabilizing and consolidating activities and acts alike. Yet many of the activities emerging in community performance share certain features. Community arts, environmental arts and civil rights performance projects often foreground concepts such as democratic or collaborative practices, everyday life, the local and the private as spaces of agency, engagement with dominant stereotypes, the merging of educative and creative aims, and the respect for multiple voices.

The histories of art practices, however, show that these features do not exempt community arts from co-option and commodification. Indeed, many recent and ongoing anti-war/pro-war/think-about-war art actions, processions or demonstrations in the UK, the US, Germany, Spain, Brazil and other countries provide interesting material for analysis in terms of the issues that define this collection: are these actions univocal, or multivocal? Are they collaboratively created, and, if so, is the collaborating group made up of people who fundamentally agree? How is access assured, safe-guarded and kept alive when differences of opinion occur? Who speaks/performs, who is spoken for? These community performance questions can provide valuable insights into public performances of political action, and an attentiveness to these issues subtends many contributions in this Reader.

Other important issues that emerge at times in these texts include the relative positioning of community arts in the value scheme of the art market and arts funding bodies. Funding schemes can often provide problems for art workers in these fields, who might find themselves on the sidelines, and need appropriate networks and language to educate funders and critics. Similarly, the collection attempts to explain to potentially skeptical voices at the university or museum level that community performance is a valid artistic expression that shares intellectual roots with some of the most influential thinkers of the last hundred years.

This collection (and its sister publication, *Community Performance: An Introduction*) therefore aims to give artists, funders, critics, students and others the necessary critical vocabulary to reflect on and argue effectively and reflectively for this kind of art practice. The Community/Performance conference did not just come and go – one important aspect of its organization was to find a way to make the visits of so many scholars and practitioners resonate in our locality, and in the everyday lives of local community performance artists. And so, for over a year after the conference, local artists, activists and representatives of funding bodies met regularly every three weeks to network, have fun, and to hone our critical skills by presenting and then discussing our respective practices. Some of the members of this community performance network share their work in these pages.

This reverberation in the local and the everyday is a significant component not only of this Reader, but also of the aesthetic with which we as editors approached our task. We wanted to provide core readings that we had found deeply useful in our teaching (Petra has taught community dance and community performance classes at universities and in non-academic settings in the UK, Germany, the US, New Zealand and Australia, and Gwen has taught university courses on public art, art policy and community art business).

At the same time, though, we did not wish to rank community performers, nor create a sense of 'best practice'. Much of what goes on in community performance exists outside the networks of adjudication, judgment and dissemination associated with other art forms. And, while this can be a problem (in particular when it comes to finding funding, or to connecting with other practitioners) it is also a strength. It allows for particularization, for a concentration on the here-and-now, and a responsiveness to the specific local situation. In the Reader, we have tried to balance overview and authority with specificity and the playfulness of the individual voice.

The Reader is organized into five sections: Pedagogies/communities; Relations; Environments; Rituals, embodiment, challenge, and Practices. These sections present emphases rather than exclusive categories: many of the contributions stretch their thematic or methodological grasp across various fields. In each section, we combine excerpts from foundational texts with the voices of contemporary scholars and artists. We have encouraged our contributors to use their own, specific writing genre, appropriate to the kind of writing they engage in for their practice: some of the material is governed by the demands of practice or acquittal reports (shaped to the demands of a general collection), some writers use a very personal voice to talk about their experiences, and some embed their work in other frames. We offer this multivoicing as a microcosm of the field: a reflection of the field in its language, a multiplicity in the face of static definition. There are many voices missing here, for many reasons (logistically, financially, in terms of the networks we access, and the specific practices we know), and we want to acknowledge these voices too: there are many specialists, skilled and engaged, and we hope that our readers will seek out their local, regional and national community performance artists. This Reader is also intended to reflect the everyday experiences students in community arts courses in countries such as the UK, Ireland, the US, Australia and New Zealand are likely to encounter. And while (within the limits of our word-count) we made sure that most world regions had some representation in this volume, we consciously decided not to cast our net too broadly, or evenly. Indeed, many of the choices in this Reader are based on recommendations we collected via questionnaires at various conferences and practitioner meetings in the UK, US, New Zealand and Australia, in which we asked for readings that had inspired people, as well as readings they used in the classroom when teaching in community performance. And while we present a mix of writings and approaches, we also focus more on case studies rather than authorative overviews and field-defining analysis, given our strong belief in the local and specific nature of community performance.

Excellent work exists for any one art form, locality, or specific theme within community performance practices, and professional journals such as *Animated* (community dance, with a UK focus) and the US-based organization Community Arts Network and its website (communityart.net) cover a wide range of voices. The Foundation for Community Dance, host organization of *Animated*, also brought out the influential short collection *Thinking Aloud: In Search of a Framework for Community Dance* in 1996. Academic journals, such as *Research in Theatre Education* and *Research in Dance Education* (both UK-based), as well as *Theatre Topics* (US-based) and *The Applied Theatre Researcher* (Australia-based), cover and discuss many practices that are of interest to community performance practitioners, and book collections have come out of these journals.

There are also valuable collections that reflect writing on community performance internationally. Fascinating material on cross-geographical work can be found in Don Adams and Arlene Goldbard's *Community, Culture and Globalization*, an anthology of writers who came together at the Bellagio Center in Italy to reflect on the theme, and whose writings for the Rockefeller Foundation served as a companion to their influential *Creative Community: The Art of Cultural Development* (2001). This focus on community development is also at the heart of the work of John Kretzmann and John McKnight (March 1997), and, inflected more specifically through art practice, and of Julie McCarthy's and Karla Galvao's *Enacting Partici- patory Development: Theatre-based Techniques* (2005). Cultural development is a significant aspect of discussions of community performance and policy issues – a theme that alone could fill multiple Readers.

Jan Cohen-Cruz's *Local Acts* provides an in-depth account of the development of com- munity performance in theatrical contexts in the US, and Sonja Kuftinec's work on Cornerstone Theatre traces many important themes in relation to this company's practices. Jan Cohen- Cruz and Mady Schutzman's collaborative editing work gives valuable insights into Augusto Boal's theatre work, and its take-up and modulation by other contemporary practitioners (1994, 2006). Practitioners have also created 'training manuals' – Michael Rohde, for instance, models the use of theatre in community situations (1998).

In visual art debates, Grant Kester (2004) provides an in-depth critical and analytic account of the community work and dialogic practice in international visual arts, Susan Lacy's influential collection on *New Genre Public Art* (1994) presents debates within socially conscious art (with a US focus), and Miwon Kwon discussed some US-based community-based practices in relation to issues of site-specificity (2004). Beyond these, discussions of public art in the US have created a large body of work, and many of the debates surrounding it, even if not performance-based, can provide useful perspectives on our theme (for instance, in Goldstein, 2005; Finkelperl, 2001; Senie and Webster, 1998; and Bach, 2000, describing the trans- formation of a particular location in Philadelphia).

Other books focus on specific practices or regions, and often specific stories or projects provide entry into practices. For instance, Poynor and Simmonds (1997) present a wide range of work and approaches to community dance in Australia. Ten fascinating US stories about youth development work and community practice are at the core of Mat Schwarzman's *Beginner's Guide to Community-Based Arts* (with illustrator Keith Knight). A similar practical ethos shapes editions such as Warren's UK-focused *Creating a Theatre in your Classroom and Community* (2002), which has a strong emphasis on theatre-in-education approaches – an area we deliberately did not focus on for this Reader. Applied theatre is also at the heart of collections and books such as Philip Taylor (2003) and Helen Nicholson (2005). James Thompson's work on performance in prison settings, and his wider editorial practice on Applied Theatre, is focused on the UK but influential beyond the national context. Eugene van Erven's books, in particular *Community Theatre*, together with its accompanying video, documents a wide range of international practices in detail, and are valuable classroom tools.

Urban practices in relation to community performance are collected in Haedicke and Nellhaus's edition (2001). And Theatre-in-Development, especially, but not only, in African nations, has found a wide range of commentators, for instance in the material collected in Salhi (1998), and books by Byam (1999), and Epskamp (2006).

Many more excellent sources of inspiration, practical advice and conceptual thought circulate among community performance practitioners through looseleaf collections, privately printed leaflets, or policy statements handed out at workshops (and *Community Performance: An Introduction* specifically uses many of these). And so, while this is a Reader aimed at academic environments, we wish to be careful not to close the conversations on these pages, sanctioning only one kind of knowledge-production over others.

Our Reader draws on many of these works (and, indeed, a number of the essays in this collection first appeared in print in the books above), but also makes a conscious effort to find ways to bring the everyday, 'ordinary', alive experience of community performance into focus through some of our commissioned essays.

The sections of our Reader are accompanied by a number of images – stills from community performances, workshops and sharings. Many are not the high-gloss photos of mainstream professional production, but they all share instead the energy, provisionality and resourcefulness of much of the material we discuss.

In the end, community performance is a whole host of elements, practices and traditions. Rather than define it or contain it, this collection hopes to continue a dialogue that has begun all over the globe. It is a dialogue not about the limits of a practice, but instead about the potential for innovation, collaboration and human exchange.

Different readers, teachers and practitioners will find different paths through the material we have collected here – we trust that you will find much of worth. The Reader (and the *Community Performance: An Introduction* text) are the beginnings of a conversation: we are well aware that there is so much more to be said, both geographically and thematically. We hope that you can carry the conversation forward.

References

Adams, Don and Arlene Goldbard (2001) *Creative Community: The Art of Cultural Development*, New York, The Rockefeller Foundation.

Bach, Penny Balkin (ed.) (2000) *New Land Marks: Public Art, Community, and the Meaning of Place*, Washington, DC, Editions Ariel.

Byam, Dale (1999) *Community in Motion: Theatre for Development in Africa*, Westport, CT, Bergin & Garvey.

Cohen-Cruz, Jan (2005) *Local Acts: Community-Based Performance in the United States*, New Brunswick, NJ, Rutgers University Press.

Cohen-Cruz, Jan and Mady Schutzman (eds) (2006) *A Boal Companion: Dialogues on Theatre and Cultural Politics*, London and New York, Routledge.

Epskamp, Kees (2006) *Theatre for Development: An Introduction to Context, Applications and Training*, London, Zed Books.

Finkelperl, Tom (2001) *Dialogues in Public Art*, Cambridge, MA, MIT Press.

Goldstein, Barbara (2005) *Public Art by the Book*, Seattle, WA, University of Washington Press.

Haedicke, Susan C. (1998) 'Dramaturgy in Community-Based Theatre', *Journal of Dramatic Theory and Criticism*, vol. xiii, 1.

Haedicke, Susan C. and Tobin Nellhaus (eds) (2001) *Performing Democracy: International Perspectives on Urban Community-Based Performance*, Ann Arbor, MI: Michigan University Press.

Kester, Grant (2004) *Conversation Pieces: Community and Communication in Modern Art*, Berkeley, CA, University of California Press.

Kretzmann, John and John McKnight (1997) *Building Communities from the Inside Out: A Path Toward Finding and Mobilizing a Community's Assets*, Skokie, IL, ACTA Publications.

Kuftinec, Sonja (2003) *Staging America: Cornerstone and Community-Based Theatre*, Carbondale, IL, Southern Illinois Press.

Kwon, Miwon (2004) *One Place After Another: Site Specific Art and Locational Identity*, Cambridge, MA, MIT Press.

Lacy, Susan (1994) *Mapping the Terrain: New Genre Public Art*, Seattle, WA, Bay Press.

McCarthy, Julie and Galvao, Karla (2005) *Enacting Participatory Development: Theatre-based Techniques*, London, Earthscan Publications.

Nicholson, Helen (2005) *Applied Drama: The Gift of Theatre*, New York: Palgrave Macmillan.

Poynor, Helen and Jacqueline Simmonds (eds) (1997) *Dancers and Communities: A Collection of Writings About Dance as a Community Art*, Walsh Bay, Ausdance.

Rohde, Michael (1998) *Theatre for Community Conflict and Dialogue: The Hope Is Vital Training Manual*, Portsmouth, NH, Heinemann Drama.

Salhi, Kamal (ed.) (1998) *African Theatre for Development*, Exeter, Intellect Books.

Senie, Harriet and Webster, Sally (eds) (1998) *Critical Issues in Public Art: Content, Context, and Controversy*, Washington, DC, Smithsonian Books.

Schutzman, Mady and Jan Cohen-Cruz (eds) (1994) *Playing Boal: Theatre, Therapy, Activism*, London and New York, Routledge.

Schwarzman, Mat and Keith Knight (2005) *Beginner's Guide to Community-Based Arts*, Oakland, CA, New Village Press.

Taylor, Phillip (2003) *Applied Theatre: Creating Transformative Encounters in the Community*, Portsmouth, NH, Heinemann Drama.

Thompson, James (2003) *Applied Theatre: Bewilderment and Beyond*. New York and Oxford, Peter Lang Publishing.

Thompson, James (2005) *Digging Up Stories: Applied Theatre, Performance and War*, Manchester, Manchester University Press.

Thompson, James (ed.) (1998) *Prison Theatre: Perspectives and Practices*, London, Jessica Kingsley Publishers.

Van Erven, Eugene (2001) *Community Theatre: Global Perspectives*, London, Routledge.

Warren, B (ed.) (2002) *Creating a Theatre in Your Classroom and Community*, North York, Captus University Publications.

PART ONE

Pedagogical communities

Introduction to Part One

■ Petra Kuppers and Gwen Robertson

TO OPEN THE COMMUNITY/PERFORMANCE discussion, we begin with the pedagogies of communities, the kind of engagement opportunities that reside in the concept of 'community', and the practices that can meld people together into political aesthetic action. Defining 'community' is hard, indeed, and it is even harder to escape an unreflective celebration of communality. Victor Turner identified 'communitas' as a limit experience: as a state of being with others that transcends differences. In this state, it is easy to feel warmth and love towards others. It is much harder to sustain this communality into political engagement, and into a serious reflection on the differences that need to stay visible and experiential if a community is to sustain itself and grow. Many of the writers in this section address these problems, and present processes and ways of thinking about ethics of engagement that try to remain open to difference.

The section presents core texts in which the specific nature and charge of community performance as an empowering tool for the oppressed emerges. **Augusto Boal**'s work in Brazil has created a foundation for many practitioners who want to foreground free and democratic expressive exchange, as well as reflect on the problems inherent in such terms. **Paulo Freire**'s pedagogy of the oppressed developed out of his work on literacy campaigns with landless peasants in Brazil, and speaks eloquently about the need to address the power structures inherent in teaching and transmission. **Gerard Delanty**, in contrast, looks at how modernist theorists Habermas, Touraine and Bauman distrust the equation of community with democracy and instead call for a stronger link between community and communication. **Jessica Berson** discusses the political charge of Rudolf von Laban's work, which, in a different tradition, has created a touchstone for community dance practice that is not based on technique and exclusivity.

The Pedagogical communities section also reflects shifts in the theorization of performance, and a changing emphasis in the nature of 'the political' in performance. Building on the legacy of Bertolt Brecht and the epic theatre, many writings on the political nature of drama focus on didactic elements in the interplay of the performance and an audience. **Baz Kershaw**, writing on political theatre in Britain in the 1960s to early 1990s (including community theatre), addresses the potential ideological differences between target groups (audiences) and the presenters of material. His intricate discussion of stage aesthetics emerges from a belief in the ability of performance to manipulate and challenge its audience – so much so that audiences become co-creators of community performance in a shared world.

The personal ethics of the facilitator become central in **Dwight Conquergood**'s reflection on ethnography, performance and performing other people's stories.

Anita Gonzalez writes on the multiple meanings of community in the Urban Bush Women's work, a black US group that affirms black women's aesthetics, and **Petra Kuppers** discusses Jean Luc Nancy's politics of community in relation to a long-term Welsh community project with mental-health system survivors. In both of these essays, the group dynamics of creation take precedence over a calculated audience address in a performance age where shared communal politics and identifications are hard to come by. Forms of modeling and an invitation to sharing become the experiential dimension of these pedagogies of community.

All community performance practitioners have to find answers to questions about agency, impact, collaboration, access and engagement. The writings in this section show how searching for answers, not merely in the created art work, but in the processes that lead to the work, become the shared creative act.

CHAPTER 1

Augusto Boal

Poetics of the oppressed

G EORGE IKISHAWA USED TO SAY that the bourgeois theater is the finished
theater. The bourgeoisie already knows what the world is like, *their* world, and
is able to present images of this complete, finished world. The bourgeoisie presents
the spectacle. On the other hand, the proletariat and the oppressed classes do not
know yet what their world will be like; consequently their theater will be the rehearsal,
not the finished spectacle. This is quite true, though it is equally true that the theater
can present images of transition.

I have been able to observe the truth of this view during all my activities in the
people's theater of so many and such different countries of Latin America. Popular
audiences are interested in experimenting, in rehearsing, and they abhor the "closed"
spectacles. In those cases they try to enter into a dialogue with the actors, to interrupt
the action, to ask for explanations without waiting politely for the end of the play.
Contrary to the bourgeois code of manners, the people's code allows and encourages
the spectator to ask questions, to dialogue, to participate.

All the methods that I have discussed are forms of a rehearsal theater, and not a
spectacle theater. One knows how these experiments will begin but not how they
will end, because the spectator is freed from his chains, finally acts, and becomes a
protagonist. Because they respond to the real needs of a popular audience they are
practiced with success and joy.

But nothing in this prohibits a popular audience from practicing also more "finished"
forms of theater. In Peru many forms previously developed in other countries,
especially Brazil and Argentina, were also utilized and with great success. Some of
these forms were:

Figure 1 Boal workshop. Setting up changes in an opening fluid image to show how awareness of exposure pathways and environmental health risks can transform a neighborhood (Teatro Luca/de Madres a Madres at Holy Name parish, Houston, TX, 2005).
Photo: Karla Hold.

1) *Newspaper theater:* It was initially developed by the Nucleus Group of the Arena Theater of Sao Paulo, of which I was the artistic director until forced to leave Brazil.[1] It consists of several simple techniques for transforming daily news items, or any other non-dramatic material, into theatrical performances.

a) Simple reading: the news item is read detaching it from the context of the newspaper, from the format which makes it false or tendentious.

b) Crossed reading: two news item are read in crossed (alternating) form, one throwing light on the other, explaining it, giving it a new dimension.

c) Complementary reading: data and information generally omitted by the newspapers of the ruling classes are added to the news.

d) Rhythmical reading: as a musical commentary, the news is read to the rhythm of the samba, tango, Gregorian chant, etc., so that the rhythm functions as a critical "filter" of the news, revealing its true content, which is obscured in the newspaper.

e) Parallel action: the actors mime parallel actions while the news is read, showing the context in which the reported event really occurred; one hears the news and sees something else that complements it visually.

f) Improvisation: the news is improvised on stage to exploit all its variants and possibilities.

g) Historical: data or scenes showing the same event in other historical moments, in other countries, or in other social systems, are added to the news.

h) Reinforcement: the news is read or sung with the aid or accompaniment of slides, jingles, songs, or publicity materials.

i) Concretion of the abstract: that which the news often hides in its purely abstract information is made concrete on the stage: torture, hunger, unemployment, etc., are shown concretely, using graphic images, real or symbolic.

j) Text out of context: the news is presented out of the context in which it was published; for example, an actor gives the speech about austerity previously delivered by the Minister of Economics while he devours an enormous dinner: the real truth behind the minister's words becomes demystified — he wants austerity for the people but not for himself.

2) *Invisible theater:* It consists of the presentation of a scene in an environment other than the theater, before people who are not spectators. The place can be a restaurant, a sidewalk, a market, a train, a line of people, etc. The people who witness the scene are those who are there by chance. During the spectacle, these people must not have the slightest idea that it is a "spectacle," for this would make them "spectators."

The invisible theater calls for the detailed preparation of a skit with a complete text or a simple script; but it is necessary to rehearse the scene sufficiently so that the actors are able to incorporate into their acting and their actions the intervention of the spectators. During the rehearsal it is also necessary to include every imaginable intervention from the spectators; these possibilities will form a kind of optional text.

The invisible theater erupts in a location chosen as a place where the public congregates. All the people who are near become involved in the eruption and the effects of it last long after the skit is ended.

A small example shows how the invisible theater works. In the enormous restaurant of a hotel in Chiclayo, where the literacy agents of ALFIN were staying, together with 400 other people, the "actors" sit at separate tables. The waiters start to serve. The "protagonist" in a more or less loud voice (to attract the attention of other diners, but not in a too obvious way) informs the waiter that he cannot go on eating the food served in that hotel, because in his opinion it is too bad. The waiter does not like the remark but tells the customer that he can choose something *à la carte*, which he may like better. The actor chooses a dish called "Barbecue a la pauper." The waiter points out that it will cost him 70 *soles*, to which the actor answers, always in a reasonably loud voice, that there is no problem. Minutes later the waiter brings him the barbecue, the protagonist eats it rapidly and gets ready to get up and leave the restaurant, when the waiter brings the bill. The actor shows a worried expression and tells the people at the next table that his barbecue was much better than the food they are eating, but the pity is that one has to pay for it. . . .

"I'm going to pay for it; don't have any doubts. I ate the 'barbecue a la pauper' and I'm going to pay for it. But there is a problem: I'm broke."

"And how are you going to pay?" asks the indignant waiter. "You knew the price before ordering the barbecue. And now, how are you going to pay for it?"

The diners nearby are, of course, closely following the dialogue — much more attentively than they would if they were witnessing the scene on a stage. The actor continues:

"Don't worry, because I *am* going to pay you. But since I'm broke I will pay you with labor-power."

"With what?" asks the waiter, astonished. "What kind of power?"

"With labor-power, just as I said. I am broke but I can rent you my labor-power. So I'll work doing something for as long as it's necessary to pay for my 'barbecue a la pauper,' which, to tell the truth, was really delicious — much better than the food you serve to those poor souls. . . ."

By this time some of the customers intervene and make remarks among themselves at their tables, about the price of food, the quality of the service in the hotel, etc. The waiter calls the headwaiter to decide the matter. The actor explains again to the latter the business of renting his labor-power and adds:

"And besides, there is another problem: I'll rent my labor-power but the truth is that I don't know how to do anything, or very little. You will have to give me a very simple job to do. For example, I can take out the hotel's garbage. What's the salary of the garbage man who works for you?"

The headwaiter does not want to give any information about salaries, but a second actor at another table is already prepared and explains that he and the garbage man have gotten to be friends and that the latter has told him his salary: seven *soles* per hour. The two actors make some calculations and the "protagonist" exclaims:

"How is this possible! If I work as a garbage man I'll have to work ten hours to pay for this barbecue that it took me ten minutes to eat? It can't be! Either you increase the salary of the garbage man or reduce the price of the barbecue! . . . But I can do something more specialized; for example, I can take care of the hotel gardens, which are so beautiful, so well cared for. One can see that a very talented person is in charge of the gardens. How much does the gardener of this hotel make? I'll work as a gardener! How many hours work in the garden are necessary to pay for the 'barbecue a la pauper'?"

A third actor, at another table, explains his friendship with the gardener, who is an immigrant from the same village as him; for this reason he knows that the gardener makes ten *soles* per hour. Again the "protagonist" becomes indignant:

"How is this possible? So the man who takes care of these beautiful gardens, who spends his days out there exposed to the wind, the rain, and the sun, has to work seven long hours to be able to eat the barbecue in ten minutes? How can this be, Mr. Headwaiter? Explain it to me!"

The headwaiter is already in despair; he dashes back and forth, gives orders to the waiters in a loud voice to divert the attention of the other customers, alternately laughs and becomes serious, while the restaurant is transformed into a public forum. The "protagonist" asks the waiter how much he is paid to serve the barbecue and offers to replace him for the necessary number of hours. Another actor, originally from a small village in the interior, gets up and declares that nobody in his village makes 70 *soles* per day; therefore nobody in his village can eat the "barbecue a la pauper." (The sincerity of this actor, who was, besides, telling the truth, moved those who were near his table.)

Finally, to conclude the scene, another actor intervenes with the following proposition:

"Friends, it looks as if we are against the waiter and the headwaiter and this does not make sense. They are our brothers. They work like us, and they are not to blame for the prices charged here. I suggest we take up a collection. We at this table are going to ask you to contribute whatever you can, one *sol*, two *soles*, five *soles*, whatever you can afford And with that money we are going to pay for the barbecue. And be generous, because what is left over will go as a tip for the waiter, who is our brother and a working man."

Immediately those who are with him at the table start collecting money to pay the bill. Some customers willingly give one or two *soles*. Others furiously comment:

"He says that the food we're eating is junk, and now he wants us to pay for his barbecue! . . . And am I going to eat this junk? Hell no? I wouldn't give him a peanut, so he'll learn a lessons. Let him wash dishes. . . ."

The collection reached 100 *soles* and the discussion went on through the night. It is always very important that the actors do not reveal themselves to be actors! On this rests the *invisible* nature of this form of theater. And it is precisely this invisible quality that will make the spectator act freely and fully, as if he were living a real situation — and, after all, it is a real situation!

It is necessary to emphasize that the invisible theater is not the same thing as a "happening" or the so-called "guerrilla theater." In the latter we are clearly talking about "theater," and therefore the wall that separates actors from spectators immediately arises, reducing the spectator to impotence: a spectator is always less than a man! In the invisible theater the theatrical rituals are abolished; only the theater exists, without its old, worn-out patterns. The theatrical energy is completely liberated, and the impact produced by this free theater is much more powerful and longer lasting.

Several presentations of invisible theater were made in different locations in Peru. Particularly interesting is what happened at the Carmen Market, in the *barrio* of Comas, some 14 kilometers away from downtown Lima. Two actresses were protagonists in a scene enacted at a vegetable stand. One of them, who was pretending to be illiterate, insisted that the vendor was cheating her, taking advantage of the fact that she did not know how to read; the other actress checked the figures, finding them to be correct, and advised the "illiterate" one to register in one of ALFIN's literacy courses. After some discussion about the best age to start one's studies, about what to study and with whom, the first actress kept on insisting that she was too old for those things. It was then that a little old woman, leaning on her cane, very indignantly shouted:

"My dears, that's not true? For learning and making love one is never too old!"

Everyone witnessing the scene broke into laughter at the old woman's amorous outburst, and the actresses were unable to continue the scene.

3) *Photo-romance:* In many Latin-American countries there is a genuine epidemic of photo-romances, sub-literature on the lowest imaginable level, which furthermore always serves as a vehicle for the ruling classes' ideology. The technique here consists in reading to the participants the general lines in the plot of a photo-romance without telling them the source of this plot. The participants are asked to act out the story. Finally, the acted-out story is compared to the story as it is told in the photo-romance, and the differences are discussed.

For example: a rather stupid story taken from Corin Tellado, the worst author of this brutalizing genre, started like this:

A woman is waiting for her husband in the company of another woman who is helping her with the housework. . . .

The participants acted according to their customs: a woman at home expecting her husband will naturally be preparing the meal; the one helping her is a neighbor, who comes to chat about various things; the husband comes home tired after a long day's work, the house is a one room shack, etc., etc. In Corin Tellado on the contrary, the woman is dressed in a long evening gown, with pearl necklaces, etc.; the woman who is helping her is a black maid who says no more than "Yes, ma'am"; "The dinner is served, ma'am"; "Very well, ma'am"; "Here comes Mr. X, ma'am", and nothing else. The house is a marble palace; the husband comes home after a day's work in his factory, where he had an argument with the workers because they, "not understanding the crisis we are all living through, wanted an increase in salaries . . . ," and continuing in this vein.

This particular story was sheer trash, but at the same time it served as magnificent example of ideological insight. The well dressed woman received a letter from an unknown woman, went to visit her, and discovered her to be a former mistress of her husband; the mistress stated that the husband had left her because he wanted to marry the factory owner's daughter, that is, the well-dressed woman. To top it all, the mistress exclaimed:

"Yes, he betrayed rue, deceived me. But I forgive him because, after all, he has always been very ambitious, and he knew very well that with me he could not climb very high. On the other hand, with you he can go very far indeed!"

That is to say, the former mistress forgave her lover because he had in the highest degree that capitalistic eagerness to possess everything. The desire to be a factory owner is presented as something so noble that even a few betrayals on the way up are to be forgiven. . . .

And the young wife, not to be outdone, pretends to be ill so that he will have to remain at her side, and so that, as a result of this trick, he will finally fall in love with her. What an ideology! This love story is crowned with a happy ending rotten to the core. Of course the story, when told without the dialogues and acted out by peasants, takes on an entirely different meaning. When at the end of the performance, the participants are told the origin of the plot they have just acted out, they experience a shock. And this must be understood: when they read Corin Tellado they immediately assume the passive role of "spectators"; but if they first of all have to act out a story themselves, afterwards, when they do read Corin Tellado's version, they will no longer assume a passive, expectant attitude, but instead a critical, comparative one. They will look at the lady's house, and compare it to their own, at the husband's or wife's attitudes and compare them with those of their own spouses, etc. And they will be prepared to detect the poison infiltrating the pages of those photo-stories, or the comics and other forms of cultural and ideological domination.

I was overjoyed when, months after the experiments with the educators, back in Lima, I was informed that the residents of several *barrios* were using that same technique to analyze television programs, an endless source of poison directed against the people.

4) *Breaking of repression:* The dominant classes crush the dominated ones through repression; the old crush the young through repression; certain races subjugate certain others through repression. Never through a cordial understanding, through an honest interchange of ideas, through criticism and autocriticism. No. The ruling classes, the old, the "superior" races, or the masculine sex, have their sets of values and impose them by force, by unilateral violence, upon the oppressed classes, the young, the races they consider inferior, or women.

The capitalist does not ask the working man if he agrees that the capital should belong to one and the labor to another; he simply places an armed policeman at the factory door and that is that — private property is decreed.

The dominated class, race, sex, or age group suffers the most constant, daily, and omnipresent repression. The ideology becomes concrete in the figure of the dominated person. The proletariat is exploited through the domination that is exerted on all proletarians. Sociology becomes psychology. There is not an oppression by the masculine sex in general of the feminine sex in general: what exists is the concrete oppression that men (individuals) direct against women (individuals).

The technique of breaking repression consists in asking a participant to remember a particular moment when he felt especially repressed, accepted that repression, and began to act in a manner contrary to his own desires. That moment must have a deep personal meaning: I, a proletarian, am oppressed; we proletarians are oppressed; therefore the proletariat is oppressed. It is necessary to pass from the particular to the general, not vice versa, and to deal with something that has happened to someone in particular, but which at the same time is typical of what happens to others.

The person who tells the story also chooses from among the rest of the participants all the other characters who will participate in the reconstruction of the incident. Then, after receiving the information and directions provided by the protagonist, the participants and the protagonist act out the incident just as it happened in reality — recreating the same scene, the same circumstances, and the same original feelings.

Once the "reproduction" of the actual event is over, the protagonist is asked to repeat the scene, but this time without accepting the repression, fighting to impose his will, his ideas, his wishes. The other participants are urged to maintain the repression as in the first performance. The clash that results helps to measure the possibility one often has to resist and yet fails to do so; it helps to measure the true strength of the enemy. It also gives the protagonist the opportunity of trying once more and carrying out, in fiction, what he had not been able to do in reality. But we have already seen that this is not cathartic: the fact of having rehearsed a resistance to oppression will prepare him to resist effectively in a future reality, when the occasion presents itself once more.

On the other hand, it is necessary to take care that the generic nature of the particular case under study be understood. In this type of theatrical experiment the particular instance must serve as the point of departure, but it is indispensable to reach the general. The process to be realized, during the actual performance or afterward during the discussion, is one that ascends from the *phenomenon* toward the *law*; from the phenomena presented in the plot toward the social laws that govern those phenomena. The spectator-participants must come out of this experience enriched with the knowledge of those laws, obtained through analysis of the phenomena.

5) *Myth theater:* It is simply a question of discovering the obvious behind the myth: to logically tell a story, revealing its evident truths.

In a place called Motupe there was a hill, almost a mountain, with a narrow road that led through the trees to the top; halfway to the top stood a cross. One could go as far as that cross: to go beyond it was dangerous; it inspired fear, and the few who had tried had never returned. It was believed that some sanguinary ghosts inhabited the top of the mountain. But the story is also told of a brave young man who armed himself and climbed to the top, where he found the "ghosts." They were in reality some Americans who owned a gold mine located precisely on the top of that mountain.

Another legend is that of the lagoon of Cheken. It is said that there was no water there and that all the peasants, having to travel for several kilometers to get a glass of water, were dying of thirst. Today a lagoon exists there, the property of a local landowner. How did that lagoon spring up and how did it become the property of one man? The legend explains it. When there was still no water, on a day of intense heat all the villagers were lamenting and praying to God to grant them even a tiny stream of water. But God did not have pity on that arid village. At midnight of the same day, however, a man dressed in a long black poncho and riding a black horse arrived and addressed the landowner, who was then only a poor peasant like the others:

"I will give a lagoon for all of you, but you, friend, must give me your most precious possession."

The poor man, very distressed, moaned:

"But I have nothing; I am very poor. We all here suffer from the lack of water, live in miserable shacks, suffer from the most terrible hunger. We have nothing precious, not even our lives. And myself in particular, my only precious possession is my three daughters, nothing else."

"And of the three," responded the stranger, "the oldest is the most beautiful. I will give you a lagoon filled with the freshest water of all Peru; but in exchange you will give me your oldest daughter so that I may marry her."

The future landlord thought for a long while, cried a lot, and asked his frightened eldest daughter if she would accept such an unusual marriage proposal. The obedient daughter expressed herself in this way:

"If it is for the salvation of all, so that the thirst and hunger of all the peasants will come to an end, if it is so that you may have a lagoon with the freshest water of all Peru, if it is so that that lagoon will belong to you alone and bring you personal prosperity and riches — for you will be able to sell this wonderful water to the peasants, who will find it cheaper to buy from you than to travel so many kilometers — if it is for all this, tell the gentleman in the black poncho, astride his black horse, that I will go with him, even if in my heart I am suspicious of his true identity and of the places he will take me."

Happy and contented, and of course somewhat tearful, the kind father went to inform the man in black of the decision, meanwhile asking the daughter to make some little signs showing the price of a liter of water, in order to expedite the work. The man in black undressed the girl, for he did not want to take anything from that house besides the girl herself, and placed her on his horse, which set off at a gallop toward a great depression in the plains. Then an enormous explosion was heard, and a large cloud of smoke remained in the very place where the horse, horseman, and naked girl had disappeared. From the huge hole that had been made in the ground, a spring started to flow and formed the lagoon with the freshest water of all Peru.

This myth no doubt hides a truth: the landlord took possession of what did not belong to him. If formerly the noblemen attributed to God the granting of their property and rights, today explanations no less magical are still used. In this case, the property of the lagoon was explained by the loss of the eldest daughter, the landlord's most precious possession — a transaction took place! And serving as a reminder of that, the legend said that on the nights of the new moon one could hear the girl singing at the bottom of the lagoon, still naked and combing her long hair with a beautiful golden comb. . . . Yes, the truth is that for the landlord the lagoon was like gold.

The myths told by the people should be studied and analyzed and their hidden truths revealed. In this task the theater can be extraordinarily useful.

6) *Analytical theater:* A story is told by one of the participants and immediately the actors improvise it. Afterward each character is broken down into all his social roles and the participants are asked to choose a physical object to symbolize each role. For example, a policeman killed a chicken thief. The policeman is analyzed:

a) he is a worker because he rents his labor-power; symbol: a pair of overalls;

b) he is a bourgeois because he protects private property and values it more than human life; symbol: a necktie, or a top hat, etc.;

c) he is a repressive agent because he is a policeman; symbol: a revolver.

This is continued until the participants have analyzed all his roles: head of a family (symbol: the wallet, for example), member of a fraternal order, etc., etc. It is important that the symbols be chosen by the participants present and that they not be imposed "from above." For a particular community the symbol for the head of the family might be a wallet, because he is the person who controls the household finances, and in this way controls the family. For another community this symbol may not communicate anything, that is, it may not be a symbol; then an armchair may be chosen. . . .

Having analyzed the character, or characters (it is advisable to limit this operation to the central characters only, for the sake of simplicity and clarity), a fresh attempt to tell the story is made, but taking away some of the symbols from each character, and consequently some social roles as well. Would the story be exactly the same if:

a) the policeman did not have the top hat or the necktie?

b) the robber had a top hat or necktie?

c) the robber had a revolver?

d) the policeman and the robber both had the same symbol for the fraternal order?

The participants are asked to make varying combinations and the proposed combinations must be performed by the actors and criticized by all those present.

In this way they will realize that human actions are not the exclusive and primordial result of individual psychology: almost always, through the individual speaks his class!

7) *Rituals and masks:* The relations of production (infrastructure) determine the culture of a society (superstructure).

Sometimes the infrastructure changes but the superstructure for a while remains the same. In Brazil the landlords would not allow the peasants to look them in the face while talking with them: this would mean lack of respect. The peasants were accustomed to talking with the landlords only while staring at the ground and murmuring: "yes, sir; yes, sir; yes, sir." When the government decreed an agrarian reform (before 1964, date of the facist *coup d'etat*) its emissaries went to the fields to tell the peasants that now they could become landowners. The peasants, staring at the ground, murmured: "yes, friend; yes, friend; yes, friend." A feudalistic culture had totally permeated their lives. The relationships of the peasant with the landlord were entirely different from those with the agent of the Institute of Agrarian Reform, but the ritual remained unchanged.

This particular technique of a people's theater ("Rituals and masks") consists precisely in revealing the superstructures, the rituals which reify all human relationships, and the masks of behavior that those rituals impose on each person according to the roles he plays in society and the rituals he must perform.

A very simple example: a man goes to a priest to confess his sins, how will he do it? Of course, he will kneel, confess his sins, hear the penitence, cross himself, and leave. But do all men confess always in the same way before all priests? Who is the man, and who is the priest?

In this case we need two versatile actors to stage the same confession four times:

First scene: the priest and the parishioner are landlords;
Second scene: the priest is a landlord and the parishioner is a peasant;
Third scene: the priest is a peasant and the parishioner is a landlord;
Fourth scene: the priest and the parishioner are peasants.

The ritual is the same in each instance, but the different social masks will cause the four scenes to be different also.

This is an extraordinarily rich technique which has countless variants: the same ritual changing masks; the same ritual performed by people of one social class, and later by people of another class; exchange of masks within the same ritual; etc., etc.

Conclusion: "spectator," a bad word!

Yes, this is without a doubt the conclusion: "Spectator" is a bad word! The spectator is less than a man and it is necessary to humanize him, to restore to him his capacity of action in all its fullness. He too must be a subject, an actor on an equal plane with those generally accepted as actors, who must also be spectators. All these experiments of a people's theater have the same objective — the liberation of the spectator, on whom the theater has imposed finished visions of the world. And since those responsible for theatrical performances are in general people who belong directly or indirectly to the ruling classes, obviously their finished images will be reflections of themselves. The spectators in the people's theater (i.e., the people themselves) cannot go on being the passive victims of those images.

[T]he poetics of Aristotle is the *poetics of oppression:* the world is known, perfect or about to be perfected, and all its values are imposed on the spectators, who passively delegate power to the characters to act and think in their place. In so doing the spectators purge themselves of their tragic flaw — that is, of something capable of changing society. A catharsis of the revolutionary impetus is produced! Dramatic action substitutes for real action.

Brecht's poetics is that of the enlightened vanguard: the world is revealed as subject to change, and the change starts in the theater itself, for the spectator does not delegate power to the characters to think in his place, although he continues to delegate power to them to act in his place. The experience is revealing on the level of consciousness, but not globally on the level of the action. Dramatic action throws light upon real action. The spectacle is a preparation for action.

The *poetics of the oppressed* is essentially the poetics of liberation: the spectator no longer delegates power to the characters either to think or to act in his place. The spectator frees himself; he thinks and acts for himself! Theater is action!

Perhaps the theater is not revolutionary in itself; but have no doubts, it is a rehearsal of revolution!

Note

1   Under the author's leadership the Arena Theater developed into one of Brazil's — indeed, one of Latin America's — most outstanding theaters. After 1964, when military rule was established in that country, Boal's work continued, though hampered by censorship and other restrictions imposed by the government. His outspoken position against the authoritarian regime led to his imprisonment and torture in 1971. Released after three months and acquitted of all charges, he was nevertheless compelled to leave Brazil in order to insure the safety of himself and his family. After political circumstances also forced him to leave Buenos Aires, Argentina, he took up residence in Portugal.

CHAPTER 2

Paulo Freire

Pedagogy of the oppressed

IT IS ONLY WHEN THE OPPRESSED find the oppressor out and become involved in the organized struggle for their liberation that they begin to believe in themselves. This discovery cannot be purely intellectual but must involve action; nor can it be limited to mere activism, but must include serious reflection: only then will it be a praxis.

Critical and liberating dialogue, which presupposes action, must be carried on with the oppressed at whatever the stage of their struggle for liberation.[1] The content of that dialogue can and should vary in accordance with historical conditions and the level at which the oppressed perceive reality. But to substitute monologue, slogans, and communiqués for dialogue is to attempt to liberate the oppressed with the instruments of domestication. Attempting to liberate the oppressed without their reflective participation in the act of liberation is to treat them as objects which must be saved from a burning building; it is to lead them into the populist pitfall and transform them into masses which can be manipulated.

At all stages of their liberation, the oppressed must see themselves as women and men engaged in the ontological and historical vocation of becoming more fully human. Reflection and action become imperative when one does not erroneously attempt to dichotomize the content of humanity from its historical forms.

The insistence that the oppressed engage in reflection on their concrete situation is not a call to armchair revolution. On the contrary, relection—true reflection —leads to action. On the other hand, when the situation calls for action, that action will constitute an authentic praxis only if its consequences become the object of critical reflection. In this sense, the praxis is the new *raison d'être* of the oppressed, and the revolution, which inaugurates the historical moment of this *raison d'être*, is not viable apart from their concomitant conscious involvement. Otherwise, action is pure activism.

To achieve this praxis, however, it is necessary to trust in the oppressed and in their ability to reason. Whoever lacks this trust will fail to initiate (or will abandon) dialogue, reflection, and communication, and will fall into using slogans, communiqués, monologues, and instructions. Superficial conversions to the cause of liberation carry this danger.

Political action on the side of the oppressed must be pedagogical action in the authentic sense of the word and, therefore, action *with* the oppressed. Those who work for liberation must not take advantage of the emotional dependence of the oppressed—dependence that is the fruit of the concrete situation of domination which surrounds them and which engendered their unauthentic view of the world. Using their dependence to create still greater dependence is an oppressor tactic.

Libertarian action must recognize this dependence as a weak point and must attempt through reflection and action to transform it into independence. However, not even the best-intentioned leadership can bestow independence as a gift. The liberation of the oppressed is a liberation of women and men, not things. Accordingly, while no one liberates himself by his own efforts alone, neither is he liberated by others. Liberation, a human phenomenon, cannot be achieved by semihumans. Any attempt to treat people as semihumans only dehumanizes them. When people are already dehumanized, due to the oppression they suffer, the process of their liberation must not employ the methods of dehumanization.

The correct method for a revolutionary leadership to employ in the task of liberation is, therefore, *not* "libertarian propaganda." Nor can the leadership merely "implant" in the oppressed a belief in freedom, thus thinking to win their trust. The correct method lies in dialogue. The conviction of the oppressed that they must fight for their liberation is not a gift bestowed by the revolutionary leadership, but the result of their own *conscientização*.

The revolutionary leaders must realize that their own conviction of the necessity for struggle (an indispensable dimension of revolutionary wisdom) was not given to them by anyone else—if it is authentic. This conviction cannot be packaged and sold; it is reached, rather, by means of a totality of reflection and action. Only the leaders' own involvement in reality within an historical situation, led them to criticize this situation and to wish to change it.

Likewise, the oppressed (who do not commit themselves to the struggle unless they are convinced, and who, if they do not make such a commitment, withhold the indispensable conditions for this struggle) must reach this conviction as Subjects, not as objects. They also must intervene critically in the situation which surrounds them and whose mark they bear; propaganda cannot achieve this. While the conviction of the necessity for struggle (without which the struggle is unfeasible) is indispensable to the revolutionary leadership (indeed, it was this conviction which constituted that leadership), it is also necessary for the oppressed. It is necessary, that is, unless one intends to carry out the transformation *for* the oppressed rather than *with* them. It is my belief that only the latter form of transformation is valid.

The object in presenting these considerations is to defend the eminently pedagogical character of time revolution. The revolutionary leaders of every epoch who have affirmed that the oppressed must accept the struggle for their liberation—an obvious point—have also thereby implicitly recognized the pedagogical aspect of this struggle. Many of these leaders, however (perhaps due to natural and understandable biases against pedagogy), have ended up using the "educational" methods employed by the oppressor. They deny pedagogical action in the liberation process, but they use propaganda to convince.

It is essential for the oppressed to realize that when they accept the struggle for humanization they also accept, from that moment, their total responsibility for the struggle. They must realize that they are fighting not merely for freedom from hunger, but for

> . . . freedom to create and to construct, to wonder and to venture. Such
> freedom requires that the individual be active and responsible, not a slave
> or a well-fed cog in the machine. . . . It is not enough that men are not
> slaves, if social conditions further the existence of automatons, the result
> will not be love of life, but love of death.[2]

The oppressed, who have been shaped by the death-affirming climate of oppression, must find through their struggle the way to life affirming humanization, which does not lie *simply* in having more to eat (although it does involve having more to eat and cannot fail to include this aspect). The oppressed have been destroyed precisely because their situation has reduced them to things. In order to regain their humanity they must cease to be things and fight as men and women. This is a radical requirement. They cannot enter the struggle as objects in order *later* to become human beings.

The struggle begins with men's recognition that they have been destroyed. Propaganda, management, manipulation—all arms of domination—cannot be the instruments of their rehumanization. The only effective instrument is a humanizing pedagogy in which the revolutionary leadership establishes a permanent relationship of dialogue with the oppressed. In a humanizing pedagogy the method ceases to be an instrument by which the teachers (in this instance, the revolutionary leadership) can manipulate the students (in this instance, the oppressed), because it expresses the consciousness of the students themselves.

> The method is, in fact, the external form of consciousness manifest in acts,
> which takes on the fundamental property of consciousness—its intentionality.
> The essence of consciousness is being with the world, and this behavior
> is permanent and unavoidable. Accordingly, consciousness is in essence a
> 'way towards' something apart from itself, outside itself, which surrounds
> it and which it apprehends by means of its ideational capacity. Consciousness
> is thus by definition a method, in the most general sense of the word.[3]

A revolutionary leadership must accordingly practice *co-intentional* education. Teachers and students (leadership and people) co-intent on reality are both Subjects, not only in the task of unveiling that reality, and thereby coming to know it critically, but in the task of re-creating that knowledge. As they attain this knowledge of reality through common reflection and action, they discover themselves as its permanent re-creators. In this way, the presence of the oppressed in the struggle for their liberation will be what it should be: not pseudo-participation, but committed involvement.

Notes

1   Not in the open, of course; that would only provoke the fury of the oppressor and lead to still greater repression.
2   Erich Fromm (1966) *The Heart of Man*, New York, Harper & Row, pp. 52–53.
3   Alvaro Vieira Pinto, from a work in preparation on the philosophy of science. I consider the quoted portion of great importance for the understanding of problem-posing pedagogy (to be presented in chapter 2), and wish to thank Professor Vieira Pinto for permission to cite his work prior to publication.

CHAPTER 3

Gerard Delanty

Critiques of community

Habermas, Touraine and Bauman

THE SOCIAL THEORIES of Habermas, Touraine and Bauman are all marked
by a distrust of the very idea of community. At this juncture some consideration
will be given to their critiques of community, which offer a perspective that is neither
liberal nor communitarian. Habermas' and Touraine's critique of community is aimed
largely at communitarianism and more generally at nationalism, while Bauman's critique
of community is aimed at the nostalgia for community in contemporary society where
the problem of insecurity has become acute.

Habermas' position on community is ambivalent. On the one side, he rejects some
of the basic premises of communitarianism, in particular the tendency in communitarian
thought to conceive of society as a moral totality, and, on the other side, he wants
to retrieve the notion of a communication community, which is in danger of instru-
mentalization by commodified social relations. Communication as a form of social
action is the central concept in his work (Habermas, 1984, 1987). Social action is
based on language and, in this view, society is a linguistically created and sustained
entity. For Habermas communication is open-ended and is the basis of all social action;
it can never be reduced to an instrumental relationship since the communicative process
always resists closure and thus ultimately resists domination. This transcendental
component of communication means that it contains within it a degree of critique
and reflexivity. The aim of Habermas' social theory of modernity is to uncover the
communicative rationality in modern society and to demonstrate how American
tradition of communitarianism, community has been seen largely as appropriate to a
modern urban society in its retreat from the social ills of modernity. However, despite
this search for a modern kind of community that may be capable of offering an antidote
to the malaise of modernity, communitarianism has reflected a very anti-political view

of community. [I]n its civic republican formulations, it is a view of community that is very much disengaged from the state, locating community in the voluntaristic domain. Other versions of communitarianism stress the importance of the state to give some official status to particular cultural communities in order to foster a civic patriotism. This is clearly not a view of community as a basis of an alternative vision of society but an accommodation of groups within the larger framework.

This chapter addresses the radical dimension of community as expressed in protest, in the quest for an alternative society or the construction of collective identity in social movements. What is suggested by this conception of community as dissent is a more communicative model. Communities of dissent, or 'communities of resistance', are essentially communicative in their organization and composition, and in this they contrast with the emphasis on the symbolic, the civic and the normative in the other major models. In this sense of community, what is distinctive is not merely a normative vision of an alternative society, as in some of the great ideologies of modernity discussed in Chapter 1, but the construction of a communicative project that is formed in the dynamics of social action.

The chapter proceeds as follows. The first section looks at some critical theories of community (Habermas, Touraine and Bauman) and argues, following Habermas, for a notion of communication community. The second section discusses the connection between community and social movements. In this view community emerges out of the mobilization of people around a collective goal. In the third section, an attempt is made to reassess the idea communicative structures provide the basis of political possibilities. His theory of modernity thus aims to reconstruct modernity in terms of the expansion of critical forms of communication that are capable of resisting the other face of modernity, namely the instrumentalized forces of capitalism. More generally, this theorization of modern society is also one of a conflict of system and life-world whereby the communicative structures of the latter resist the instrumental rationality of the system.

Communication for Habermas operates on two levels. It is the basic medium of social integration and is the means of reconciling conflict, including competing political positions. On the first level, communication is embedded in the basic linguistic nature of social action. All social action is mediated by language and the essence of language is the social act of shared worlds. Although power relations and various pathologies disguise and distort communicative structures, it is always in principle possible that people, despite their differences, can agree on certain things. The very fact that social action is articulated through language implies the possibility of a shared conception of truth, justice, ethics and politics. The very capacity to speak entails an orientation to a possible agreement with another person and the tacit assumption of a shared world. Indeed, the very idea of the life-world is a communitarian notion. Although a consensus will never be arrived at, the capacity for people to deliberate in communicative modes of action can never be excluded in principle. This constitutes the second level of language, the reflective and critical dimension of deliberative communication, which is a point removed from, but always presupposed in, everyday life. In his study of the public sphere, Habermas argued how modern societies institutionalized spaces for public discourse (Habermas, 1989). His idea of discursive democracy reflects this basic communitarian understanding of politics as a dialogic process.

The ambivalence of community is that it can either be the expression of the communicative action of the life-world or it can be a retreat from communication in a purely moral stance that leaves the structure of domination untouched. As a communicative concept, then, community has been quite important in Habermas' social theory. The idea of a 'communication community' means that social relations in modern society are organized around communication rather than by other media such as authority, status or ritual. While of course power and money – along with law – are the most important media in steering modern society, it is a basic premise of Habermas' work that such systemic forms of reproduction always face resistance from the recalcitrant life-world which is reproduced by different logics and which are inextricably linked with communication. In modern society, there are more and more communicative spaces, the most significant being the public sphere and science. The public sphere consists of a multiplicity of communicative sites, which can exist at all levels of society ranging from nationally specific forms of civil society to transnational discourses. Science and the institution of the modern university, too, is an open communication community, according to Habermas, since it is characterized by a commitment to truth that can in principle be settled only by consensus. The notion that truth can be arrived at only in a deliberative manner and settled by consensus is the kernel of Habermas' theory of communication. It is this idea that leads him to reject communitarianism and to look to an alternative and more communicative idea of community. If community is what is shared, this must take a communicative form. This is the implication of Habermas' theory of communicative action. It also points to a transformative idea of community as the bringing to expression of communicative competences. Community is never complete but is always emergent.

For Habermas, communitarians such as, for instance, Charles Taylor or Hannah Arendt reduce the social to a moral totality rather than see it as a communicative structured process that is always in tension with the existing society. In fact, communitarianism ignores the communicative dimension of community, seeing it instead as merely moral or civic. For Habermas this reductive and highly normative stance in communitarianism denies the transformative moment in modern society, which derives from the very structures of communication. His critique of communitarianism does not share the liberal position, since the point is not the loss of moral individualism but the denial of the critical reflective capacity of society. In fact, Habermas shares with communitarians the desire to go beyond liberalism's moral individualism but does not agree with their commitment to an underlying morality. The morality of a community not only lays down how its members should act: it also provides grounds for the consensual resolutions of relevant conflicts (Habermas, 1998, p. 4). His position, especially in his recent work, stresses the existence of multiple communication communities and, in his more recent works, a multi-dimensional view of political community as also existing at the level of global society.

While Habermas' critique of communitarism has been shaped by his support for European integration and the recognition that cosmopolitan forms of community are becoming more and more important today, he is also responding to the dangers that community has represented in the context of Germany. Community has been one of the major legitimations of nationalism and in the extreme case it has provided a justification for fascism. As a moral totality, community is a dangerous sentiment since it reduces society to a non-social principle and it binds modernity to a premodern conception of society. For all these reasons, his social theory is very uneasy with the term community, although he never explicitly rejects it. Indeed, the very assumptions of his theory of communicative action presuppose the social and cultural context of a shared life-world. Shifting the focus from community to communication solves some of the difficulties with which community is beset. In this sense, then, the idea of community as communication community recalls the more variable and fluid notion of communitas discussed above.

This critical position on community is also found in Alain Touraine's work on democracy and modernity. Community and nationalism are very close, he argues. One of the most common expressions of community is *völkisch* sentiment and the notion that society is based on a pre-established unity over and above the individual and all social groups whose diversity must be denied in the assertion of wholeness. Touraine sees as the main challenge to democracy conceptions of politics that appeal to cultural heritage, community and nationalism. This does not mean that he is opposed to community in the sense of collective goals or the common good. The problem is that community has been debased by nationalism: 'Has not the pursuit of the common good become an obsession with identity and do we not need stronger institutional guarantees of respect for personal liberty and human rights rather than more integrated communities?' (Touraine, 1997, p. 112; see also pp. 65–8 and Touraine, 2000).

His theory of modernity sees society today as divided between a struggle of community versus markets and individualism (Touraine, 1995). In this situation, democracy is denied a social space, since it can exist in neither markets nor in community. A world dominated by community seeks only integration, homogeneity and consensus, rejecting democratic debate: 'A communitarian society is suffocating and can be transformed into a theocratic or nationalist despotism', he argues, and something like a 'cultural totalitarianism' is emerging today with community being resurrected by authoritarian forms of religion (Touraine, 1995, pp. 304, 311–12).

In contrast to community democracy allows a society to be both united and at the same time divided in the sense of a pluralist democracy consisting of many voices. However, this is not to say that Touraine is opposed to the principle of unity, which is in fact quite central to his thought. It might be suggested that like Habermas he is looking for an alternative conception of political community that does not reduce community to an underlying unity but builds upon diversity and communicative possibilities. Community alone will not achieve unity, according to Touraine, who is looking for a contemporary equivalent to the great social movements of modernity. The problem with community is that it places too much weight on identity: 'A society which defines itself primarily in terms of its identity cannot be democratic. Still less a society which defines itself in terms of its uniqueness. Such a society is too caught up in a logic that benefits only the State, which then reduces society to the nation and the multiplicity of social actors to the unity of the people' (Touraine, 1995, p. 343). Identity is central to community and to social movements, but when it becomes the sole component of a movement the result can only be an excessive preoccupation with the self and political impotence.

Zygmunt Bauman shares with Touraine and Habermas a deep scepticism of community. Community promises security but delivers only nostalgia and illusion, he argues in a recent book on community. It is, he says, merely a word that conveys a feeling of security that makes the world a warm and cosy place: 'We miss community because we miss security, a quality crucial to a happy life, but one which the world we inhabit is ever less able to offer and ever more reluctant to promise' (Bauman, 2001, p. 144). It is also a place where nobody is a stranger and where there is a shared understanding of society. However, it comes at a price, for security and freedom do not fit too easily together. In a true community there is no criticism or opposition. But this community does not exist as a natural entity, except perhaps as a utopia. The really existing community is a besieged fortress defending itself against the outside world. Bauman sees the contemporary world as one obsessed with digging cultural trenches. In fact, community is being resurrected today as the problem of identity becomes more acute. As real communities decline, identity replaces it around a new understanding of community. As a surrogate for community, it has reinvented identity (Bauman, 2001, p. 15). This is a point Eric Hobsbawm has made in *The Age of Extremes*: 'Never was the word "community" used more indiscriminately and emptily than in the decades when communities in the sociological sense became hard to find in real life' (Hobsbawm, 1994, p. 428).

The problem is that community is impossible because it cannot solve the problems with which it is confronted, in particular the problem of moral choice and uncertainty. Rather than facing these challenges directly, community offers only a comfortable illusion. In this sense, then, community was never lost – it was never born. Community is constantly appealed to by a present, dissatisfied with itself and needing the illusion of an alternative whether redeemed from the past or the promise of a utopia.

Communitarian thought, he argues, merely uncritically takes over the discourse of community and thereby simplifies greatly the social and existential problems of insecurity. Bauman shares with Habermas and Touraine a belief that something resembling community is possible but it needs to be redeemed from communitarianism and nationalism. 'If there is to be a community in the world of individuals, it can only be (and needs to be) a community woven together from sharing and mutual care; a community of concern and responsibility for the equal right to be human and the equal ability to act on that right' (Bauman, 2001, pp. 149–50). Against community and its false promises, Bauman argues for a postmodern ethics based on individual autonomy and in which the exclusion of the other is not the price to be paid for the identity of the self. Such a postmodern ethics cannot hide from the fact of insecurity but must live up to it.

In sum, the critical approaches to community in the work of Habermas, Touraine and Bauman might urge us to abandon community altogether. It would appear that community is not entirely compatible with a conception of modernity that stresses the critical power of communication and reflexivity. However, much of the problem with community can be resolved by taking a communicative approach to it. In this respect Habermas' notion of a communicatively constituted community offers an alternative to Bauman's stronger ethical position. The idea of a communication community can be theorized in a way that lends itself to a world of multiple belongings and one in which integration is achieved more by communication than by an already existing morality and consensus. In this context social movement theory – with its themes of dissent and identity as practice – has much to offer such a theory of community as communication.

References

Bauman, Z. (2001) *Community: Seeking Safety in an Insecure World*, Cambridge: Polity Press.

Habermas, J. (1984) *The Theory of Communicative Action, Vol. 1: Reason and the Rationalisation of Society*, Cambridge: Polity Press.

Habermas, J. (1987) *The Theory of Communicative Action, Vol. 2: Liveworld and System: A Critique of Functionalist Reason*, Cambridge: Polity Press.

Habermas, J. (1989) *The Structural Transformation of the Public Sphere*, Cambridge: Polity Press.

Habermas, J. (1998) *The Inclusion of the Other: Studies in Political Theory*, Cambridge, MA: MIT Press.

Hobsbawm, E. (1994) *The Age of Extremes: The Short Twentieth Century, 1914–1991*, London: Michael Joseph.

Touraine, A. (1995) *Critique of Modernity*, Oxford: Blackwell.

Touraine, A. (1997) *What is Democracy?*, Oxford: Westview Press.

Touraine, A. (2000) *Can We Live Together? Equal and Different*, Cambridge: Polity Press.

CHAPTER 4

Petra Kuppers

Community arts practices

Improvising being-together

SOCIAL THEORY'S RENEWED INTEREST in issues of community coincides with a new visibility for community arts and participatory art-making as alternative to high modernist art practice and the romantic legacy of the individual artist. In this chapter, I want to bring these areas of social thought into contact with one another, by asking what is at stake in the definitions of 'community' at work in community art practice, and in what way these definitions refract and intersect with the turn-away from essentialized identities and 'the nation'.

At the heart of this chapter are two art projects: 'Earth Stories' and 'Sleeping Giants' – two digital videos that emerged out of a two-year-long workshop series with a group of survivors of the mental health system in Wales, in the United Kingdom. As a resident of a small Welsh village, and a fellow disabled person, I collaborated with people using the village's mental health self-help center, and we created communal poetry, dance, performance, traditional music and a video.[1] In the following, I use 'we' when I speak about our practices and intents, and I use it advisedly – there is of course a tension between our art work and my academic writing about it, claiming a communal voice that cannot be anything but my own single one. But, given both our experiences together and the theme of this chapter, I have chosen to stay with this precariously positioned 'we'.

We used local legends and myths to find new ways of affirming our presence in our environment. With this, we found concrete ways of intervening in the negative representation of disabled people, and in particular survivors of the mental health system, in our locality and beyond. Acts of storytelling allow me to discuss our work as a meditation on how to approach community art work that wants to speak from a

Figure 2 The Olimpias: 'Earth Stories' video still, remembering the 'Lady of the Lake',
2004.

Photo: Richard Rogers.

group, and from individuals, without canceling out experiences, showing the longing
to 'belong' and yet the inability to completely merge with one another. As individuals,
we exist *in relation* – we are neither fully separate, nor fully embraced within a group.
So how can we both create and query 'community'?

Philosopher Jean-Luc Nancy provides theoretical tools to consider community
beyond self/other relations. In *The Inoperative Community*, he configures community by
thinking about the way that being-together can resist and deconstruct dominant power
relations, which attempt to weld the process of being-together into a fixed state.
Community exists in relationship and negotiation, and in an openness:

> Community is what takes place always through others and for others. It is
> not the space for the *egos* – subjects and substances that are at bottom
> immortal – but of the *I*'s who are always *others* (or else are nothing).
> (Nancy, 1991: 15)

The Others of the I emerge because of the finite nature of the singular: for Nancy,
singular beings lean towards others, searching 'contact of the skin (or the heart) of
another singular being, . . . [another finite being] always *other*, always shared, always
exposed' (1991: 28). This community is inoperative because the moment of sharedness,
of an absolute connection, is sundered as it emerges: it is negated by the singularity
of the I just as the I leans and cannot help but lean towards the other. There are no
egos that claim immortality, only I's that know of their limit and seek others who
share this limit, too.

Storytelling and myth-making are important parts of Nancy's articulation of the inoperative community, a community that becomes inoperative at the same moment at which it offers relation.

> We know the scene: there is a gathering, and someone is telling a story . . . They were not assembled like this before the story; the recitation has gathered them together. . . . In the speech of the narrator, their language for the first time serves no other purpose than that of presenting the narrative and of keeping it going. It is no longer the language of their exchanges, but of their reunion – the sacred language of a foundation and an oath. The teller shares it with them and among them.
>
> (1991: 43–4)

Storytelling, sharing language and myth-making are the offerings that allow the horizon of community to appear: 'That the work must be offered to communication means that it must in effect be *offered*, that is to say, presented, proposed, and abandoned on the common limit where [singularities] share one another' (1991: 73).

In storytelling (and Nancy uses the 'foundational scene' of a circle, and a male storyteller), singularities can experience the shared limit: foundational stories make community inoperative, as the distance between the story's ontological claim is thrown back onto the experience of the singularity's limit, and the possibility of the I's death. Wanting to listen, hear, and tell, we are abandoned to the distance between the story and our I's, but we lean in, move our heads into the circle, hovering in the space between the I and the communal story.

To me, Nancy's account of community speaks of continuous flows – of a leaning movement, of responsibility, of meanings. These I's who are others – singularities constantly in negotiation, touching their limit – are provisional, temporal. Life flows – no point of standing still, definition, or grounding of identity in ontology is possible in this conception of improvisational community. In this chapter, this emphasis on the I's who are others informs the discussion of art-making as improvisational flow.

In the two art projects, everyday performance was the ground on which we built our communal art work: being unconsciously and consciously in spaces that have histories, dominant narratives, dominant ways of being seen. Our disabilities meant exclusion from some of the spaces we were investigating. Our environment was a Welsh village, surrounded by the green hills of a national park: the Brecon Beacons. The exclusions we experienced worked on a variety of levels, from physical access to do with stairs, public transport or stamina, to imaginary access, to do with patterns of usage, ownership of a locale's imagination and the use it is put to. Through performance, and, importantly, through mediation of those performances in public environments, we inscribed our right of access to these spaces, we made our presences felt. The performance act became the performative act: a conscious inscription of difference into sedimented patterns of naturalized 'law'. With this, our work is not located within art therapy, changing ourselves, but within political labor, changing ourselves and our world.

Our communal practice refused to be singularly authored, and this anti-romantic tactic links our work back to everyday practices of story-telling. Community, this impossible goal, is tactically erected as a place to momentarily speak from.

With this chapter, I am offering a contemplation not (only) of a community of minds, but of co-habitation, embodiment and enworldedness as necessary aspects of a thinking towards a coming community.

Local stories

To speak about 'community', I find it important to establish the ecology of the specific example of an intervention into the formation and articulation of community as a process. 'Community' emerges as many things in the following: as an ideal, a marketing tool, an experience, a hope and a problem.

The village of Ystradgynlais, where all the activities I am discussing here took place, is situated on the edges of the Brecon Beacons, a national park in the middle of Wales. Ystradgynlais used to support itself through the mining industry, and the rolling hills surrounding it have been changed by Roman soldiers, Celtic inhabitants, sheep grazing, canals and now disused railway lines. The people supported by this land include a Welsh-speaking minority and a majority of English-speaking inhabitants. The language of Wales suffered under Great Britain's imperialist policy, and has been rooted out by various historical practices, such as forbidding the language to be spoken in schools or in public meetings. More recently, the language has been re-introduced into school curricula, and a culture war surrounds its problematic position in modern Wales. Against an image of Wales as a country of anti-imperialistic segregationist politics stands the image of Wales perpetuated in tourist brochures. This image is the rural idyll, with bucolic pastoral characters such as sheepdog owners, and craftspeople, who make things with their hands out of wood and reed.

All of these images, though, do not capture the reality for many of the people living in Ystradgynlais, and, in particular, the experiences of people hidden on the economic margin, unemployed or disabled. Both the fiercely national and the bucolic image rely on segregationist and exclusionary concepts of community, on a single vision that references historical origin and continuity. This kind of mobilization of 'community' is deeply suspect to feminists and others who wish to consider social change in conjunction with collective action. Thus Iris Marion Young critiques 'community' ideals when they become a desire for social wholeness and identification – a form of politics that relies on sameness, and which in turn erects exclusionary zones and borders (1990). Benedict Anderson, in *The Imagined Community*, sees the problem of national community and its seductiveness in a different light: here, '[I]t is imagined as a *community*, because, regardless of the actual inequality and exploitation that may prevail in each, the nation is always conceived as a deep, horizontal comradeship' (1991: 5–7). But how can a community politics that keeps openness, provisionality and respect for difference alive be mobilized?

In order to address this question, I collaborated with fellow disabled people in Wales. We realized that to create affective and effective arts for social change, we needed to find points of entry into the representational canon, into the images and stories of Wales.

Many disabled people in Wales became so due to their labor in coal mines: white-finger vibration symptoms and lung diseases are common, as is arthritis. Depression and other mental health symptoms are also common in Wales, one of the poorest regions in Britain. Nationally and internationally, though, mental health issues in the countryside are marginalized – mental health has become increasingly focused upon as an urban problem, one associated with the rise of modernity's social arrangements and alienations. Studies (such as Torrey and Miller (2001)) bear out this trend: epidemiologically, mental health and in particular schizophrenia, tend to be associated with the city. The rise of the city and the rise and visibility of institutional practice around mental health technologies are linked in the cultural imagination.

Few of these realities of contemporary rural life find their way into the romanticized images of Wales. Television images of the Brecon Beacons, for many the main access to their local landscape, emphasize a place set apart from the everyday, a place of Sunday TV programming with English voices and tweed. Fishing, sheep husbandry and farming form the mainstream images – and the visible reality of these occupations tend to be male-dominated. Many of the participants of the mental health self-help group were female, and they found their voices marginalized not only by disability and class, but also by gender.

The answer to access is not to bring a bus onto the heath, but to find meaning-ful ways of structuring activity within the national park, and of finding connections between the park and the everyday. In the first meetings within the group, we agreed that one of our prime objectives for the creation of art works was to re-image ourselves, to speak for us and for others about our lived reality of mental health as people living where we did. Everybody in the group had had significant mental health experiences, and encounters with the mental health system. Life experiences included voice-hearing, the diagnosis of schizophrenia, manic depression, anxiety disorders, etc. Some had been hospitalized in the past, and knew at first hand the horror of some institutions. Many were on drug regimes. Some had prison experiences, others had been homeless. Among us were retired miners, factory workers, one teacher, and homemakers. For many of us, loneliness and the experience of the I as singular stood in tension with a way of life that romanticizes village life, communality and community. As we began our work together, we had to assert to each other again and again 'you cannot know . . . you know', that double bind of singular beings and community that Nancy offers.

In our initial meetings and discussions, over tea, we decided that we wanted to use the vocabulary that surrounded us in our media world, the vocabulary of land, myths and history, both personal and national. These were the important, foundational stories of our environment, and we wanted to approach ownership of them – even though we were aware of their problematic nature. Our lives were not apart from these images, and the desire to be seen mixed uneasily with the desire to use the images and narratives that shape the mediation of our world to ourselves.

The initial idea of working in the mental health self-help center was, then, to combine elements of disability politics and storytelling. We wanted to break the silence surrounding mental health issues, in particular in rural areas, but we wanted to present our experiences in an ambivalent way, not merely to stress the negative experiences, but to retain our dignity and pride. Negotiating the tensions and opportunities between the individual voice and a communal myth-making became central elements of the poetics we built together.

Methods: the 'Lady of the Lake'

The focus of our first sets of workshops, in 2001, was the story of the 'Lady of the Lake'. This story is centered on a lake high up in the hills of the Brecon Beacons, in an area of moors and high fens. The story mirrors similar myths in various British and international locations: a female fairy steps out of the waters, leaves her kingdom, to marry a mortal, and not fit in, or to marry a mortal not worthy of her; and then to vanish again, having transformed aspects of human experience. A local fish-and-chip shop displays the following summary of the Brecon Beacon 'Lady of the Lake' story, painted as part of a mural and written in 'heritage' script on its walls:

> In the midst of beautiful mountain scenery, about 16 miles from here, is the lovely lake of Llyn y fan fach. Here, legend has it that a beautiful woman appeared to a poor shepherd boy who was so taken by her that he asked for her hand in marriage. She agreed, but only on condition that he wouldn't strike her 3 times. However, he found cause to and she returned to the lake with her dowry of animals. Behind her were left 3 sons who became the famous doctors of Wales.
> (Mural at the Bwyty West End Café, Llandovery)

In the imagination of local people, the story of the 'Lady of the Lake' has, naturally, many more facets, subsets, versions and events than the bare-bones story narrated on this local wall. In the self-help group, we found in particular that stories that emphasized the *reasons* for the violence of the husband on his fairy wife were of interest in many of the versions the women in the group knew and had selected to remember.

In the workshops that followed, we used performance tableaux, rituals, creative writing methods and spatial chorus work to create moments out of the legend's connection with our lives. Through this legend work, we accessed a realm of political practice similar to the kind of practices that de Certeau calls 'tactical', which undermine the 'strategic' – the central force, inscribing its laws legitimately. The strategic is forceful, dominant; it can lay down rules, generalize these and make them work. The tactical is the work of the minority, the non-dominant. 'A tactic insinuates itself into the other's place, fragmentarily, without taking it over in its entirety, without being able to keep it at a distance' (de Certeau, 1988: xix).

de Certeau offers the distinction between the strategy and the tactic as a way of understanding the nature of resistance within the field of discourse. Resistance is not conceptualized as fully there, conscious, strategic, an organized political practice. Instead, de Certeau sees everyday practices as tactical interventions: he likens walking and talking to acts that momentarily, locally, impact on power structures. An embodied knowledge of the street allows a way of living that negotiates the dictates of street grids, and the vision of social planning, abstraction or metaphorization of life: by walking the street, the 'soulless' plan becomes a lived experience that could, potentially, open up a moment of difference. People get away with things:

> (v)ictories of the 'weak' over the 'strong' (whether the strength be that of powerful people or the violence of things or of an imposed order, etc.), clever tricks, knowing how to get away with things, 'hunter's cunning', maneuvers, polymorphic situations, joyful discoveries, poetic as well as warlike.
>
> (de Certeau, 1984: xix)

de Certeau's work on the politics and poetics of the everyday outlines how Foucault's resistances can function in practice. His work shows how life deals with rules and how these rules can only be bound by temporality given the force of life running through them, leavening their strength.

Legends and myths, the energies expended on 'storytelling' a location and thereby making it 'human', play an important part in this interaction between strategies and tactics. The absolute rule of 'history' as a monolithic discourse, one that has naturalized itself into truth, is put into question by the power of the minor story, the legend. de Certeau writes: '[W]hereas historiography recounts in the past tense the strategies of instituted powers, these 'fabulous' stories offer their audience a repertory of tactics for future use' (de Certeau, 1984: 23).

de Certeau sees hollow places in the everyday, moments of layering that become accessible in the activity of the everyday, that make the everyday habitable by creating 'depth' and 'space', spatial metaphors that create 'habitation' – a space where one *can* be, rather than having to be in one way only. Legends have an important function in this desire to make a space out of a place, making it human-shaped, habitable, weaving it into the practices of the everyday. They help to create a phenomenological, lived experience of a location.

> It is through the opportunity they offer to store rich silences and wordless stories, or rather through their capacity to create cellars and garrets everywhere, that local legends . . . permit exists, ways of going out and coming back in, and thus habitable spaces.
>
> (de Certeau, 1984: 106)

Legends are seen here as 'exits': as *Spielraum*, room to play, offering the potential to not be caught in an endless, dominant signification. They allow for a place to be seen differently. This ability of legends to open up spaces for difference were used in the process of 'Earth Stories': using the make-believe of the legend allowed our group to make-believe about our own situation, and therefore to allow our imaginations to soar. Ultimately, this strategy allows us to see ourselves as not fixed *in* discourse, but to *experience* discourse as a *Spielraum*. And yet this 'freedom' also highlighted again and again the distance between myth and the limited I, the inoperable nature of storytelling that haunts our gatherings.

de Certeau links this ability of stories and their historical, layered ghosting of a specific location to tactics, evading the fixed knowledges of Foucault's *Panopticon*:

> There is no place that is not haunted by many different spirits hidden there
> in silence, spirits one can 'invoke' or not. Haunted places are the only
> ones people can live in – and this inverts the schema of the *Panopticon*.
> (de Certeau, 1984: 108)

These local stories create forms of knowledge that are minor, local, momentarily evoked – in tension with the 'public'.

These links between knowledge and minor discourses, and between practice and transformatory repetition, became graspable in the workshops. Every time we joke about the woman's perception of the strikes her husband gives her, the perspective shifts momentarily from the 'inevitable' difference between human and fairy to gender issues: traditional tellings of the story use the point of view of the young man who wants to wed the lovely lady he saw in the lake while he was herding his sheep. Every time we transpose our local environment into the gothic genre, we see our world with different eyes, and the 'normal' loses its hold temporarily. Nancy's community of I's who are others, who journey together to see themselves shifting, becoming, and yet are part of a common place, emerges in this improvisatory play. Becoming other, stepping outside the rules of place and space, means being both more and more fully the I's we already are: our imaginations and ways of being allow for more than one facet of subject position, but are always bound back to the conditions of singularity, subjectivity, imagination and context that we live in. We can recognize the strangenesses and familiarities in each other, the moment where the story and the I are cast asunder, where the experience of the limit exiles us from full presence in the myth we make. But instead of retreating to disappointed selves, we can see otherness within ourselves, and we can begin to build community that is both located in specific conditions and yet open to difference. The tactical uses of holding open the multiplicity of the I are not without serious discomfort, though: no place of rest and certainty is available.

In our projects, all of us weld our identities in new provisional alignments: Welsh, English, German, farmer, miner, unemployed, academic, artist, writer, performer, family member, patient, victim, survivor, client and many more. When we work together, paying careful heed to the multiple identities means that we strive to hold open the unknown: a sense of difference within the known, within the warm atmosphere of our meetings. Listening to the poetry we write, many of these singularities as multiple, in new constellation, emerge as we trust ourselves to share. The sharing is the core part of this relation: not the content of what is shared, or the reception of the shared content and its understanding. The *act of leaning* anchors our circle. Nancy's leaning towards community allows me to think of these differences and otherings, as well as those that swing among us unsaid, unwritten, and as yet unthought, as potentialities that feed our community, and question its boundaries and definitions.

de Certeau offers a phenomenology of resistance: of the embodiment of living within structures, opening up spaces for people to live in. The political hope I hold is that the accumulation of layers, distancing us from the 'dominant' story of our world and its relation, and from our story of our self, doesn't just alienate us, but opens up Nancy's I's as others. This offers up a reservoir of richness that binds us with different ties to one another and to our locality. I believe that a stronger grasp of the potential of group communication and a sense of pride in the 'deep' location surrounding us can awaken social processes and political consciousness. Art-making plays a significant part in this transformatory process: the workshops were process-based, but over a period of time, we shaped aspects of our work together into a product that could leave the circle of the self-help center and travel into the wider social world. Early on in one workshop, we created a short performance piece about the lady of the lake, consisting of a number of tableaux and transitions and a narrative recited as a choral, with individual voices taking on different 'characters'. The group showed great pride in their creation after a number of run-throughs, and the moving together, creating spaces and openings for one another set a new tone of intimacy and openness in the following workshops. As we talked about the experience it became clear that, while we felt a desire to show our work, we acknowledged a multitude of problems in bringing the performance 'live' to local events. And thus, our version of the 'Lady of the Lake' traveled to the outside as a video, combining spoken poetry and visuals, recording us in the countryside we were talking about. This provided a very useful vehicle for allowing our imaginations to soar, and our writing and our stories became wilder, as we all realized that a different set of rules (strategies) governs the universe of video-making when compared with live art.

Embodiment as a reservoir and repetition of knowledge played an interesting part in the way that memories became retrievable, and entered from the private into the social: when we were exploring the connection between our childhood memories and the story, most of us pointed to moments of outside physical activity as a pivotal point in our memories: walking in a group of schoolchildren, standing by a gate in the garden, playing in a field. Meditating on the myth brought many of the participants to recall the feeling of grass under their fingers, or their emotions as they sat amongst rocks. We discussed how video would allow us to show intimate perspectives, including the touch of hand on stone, in close-up.[2] Sensations usually characterized as 'minor' or 'private' took on a different charge as we gave ourselves permission to focus on *our* way of telling, and how it felt right to *us*. Soon our workshops moved outside, from the living room of the community center to the small garden. We collected sensations, feelings, stories, moments, images and scenes. I acted as a facilitator and scribe: recording with whatever means possible what we hoarded, moderating discussions that edited our collection of everyday practices and local retellings down to manageable size. Our poems were all communal: we agreed on a theme to write about, and then we all produced four lines, with sometimes only single words in each line. Then we read them out to each other. And finally read them communally: in a circle, everybody reading their first line, then as the circle came round again the second one. In this way, a communal theme created a coherence in the poem, but one that was beyond the individual author. In these poetry rounds, the I's do not share their singularity, but we lean in, from our own singularities into a rhythm, a round.

> Giant river boulders, round hollows ground into them, by the rushing
> river twirling into deep dark pools.
> Branches bent, fingers grip, fear flings me into the hole.
> Grass bends into the earth.
> In the craggy rocks, an opening to an underground tunnel.
> I am frightened of the darkness.
> The sense of not knowing where will it lead to, how long will it go on
> for.
> Suddenly there is light ahead – a cave in the mountainside.
> Deliver me from the fear of darkness, lady of the lake.
> The lady of the lake appears in the garden, and flies to the moon and the
> stars, and promises, good times will appear once more.
> (from 'Earth Stories' video-poem)

Anxieties: 'Sleeping Giants'

If 'Earth Stories' was our summer story, our celebration, and our engagement with mainstream aesthetics, the next video we created, 'Sleeping Giants', was our winter work. It is harsher, its production is even further removed from 'the professional' as we took the camera with us all the time, with different videographers amongst us capturing the shots.

The video-poem deals with another local story: as you move towards Ystradgynlais and through it, you can see a hill above the village. The outline of the hill is like a lying man – and the formation is called the 'Sleeping Giant'.

> I wish I could lie still
> For a long long time like you do
> Is the sleeping giant going to wake up?
> Is the sleeping giant going to wake up?
> Head in the clouds
> Stone body
> tilting feet first
> down into the earth
> (from 'Sleeping Giants' video-poem)

This 'mountain man' is not visible from any static point – the best views can only be gained by traveling in a car. The route follows the closed and disused line of the canal that used to transport coal from the Beacons and Ystradgynlais to the ironworks. And this connection between the giant and the coal, the hill and the mineworkings, the cave, the weight of history, the lost grandeur of Welsh economic power, is the back-story of our second video-poem. In it, we search: our original idea was anchored in the detective genre, searching compulsively for the Giant. Compulsion disorders and anxiety is something many of us in the group share, and we saw here a way of again transforming individual mental habits into an artistic vision.

> Find a deep cave to the heart of the giant
> It is dark but my eyes adjust
> Two small points of light in the darkness
> I can see the light through the crevices of his fingers
> Heart beating faster, I could feel the warmth and the need to get closer
>   to the giant's heart.
> The giant's heart is a cave of stalagmites, an unchartered country.
> (from 'Sleeping Giants' video-poem)

By reading de Certeau, I shored up my sense of the communal importance of our art-making. I can make sense of the empowerment, the euphoria of re-imaging ourselves.

But, of course, the act of labor itself is always visible, the tactic remains momentary, minor, a forced insertion. Performance substitutes, cites, re-creates. However performance does not offer an easy substitute; it offers a labored one. To quote Joseph Roach: 'a stand-in for an elusive entity that it is not but that it must vainly aspire both to embody and to replace' (1996: 3). This Sleeping Giant isn't mythical, ritualistic, always-already-there, outside history. In our practice, the Giant becomes discursive, historically contingent, an oratorical procedure. By recounting when we saw him, we historicize him, binding his presence to the time of our lives – bridging distances between I's and myths. With this, our Giant as myth, retold, offers us a process of community communication. By destabilizing the founding story, we fight for entry into the realm where new meaning can be founded at the same time as we continue to be suspicious of founding stories and their exclusionary effects. And it is our loss of certainty, our anxiety, that allows for new community to come into being, in being-together, and in joint exploration.

> Here the mythic hero – and the heroic myth – interrupts his pose and his epic. He tells the truth: that he is not a hero, not even, or especially not, the hero of writing or literature, and that there is no hero, there is no figure who alone assumes and presents the heroism of the life and death of commonly singular beings. He tells the truth of the interruption of his myth, the truth of the interruption of all founding speeches, of all creative and poietic speech, of speech that schematizes a world and that fictions an origin and an end. He says, therefore, that foundation, poiesis and scheme are always offered, endlessly, to each and all, to the community, to the absence of communion through which we communicate and through which we communicate to each other not *the* meaning of community, but *an infinite reserve of common and singular meanings*.
> (Jean-Luc Nancy, 1991: 79)

When we as a group engage our local myths, we do so with an agenda and a tactical sense. We substitute the dominant myth, but the act of substitution creates a new anxiety and liminality, new impossible desires for wholeness and plenitude: a traumatics of political art labor. The mythological fullness of mythology is not available to us. Our myth is a substitute myth, hewn out of dominant images as a response to them.

Conclusion: community art

In 'Earth Stories' and 'Sleeping Giants' we translate. We transpose perceptual or cognitive difference into sources of artistic endeavor. Our communal practice that refuses to be singularly authored binds our work back to everyday practices of storytelling. And, ultimately, our work also came back to the traditional places of storytelling. Eventually, both 'Earth Stories' and 'Sleeping Giants' had very successful exhibition records, traveling to the British National Film Theatre (as part of different years of the National Disability Film Festival), and to many other international film festivals, conferences, and disability culture meetings. But these circuits were quite far removed from the realities of the Welsh village, and the everyday funding and acceptance struggles of a mental health self-help organization in its own locality. More importantly, then, our videos played and continue to play locally. The mental health self-help center uses the video as part of its regular stand at the local markets, where the stand functions to raise awareness of the center and its function in the community. The videos have also helped the center to raise funds: they provide excellent marketing material, and give an insight into the abilities, depth and creativity of the people using the center. In all of these marketplaces, where information is exchanged and public visibility tested, our re-visions of ourselves tactically undermine stereotypes of disability. In the video interviews that accompany the video-poem about the 'Lady of the Lake', two participants say this about their experiences in the project:

> When we began this project, I was very apprehensive about starting it. I've always written, but it was always personal, private to me. But I never ever dreamed that anything like this could have come out of it. Because people with a mental health problem, there is such a stigma attached to it. It is like people with a mental health problem are non-achievers, but that's not true to all. Because what we achieve in doing this project is more that I could ever dreamed of doing!

> Being part of this project has been a revelation. I worked in a group, which wasn't something I was used to doing when I had my own mental distress, disability. I always had the feeling that something good could come out of something that at the time was so very bad and black and terrible. But I know that if we go really deep inside ourselves, we can reach a creative point and that is what working in this group has revealed to me.
>
> (video transcript)

In the processes of the project, its products and in the use we make of these products in the locality, the impossible goal of community emerges as a provisional place from which to speak. Working and re-working the connections between the everyday, the artistic, the land and the people, the village and the mental health self-help group, images of mental health and conceptual or temporal difference, plenitude and desire, we again and again start to knit places to live in, and we do so in being-together. We lean, connecting I's and others, singular story and myth. The last words of this chapter, then, come from our group rather than from one single voice:

> This is not a giant of despair,
> this is a giant of hope
> I saw him after the snowfall
> silent and frozen in time
> His cheek was wet
>
> He lay there like a monster,
> quiet and still
> I thought if he yawned,
> his arms would reach the sky

Notes

1   The work was initially funded by a MIND Millennium Award, a fund that allowed people to create work that strengthened their communities, without a salary or artist's fee component for the organizer. Later, additional funds from the University of Wales, Swansea, Adult Outreach Department and, most significantly, from the National Endowment for Science, Technology and the Arts, allowed us to extend our work. My academic appointments allow me to work in this collaborative and research-focused manner, without the expectation of 'peer-reviewed' outcomes or venues for 'my' art practice. It is important to stress, though, that while community arts are (relatively speaking) thriving in many countries, community artists often struggle to make a living.
     In the case of the Olimpias projects in Wales, the fact that I do not necessarily get paid for projects I facilitate can be an important feature of building trust and working together. In other projects, and always dependent on funding structures, this issue is dealt with differently: in the Olimpias projects in Rhode Island, every participant gets paid for participation in every workshop, as a recognition of their creative labor, appropriate to the way that recognition is usually bestowed in the US.

2   Participants and collaborators in the Olimpias projects are aware that I am an academic, and (in some way) of the ways that value and recognition flow within the academy. But they also know that I do not write about projects immediately, or after only short contact, and that I carefully guard privacy and confidences. When I do write about projects, it is with permission, and usually after a long period of reflection. In the main, collaborators know me as a fellow disabled woman, with many stories and issues that I share with them, but are not for publication or public consumption,

just like their own. They know me as a disability culture activist, and they know that my writing is always in aid of a larger political project: the validation and celebration of disability culture and community arts.

References

Anderson, Benedict (1991) *Imagined Communities: Reflections on the Origin and Spread of Nationalism*, London and New York: Verso.

de Certeau, Michel (1988) *The Practice of Everyday Life*, Berkeley, Los Angeles, CA, and London: University of California Press.

Nancy, Jean-Luc (1991) *The Inoperative Community*, translated by Peter Connor, Lisa Garbus, Michael Holland and Simona Sawhney, Minneapolis, MI: University of Minnesota Press.

Roach, Joseph (1996) 'Cities of the Dead', *Circumatlantic Performance*, New York: Columbia University Press.

Torrey, E. Fuller and Miller, Judy (2001) *The Invisible Plague: The Rise of Mental Illness from 1750 to the Present*, Brunswick, NJ, and London: Rutgers University Press.

Young, Iris Marion (1990) 'The Ideal of Community and the Politics of Difference', in Linda J. Nicholson (ed.), *Feminism/Postmodernism*, New York and London: Routledge.

CHAPTER 5

Anita Gonzalez

Tactile and vocal communities in Urban Bush Women's *Shelter* and *Praise House*

COMMUNITIES, PERFORMED OR OTHERWISE, are created and maintained through verbal as well as non-verbal associations. In the world of dance performance, the tactile nature of the work creates physical touching and sharing that help to bond the performers. For a black dance company such as the Urban Bush Women, the physical and emotional bonds enacted on-stage replicate somewhat the physical and emotional traumas that emerge from a historically troubled past. Political implications of the Urban Bush Women's work surface from the company's depiction of humor, yearning, joy, grief, anger and frustration characteristic of African American womanhood. Many Bush Women dances humanize black women as a 'way of reclaiming history and paying attention to erasures and misconceptions about the "bush people" in colonial narratives' (Chatterjea, 2003: 452).[1]

I am particularly interested in how the tactile operates within several signature Urban Bush Women works. Sound, movement and body-to-body contact serve to unite dancers on-stage and to create a subjective sense of communal fortitude or struggle. Because the unified bodies are African-American women, audiences are often moved to see these dances as testaments to African-American communal solidarity. In many dances from the company's early repertoire (1984–94), the tight sweaty unity of bodies creates an on-stage ambience that marks identity for performers and, at times, audience members. The company's aesthetic of depicting unity through collective group movement may carry political overtones. Historically, unified blacks have meant trouble for the white majority. In the Urban Bush Women's work, the choral nature of the ensemble also provides a space in which dancers/performers can experience the utopia of communal support even as they perform their individual parts.

The African-American collective

Early Urban Bush Women repertory works such as *River Songs* (1984), *Marinesa* (1985) and *Song of Lawino* (1988) emphasized black women's unity in the face of adversity. Nearly stationary images of women as supportive clusters are peppered throughout the dances like still photos. Sometimes the choreographic moments capture the women in encounters of gentle touching; sometimes they are united in their angry and menacing rage. In *River Songs*, for example, a group of women gather by the edge of an unnamed river to sing, chant, comfort each other and comb one another's hair. One woman, in a moment of grieving, is embraced, rocked and eventually supported as the collective bathes her and releases her inner pain.[2] *Song of Lawino* (1988), based upon the writings of Okot b'Pitek, was a play with music in which the collective voices of multi-ethnic women spoke the thoughts of a single African woman.[3] In the play the central character questions her husband's treatment of her after his return from Europe. She expresses her rage and confusion about his abusive behaviors through songs, text and gestured actions performed by the entire cast.

Jawole Willa Jo Zollar, the Artistic Director and founder of the Urban Bush Women, by having a single woman's experience fragmented and then represented by an entire community, aesthetically demonstrates that women can collectively triumph over the challenges of life. In her work it is through community ensemble and connection rather than heroism that people are able to survive. Sally Banes, describing Urban Bush Women's work writes: 'It offers a utopian vision in which strong women magically save the world, but it is also a celebration of the real communities that have enabled black women's survival'.[4] While other artists of the same time (the 1980s) were engaging in solo performance work and the project of articulating autobiographical texts as representations of multi-cultural experiences, Zollar was using the collective ensemble to represent the African-American community. Banes describes the utopian vision of the Urban Bush Women as one in which strength will save the world, but I see the utopia of the company as a complex interweaving of emotion and solidarity that establishes the performing community, a community of black women, as something separate and apart from the rest of the world. This project of depicting unity within the African-American experience was (is) particularly important because of the social and political history of the United States that has resulted in the fragmentation of black families. Zollar, relating this sense of collective action to the African-American community, says:

> We have always turned to the community. I think it's just been a tradition
> . . . and in all the things I've read, the community, particularly the working
> class or poor community, is that place where black culture really bubbles
> up, and goes out.[5]

This ideal of linking a sociopolitical community with a performance collective is somewhat troubling because individual politics do not always mesh with the project of making art. Making theatre involves bringing people together in a room to experience the world of the production. The political preferences of the individual artists involved

Figure 3 Urban Bush Women lead Summer Institute performance, *Are We Democracy?*
Photo: James Burwell.

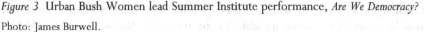

may or may not relate to the production's ideals. At the same time, assuming that a group of black artists share common perspectives is problematic as class and other social categories greatly influence African-American perspectives. The impact of the African-American community on the Urban Bush Women's productions (or the Urban Bush Women's productions on the African-American community) is difficult to measure, as audience response is diverse, fluid, and dependent upon a variety of social and political factors. In some dances, the community most affected by Zollar's communal ideals was that of the performers who participated in the dance project.

The physicality of *Shelter*

The Urban Bush Women dance *Shelter*, in particular, reflects the artistic director's desire to create, through collective ensemble movement, a shared history of fortitude in times of trauma. *Shelter* was a dance about homelessness that aimed to depict the desperation of the disenfranchised. It was presented as a 'work in progress' at the Israel Festival in May 1988 before its official première at 'Montpellier Dance Festival' (in France) in June 1988. Performances in France were followed by a second première at The Kitchen in New York within an evening entitled 'Heat' (September 1988). After its New York opening *Shelter* became a part of the Urban Bush Women's repertory and toured nationally for nearly a decade (1988–96).

Emotive connections were strong in *Shelter* because some of the physical feats within the dance could only be achieved through heightened emotion. For example, in one section of the dance, the physical was used to create a visceral sense of fear when dancers were asked to create a tremble in their stomachs and then move that tremble throughout the entire body. The rapid vibrations escalated until they shook the entire body and influenced the bodies and emotions of other dancers in the immediate vicinity. Choreographer Zollar chose to accentuate the effect of the vibrating tremble by having the dancers work in huddles and tight groupings so that the individual, corporeal feelings of fear could become collective responses to the imaginary events of the dance. For most of us, the trembles also created an emotional connection to past moments of fear. Once each dancer had created a sense of panic within herself, then this panic was directed towards a specific space – perhaps an empty corner of the room, or towards the musician – so that each person's individual emotion could be collectively focused toward a common goal.

The high point of the dance is an attack sequence in which the dancers run furiously backwards and forward in a diagonal line throwing their fearful anger towards an imaginary foe. The attack sequence was the culmination of the internalized fear evoked in the previous section. After holding the feeling of panic in the belly for the opening sequence of the dance, the forceful energy of the attack allowed the body to jettison the fear towards a collective target. The dance directive for the attack was to throw the energy of the body toward the imagined enemy until the body was exhausted, incapable of further resistance. Later in the dance, after the attack sequence, the dancers, who had reached a heightened emotional state because of the physical enactments of fear and anger, found release in the comforting community of the clump. This was a transformative moment in which the dancers achieved a collective feeling of utopia within their performance.

Earlier I described *Shelter* as a dance in which the collective ensemble could experience a shared history of fortitude in times of trauma. This moment was achieved when the dancers, physically and emotionally spent after executing the attack, could find others, equally exhausted, to lean upon. The closing phrases of the dance contained moments of caressing, huddling and other forms of physical contact. These responses were almost spontaneous as the distressed community of performers sought solace in one another. The word community was never used within the ensemble to describe this feeling of solidarity, but the pleasure of finding another human being for support had both physical and emotional ramifications. Once immersed in the temporary nightmare of hopelessness and desperation, it was gratifying to feel the presence of other bodies moving in synchronicity on the stage. To take a step forward one dancer could lean upon another to ease the pain in the lower back. The descent to the floor (a metaphor for the hard sidewalks of the street) was softened as sweaty bodies helped to support the weight of each individual dancer. An extended arm, a caressing hip – these leans and supports became an intuitive way of feeling the safety net of human presence.

The use of collective groupings in *Shelter* was not accidental. Zollar frequently uses the 'clump', a tight choreographic composition of bodies huddled together, to physically and visually demonstrate the communal unity of the artists.[6] This huddled mass appears in many Urban Bush Women's works and for some, such as *Girlfriends* (1986), it becomes the primary choreographic structure. The grouping is intended to be 'organic, like particles clustered together for strength'.[7] Dancers gather together in a clump and exchange breath, song, or unison phrases. Sometimes they simply lean upon one another. Afterwards the dancers usually move away from the group and out on their own with renewed vigor. Therefore, the clump becomes a physical and visual symbol of gathering strength before the fray. By staging dances with collective groupings of performers, Zollar underscores the close connections between social consciousness, emotionality, and performance – connections that are reinforced within the African-American experience. The dancers perform movements that are linked to individual emotional expressions, the individual emotive bodies are united through clumping, and the emotive clumps are then manipulated by the choreographer to make social statements about female bonding, African-American and other communities, and the politics of disenfranchisement.

Praise House as vocal ensemble

The collective community was used very differently in the 1990 musical theatre work *Praise House*. Once again, Zollar established a community of African-American performers; however, this time, the community united around shared senses of ecstasy based upon southern black church rituals. *Praise House* deliberately uses the theatrical dance structures of church rituals to illustrate a dramatic tale while at the same time provoking transformation of the spirit within the characters on-stage. Because the genre of the work was a dance theatre, both sound and touch were used to create the sense of communal ensemble that is characteristic of the company's style.

Jawole Zollar describes a 'praise house' as:

> . . . a place that people went to worship, a kind of leaderless church. It didn't have a preacher, but it was a gathering where you testified you gave witness to the energy that was created, so it was the idea of raising the energy to have this, experience together to glorify something higher than your self.[8]

She transformed this conception of a 'praise house' into a musical theatre work based upon the real-life story of Minnie Evans, a North Carolina artist who lived between 1890 and 1987. It had its first full production at the Spoleto Festival in 1990, was premiered at the Brooklyn Academy of Music in November 1991, and was later filmed by Julie Dash for the 'Alive from off Center' PBS series in summer 1991. It featured an elaborate set by Leni Schwendinger, text by Angelyn DeBord, music by Tiye Giraud and Carl Riley, and was co-choreographed by Jawole Zollar and Pat Hall Smith. As a woman-centered exploration of how black church ritual can transform its participants, the work both evokes the iconographic African-American community and unites the performing community of artists through collective song and dance.

A 'praise house', as Zollar states above, is a local, colloquial African-American church where members find respite from the trials and tribulations of daily life. Neighborhood folk gather in the 'praise house' whenever work is over and the spirit is weary. During and after the era of slavery in the United States, worshipers would congregate in small churches to celebrate God with singing and dancing rituals. The ceremonies featured handclapping, ring dances, and shouts – ecstatic moments of spiritual possession expressed through body and voice. Within the space of the 'praise house' existed the possibility for renewal and liberation through communion with like-minded people. The staging of *Praise House* created a space where Urban Bush Women and other guest artists could perform and experience this congregational ecstasy.

The real-life Hannah (Minnie Evans) was a folk artist and mystic who lived in North Carolina. She received her first 'vision dream' on Good Friday 1925 when 'she completed two small pen-and-ink drawings . . . dominated by concentric circles and semi-circles against a background of unidentifiable linear motifs'.[9] Her designs, drawn in crayons and pen, depicted ancestral figures, demons, angels and chimeras. Because the drawings sprang from spiritual sources they underscored the permeable boundaries between the spiritual and natural worlds. Minnie Evans was compelled to 'draw or die', to communicate with the spirit world through her art, or else risk losing her sanity in the earthly sphere. As an early descendant of enslaved Africans, Minnie Evans is representative of a continuity of African beliefs about how art, spirituality and community interact. Her community of rural folk at first rejected Minnie for her strangeness and for her visions. However, she was eventually able to reconnect with her people through the community of spirits and ancestral beings that inspired her art.

Zollar's *Praise House*, like the community churches of the same name, enabled emotive expression of African-American cultural values. Underlying both the stage production and the film were three important motifs from the African-American world-view, each tied to a perspective about community: (1) communication can be established between the world of the living and the spiritual world, and this dialogue creates a metaphysical as well as physical community; (2) ancestral storytellers or guides link modern communities with ancient communities through stories; and (3) heightened and emotive collective music and dance can help people correspond with the metaphysical community mentioned above. The production used all three of these African-American performance concepts to underscore the importance of spirituality in black American life. Both the expression of artistry and the acknowledgement of extended communities have been important components of the African-American struggle for survival. In the fictional story, Hannah, the character who represents the younger generation, was able to overcome her personal challenges through her increasing acceptance of the spirit world as an extension of the family and the community. In return, her spirit guides helped her to cope with her special gift of artistry.

Communication between the world of the living and the spiritual world is presumed in religious texts and accomplished in African-American Christian practice through congregational gathering that center around the words of a preacher. His sermons, or inspired words, are often underscored by communal chants, hymns and praise songs recited by the congregation. On a personal level spirit guides (or angels in Christian theology) are known to speak to adherents and give them insights into their lives. The central character of *Praise House* (Hannah) exists in a world in which the borders between the spirit world and the material world are always permeable. At the same time, the production deploys a West African (Yoruba) perspective of the spirit world siphoned through the African-American experience. Although the images are couched in Christian iconography – crosses, angels and Jesus figures – the metaphysical concepts are strongly grounded in an world-view in which the relationship between spirit gods and human beings is multilateral: angels and other religious figures communicate with human beings on a daily basis and help to ease the earth-born troubles of the worshipers.

The second component of the African-American world-view, the presence of ancestral storytellers or guides, is evident in the play in a character that serves as a 'Griot' or storyteller. The Griot, in traditional African society, is a kind of community archive. Through song and story he recites the history of a cultural community while at the same time passing on ethical or moral codes to the listeners.[10] Two familiar examples of the Griot-like personage would be the character of Gabriel in August Wilson's play *Fences*, and the similarly-named character of Gabe in *No Place to be Somebody* (by Charles Gordone). Both of these characters speak of incidents from the past and explain how lessons learned from times before continue to have relevance in the dramatic present. Both of these characters are slightly crazed outsiders who are able to see both the future and the past lives of the other characters in the plays. Metaphorically they connect the realities of present dramatic circumstances to the experiences of generations that have come before. In *Praise House* the ancestral Griot is Brother Meshak, the storyteller/narrator, who guides the audience into the world of the central protagonist.

It is the third component, the use of heightened music and dance to commune with the spiritual world, that most evokes the sense of tactile and vocal community that is the subject of this essay. Within African-American church rituals, music and dance are used to connect worshipers to one another, to raise the emotions and to punctuate moments of ecstasy. The sound and timbre of the voices create a harmonic resonance that moves through the congregation. Often the vibrations of the voices become kinesthetic responses that result in physical leaps, shivers or arm-raising. *Praise House* recreates the language and rhythmic patterns of the church service in both form and content. The musical themes are drawn from a repertory of rural revivalist chants and songs, while, at the same time, the action of the play is advanced by musical transitions that are enhanced renditions of soul-stirring gospel music. In addition, characters use spirituals and blues songs to 'shout', in the process, freeing themselves emotionally from their individual fears and frustrations. When they emote through the songs the audience is expected to feel the emotional release offered by the sung rituals. At the same time, for the performers in *Praise House*, the communal singing unites the chorus and dramatically connects their feelings to those of the central character. When Hannah shouts, the chorus of angels joins in; when the mother complains of aching feet, the angels moan along with her. Often the dancing, interspersed throughout the play, emerges from the bursts of frustration/pain/joy expressed by the central characters.

The opening moment of the 1991 production at the Brooklyn Academy of Music provides an excellent example of this process. The entire cast enters the space individually, each one bringing with them an internal hum or vibration. They find one another in the dimly lit stage and wave or embrace in a pedestrian manner. The sounds guide them towards one another and solidify moments of companionship on stage. Groupings and pairings of bodies pepper the space. A single guitar strum stops the dancers on their spots. They acknowledge the harmonic resonance of the guitar by beginning to wail – expressing emotions through a single disharmonious note that carries with it a sense of pain. At first the wail is shared outwards towards the audience, with some of the performers looking up, as if seeking inspiration from god. Then, each performer extends an arm as if searching for someone else who might provide a sense of comfort. The performers come together to form a circle with the arms connecting in the center. Something about the arrangement feels as if they are in a séance preparing to call down the spirits. The wail resolves into silence. They stand and breathe.

Now a melodic note emerges from the group of performers. It is the first pitch of the song 'Bring the Spirit Child', an a cappella spiritual that resonates and visibly rises through their bodies. The huddle sways and communes until the voices blend and become essential movement within the dancer's bodies. When the song finally does emerge, it is full, harmonious, and laden with overtones. Handclapping starts. At first it is communal and unison, however it quickly disintegrates into individual, punctuated expressions of foot-stomping, jumping or head rolls. In effect, the moment of united community has provoked individual, emotional improvisations that allow the undefined spirit to enter the community of dancers and intoxicate all within it. As they clap and sing, the lyrics become distinguishable. And the pace of the lyrics accelerates until the characters are performing an active ring-shout – dancing, singing and stomping their feet in a repeating rhythm pattern with a percussive underscore.[11]

Ring-shouts are remnants of African-American plantation dances and are still practiced today in rural and folk churches. Dancers participating in a ring-shout form a circle, and slide and drag their feet while rhythmically clapping their hands, often to chants, spirituals or to a percussive underscore. The accompaniment helps to set the pacing of the dance circle; it unites the performers around a common cadence. In *Praise House* the percussion is the conga drums played by the musicians that support the emotive gesturing that occurs on the stage. The ring-shout, both in the production and in actual practice, is the form that allows the performer to emote beyond the physical world and begin to commune with the spiritual/metaphysical forces. Community, spirit and emotion interact to create a sacred place for cultural expression.

In both *Praise House* and *Shelter*, the Urban Bush Women create tactile communities of African-American womanhood that unite the performers in shared experiences. In *Shelter*, the community unites through touch to create an emotional utopia within a world of fear. Gestures of support and huddles of physical closeness provide fortitude against imaginary outside forces. *Praise House* complements this approach by using both vocal and tactile encounters to bring an imagined community of characters together in spiritual musical moments of ecstasy. In this dance, both the aural and the physical senses are engaged in the depiction of a rural Christian community. Through the simple enactment of communal gathering and ecstatic shout, the *Praise House* community is able to evoke several communities: a corporeal community of vocal and physical contact, a spiritual community of sacred celebration, and an ancestral/cultural community of African-American kinship. Each of these communities is ultimately mobilized to help the performers, as a representatives of a wider consciousness, transform. The transformation of the body and spirit leads to personal growth of both artists and viewers. In effect, through shared transformation, Bush Women productions establish a new community of involved arts participants.

Notes

1   Chatterjea, Ananya (2003) 'Subversive Dancing: The Interventions in Jawole Willa Jo Zollar's *Batty Moves*', *Theatre Journal* 55: 451–465.
2   *River Songs* was based upon a novel written by the Caribbean author Jamaica Kincaid. Events of the novel, which was set by a river, were loosely interpreted in the theatrical work through dance and gestured movement.
3   *Song of Lawino* was based upon a long poem written by Ugandan poet Okot p'Bitek. The work was scripted and directed by Valeria Wasiliewski and composed by Edwina Lee Tyler and Tiye Giraud. It premièred at Dance Theater Workshop, New York, in 1988.
4   Sally Banes (1988) *Dancing Women*, New York, Routledge, p. 228, is specifically referencing the 1995 Urban Bush Women's dance theatre work *Bones and Ash: A Gilda Story*.
5   Jawole Zollar (March 2001) personal interview, Tallahassee, Florida.
6   The phrase 'clump' is a term that was coined within the company by the performers to describe the grouped formation of dancers.
7   Tiye Giraud (15 July 2003) personal telephone interview.
8   This is an excerpt from a March 2001 interview with Jawole Zollar.
9   Regina Perry (1992) *Free Within Ourselves: African American Artists in the Collection of the National Museum of American Art*, Washington, DC, Smithsonian Institution Press, p. 70.
10 Oscar Brockett (ed.) (2003) *History of the Theater*, ninth edition, New York, Allyn & Bacon, p. 581.
11 For further information about the ring-shout see Lynne Fauley Emery (1988) *Black Dance from 1619 to Today*, Princeton, NJ, Dance Horizons, pp. 92–3 or Jacqui Malone (1996) *Steppin' on the Blues: The Visible Rhythms of African American Dance*, Chicago, IL, University of Illinois Press, pp. 41–5.

CHAPTER 6

Dwight Conquergood

Performing as a moral act[1]

Ethical dimensions of the ethnography of performance

> For the story of my life is always embedded in the story of those
> communities from which derive my identity. . . . The self has to find
> its moral identity in and through its membership in communities
> such as those of the family, the neighborhood, the city, and the tribe.
> . . . Without those moral particularities to begin from there would
> never be anywhere to begin; but it is in moving forward from such
> particularity that the search for the good, for the universal, consists.
> —Alasdair MacIntyre[2]

> During the crucial days of 1954, when the Senate was pushing for
> termination of all Indian rights, not one single scholar, anthropologist,
> sociologist, historian, or economist came forward to support the
> tribes against the detrimental policy.
> —Vine Deloria, Jr.[3]

ETHNOGRAPHERS STUDY THE DIVERSITY and unity of cultural
performance as a universal human resource for deepening and clarifying the
meaningfulness of life. They help us see performance with all its moral entailments,
not as a flight from lived responsibilities. Henry Glassie represents the contemporary
ethnographer's interest in the interanimation between expressive art and daily life,
texts, and contexts:

> I begin study with sturdy, fecund totalities created by the people themselves,
> whole statements, whole songs or houses or events, away from which life

expands, toward which life orients in seeking maturity. I begin with texts, then weave contexts around them to make them meaningful, to make life comprehensible.[4]

Joining other humanists who celebrate the necessary and indissoluble link between art and life, ethnographers present performance as vulnerable and open to dialogue with the world.

The repercussions for "thinking," which Clifford Geertz attributes to Dewey, can be transposed to a socially committed and humanistic understanding of "performing":

> Since Dewey, it has been much more difficult to regard thinking as an abstention from action, theorizing as an alternative to commitment, and the intellectual life as a kind of secular monasticism, excused from accountability by its sensitivity to the Good.[5]

This view cuts off the safe retreat into aestheticism, art for art's sake, and brings performance "out into the public world where ethical judgment can get at it."[6]

Moral and ethical questions get stirred to the surface because ethnographers of performance explode the notion of aesthetic distance.[7] In their fieldwork efforts to grasp the native's point of view, to understand the human complexities displayed in even the most humble folk performance, ethnographers try to surrender themselves to the centripetal pulls of culture, to get close to the face of humanity where life is not always pretty. Sir Edward Evans-Pritchard wrote that fieldwork "requires a certain kind of character and temperament. . . . To succeed in it a man must be able to abandon himself to native life without reserve."[8] Instead of worrying about maintaining aesthetic distance, ethnographers try to bring "the enormously distant enormously close without becoming any less far away."[9]

Moreover, ethnographers work with expressivity, which is inextricable from its human creators. They must work with real people, humankind alive, instead of printed texts. Opening and interpreting lives is very different from opening and closing books. Perhaps that is why ethnographers worry more about acquiring experiential insight than maintaining aesthetic distance. Indeed, they are calling for empathic performance as a way of intensifying the participative nature of fieldwork, and as a corrective to foreshorten the textual distance that results from writing monographs about the people with whom one lives and studies.[10] When one keeps intellectual, aesthetic, or any other kind of distance from the other, ethnographers worry that other people will be held at an ethical and moral remove as well.

Whatever else one may say about ethnographic fieldwork, Geertz reminds us, "one can hardly claim that it is focused on trivial issues or abstracted from human concerns."[11] This kind of research "involves direct, intimate and more or less disturbing encounters with the immediate details of contemporary life."[12] When ethnographers of performance complement their participant observation fieldwork by actually performing for different audiences the verbal art they have studied *in situ*, they expose themselves to double jeopardy. They become keenly aware that performance does not proceed in ideological innocence and axiological purity.

Most researchers who have extended ethnographic fieldwork into public performance will experience resistance and hostility from audiences from time to time.[13] This disquieting antagonism, however, more than the audience approval, signals most clearly that ethnographic performance is a form of conduct deeply enmeshed in moral matters. I believe that all performance has ethical dimensions, but have found that moral issues of performance are more transparent when the performer attempts to engage ethnic and intercultural texts, particularly those texts outside the canon and derived from fieldwork research.

For three and a half years I have conducted ethnographic fieldwork among Lao and Hmong refugees in Chicago. The performance of their oral narratives is an integral part of my research project and a natural extension of the role of the ethnographer as participant to that of advocate. When working with minority peoples and disenfranchised subcultures, such as refugees, one is frequently propelled into the role of advocate. The ethnographer, an uninvited stranger who depends upon the patient courtesies and openhearted hospitality of the community, is compelled by the laws of reciprocity and human decency to intervene, if he can, in a crisis. Further, the stories my Laotian friends tell make claims on me. For example, what do you do when the coroner orders an autopsy on a Hmong friend and the family comes to you numb with horror because according to Hmong belief if you cut the skin of a dead person the soul is lost forever, there can be no hope of reincarnation? Moreover, that disembodied soul consigned to perpetual limbo will no doubt come back to haunt and terrorize the family.

I have performed the stories of the refugees for dozens of audiences. In addition to academic audiences, where the performance usually complements a theoretical argument I want to make about the epistemological potential of performance as a way of deeply sensing the other, I have performed them before many and varied nonacademic audiences. I have tried to bring the stories of the Lao and Hmong before social service agencies, high schools where there have been outbreaks of violence against refugee students, businessmen, lawyers, welfare case workers, public school teachers and administrators, religious groups, wealthy women's clubs, and so forth. Often I have been gratified to see the way the performance of a story can pull an audience into a sense of the other in a rhetorically compelling way. Many times, however, the nonacademic audiences are deeply disturbed by these performances. I have been attacked, not just in the sessions of discussion and response immediately following these performances. One time the anger and hostility was so heated that I was invited back to face the same group two weeks later for a three-hour session that began with attack and abuse but moved gradually, and painfully, to heightened self-reflexivity (for me, as well as them). The last hour we spent talking about ourselves instead of the refugees.

Here is a partial list of the offenses for which I am most frequently condemned. Members of certain religious groups indict me for collaborating in the "work of the devil." My refugee friends are not Christian, and their stories enunciate a cosmology radically different from Judeo-Christian traditions. Fundamentalist Christians perceptively point out that by the very act of collecting, preserving, and performing these stories, I am legitimizing them, offering them as worthy of contemplation for Christians, and encouraging the Lao and Hmong to hold fast to their "heathenism." Welfare workers despise me for retarding the refugees' assimilation into mainstream America and thereby making the caseworker's job more difficult. From their point of view, these people must be Americanized as quickly as possible. They simply must drop their old ways of thinking, "superstitions," and become American. Developing resettlement programs that involve careful adjustments and blends between the old and new would require too much time or energy or money. Some social workers and administrators clearly emphasize that videotaping ancient rituals, recording and performing oral history are not morally neutral activities. Some public school educators interrogate me for performing in a respectful tone a Lao legend that explains the lunar eclipse as a frog in the sky who swallows the moon. After one performance I was asked, "How do the Lao react when you tell them they are wrong?" When I replied that I do not "correct" my Lao friends about their understanding of the lunar eclipse, the audience was aghast. Some stormed out, but some stayed to chastise me. I've been faulted for not correcting the grammar and pronunciation of the narrative texts I've collected and thus making the people "sound stupid and backward." Weeks after a performance I've received letters from people telling me how angry they were, that they "couldn't sleep" when thinking about the performance, and that it had given them "bad dreams."

In another vein, from audiences who are moved by the performance, I am sometimes challenged in an accusing tone, "How can you go back to being a professor at a rich university? Why don't you spend full time trying to help these people learn English, get jobs, find lost relatives?" In comparison to nonacademic audiences, the criticism from academic audiences pales. Nevertheless, remarks get back to me about how I'm "moving the field off center." The ostensibly neutral question, "What does this have to do with oral interpretation of literature?" thinly veils deep misgivings. One specialist in eighteenth-century literature was more direct, and I respect him for that. At a Danforth conference, this senior gentleman rose to his feet after my presentation and in authoritative and measured tones declared: "You have confused art and nature, and that is an abomination!"

The one question I almost never get, however, is the "white guilt" accusation, "What right do you, a middle-class white man, have to perform these narratives?" Usually whoever introduces me gives some background information about my participant observation research. One time some audience members came in late, after the introduction, and sure enough, one of them was the first to raise his hand after the performance and accuse me of white man's presumptuousness. However, other audience members came to my defense before I had a chance to respond. They explained to him that I had lived with the people for more than three years, that I was not a weekend commuter from a comfortable suburban house. This information seemed to subdue him.

Even though my ego is probably as vulnerable as the next person's, I take courage in knowing that negative response, more than approving applause, testifies to the moral implications of this kind of work. I can be grateful to my detractors for forcing into my awareness the complex ethical tensions, tacit political commitments, and moral ambiguities inextricably caught up in the act of performing ethnographic materials. Indeed, I began doing this kind of work focused on performance as a way of knowing and deeply sensing the other. Hostile audiences have helped me see performance as the enactment of a moral stance. Now I have become deeply interested in the ethical dimensions of performing the expressive art that springs from other lives, other sensibilities, other cultures.

I agree with Wallace Bacon that the validity of an intercultural performance is "an ethical concern no less than a performance problem."[14] Good will and an open heart are not enough when one "seeks to express cultural experiences which are clearly separate from his or her lived world."[15] I would like to sketch four ethical pitfalls, performative stances towards the other that are morally problematic. I name these performative stances "The Custodian's Rip-Off," "The Enthusiast's Infatuation," "The Curator's Exhibitionism," and "The Skeptic's Cop-Out." These four problem areas can be graphically represented as the extreme corners of a moral map articulated by intersecting axes of ethnographic tensions. The vertical axis is the tensive counterpull between Identity and Difference, the horizontal axis between Detachment and Commitment (see Figure 6.1). The extreme points of both sets of continuua represent "dangerous shores" to be navigated, binary oppositions to be transcended. The center of the map represents the moral center that transcends and reconciles the spin-off extremes. I call this dynamic center, which holds in tensive equipoise the four contrarities, "Dialogical Performance."[16] After mapping the five performative stances in order to see their alignments, I will discuss each one in more detail.

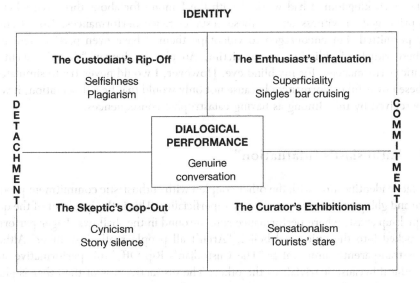

Figure 4 Moral mapping of performative stances towards the other.*

*This graphic representation is derived from Mary Douglas' method of grid group analysis. See *Cultural Bids* (1978) and *In the Active Voice* (1982).

"The Custodian's Rip-Off"

The sin of this performative stance is Selfishness. A strong attraction toward the other coupled with extreme detachment results in acquisitiveness instead of genuine inquiry, plunder more than performance. Bacon provided a striking example of this performative stance when he cited the case of the Prescott Smoki cultural preservation group who continued to perform the Hopi Snake Dance over the vigorous objections of Hopi elders. This group appropriated cherished traditions, reframed them in a way that was sacreligious to the Hopi, and added insult to injury by selling trinkets for $7.50, all in the name of preserving "dying cultures."[17] The immorality of such performances is unambiguous and can be compared to theft and rape.

Potential performers of ethnographic materials should not enter the field with the overriding motive of "finding some good performance material." An analogy from my fieldwork situation would be my performance of some of the stunningly theatrical shaman chants of Hmong healers replete with black veil over face and sacred costume. Not even a Hmong man or woman may perform these sacred traditions at will. You must be called to shamanic performance, which typically is signalled by a life-threatening illness, during which you have tremors, "shake" (*oy nang*, the Hmong word for "shaman," is the same word for "shake"). When the shaman shakes and chants, he or she is talking and pleading with the spirits that control the world. These ecstatic performances are extraordinarily delicate and dangerous affairs. A Hmong Shaman risks his or her life each time the soul leaves the body and ascends the tree of life on the ecstatic journey to the spirit kingdom. I had worked with the Hmong for about three years before I was privileged to witness one of these ecstatic trance performances. Now I am not only permitted, but encouraged to videotape them. I have even participated in one of these rituals of affliction as the victim. An elderly shaman "shook"—went into ecstatic performance—for my blind eye. However, I would never try to simulate one of these powerful performances because not only would that be a desecration, it would be perceived by the Hmong as having catastrophic consequences.

"The Enthusiast's Infatuation"

Too facile identification with the other coupled with enthusiastic commitment produces naive and glib performances marked by superficiality. This is the quadrant of the quick-fix, pick-up artist, where performance runs aground in the shallows. Eager performers get sucked into the quicksand belief, "Aren't all people really just alike?" Although not as transparently immoral as "The Custodian's Rip-Off," this performative stance is unethical because it trivializes the other. The distinctiveness of the other is glossed over by a glaze of generalities.

Tzvetan Todorov unmasks the moral consequences of too easy and eager an identification with the other:

> Can we really love someone if we know little or nothing of his identity,
>   if we see, in place of that identity, a projection of ourselves or ideals?

We know that such a thing is quite possible, even frequent, in personal relations; but what happens in cultural confrontations? Doesn't one culture risk trying to transform the other in its own name, and therefore risk subjugating it as well? How much is such love worth?[18]

"The Enthusiasts Infatuation," which is also the quadrant where "fools rush in where angels fear to tread," is neither innocent nor benign.

Fredric Jameson, to whom we are indebted for naming the Identity-Difference interpretive dilemma,[19] complements Todorov by showing how too easy affirming of identity not only banalizes the other, but seals off the self from any moral engagement:

> . . . if we choose to affirm the identity of the alien object with ourselves—
> if, in other words, we decide that Chaucer, say . . . or the narratives of
> nineteenth-century Russian gentry, are more or less directly or intuitively
> accessible to us . . . then we have presupposed in advance what was to
> have been demonstrated, and our apparent comprehension of these alien
> texts must be haunted by the nagging suspicion that we have all the while
> remained locked in our own present with its television sets and super-
> highways . . . and that we have never really left home at all, that our
> feeling of *Verstehen* is little better than mere psychological projection, that
> we have somehow failed to touch the strangeness and the resistance of a
> reality genuinely different from our own.[20]

Secure in our protective solipsism, those of us in this performative stance will never permit the other "to come before us as a radically different life form that rises up to call our own form of life into question and to pass judgment on us, and through us, on the social formation in which we live."[21] Superficiality suffocates self as well as other.

"The Curator's Exhibitionism"

Whereas the enthusiast assumed too easy an Identity with the other, the curator is committed to the Difference of the other. This is the "Wild Kingdom" approach to performance that grows out of fascination with the exotic, primitive, culturally remote. The performer wants to astonish rather than understand. This quadrant is suffused with sentimentality and romantic notions about the "Noble Savage." Performances from this corner of the map resemble curio postcards, souvenirs, trophies brought back from the tour for display cases. Instead of bringing us into genuine contact (and risk) with the lives of strangers, performances in this mode bring back museum exhibits, mute and staring.

Jameson explains that when one affirms "from the outset, the radical Difference of the alien object from ourselves, then at once the doors of comprehension begin to swing closed. . . ."[22] The manifest sin of this quadrant is Sensationalism, and it is an immoral stance because it dehumanizes the other. Todorov makes strikingly clear the moral consequences of exoticizing the other in his brilliant case study of the most dramatic encounter with the other in our history, the discovery and conquest of America.[23] He clarifies how the snap-shot perspectives of "Noble Savage" and "dirty dog" can come from the same view-finder:

> How can Columbus be associated with these two apparently contradictory myths, one whereby the other is a 'noble savage' (when perceived at a distance) and one whereby he is a 'dirty dog,' a potential slave? It is because both rest on a common basis, which is the failure to recognize the Indians, and the refusal to admit them as a subject having the same rights as oneself, but different. Columbus has discovered America but not the Americans.[24]

Too great a distance—aesthetic, romantic, political—denies to the other membership in the same moral community as ourselves.

"The Skeptic's Cop-Out"

The fourth corner of the map is the prison-house of Detachment and Difference in which, according to Jameson, "we find ourselves separated by the whole density of our own culture from objects or cultures thus initially defined as other from ourselves and thus as irremediably inaccessible."[25] Instead of a performative stance, it is an easy bail-out into the no man's land of paralyzing skepticism. This corner of the map is the refuge of cowards and cynics. Instead of facing up to and struggling with the ethical tensions and moral ambiguities of performing culturally sensitive materials, the skeptic, with chilling aloofness, flatly declares, "I am neither black nor female: I will not perform from *The Color Purple*."

When this strange coupling of naive empiricism and sociobiology—only blacks can understand and perform black literature, only white males John Cheever's short stories—is deconstructed to expose the absurdity of the major premise, then the "No Trespassing" disclaimer is unmasked as cowardice or imperialism of the most arrogant kind. It is only the members of the dominant culture who can hold to this high purity argument regarding cultural intercourse. It is a fact of life of being a member of a minority or disenfranchised subculture that one must and can learn how to perform cultural scripts and play roles that do not arise out of one's own culture. As a matter of sheer survival refugees must learn how to play American ways of thinking and social conduct. "Code-switching" is a commonplace ethnographic term used to describe the complex shifts minority peoples deftly and continuously negotiate between the communication styles of dominant culture and subculture. Todorov, who refers to his own "simultaneous participation in two cultures,"[26] offers a strong rebuttal to the skeptic's position:

> Ultimately, understanding between representatives of different cultures (or between parts of my own being which derive from one culture or the other) is possible, if the will-to-understand is present: there is something

beyond 'points of view,' and it is characteristic of human beings that they can transcend their partiality and their local determinations.[27]

There is no null hypothesis in the moral universe. Refusal to take a moral stand is itself a powerful statement of one's moral position. That is why I have placed squarely on the moral map the skeptic's refusal to risk encounter to show that nihilism is as much a moral position as its diagonal counterpart, naive enthusiasm. In my view, "The Skeptic's Cop-Out" is the most morally reprehensible corner of the map because it forecloses dialogue. The enthusiast, one can always hope, may move beyond infatuation to love. Relationships that begin superficially can sometimes deepen and grow. Many of my students begin in the enthusiast's corner of the map. It is the work of teaching to try to pull them toward the center. The skeptic, however, shuts down the very idea of entering into conversation with the other before the attempt, however problematic, begins. Bacon, who is keenly aware of the "deep and difficult and enduring problems,"[28] rejects the skeptic's cop-out when facing up to the alternatives for action in the world:

> What, then, do we do? Do we give up performing ethnic materials? Do we say, with Anaya, that to the Hispanics belong Hispanic treasures?
> Surely not, because our world has never before cried out so needfully for understanding among us all. Never has a sense of the other seemed more crucial for our own humanity. The embodiment of texts of all kinds is one real path to the understanding of others.[29]

The skeptic, detached and estranged, with no sense of the other, sits alone in an echo-chamber of his own making, with only the sound of his own scoffing laughter ringing in his ears.

"Dialogical Performance"

One path to genuine understanding of others, and out of this moral morass and ethical minefield of performative plunder, superficial silliness, curiosity-seeking, and nihilism, is dialogical performance.[30] This performative stance struggles to bring together different voices, world views, value systems, and beliefs so that they can have a conversation with one another. The aim of dialogical performance is to bring self and other together so that they can question, debate, and challenge one another. It is a kind of performance that resists conclusions, it is intensely committed to keeping the dialogue between performer and text open and ongoing. Dialogical understanding does not end with empathy. There is always enough appreciation for difference so that the text can interrogate, rather than dissolve into, the performer. That is why I have charted this performative stance at the center of the moral map. More than a definite position, the dialogical stance is situated in the space between competing ideologies. It brings self and other together even while it holds them apart. It is more like a hyphen than a period.

The strength of the center is that it pulls together mutually opposed energies that become destructive only when they are vented without the counterbalancing pull of their opposite. For example, good performative ethnographers must continuously play the oppositions between Identity and Difference. Their stance toward this heuristically rich paradox of fieldwork (and performance) is both/and, yes/but, instead of either/or. They affirm cross-cultural accessibility without glossing very real differences. Moreover, they respect the Difference of the other enough to question and make vulnerable her own *a priori* assumptions. When we have true respect for the Difference of other cultures, then we grant them the potential for challenging our own culture. Genuine dialogical engagement is at least a two-way thoroughfare. Glassie insists that the ethnographer's home culture should be as open to interpretation, questioning, weighing of alternatives, as the host culture.

> Old societies alienated from us by chronology become but academic curios, no challenge at all to the status quo. The outward search for alternatives can likewise die into thrills and souvenirs, but when the traveler is serious, the quest through space leads through confrontation into culture, into fear, and it can prove trying, convincing, profoundly fruitful. The reason to study people, to order experience into ethnography, is not to produce more entries for the central file or more trinkets for milord's cabinet of curiosities. It is to stimulate thought, to assure us there are things we do not know, things we must know, things capable of unsettling the world we inhabit.[31]

In order to keep fieldwork dialogically alive, Glassie construes it as "intimate conversation" a description that resonates both literally and metaphorically with the praxis of ethnography:

> Ethnography is interaction, collaboration. What it demands is not hypotheses, which may unnaturally close study down, obscuring the integrity of the other, but the ability to converse intimately.[32]

Todorov makes the same point about the dialogical stance towards textual criticism:

> Dialogic criticism speaks not *of* works but *to* works, rather *with* works. It refuses to eliminate either of the two voices present . . . The author is a 'thou,' not a 'he,' an interlocutor with whom one discusses and even debates human values.[33]

He argues that the honesty of dialogic criticism lies in two voices that can speak simultaneously and interactively. Like good conversation, the event is a cooperative enterprise between two voices, neither of which succumbs to monologue: ". . . as in personal relations, the illusion of fusion is sweet, but it is an illusion, and its end is bitter, to recognize others *as* others permits loving them better."[34]

Dialogical performance is a way of having intimate conversation with other people and cultures. Instead of speaking about them, one speaks to and with them. The sensuous immediacy and empathic leap demanded by performance is an occasion for orchestrating two voices, for bringing together two sensibilities. At the same time, the conspicuous artifice of performance is a vivid reminder that each voice has its own integrity. The performer of a Laotian cosmological legend stands before an audience in all his Scots-German facticity. Dialogical performance celebrates the paradox of "how the deeply different can be deeply known without becoming any less different."[35] Bacon quoted Auden, who evocatively etched the moral lineaments of dialogical performance: "When truly brothers/men don't sing in unison/but in harmony."[36]

Dialogical performance is a way of finding the moral center as much as it is an indicator that one is ethically grounded. One does not have to delay entering the conversation until self and other have become old friends. Indeed, as the metaphor makes clear, one cannot build a friendship without beginning a conversation. Dialogical performance is the means as much as the end of honest intercultural understanding. But what are the qualities one absolutely needs before joining the conversation? Three indispensables, according to Glassie: energy, imagination, and courage.

> Scholars need energy to gather enough information to create full portraits. They need imagination to enter between facts, to feel what it is like to be, to think and act as another person. They need courage to face alternatives, comparing different experiences to help their fellows locate themselves.[37]

If we bring to our work energy, imagination, and courage—qualities that can be exercised and strengthened through dialogical performance—then we can hope not to trample on "the sweet, terrible wholeness of life."[38]

Finally, you don't have to do years of fieldwork with a people before you can perform their verbal art. Fieldwork is enormously time-consuming and labor-intensive; it appeals to a certain kind of person and temperament, but certainly it is not for everyone. Ethnographers would be selfish and arrogant to set themselves up as cultural game wardens, insisting that you have to have "been there" before you understand. Geertz is quite insistent that good ethnography is not dependent on the fieldworker's being possessed of some mystical powers that enable her to "commune with natives"; good ethnography can be done "without recourse to pretensions to more-than-normal capacities for ego-effacement and fellow-feeling."[39] He argues that ethnographic understanding "is more like grasping a proverb, catching an allusion, seeing a joke— or, as I have suggested, reading a poem—than it is like achieving communion."[40]

It is the responsibility of the ethnographer of performance to make performance texts derived from fieldwork that are accessible—and that means performable—for responsible interpreters of texts who have callings other than fieldwork.[41] The ethnographic movement in performance studies will die if it does not reach out to share the human dignity of the other, the other-wise, with audiences larger than a coterie of specialists. If it turns in upon itself, then, quite appropriately, it will become an "inside joke" that only fieldworkers can "get." The ethnographic movement is dependent on the existence of traditional interpreters and teachers of literature, who continue to deepen in new generations of students sensitivity to the other of a Renaissance text, or a contemporary poem, so that when performance texts from nonliterate cultures are produced and made available, it will be possible for more voices to join the human dialogue.

Notes

1   This essay is the result of an ongoing dialogue with three voices other than my own. My transposition of Clifford Geertz' title, "Thinking as a Moral Act: Ethical Dimensions of Anthropological Fieldwork in the New States," *Antioch Review*, 28 (Summer, 1968), 139–158, explicitly signals the deep impact that essay has had on my own fieldwork project. Wallace Bacon first introduced me to "the sense of the other," an idea that changed my life and is a luminous demonstration of "thinking as a moral act." For more than a decade, Mary Strine has given me lists of difficult books that ask hard questions, and insisted that I read them. Particularly the dialogical marxism of Mikhail Bakhtin, which she introduced to the field, has challenged me, and even though not explicitly cited, I hope its presence is felt by the very nature of the questions that shaped this paper.

2   *After Virtue: A Study in Moral Theory*, 2nd ed. (Notre Dame: Univ. of Notre Dame Press, 1984), p. 221.

3   *Custer Died for Your Sins: An Indian Manifesto* (New York: Avon, 1969), p. 98.

4   *Passing the Time in Ballymenone: Culture and History of an Ulster Community* (Philadelphia: Univ. of Pennsylvania Press, 1982), p. xvi.

5   "Thinking as a Moral Act," p. 140.

6   "Thinking as a Moral Act," p. 139.

7   For an incisive historical explanation of this concept, see Beverly Whitaker Long, "A 'Distanced' Art: Interpretation at Mid-Century," *Performance of Literature in Historical Perspectives*, ed. David Thompson (Lanham, MD: University Press of America, 1983), pp. 567–588. See also the provocative discussion of "moral distance" in Mary Frances Hopkins, "From Page to Stage: The Burden of Proof," *The Southern Speech Communication Journal*, 47 (Fall 1981), 1–9.

8   Quoted in Clifford Geertz, "Slide Show: Evans-Pritchard's African Transparencies," *Raritan*, 3 (Fall 1983), 72–73.

9   Clifford Geertz, *Local Knowledge; Further Essays in Interpretive Anthropology* (New York: Basic Books, 1983), p. 48.

10   Cf. Victor Turner, *From Ritual to Theatre: The Human Seriousness of Play* (New York: Performing Arts Journal Publications, 1982).

11   "Thinking as a Moral Act," p. 139.

12   "Thinking as a Moral Act," p. 141.

13   See Joan Speer and Elizabeth Fine, "What Does a Dog Have to do with Humanity?: The Politics of Humanities Public Programming," paper presented at the Eastern Communication Association Convention, Ocean City, MD, 1983.

14   "The Interpretation of Oral and Ethnic Materials: The Ethical Dimension," *Literature in Performance*, 4 (April 1984), 94–97.

15   Bacon, p. 95.

16 I have discussed "dialogical performance" in the philosophical context of the theories of Martin Buber, Mikhail Bakhtin, and Wallace Bacon in " Performance and Dialogical Understanding: In Quest of the Other," *Proceedings of the Ninth International Colloquium on Communication*, ed. Janet McHughes (Tempo: Arizona State Univ., 1984).

17 Bacon, p. 94–95.

18 *The Conquest of America: The Question of the Other*, trans. Richard Howard (New York: Harper and Row, 1984), p. 168. It is noteworthy that two other books have appeared recently that deal centrally with the concept of "the other": Johannes Fabian, *Time and the Other: How Anthropology Makes its Object* (New York: Columbia Univ. Press, 1983); Michael Theunissen, *The Other: Studies in the Social Ontology of Husserl, Heidegger, Sartre, and Buber*, trans. Christopher Macann (Cambridge, MA: MIT Press, 1984).

19 "Marxism and Historicism," *New Literary History*, 11 (Autumn 1979), 41–73.

20 Jameson, p. 45.

21 Jameson, p. 70.

22 Jameson, p. 43.

23 Todorov writes, "My main interest is less a historian's than a moralist's, the present is more important to me than the past," p. 4.

24 Jameson, p. 49.

25 Jameson, p. 43–44.

26 "A Dialogic Criticism?" *Raritan*, 4 (Summer 1984), 69.

27 "A Dialogic Criticism?" p. 70.

28 Bacon, p. 96.

29 Bacon, p. 97.

30 The recent explosion of interest in the works of Mikhail Bakhtin now being translated from the original Russian and made accessible to western readers has given wide-spread currency to the idea of "dialogue" as a way of being in the world. Two of Bakhtin's works now available in translation are useful starting points for engaging the complexities of his thinking: *The Dialogic Imagination*, trans. Caryl Emerson and Michael Holquist, ed. Michael Hoiquist (Austin: Univ. of Texas Press, 1981), and *Problems of Dostoevsky's Poetics*, ed. and trans. Caryl Emerson (Minneapolis: Univ. of Minnesota Press, 1984). I recommend also two invaluable scholarly tools for anyone working with Bakhtin: the intellectual biography by Katerina Clark and Michael Holquist, *Mikhail Bakhtin* (Cambridge: Harvard Univ. Press, 1984), and the critical assessment of his ideas in their programmatic context by Tzvetan Todorov, *Mikhail Bakhtin: The Dialogical Principle*, trans. Wlad Godzich (Minneapolis: Univ. of Minnesota Press, 1984). Clark and Holquist point out in their biography that Bakhtin had a lifelong involvement with performance and theatre ranging from the German governess who organized the young Bakhtin brothers in dramatic renderings of the *Iliad* to his dramatic performances in the Nevel theatre groups long after his university days (p. 21). Todorov concludes his assessment of Bakhtin's lifelong career by arguing that the term that most richly encompasses the scope and depth of his intellectual protect is "philosophical anthropology": "I have reserved for this last chapter those ideas of Bakhtin that I value most and that, I believe, hold the key to his whole work: they constitute, in his own terms, his 'philosophical anthropology,'" (p. 94).

31 Glassie, pp. 12–13.

32 Glassie, p. 14.

33 "A Dialogic Criticsim?" p. 72.

34 "A Dialogic Criticism?" p. 73.

35 *Local Knowledge*, p. 48.

36 Bacon, p. 94.

37 Glassie, p. 12.

38 Glassie, p. xiv.

39 "'From the Native's Point of View': On the Nature of Anthropological Understanding," *Symbolic Anthropology*, eds. Janet L. Dolgin, David S. Kemnitzer, and David M. Schneider (New York: Columbia Univ. Press, 1977), p. 492.

40 "'From the Native's Point of View,'" p. 492.

41 See Elizabeth C. Fine, *The Folklore Text: From Performance to Print* (Bloomington: Indiana Univ. Press, 1984), and Dennis Tedlock, *The Spoken Word and the Work of Interpretation* (Philadelphia: Univ. of Pennsylvania Press, 1983).

CHAPTER 7

Jessica Berson

Mass movement

Laban's movement choirs and community dance

DURING THE 1920S AND 1930S, while he was developing his system of movement analysis and notation, Rudolf Laban also began to form and direct amateur movement choirs (*bewergungschore*). The movement choirs were large groups of working men and women, who, Laban believed, came together for 'the delight of the shared experience'.[1] Laban's movement choirs offer an early model of community dance: dance that grew out of and shaped community experience but was not based on specific ethnic or regional folk dance forms. At the same time, the National Socialist Party brought together large groups of moving bodies with a different agenda: it sought to demonstrate its power, to visualize its ideal of the people, and to "aestheticize the political."[2]

It seems crucial to our historical understanding of community performance to explore the relationship between these two conceptions of mass movement and examine the ways Laban's choreography was both continuous with and resistant to Nazi ideology. Laban's understanding of universal movement foreshadows and can illuminate that of contemporary community dance leaders. However, his complex notion of the role of the individual in the movement choir diverges from that of contemporary artists: while the movement choirs aimed to transcend individuality in order to achieve a 'mystical sense of unity', contemporary community dance often conceives of the group working together to support the individual's understanding of his or her own experience. Finally, the appropriation of Laban's methodology by an oppressive political regime can serve as a stark example of the potential dangers of the universalist rhetoric that sometimes pervades community performance.

Laban sought a new mode of dance that could include professionals and amateurs, old and young. He asked: 'was it really necessary at all to find a frame in the shape of a theater stage for the kind of performing works I had in mind? Are not groups of moving people much more impressive when they speak for themselves?'[3] In his memoir *A Life for Dance*, Laban recounts a journey from the urban chaos of Munich to the peaceful countryside that points toward some of the sources of his inspiration:

> After all the smooth parquet floors, the dust and the clamor, once again there were trees and earth, rocks and silence, and a clear sky above me . . . some peasants arrived for a dance . . . every movement was filled through and through with lively enjoyment.[4]

Laban's rhapsodies about the beauty of nature, and his admiration for the *Volk* and their dancing, bear a discomforting similarity to some aspects of the aesthetic and spiritual values of the National Socialist Party. The Nazis looked to the unaffected lifestyle of the *Volk* as a site of pre-Christian Germanic virtue, and embraced folk traditions that seemed to advance this vision of German history and culture. The tradition of German Romanticism (exemplified by Goethe and Wagner) that infused Nazi ideology claimed Laban as an enthusiastic devotee. But like many of his contemporaries, Laban imagined this tradition yielding innovations other than those that the Nazis had in mind.

By 1927, there were more than one hundred schools teaching Laban's theories and supporting movement choirs. Laban envisioned the choirs as reclaiming an ancient ritualized culture (*Festkulture*) that would return the people to a mystical connection with nature. Through dancing in the choirs,

> the individual was seen to access a higher reality beyond the material world of superficial reason and Enlightenment thought. This fusion was seen as the source of individual creativity through union with the creative process of a higher life force, a process that would simultaneously invigorate the wider *Volk* culture.[5]

This notion of dance ritual as an instrument for breaking free from the constraints of rationality and materiality towards a mystical union with the cosmos clearly grew out of romantic thought, and might seem inexorably affixed to its place and time. However, this notion resurfaced in the 1960s and 1970s in the United States and Europe and continues to permeate much contemporary community-based dance.

In the choreography for the choirs, large numbers of dancers were divided into several smaller groups, arranged in organic clusters rather than in the rows and columns typical in classical ballet. Although groups within the choir moved together in clearly choreographed phrases – as opposed to a solely improvised approach – individuals within the groups performed the movement with different qualitative emphases. There was unison in Laban's choreography, but not uniformity. In her essay 'Relational Movement Patterns: The Diversity of Movement Choirs and their Social Potential in the Weimar Republic', German dance scholar Yvonne Hardt analyzed a number of photographs of Laban's choirs:

> Contrasting movement patterns are found in most photos of the movement choirs. Laban differentiated between so-called low, middle, and high

Figure 5 Thread by Daniel McCusker, September 2004 at Chateau-sur-Mer in Newport, Rhode Island, as part of Island Moving Co.'s Open for Dancing 2002, a biennial site-specific dance festival of works created and performed by participants of all levels of dance experience, open to everyone.

Photo: Thomas Palmer.

dancers. This differentiation took the physical differences of dancers into consideration. Laban did not try to give priority to any of them and accordingly did not try to force a coherent movement quality on all dancers.[6]

While the choirs developed a vision of community cohesion, each dancer performed Laban's choreography with personal stylistic variations. This led to what Hardt calls the choirs' 'messy appearance',[7] quite antithetical to the Nazi ideal of order.

Laban's movement choirs were easily turned towards a Nazi vision of 'community dance' because of the continuity of his belief in dance as a conduit for cosmic unity and communal integrity with beliefs central to the Nazi regime. However, the nature of community as articulated by the choirs was different from that advanced by the Reich. Karl Toepfer writes:

> Movement choirs attempted to construct a dynamic image of community that preserved the amateur status of performers yet transmitted a convincing, almost ritualistic aura of modernity, grounding an idealized communal identity in a common appreciation of bodily expressivity. Indeed, these lay productions probably appealed more to persons who performed in them than to those who watched them.[8]

Although the choirs performed, their activities were aimed at their own communion with nature than eliciting specific responses in the audience. Laban himself declared that 'the lay dance choir is a recovery of a much earlier artistic community' in which the 'spectator played a secondary role'.[9] Because the choirs were focused on the internal experiences of the participants, the meanings generated by the choreography were not fixed, and could be read differently by different viewers. The instability of the choreographic content and its availability to interpretation made the choirs difficult to incorporate into a vision of dance in which 'shared communal experience was paramount'.[10] Additionally, Laban's allowance for individuation within the group confounded Nazi expectations of perfect unison. Most importantly, however, the choirs refuted the Nazi exultation of leadership. Laban's choreography employed groups moving with and opposed to each other, but did not delineate a single authority, either within or outside of the community.

Both Laban and the National Socialist Party pursued mass movement as a means of creating community. But the notion of community, the understanding of how people are bound together, and for what purpose, was deeply contested in the give and take of their interactions. For Laban, building community through dance honored the coming together of individuals in order to celebrate a mystical connection with the universe. His choreography for the choirs engendered individual, spiritual experiences of movement, rather than on the rigid training and discipline prescribed by National Socialism. Laban ardently believed that the experience of the amateur dancers, rather than their effect on an audience, was the primary goal of community dance. Nazi mass movement, on the other hand, was made for the audience: the spectacle of order and precision operated on the viewer, not just the performer, functioning as a clear expression of ideology, the sort of 'invisible propaganda' for which Goebbels longed. Both Laban and the Nazi Party used large groups of amateur dancers to produce a concept of community, but the communities that they created were fundamentally discordant.

Contemporary community dance continues to struggle with Laban's legacy, in multiple, and sometimes unexpected, ways. In the early 1990s, the Berlin Laban Center (Eurolab) revived its amateur movement choir, and hired an expert from Britain, where Laban's ideas about community dance continued to be taught, to choreograph its inaugural dance. But the choreographer was frustrated in his attempts to recreate the tone of Laban's work, because the dancers in the choir absolutely refused to perform any movement in unison.[11] The images of the Nazi parades still haunted these German dancers, even sixty years after Laban's vision of amateur dance had clashed with the Reich's. Susan Manning describes another echo of the choirs in the 'coda' to her essay 'Modern Dance in the Third Reich: Six Positions and a Coda'. Participating in a dance ritual staged by Anna Halprin at the 'Choreographing History' conference in 1992, Manning took hands with other members of the large group – over a hundred people – and danced in circular patterns on the open grassy space. Halprin told the participants that they would engage in a 'spontaneous ritual', whose purpose was nothing less than to serve as 'a prayer to deepen our commitment to and enact our faith in the survival of our planet, of each other and all of life'.[12] At the same conference, Manning had been developing a model for thinking about dance that 'conceptualizes form as variously mutable across time and space and as deceptively mobile from one ideological context to another'.[13] But despite the multiple contextual differences between this event and the movement choirs that had taken place in Germany over a half-century earlier, she writes:

> what did surprise me was the moment when I experienced the immutability of the form of the movement choir, a seemingly direct connection between its use in Nazi spectacle and in Earth dance . . . It was when the group gathered around the base of the tree and reached up to touch its bark that I pulled back, attempting to drag a friend along with me. The association with Nazi nature worship – all those groups of Hitler youth camping out together – seemed so direct that I couldn't remain a part of the event. I did later continue, mostly because in that moment of pulling back I had begun to meditate on exactly how mutable was the form of the movement choir.[14]

Manning is dismayed not just by the association of Halprin's dance ritual with Nazi movement choirs, but by the visceral reminder that 'form too [has] a history and a memory'.[15]

The movement choirs carry the memory of a discomforting continuum between a vision of community dance as made up of individuals moving together to achieve a 'mystical sense of unity' and one of orderly masses turning towards an all-powerful leader. Tracking the genealogy of the choirs is essential to developing an understanding of their implications for contemporary community dance, as Manning attests. It is important to name the traces of Laban's construction of amateur dance as a ritual to create cosmic harmony that can be felt in Halprin's 'prayer' for planetary unity. However, dance 'speaks both *to* and *of*' the societies in which it is created[16] – the meanings of the form, of large groups gathered to dance together, changes in different contexts and for different people.

Notes

1   John Hodgson and Valerie Preston-Dunlop (1990) *Rudolf Laban: An Introduction to his Work and Influence*, Plymouth: Northcote House, pp. 43–4.
2   Richard Golson (1995) 'Fashionable Fascism', *Utne Reader* (Nov.–Dec.): 60.
3   Rudolf Laban (1975) *A Life for Dance*, London: MacDonald & Evans, pp. 88–9.
4   Laban (1975), p. 78.
5   Carole Kew (1999) 'From Weimar Movement Choir to Nazi Community Dance: The Rise and Fall of Rudolf Laban's Festkultur', *Dance Research: The Journal of the Society for Dance Research*, XVII (2), Winter: 75.
6   Yvonne Hardt (2003) 'Relational Movement Patterns: The Diversity of Movement Choirs and their Social Potential in the Weimar Republic', in *Proceedings of the 2003 Conference of the Society of Dance History Scholars*, Stoughton, WI: The Printing House, p. 47.
7   Hardt (2003), p. 49.

8   Toepfer, Karl (1997) *Empire of Ecstasy: Nudity and Movement in German Body Culture 1910–1935*, Berkeley, CA: University of California Press, p. 300.
9   Toepfer (1997), p. 300.
10 Kew (1999), p. 79.
11 Peggy Hackney, Interviews by author, November 1997 to January 1999.
12 Susan Manning (1995) 'Modern Dance in the Third Reich: Six Positions and a Coda', in Susan Leigh Foster (ed.), *Choreographing History*, Bloomington, IN: Indiana University Press, p. 172.
13 Manning (1995), p. 172.
14 Manning (1995), p. 173.
15 Manning (1995), p. 173.
16 Thomas, Helen (2003) *The Body, Dance, and Cultural Theory*, Hampshire, Palgrave/Macmillan), p. 21.

CHAPTER 8

Baz Kershaw

Performance, community, culture

> I think the fringe has failed. Its failure was that of the whole dream
> of the 'alternative culture' – the notion that within society as it exists
> you can grow another way of life . . . What happens is that the
> 'alternative society' becomes hermetically sealed, and surrounded. A
> ghetto-like mentality develops. It is surrounded, and, in the end,
> strangled to death.
>
> —Brenton 1981: 91–2

> if we think in terms of an expressive, rather than political revolution,
> then it is clear that the fringe, and the rest of the counter-culture,
> has not failed. It never had a coherent programme or a single identity,
> which is why single issues – feminism, ecology, community art –
> have become individual themes, rather than part of some overall
> strategy for change. But that does not detract from their significance.
>
> —Hewison 1986: 225

The roots of a theory

WHATEVER JUDGEMENT IS PASSED on the social and political effects
of British alternative and community theatre, it must be informed by the fact
that the movement was integral to a massive cultural experiment. From this perspective
the leading edge of the movement was not stylistic or organisational innovation (though
both these were fundamental to its growth); rather, its impact resulted from a cultural

ambition which was both extensive and profound. It was extensive because it aimed to alter radically the whole structure of British theatre. It was profound because it planned to effect a fundamental modification in the cultural life of the nation. Hence, the nature of its success or failure is not a parochial issue of interest only to students of theatre. In attempting to forge new tools for cultural production, alternative theatre ultimately hoped, in concert with other oppositional institutions and formations, to re-fashion society.

The chief purpose of this chapter is to construct a theory which will facilitate our investigations into alternative theatre's potential for efficacy, both at the macro-level of the movement as a whole. This requires that we address a number of basic questions about the relationships between performers and audiences, between performance and its immediate context, and between performances and their location in cultural formations. The answers will show how the nature of performance enables the members of an audience to arrive at collective 'readings' of performance 'texts', and how such reception by different audiences may impact upon the structure of the wider socio-political order. The focus will be on oppositional performances because the issue of efficacy is highlighted by such practices, but the argument should be relevant to all kinds of theatre.

My central assumption is that performance can be most usefully described as an *ideological transaction* between a company of performers and the community of their audience. Ideology is the source of the collective ability of performers and audience to make more or less common sense of the signs used in performance, the means by which the aims and intentions of theatre companies connect with the responses and interpretations of their audiences. Thus, ideology provides the framework within which companies encode and audiences decode the signifiers of performance. I view performance as a transaction because, evidently, communication in performance is not simply uni-directional, from actors to audience. The totally passive audience is a figment of the imagination, a practical impossibility; and, as any actor will tell you, the reactions of audiences influence the nature of a performance. It is not simply that the audience affects emotional tone or stylistic nuance: the spectator is engaged fundamentally in the active construction of meaning as a performance event proceeds. In this sense performance is 'about' the transaction of meaning, a continuous negotiation between stage and auditorium to establish the significance of the signs and conventions through which they interact.

In order to stress the function of theatre as a public arena for the collective exploration of ideological meaning, I will investigate it from three perspectives, drawn in relation to the concepts of *performance, community* and *culture*. I will argue that every aspect of a theatrical event may need to be scrutinised in order to determine the full range of potential ideological readings that it makes available to audiences in different contexts. The notion of 'performance' encompasses all elements of theatre, thus providing an essential starting point for theorising about theatre's ideological functions. Similarly, the concept of 'community' is indispensable in understanding how the constitution of different audiences might affect the ideological impact of particular performances, and how that impact might transfer (or not) from one audience to another. Lastly, theatre is a form of cultural production, and so the ideal of 'culture' is a crucial component in any account of how performance might contribute to the wider social and political history.

Viewed from these perspectives, British alternative and community theatre between 1960 and 1990 provides an exceptionally rich field of investigation, for three main reasons. Alternative theatre was created (initially, at least) outside established theatre buildings. Hence, every aspect of performance had to be constructed in contexts which were largely foreign to theatre, thus making it easier to perceive the ideological nature of particular projects. Next, the audiences for alterative theatre did not come ready-made. They, too, had to be constructed, to become part of the different constituencies which alternative theatre chose to address, thus providing another way of highlighting the ideological nature of the movement's overall project. Finally, alternative theatre grew out of and augmented the major oppositional cultural formations of the period. Particular performances were aligned with widespread subversive cultural, social and political activity, with the result that they were part of the most fundamental ideological dialectics of the past three decades.

This is particularly the case because, besides being generally oppositional, many individual companies and, to a large extent, the movement as a whole, sought to be popular. As well as celebrating subversive values, alternative theatre aimed to promulgate them to a widening span of social groupings. Hence, the movement continually searched out new contexts for performance in a dilating spectrum of communities. And often – particularly in the practices of community theatre – alternative groups aimed to promote radical socio-political ideologies in relatively conservative contexts. Thus, complex theatrical methods had to be devised in order to circumvent outright rejection. Inevitably, the whole panoply of performance came into play as part of the ideological negotiation, and all aspects of theatre were subject to cardinal experiment so that its appeal to the 'community' might effect cultural – and socio-political – change. In an important sense, then, we are dealing with a rare attempt to evolve an *oppositional popular culture*.

The nature and force of such a project prompt my fundamental interest in the potential efficacy of performance. So I am concerned now to see in what ways Brecht's dictum that 'it is not enough to understand the world, it is necessary to change it' might be exemplified in *both* its aspects by British community and alternative theatre, at both the micro- and macro-levels of performance. Thus, whilst it is obvious that alternative theatre did not bring about a political revolution, it is by no means certain that it failed to achieve other types of general effect. As Robert Hewison argues, the possibility that it did contribute significantly to the promotion of egalitarian, libertarian and emancipatory ideologies, and thus to some of the more progressive socio-political developments of the last three decades, cannot be justifiably dismissed.

Ideology and performance

Ideology has been described as a kind of cement which binds together the different components of the social order. It has also been likened to plaster, covering up the cracks and contradictions in society (K.T. Thompson 1986: 30). Whatever metaphor is preferred, though, the notion of shared beliefs is fundamental to most definitions of the concept. To put it at its simplest: ideology is any system of more or less coherent values which enables people to live together in groups, communities and societies. Thus, to the extent that performance deals in the values of its particular society, it is dealing with ideology. But in practice such dealing is far more complicated than this over-simple formulation suggests.

The concept of ideology has generated a minefield of interpretations regarding the ways it may relate to culture and society. The critical debates have been long and complex, as even the briefest glimpse of their major themes will show (J.B. Thompson 1990; Eagleton 1991). Marx used the term in a number of ways, but most influentially to refer to the ideas which express the interests of the dominant class of society. Durkheim broached the idea that for any society there may be a single social order which encompasses class differences, and thus a unitary ideology that can represent it. Recent Marxist theorists, following the lead of Althusser and Gramsci, generally argue that there is such an order, that it is run by a ruling class, and that it is largely the function of cultural production to reinforce the structures of power by promulgating (in many diverse and complex ways) a dominant ideology which operates in the interests of such ruling classes. Subordinate social groups accept this ideology through a process of hegemony. This concept indicates the predominance of a form of consciousness (or set of beliefs) which serves the interests of an exclusive social group, the 'ruling class'. The majority in society, however, unconsciously collude in their own subordination because hegemony reinforces the dominant form of consciousness by making it seem 'natural' or 'common sense'. Thus, hegemony works to ensure that dominant ideologies remain generally unchallenged. The ruling groups maintain their power and their control over the social system because the majority accept their predominance as the norm (Althusser 1971; Gramsci 1971: 12–13).

In complete contrast to this position, the writing of structuralist and post-structuralist theorists, such as Foucault, Derrida and Baudrillard, tend to resist the idea of ideology in a world in which, from their perspective, language has become dissociated from its object, the sign from what it signifies. For these thinkers, any notion of a stable system of meaning is anathema, and so ideological concepts, such as 'the self', imply a 'false transcendence' (Sturrock 1979: 15).

Between the post-structuralists and the neo-Marxists we can locate post-modernist theorists and cultural critics, such as Jencks and Collins. These argue for a pluralist and de-centred competition of cultures and ideologies, within a society which has a multiplicity of orders in constant conflict with each other, thus precluding the possibility of a dominant ideology (Collins 1989; Jencks 1986). Again, the debates surrounding the idea of post-modernity – in which does it consist; in what ways does it affect society; etc. – have been complex and sometimes bitter. However, for the argument here I will adopt the version advanced by Fredric Jameson, who states:

> I believe that the emergence of postmodernism is closely related to the
> emergence of [the] moment of late, consumer or multinational capitalism.
> I believe also that its formal features in many ways express the logic of
> that particular social system.
>
> (Foster 1985: 125)

Jameson's argument raises the issue of whether or not a socially critical or effectively oppositional art can be created within the 'postmodern condition'. Viewed from this perspective, the question of the potential efficacy of performance – and the nature of alternative theatre history – takes on an increasingly acute and urgent resonance as post-modernism inflects ever-widening social and cultural discourses.

Hence, the neo-Marxist position, *vis-à-vis* ideology, in part informs my argument. The evidence for at least a set of dominant ideologies, if not a single ideology, is much too great to be ignored. For example, one does not need to be a feminist to see that most aspects of Western society are organised patriarchally, or a homosexual to see that heterosexuality provides the dominant values which regulate sexual relations. The question of whether or not such dominant ideologies add up to a singularlity – a dominant ideology – is beyond the scope of this study, though I will use the phrase 'status quo' to suggest that those ideologies tend to be mutually reinforcing. However, it is obvious that British society, in common with other 'developed' societies, is far too complex to permit a monolithic hegemonic control of *every* aspect of its culture. Thus the conflictual version of ideology presented by the post-modernists will also in part inflect my argument, since the dominant ideologies of Western societies – and their ruling groups – are frequently challenged by alternatives. Within or alongside the dominant ideologies other, oppositional, ideologies may struggle for cultural space and may sometimes even modify the dominant ideologies to a significant degree.

Cultural institutions and products are clearly central to the maintenance of dominant ideologies, and are frequently the locus for ideological struggle in society. In particular, theatre and performance are major arenas for the reinforcement and/or the uncovering of hegemony. British alternative theatre generally pursued the latter course. Therefore, it is my contention that, as a result of its nature and scale, the movement offered a significant challenge to the status quo, and may even have contributed to the modification of dominant ideologies in the 1970s and 1980s. This general efficacy became possible because performance was especially well suited to the styles of celebratory protest and cultural interventionism favoured by the new oppositional cultural formations which emerged between 1965 and 1990. As the companies of the alternative theatre movement were usually aligned with these formations they had, in one way or another, ideological designs on their audiences. And whether they aimed to celebrate or to protest against the ideologies of their different audiences, their over-riding purpose was to achieve ideological efficacy.

Performance and efficacy

To have any hope of changing its audience a performance must somehow connect with that audience's ideology or ideologies. However, the longer-term effects – ideological or otherwise – that a performance actually might have on its audience, and their community or communities, are notoriously difficult to determine. This is ironic, given that we usually have little or no difficulty in observing, and even sometimes accurately describing, the immediate responses a performance provokes. It is doubly ironic in view of the well-documented power of performance to cause riots on occasion, and in view of the long history of censorship that theatre has suffered. If performance is powerless to affect the socio-political future, why then has it been taken so seriously by the successive powers that be? Despite this circumstantial evidence there has often been a widespread nervousness among theatre historians and critics about making claims for the efficacy of performance.

Nonetheless, the ghost of Aristotelian catharsis has haunted generations of writers on theatre. The most serious theorists of theatre, like addictive exorcists, have been drawn back continually to address the issue of the effects that performance might achieve. Recently, new arguments for performance efficacy have been evolved in the field of performance theory, the discipline born out of a fruitful coupling of anthropology and alternative theatre practices, initially in the work of the American director-academic Richard Schechner. Schechner aims to describe the structural and functional links between performance, community and culture in a variety of societies, and the admirable inclusiveness of this ambition leads to a fundamental tenet of performance theory: namely, that no item in the environment of performance can be discounted as irrelevant to its impact. Schechner thus defines performance as:

> The whole constellation of events . . . that take place in/among performers
> and audience from the time the first spectator enters the field of performance
> – the precinct where the theatre takes place – to the time the last spectator
> leaves.
>
> (Schechner 1988: 39)

Obviously he wishes 'field' and 'precinct' to be indeterminate, so that performance may include events physically quite remote from the place in which performing itself happens. In Western theatrical terms, the *production* is simply the most concentrated part of the performance event. If we extend Schechner's logic, it follows that everything else which is done in preparation for, and in the aftermath of, the production is part of the performance and may effect its socio-political significance, and its potential efficacy, for the spectators.

Many theatre managers and entrepreneurs would find such claims unexceptional. In the hard-headed world of commercial theatre the full house, the open-ended run, and the cash till are measure enough of a show's social effects. Schechner would concur that theatre can be indisputably efficacious when viewed from this perspective:

> a Broadway musical is entertainment if one concentrates on what happens
> onstage and in the house. But if the point of view expands – to include
> . . . the function of the roles in the careers of each performer, the money
> invested by backers, the arrival of the audience, their social status, how
> they paid for their tickets (as individuals, expense accounts, theatre parties,
> etc.) and how this indicates the use they are making of the performance
> (as entertainment, to advance their careers, to support a charity, etc.) –
> then the Broadway musical is more than entertainment; it reveals many
> ritual elements.
>
> (Schechner 1988: 75)

Schechner draws a line between entertainment and efficacy (and by excluding entertainment thus undermines the case that performance *per se* may achieve a lasting effect), but his points about the functional links between theatre economics and social structuring are vividly valid. During recent years arts bureaucrats world-wide have latched onto this 'justification' for the 'value' of culture (Pick 1988). New and refurbished theatre buildings invariably include a 'corporate entertainment suite', while the once-shunned street entertainer is now encouraged as an index of inner-city regeneration. Hence, arguments for the 'economic importance of the arts' assume the efficacy of theatre as an institution of cultural production. However, the influence of a cultural institution may operate independently of the particular aesthetic artefacts it produces or displays. This type of institutional efficacy does not necessarily reinforce the harder case for the efficacy of the artefact, the performance itself.

Nevertheless, the wider perspective of performance theory is particularly apposite for the analysis of alternative theatre, given that generally it constructs its own performance contexts. So we find a leading practitioner in the field, John McGrath, echoing Schechner when he writes:

> There are elements in the language of the theatre beyond the text, even beyond the production, which are often more decisive, more central to one's experience of the event than the text or the production . . . notably the choice of venue, audience, performers, and the relationship between audience and performer . . .
>
> (McGrath 1981b: 7)

Hence, in suggesting how community theatre performances may achieve ideological efficacy we will need to take into account all aspects of the event which bear on the ideological transaction between a theatre company and the community of the audience in any cultural context. How the audience gathers for a performance, and disperses when it is over, may be as important to its ideological reception of the show as, say, the style of performing itself.

In all forms of Western theatre the gathering phase is designed to produce a special attitude of reception, to encourage the audience to participate in the making of the performance in a particular frame of mind. In other words, the conventions of gathering for a performance are intended to effect a transition from one social role into another, namely, the role of audience member of spectator. A crucial element in the formation of the role is the 'horizon of expectation' which performative conventions create for the audience; that is to say, the framework within which a piece of theatre will be understood as one type of performance event rather than another (a pageant, a pantomime, a classical tragedy) (Bennett 1990). So the precise nature of the audience's role will vary. However, the anthropologist Victor Turner (who worked with Schechner) has pointed out that in some aspects the role is always similar to that experienced by participants in ritual. It is a *liminal* role, in that it places the participant 'betwixt and between' more permanent social roles and modes of awareness. Its chief characteristic is that it allows the spectator to accept that the events of the production are *both real and not real*. Hence it is a *ludic* role (or frame of mind) in the sense that it enables the spectator to participate in playing around with the norms, customs, regulations, laws, which govern her life in society (Turner 1982: 11). Thus, the ludic role of spectator turns performance into a kind of ideological experiment in which the outcome has no *necessary* consequence for the audience. Paradoxically, this is the first condition needed for performance efficacy.

The nature of the audience and its responses has recently attracted the attention of critics such as Herbert Blau, Susan Bennett and Julian Hilton, who in part elaborate aspects of reception theory previously developed by Robert C. Holub, Hans Jauss, and others (Blau 1990; Bennett 1990; Hilton 1987). These writers tend to focus on the exceptional nature of the audience's role in theatre. For example, Julian Hilton argues that it produces what he calls 'performance consciousness', by which he means a collective imaginative capacity to engage in the construction of 'potential worlds' through the interaction of performer and spectator. He also notes that his interaction occurs on two levels simultaneously:

> There is the on-stage conflict of forces which constitutes the plot of the drama, and there is the engagement with the audience in an imaginative act of constructing a possible world . . . Performers state by their actions that what they are performing is both real and not real, is in effect simply 'possible'. The audience . . . test the validity of the perceived meanings [of the performance] within the wider context of culture as a whole.
>
> (Hilton 1987: 132–3)

Whilst I would argue that how the performers perform may often be less important than the conventions of gathering in creating 'performance consciousness', it seems to me that Hilton's account is at root an accurate one. Unfortunately, though, he spends little time discussing the ways in which the structural dualism of the performance experience might produce potential efficacy for its audience. In order to approach a fuller account, then, we need to theorise the relationship between the 'real' and 'not real' aspects of performance, for it is that relationship which determines the audience's reading of the significance of theatrical signs, and thus their potential effect on the future.

In *Theatricality* Elizabeth Burns provides a very useful protosemiotic analysis of theatrical duality. Her account matches Schechner's and Hilton's in noting that performance takes place simultaneously on two levels. She describes these as 'interaction between performers and spectators and interaction between characters in the play' (Burns 1972: 31). Burns' model for analysis is the traditional mainstream one that sees theatre primarily in terms of character, dialogue, plot and so on. Nonetheless, her sociological perspective leads her to make a very useful distinction between two different types of convention which govern the audience's reading of performance. The first type she calls 'rhetorical conventions':

> Between actors and spectators there is an implicit agreement that the actors will be allowed to conjure up a fictitious world . . . This agreement underwrites the devices of exposition that enable the audience to understand

the play. These conventions . . . can be described as *rhetorical*. They are the means by which the audience is persuaded to accept characters and situations whose validity is ephemeral and bound to the theatre.

(Burns 1972: 31)

Clearly the notion of rhetorical conventions, or signs, is applicable to all types of theatrical event. They produce the signals that enable us to classify different shows as belonging to the same genre or form, and to distinguish between different genres and forms. Clearly, too, rhetorical conventions are not confined solely to the performed show itself. They also structure the gathering and dispersal phases of performance, though there they tend to contribute less to the construction of genre or form, and more to the particular type of spectator/audience role that the event requires. Rhetorical conventions are thus crucial to the ideological framing, via horizons of expectation, of performing.

Burns calls the second type of convention 'authenticating conventions', which:

'model' social conventions in use at a specific time and in a specific place and milieu. The modes of speech, demeanour and action that are explicit in the play . . . have to imply a connection to the world of human action of which the theatre is only a part. These conventions suggest a total and external code of values and norms of conduct from which the speech and action of the play is drawn. Their function is, therefore, to *authenticate* the play.

(Burns 1972: 32)

Despite the rather limited mimetic model on which Burns' description is based, the notion that there is a category of theatrical sign directly engaged with the ideology of the 'real' extra-theatrical world is crucial to an account of performance efficacy. Authenticating conventions or signs are the key to the audience's successful decoding of the event's significance to their lives. They determine the audience's reading of performance by establishing more or less transparent relationships between the fictionality of performance, the 'possible worlds' created by performance, and the 'real world' of the audience's socio-political experience outside theatre. In terms of my theoretical perspective, they enable an audience to perceive the specific ideological meanings of the show in relatively explicit ways.

Now Burns' crucial distinction will allow us to extend our analysis of the interaction of theatre-as-theatre and theatre-as-social-event, between the 'not real' and 'real' dimensions of performance. In particular the distinction will enable us to describe more accurately the kinds of *crisis* that performance may provoke for an audience, and to suggest how such crises are an essential element in the ideological efficacy of performance.

Examples of the immediate effects of crises provoked by authenticating conventions are easy to find — we need only look to the history of theatre riots. Sean O'Casey's *The Plough and the Stars* sparked off disorder at Dublin's Abbey Theatre in

1926. According to all the eyewitness accounts the trouble started during Act II, and centred mainly on O'Casey's linking of the nationalist cause to the low life of Dublin pubs and prostitution. The report in the Dublin *Evening Herald* matches others in pinpointing the 'desecration' of the Irish tricolour as a crucial trigger for the violence:

> There is an effort abroad to destroy nationalism and supplant it by inter-
> nationalism, and the desecration of the National flag of a country. I should
> imagine the play would come under the Treason Act.
>
> (Lowery 1984: 42)

The example illustrates how ideology and the immediate effects of a performance may be intimately connected. That the event became especially memorable in Irish politics suggests that its impact stretched beyond the direct participants, and, at least on a symbolic level, may have achieved more than a modicum of influence in the subsequent history of Irish nationalism. If this is the case (and perhaps it is not such a big 'if' as might appear), then the connection between performative crisis and ideological efficacy would be established clearly.

The example of the Abbey riot also prompts two important qualifying points about crises and efficacy. Firstly, the kind of crises provoked by the ideological significance of the authenticating conventions of a performance can as much reinforce dominant ideologies as support oppositional ones. Secondly, the longer-term effects of a crisis of authenticating conventions will depend centrally on their success in engaging with the fundamental values of the audience: both outrage and a sense of righteousness can last a long time when the most cherished symbols of belief are desecrated or celebrated (as was seen in the Salman Rushdie affair). Unfortunately, the riot in Dublin was efficacious for *both* sides of the dispute in ways that neither O'Casey nor the Abbey Theatre desired. The riot caused O'Casey to leave Ireland for good, and W.B. Yeats accused the audience from the stage: 'You have disgraced yourselves again. Is this to be an ever-recurring celebration of the arrival of Irish genius? Once more you have rocked the cradle of genius.' He was, of course, primarily referring to the rupturing of rhetorical conventions.

Such ruptures usually signal a breakdown of the necessary duality of conventions which allows performance to 'play' with the audience's fundamental beliefs, and to provoke a potential crisis in those beliefs, *without* producing immediate rejection. For it is the *ludic* nature of the audience's role that allows it to engage with ideological difference, that allows rules to be broken (via authenticating conventions) while rules are being kept (via rhetorical conventions). This paradox links theatrical performance to carnival and other forms of public celebration which are designed to produce what Victor Turner has called *communitas*: primarily 'a direct, immediate and total confrontation of human identities' (Turner 1982: 47).

As, according to Turner, *communitas* is the foundation of community cohesiveness, then the paradox of rule-breaking-within-rule-keeping is crucial to the efficacy of performance in its contribution to the formation of (ideological) communities). It is when this paradox is operating at its most acute – when a riot of anger or ecstasy could break out, but does not – that performance achieves its greatest potential for long-term efficacy. For the 'possible worlds' encountered in the performance are carried back by the audience into the 'real' socio-political world in ways which may influence subsequent action. Thus, if a modification of the audience's ideology (or ideologies) is induced by crisis, whether as a confirmation or a radical alteration, then the function of the rhetorical conventions of dispersal is to effect a re-entry into society, usually in ways which do not lead to immediate efforts to influence the existing socio-political order, in whatever direction. In this respect, theatre which mounts a radical attack on the status quo may prove deceptive. The slow-burning fuse of efficacy may be invisible.

It should also be noted that audience members always have a *choice* as to whether or not the performance may be efficacious for them. For the ludic role of spectator permits the participant to treat the performance as of no consequence to her or his life: it's only a fiction, only a 'possible world', with no bearing on the real one. It also follows that if the spectator decides that the performance is of central significance to her or his ideology then such choice implies a commitment. It is this commitment that is the source of the efficacy of performance for the future, because a decision that affects a system of belief, an ideology, is more likely to result in changes to future action. It is in this respect that the collective impact of a performance is so important. For if a whole audience, or even a whole community, responds in this way to the symbolism of a 'possible world', then the potential of performance efficacy is multiplied by more than the audience number. To the extent that the audience is part of a community, then the networks of the community will change, however infinitesimally, in response to changes in the audience members. Thus the ideology of communities, and so their place in culture, may begin to have a bearing on the wider socio-political make-up of a nation or even a continent.

Community and performance

To pursue our quest of explaining how particular performances may achieve efficacy we need a concept which can mediate between the experiences of individual audiences and the structures that shape society as a whole. In other words, we need a concept which signifies concrete groupings of people and at the same time allows for the myriad ways in which many different social groupings may be organised. I shall argue that the idea of 'community' can supply this need, that it can be the conceptual lynch-pin which links the experience (and action) of individuals – including that of performance – to major historical changes in society. Raymond Williams reinforces this fundamental structural and ideological function of community when he writes of 'the importance of actual communities and forms of association as the necessary mediating element between individuals and large Society' (Williams 1965: 95). Hence, he conceives of community as the concrete medium of face-to-face interactions through which we transact ideological business with the wider social structure. That is to say, the networks of our mutual relations with others have inscribed in them values which may or may not be consonant with those inscribed in the larger social order. Community is thus a potential site of ideological opposition to the status quo, and a performance which engages with the ideological identity of a particular community may enlist powerful forces for change.

Obviously, the identity of any type of community can be maintained only by constant reinforcement of the values inscribed in its networks. But by what common process can communities as different, say, as pigeon-fanciers and feminists, villages and inner-city neighbourhoods, achieve their vastly differing identities? Anthony Cohen provides a stimulating and cogent thesis which addresses this question from a semiotic perspective. In *The Symbolic Construction of Community* (1985) Cohen argues that all communities identify themselves by creating boundaries between what is included and what is excluded as part of the community. These boundaries are established through the constant use of appropriate symbols by the networks of the community, including the notion of 'community' itself. All individuals in the community may not necessarily agree to exactly the same decoding of the symbols; in fact the internal ideological dynamic of communities often derives from differences of opinion in this respect. But, to establish the boundaries that provide the basis of a sense of community, any particular community's members must at least agree to use the same symbols. Obvious examples of such symbols are provided by, say, the CND peace sign or simply the name of a village or inner-city district. More complex examples are supplied by the world 'feminist' or by the topography of the local lovers' leap!

So the continual and collective making of meanings through the use of common symbols constructs the boundaries of particular communities and gives them their specific ideological complexion. As Cohen notes, this meaning-making activity:

> Continually transforms the reality of difference into the appearance of similarity with such efficacy that people can still invest 'community' with ideological integrity. It unites them in their opposition, both to each other, and to those outside.
>
> (Cohen 1985: 31)

All communities are alike in this respect, though their 'integrity' may well be built on totally differing foundations. For instance, we can identify a distinction between communities of *location* and communities of *interest*. 'Communities of interest', as the phase suggests, are formed through networks of association that are predominantly characterised by their commitment to a common interest. It follows that such communities may not necessarily be limited to a particular geographical area. It also follows that communities of interest tend to be ideologically explicit, so that even if the members of a particular community come from different geographical areas they can relatively easily recognise their common identity. 'Communities of location' are created through networks of relationships formed by face-to-face interaction within a geographically bounded area. Some communities of location are ideologically explicit – a religious order founded on a monastery, for instance – though it is much more common for their ideological values to be implied by the organisation and interaction of their networks. This is primarily because such communities usually include a variety of ideological interests within the one geographical area, and overt ideological disputes are generally avoided in the interests of the stability of the community itself.

Now, the differences between the two types of community are more a matter of tendency than absolute distinction: communities of location and interest are always intersecting, and individuals may thus be members of two or more communities simultaneously. Nonetheless, the idea of the ideological integrity of a community – whether it is constructed mainly by the location or the interests of its members – is crucial to an understanding of how performance might achieve efficacy.

Community and performance efficacy

At this juncture, the relationship between community and performance efficacy can be best demonstrated by a hypothetical example based on a community of location possessing a high level of explicit ideological integrity. Such communities will usually possess and use symbolism as a conscious part of their public domain. To identify key symbols for this type of community we need only look at any ceremonies or rituals which are regularly mounted. Take, for example, the town of Kilbroney in Northern Ireland. The town has a Protestant working-class population which lives mainly in segregated council housing estates. Each July the Twelfth, in common with many other towns and villages in the region, these people celebrate that Protestantism through a day of parades, sermons, picnics, games and music: the Glorious Twelfth as it is called. Now, according to Sangestad Larsen, the symbols central to the Glorious Twelfth represent 'cleanliness, order, responsible management of property' and commitment to the 'true faith and the Crown' (Cohen 1985: 56). The symbols thus variously signify the beliefs and behaviour which structure the community (including the rules for separation from the Kilbroney Catholic working class), but the community's central symbol is the 'fresh-coloured Ulster flag'. Given this, we can envisage how a performance might use the Ulster flag (and associated symbols) to engage in a transaction with this particular community's ideology, in the hope of influencing its patterns of behaviour.

Our theoretical perspective demands that the flag must become part of an action that provokes a crisis which has inescapable significance for the audience, and this will involve the manipulation by the performance company of the relationships between the rhetorical conventions (or 'real' aspects) of performance and the authenticating convention (or 'not real' representations) of the event. Now clearly the gathering of the Kilbroney Protestant community for a performance will be enhanced by a recognition of some of the meanings that are represented by the Glorious Twelfth. So any company mounting a performance for this audience would do well to ensure that, for instance, the performance space is neat, tidy and well organised and that the audience is admitted in an orderly and well-managed manner. In short, a company is likely to have more success in securing an effective transaction with the audience if the rhetorical conventions of performance are consonant with – confirm the boundaries of – the ideology of the community. In a sense, the company must reassure the community that it is able to represent its interests.

In contrast to this, and in order to approach efficacy, the performing itself must employ authenticating conventions/signs to discomfort or disturb the ideology of the community in ways that do not cause a riot or other kind of insuperable schism. To put this rather gnomically, the Ulster flat would somehow need to be damaged, but not destroyed (*pace* the tricolour in *The Plough and the Stars*). Moreover, in order to achieve inescapable significance for the audience, the closer the flag gets to being destroyed – the more fundamentally the community ideology is challenged – the greater the likelihood that the performance will become efficacious within the networks of the community. In other words, the ideological transaction of performance must deal with the fundamental constitution of the audience's community identity in order to approach efficacy. In so doing it may reinforce or modify that ideological identity, but in either case efficacy depends on the identity being challenged.

Now this example fundamentally reinforces a commonplace of dramatic and theatrical criticism; namely, that what may be challenging to one audience/community may be innocuous to another. To say this is simply to stress the *ideological relativity* of performance, to make the fairly obvious point that the same performance may meet with vastly different reactions in different ideological contexts: a show celebrating the IRA is one thing on the Falls Road, quite another thing in a British army camp. However, the point also underlines a crucial notion in the argument of this book: namely, that *the context of performance directly affects its perceived ideological meaning*. Consequently, in a competition to produce an especially dense formulation, we might cryptically claim that the ideological relativity of performance is a function of the potential variability of value systems inscribed in all aspects of its context. I will call this the *contextuality* of performance, by which I mean the propensity of performance to achieve different meanings/readings according to the context in which it occurs. The socio-cultural complexion of the audience, its sense of community (or lack of it) is the most crucial factor in evoking the contextuality of a text.

It should be clear that some texts are more susceptible to ideological relativity than others, and in this respect a major factor in a text's contextuality is what post-modernist critics have dubbed *inter-textuality*. As with the other concepts discussed here, different theoreticians offer varying definitions of inter-textuality. I take it to mean the ways in which a performance text gains meaning for an audience through its relationships to other texts, including the non-theatrical texts which communities produce, in the form of folklore, oral history, stories, legends and mythologies. However, inter-textuality is not simply a matter of direct allusion; the rhetorical conventions that establish a text as a member of a particular genre, say, are operating inter-textually. The same is true for the particular style created by authenticating conventions. So the construction of meaning inevitably involves inter-textuality, and the burgeoning of the mass media in the late twentieth century has made Western audiences especially skilled in inter-textual reading. We are skilful in establishing a productive relationship with texts that are allusive and multi-faceted, which break traditional rules of clarity and unity, which combine conventions from both 'high' and 'low' art forms. Thus, inter-textuality tends to make readers more active in the creation of meaning; it makes us into what John Fiske has called the 'producerly reader' (Fiske 1989: 122).

Fiske identifies the 'gaps, contradictions, and inadequacies' of popular cultural products as the source of their rich inter-textuality, and of course all texts share these characteristics to a greater or lesser degree. He quotes the pop star Madonna as a prime example of such a 'text'. The contradictions in the representations of Madonna's sexuality enable different readers to arrive at ideologically variable interpretations, in accordance with their judgements of representations of gender/sexuality by other texts. Hence:

> Madonna is circulated among some feminists as a reinscription of patriarchal values, among some men as an object of voyeuristic pleasure, and among many girl fans as an agent of empowerment and liberation. Madonna as a text . . . is incomplete until she is put into social circulation.
>
> (Fiske 1989: 124)

In a sense, inter-textuality is a foil to contextuality, in that it may feed contrasting ideologies within an audience from the same community. But also, an audience sharing the same ideological identity may utilise the inter-textuality of a performance in ways that produce collective readings. Hence, the ideological 'positioning' of the audience (or reader) in relation to the performance (or text) crucially influences both the range of what can be 'read' (via contextuality) and the types of 'reading' that may be available within the range (via inter-textuality). Contextuality/inter-textuality thus can provoke wide variations in readings of the same text.

The complexity that contextuality/inter-textuality engenders has driven some theoreticians of drama into a kind of critical reification which claims that only individual interpretations are ultimately possible. Hence, Martin Esslin write that:

> any attempts to predict what 'meaning' the performance as such contains, is bound to be doomed to failure, simply because that meaning must be different for each individual member of the audience.
>
> (Esslin 1987: 21)

Of course, there is a sense in which this line of argument is entirely valid: the particular nuances of interpretation which individuals make are bound to vary to a greater or lesser degree. But the enlargement of differences of nuance to a principle of interpretation has profound ideological ramifications. In effect, Esslin is proposing an ideology of individualism which assumes that a society can function through discourses that do not produce common meanings. In my view the contradictory nature of this proposal renders it nonsensical, particularly in the context of the study of drama and theatre, as both quintessentially assume the possibility of a collective response based on the achievement of shared readings.

Such collective responses, shaped by the ideological identity of the audiences' communities, are the very foundation of performance efficacy. They are the first link in a chain that connects the individual experience of each audience member to the wider historical development of his or her society. A further crucial link is provided by the kinds of culture which establish common identities between different communities.

Culture and performance

The idea of community as a process of ideological meaning-making helps to explain how individual performances might achieve efficacy for their audiences. However, we need also to determine how different communities might be similarly changed by a single show, or a series of shows, even given the complex variability of readings resulting from contextuality and inter-textuality. We must acknowledge, too, that this problem – which encompasses the issue of how a theatrical movement may influence society – is bound to be exacerbated in contemporary societies which are subject to post-modernist pluralism. To express this, for the moment, in terms of a post-structuralist analysis: if signs are indeed in arbitrary relationship to what they signify, then (*pace* Esslin) all we can anticipate is a riot of individual readings whose disparate nature can only reinforce the pluralistic and fragmented society which produced them in the first place.

My purpose now is to defend the possibility of common collective readings of performance on an inter-community basis, to suggest how different performances for different communities might successfully produce consonant effects in relation to society as a whole. Such an account must use the difficult concept of 'culture', which, as Raymond Williams claims, is 'one of the two or three most complicated words in the English language' (Williams 1976: 76). Now the debates within cultural studies have produced an embarrassment of riches when it comes to definitions of 'culture', but Williams' arguments have been especially influential. Hence, I will adopt his notion of culture as a 'signifying system', by which he means the system of signs via which groups, organisations, institutions, and, of course, communities recognise and communicate with each other in the process of becoming a more or less influential formation within society. In other words, 'culture' is the medium which can unite a range of different groups and communities in a common project in order to make them into an ideological force operating for or against the status quo.

The British alternative and community theatre movement was a cultural formation in the sense adopted above. However, to establish the potential significance of the movement to British society as a whole we need to investigate its place in the cultural organisation of post-war Britain. That significance is partly a question of scale, and, as we shall see in the next chapter, it was by no means negligible in this respect; but even more important were the ways in which the movement was part of the great cultural shifts of the 1960s, 1970s and 1980s. For its cultural alliances clearly have a bearing on the possible extent of its ideological influence; its potential efficacy cannot be accurately assessed if it is isolated from the very forces that brought it about in the first place. Thus, it is crucial to my argument that British alternative theatre was, at least initially, part and parcel of the most extensive, and effective, oppositional cultural movement to emerge in Western countries in the post-war period: the international counter-culture of the late 1960s and early 1970s.

Much of the debate about the nature of the counter-culture (and later similar formations) has focused on its relationship to the class structure of society. For instance, consider the following seminal text written from this perspective:

> Middle class counter cultures are diffuse, less group-centred [than sub-cultures], more individualised . . . [They] precipitate . . . a diffuse counter cultural milieu . . . [They] are distinguished precisely by their attempts to explore 'alternative institutions' to the central institutions of the dominant culture: new patterns of living, of family life, of work or even 'un-careers'.
>
> (Bennett *et al.* 1981: 72)

However, it seems very unlikely that such a phenomenon could exist within the class constraints assumed by the analysis. Indeed, the authors' perception of the full impact of the late 1960s counter-culture suggests a much more extensive basis for the formation. They argue that the counter-culture:

> represented a rupture inside the dominant culture which then became linked to the crisis of hegemony, of civil society and ultimately of the state itself. It is in *this* sense that the middle-class counter cultures, beginning from a point *within* the dominant class culture, have become an emergent ruptural force for the whole society.
>
> (Bennett *et al.* 1981: 78)

Thus, 'class' is an inadequate concept for explaining exactly *how* the counter-culture might have achieved such extensive socially disruptive potential.

A number of cultural critics have argued that generational membership may provide a better explanation for the extensive influence of counter-cultures. That is to say, a full blown counter-culture is ultimately the product of a whole generation, in that all members of a particular generation may be decisively affected by their historical positioning. The theoretical foundation for such a view has been put forward by Karl Mannheim (Mannheim 1952). He argued that under conditions of particularly accelerated social change some generations evolve an awareness, and thus ways of living, which distinguish them sharply from previous generations. In effect, there is then a major rupture in the process of historical transmission. Not all members of the generation affected will respond to the rupture in the same way, but there will be a general tendency to raise fundamental questions about socio-political organisation, and to experiment with alternatives. Cultural critics who use Mannheim's analysis to explain the impact of the late 1960s counter-culture cite a wide range of social, economic and political facts to support the case. These include the breakdown of extended families owing to increased social mobility, the relative failure of education as a socialising influence, over-production and a surplus of commodities giving a false sense of affluence, and, above all, the hardening of the Cold War for the first generation that grew up under the shadow of the nuclear apocalypse.

Now this perspective has profound implications for our assessment of the socio-political status of the institutions of the counter-culture, including the alternative theatre movement. For a start, it moves those institutions from the margins of historical change to somewhere closer to the centre, for those institutions then represent a changed generational awareness both to the generation and to the rest of society.

In addition, the institutions are a concrete embodiment and a widespread medium for the promulgation of alternative, and usually oppositional, ideologies. In addition, the generational locus provides a basis for the popularity of the institutions and their forms of production. Hence, the idea of the counter-culture thus conceived enables us to understand how the 'alternative' may become 'popular', how the socially marginal impulse of middle-class youth may become ideologically central to a whole society.

We can gain a measure of what this may mean historically by considering the nature of the cultural movements that in large part issued from the late 1960s counter-culture in the 1970s. Michael Brake gives the following succinct account:

> Ecology became a genuine political concern, leading to the development of pure-food shops, preventative medicine, organic farming and pollution campaigns against large corporations. The necessity to develop new, alternative legal, health and social services led to a new interest in community politics . . . Consciousness-raising 'rap groups' developed a recognition of oppressions outside traditional class lines, which became essential in the development of feminism and gay politics in their struggle against patriarchy and sexism.
>
> (Brake 1985: 95)

Thus, in this version the late 1960s counter-culture was a major stimulus to, and a partial source for, the ideological orientations of the great emancipatory and libertarian movements of the 1970s and 1980s. These included the gay rights and black consciousness movements, the women's and feminist movements, the community activist movement and the various movements that fought for the rights of people with disabilities, the elderly, the hospitalised and other types of socially disadvantaged group, and it may include even the campaign for a popular, grass-roots-based culture that was fought in the mid-1980s.

I am not suggesting, of course, that the late 1960s counter-culture *caused* these movements, for they have their source in a widespread and continuing dissatisfaction with the inadequacies of late-capitalism in providing for the needs of minorities and marginalised groups. However, that initial counter-culture did provide a 'model' for oppositional action against hegemony, on a grand scale. Thus it is not unreasonable to view the subsequent movements as a series of counter-cultures. I suggest, then, that the late 1960s international counter-cultural formation provided the starting point for a long-term *cultural* revolution that was not dependent on class for its effectiveness, because it impinged on the awareness of a whole generation, and its successors, in more or less decisive ways. But how could a phenomenon that was so socially diffuse and historically distended possess anything like an identifiable ideology?

Theodore Roszak, who coined the phrase, identified the late 1960s counter-culture in ideological terms drawn from a number of theorists, such as Herbert Marcuse, Alan Watts and Paul Goodman. Roszak's study is in no way a systematic theoretical treatment of these writers' ideas, but his approach allows him a kind of conceptual audacity. In short, he identifies the ideological foundation of the counter-culture as an opposition to hegemony by a utopianist idealism which promoted an egalitarian ethic through the advocacy of participative democracy on a localised level (Roszak 1969: 200).

Now the profound simplicity of Roszak's interpretation indicates how this ideological root for the counter-culture provided the formation with three major advantages for its oppositional promulgation. Firstly, the ideology was amenable to adaptation and elaboration in the phenomenally wide variety of different cultural practices, from the politically engaged activism of anti-Vietnam rallies to the rural retreating of the commune movement. Secondly, it provided the counter-culture with the principle of non-bureaucratic institutional organisation. On this principle the movement formed itself into a multiple series of 'communities', able to operate independently, but also overlapping to form a network of more or less loose associations whose boundaries are defined in broadly similar ideological terms. Thirdly, the formulation was adaptable and was adopted by the subsequent cultural formations as a central element of their ideologies. Despite their sometimes profound differences, and the contradictions between them, they can be related to a singular ideological tendency which was in deep opposition to the status quo. So, at the very least, these movements were united by resistance to the dominant order; but also they maintained at least a modicum of ideological coherence through their commitment to egalitarianism and participatory democracy.

Thus, the idea of the counter-culture provides us with a key theoretical component for understanding how particular performances connected with general social change from the 1960s to 1980s. For the British alternative theatre movement was only one, relatively small, part of the counter-cultural and emancipatory movements of the 1960s, 1970s and 1980s. As such it played, I think, a key role in promoting and popularising oppositional ideologies. And its chief tactic was allied to the emergence of the aesthetics of anti-nuclear, anti-war and civil rights demonstrations in Britain and the USA. This is best described as a carnivalesque resistance to the oppressions of affluence, as promoted by the capitalist, technocratic and meritocratic status quo. We will be talking, then, about a new mode of *celebratory protest*, which challenged dominant ideologies through the production of alternative pleasures that were particularly attractive to the generations born in the 1940s and the 1950s. And, inevitably, its audacity was greeted with an ambiguous embrace by the dominant socio-political order.

References

Althusser, Louis (1971) *Lenin and Philosophy and Other Essays*, London: Monthly Review Press.

Bennett, Susan (1990) *Theatre Audiences: A Theory of Production and Reception*, London: Routledge.

Bennett, Tony *et al.* (1981) *Culture, Ideology and Social Process*, Milton Keynes: Open University Press.

Blau, Herbert (1990) *The Audience*, Baltimore, MD: John Hopkins.

Brake, Michael (1985) *Comparative Youth Culture: The Sociology of Youth Culture and Youth Subculture in America, Britain and Canada*, London: Routledge & Kegan Paul.

Brenton, Howard (1981) 'Petrol Bombs Through the Proscenium Arch' in Simon Trussler (ed.), *New Theatre Voices of the Seventies*, London: Eyre Methuen.

Burns, Elizabeth (1972) *Theatricality: A Study of Convention in the Theatre and in Social Life*, London: Longman.

Cohen, Anthony (1985) *The Symbolic Construction of Community*, London: Ellis Horwood.

Collins, Jim (1989) *Uncommon Cultures: Popular Culture and Postmodernism*, London: Routledge.

Eagleton, Terry (1991) *Ideology: An Introduction*, London: Verso.

Esslin, Martin (1987) *The Field of Drama*, London: Methuen.

Fiske, John (1989) *Understanding Popular Culture*, Boston, MA: Unwin Hyman.

Foster, Hal (ed.) (1985) *Postmodern Culture*, London: Pluto.

Gramsci, Antonio (1971) *Selections from the Prison Notebooks*, London: Lawrence & Wishart.

Hewison, Robert (1986) *Too Much: Art and Society in the Sixties – 1960–1975*, London: Methuen.

Hilton, Julian (1987) *Performance*, London: Macmillan.

Jencks, Charles (1986) *What is Post-Modernism?*, London: Academy.

Lowery, Robert G. (1984) *A Whirlwind in Dublin: 'The Plough and the Stars' Riots*, London: Greenwood.

McGrath, John (1981) *A Good Night Out – Popular Theatre: Audience, Class and Form*, London: Methuen.

Mannheim, Karl (1952) *Essay in the Sociology of Knowledge*, London: Routledge & Kegan Paul.

Pick, John (1988) *The Arts in a State*, Bristol: Bristol Classic Press.

Roszak, Theodore (1969) *The Making of a Counter Culture*, New York: Anchor Books.

Schechner, Richard (1988) *Performance Theory*, London: Routledge.

Sturrock, John (ed.) (1979) *Structuralism and Since: From Lévi-Strauss to Derrida*, Oxford: Oxford University Press.

Thompson, Kenneth T. (1986) *Beliefs and Ideologies*, Chichester: Ellis Horwood.

Thompson, John B. (1990) *Ideology and Modern Culture*, Cambridge: Polity Press.

Turner, Victor (1982) *From Ritual to Theatre*, New York: Performing Arts Journal Publications.

Williams, Raymond (1965) *The Long Revolution*, Harmondsworth: Pelican.

—— (1976) *A Vocabulary of Culture and Society*, London: Fontana.

PART TWO

Relations

Introduction to Part Two

■ Petra Kuppers and Gwen Robertson

WHAT IS THE RELATIONSHIP between artist and audience, art and object, art world and other world? Is art inherently aesthetic? Do artists give? Do audiences receive? The writings in this section take on these questions in order to better understand, and challenge, inherited assumptions about the possibilities of artistic practice.

In the 1990s, **Nicolas Bourriaud**, a Paris-based museum curator and art critic, wrote about new practices he saw emerging in the realm of the art museum. Calling those practices 'Relational Aesthetics', Bourriaud was one of the first to critically identify a changing relationship between artists and audiences in the world of the international art museum. Unlike the formal, didactic, and inherently teleological approach of the modern art era (where artists served as cultural leaders, utopian designers, arbiters of taste, etc.), relational practices, in Bourriaud's view, reflect broad, cultural changes that have fundamentally altered what art is.

Like the other authors in this section, Bourriaud is interested in the way contemporary artists are addressing not an idealistic, utopian, world, but instead their own world(s), their own communities, our/their own time. Rather than solving problems through an idealistic aesthetic, relational practices engage what already exists and ask us – as both artists and audiences – to think about what we find, how we act, what we want. Building on the writings of similarly engaged critics and theorists, including Lucy Lippard, Susan Lacy, Miwon Kwon and Grant Kester, the authors in this section represent a growing body of practitioners and thinkers who see the artist as a critical contributor to contemporary communities.

This section offers examples of how contemporary artists are using an art world platform to interrogate the world today. Art historian **Gwen Robertson**, focusing on the work of The Encounters Group, contextualizes the changing relationship between the 'high art' realm of the traditional, museum-based art world and emergent community performance practices.

Artists **Becky Shaw**, **Cedar Nordbye** and **Devora Neumark** are visual artists who also interrogate the limits of, as well as the potential of, community performance practices. Becky Shaw reflects on her work, 'Generosity Project', which happened at the Amstelveen Center, a care home in the Netherlands, while Cedar Nordbye presents his experience exploring the assumptions and political implications of his Empire State Building-based work, 'Empire Project'. Devora Neumark explores the issues and implications involved with a work she co-developed with the residents and staff of the Feldman Foster Home in Montreal.

Each of the artists discussed in this section – in different contexts and for different reasons – questions the value and the right of the artist to work in a community context while at the same time each recognizes the value inherent in the creation of new and enriching relationships.

CHAPTER 9

Nicolas Bourriaud

Relational form

ARTISTIC ACTIVITY IS A GAME, whose forms, patterns and functions develop and evolve according to periods and social contexts; it is not an immutable essence. It is the critic's task to study this activity in the present. A certain aspect of the programme of modernity has been fairly and squarely wound up (and not, let us hasten to emphasise in these bourgeois times, the spirit informing it). This completion has drained the criteria of aesthetic judgement we are heir to of their substance, but we go on applying them to present-day artistic practices. The *new* is no longer a criterion, except among latter-day detractors of modern art who, where the much-execrated present is concerned, cling solely to the things that their traditionalist culture has taught them to loathe in yesterday's art. In order to invent more effective tools and more valid viewpoints, it behoves us to understand the changes nowadays occurring in the social arena, and grasp what has already changed and what is still changing. How are we to understand the types of artistic behaviour shown in exhibitions held in the 1990s, and the lines of thinking behind them, if we do not start out from the same *situation* as the artists?

Contemporary artistic practice and its cultural plan

The modern political era, which came into being with the Enlightenment, was based on the desire to emancipate individuals and people. The advances of technologies and freedoms, the decline of ignorance, and improved working conditions were all billed to free humankind and help to usher in a better society. There are several versions of modernity, however. The 20th century was thus the arena for a struggle between two visions of the world: a modest, rationalist conception, hailing from the 18th century, and a philosophy of spontaneity and liberation through the irrational (Dada, Surrealism, the Situationists), both of which were opposed to authoritarian and utilitarian forces eager to gauge human relations and subjugate people. Instead of culminating in hoped-for emancipation, the advances of technologies and "Reason" made it that much easier to exploit the South of planet earth, blindly replace human labour by machines, and set up more and more sophisticated subjugation techniques, all through a general rationalisation of the production process. So the modern emancipation plan has been substituted by countless forms of melancholy.

Twentieth century avant-garde, from Dadaism to the Situationist International, fell within the tradition of this modern project (changing culture, attitudes and mentalities, and individual and social living conditions), but it is as well to bear in mind that this project was already there before them, differing from their plan in many ways. For modernity cannot be reduced to a rationalist teleology, any more than it can to political messianism. Is it possible to disparage the desire to improve living and working conditions, on the pretext of the bankruptcy of tangible attempts to do as much-shored up by totalitarian ideologies and naïve visions of history? What used to be called the avant-garde has, needless to say, developed from the ideological swing of things offered by modern rationalism: but it is now re-formed on the basis of quite different philosophical, cultural and social presuppositions. It is evident that today's art is carrying on this fight, by coming up with perceptive, experimental, critical and participatory models, veering in the direction indicated by Enlightenment philosophers, Proudhon, Marx, the Dadaists and Mondrian. If opinion is striving to acknowledge the legitimacy and interest of these experiments, this is because they are no longer presented like the precursory phenomena of an inevitable historical evolution. Quite to the contrary, they appear fragmentary and isolated, like orphans of an overall view of the world bolstering them with the clout of an ideology.

It is not modernity that is dead, but its idealistic and teleological version.

Today's fight for modernity is being waged in the same terms as yesterday's, barring the fact that the avant-garde has stopped patrolling like some scout, the troop having come to a cautious standstill around a bivouac of certainties. Art was intended to prepare and announce a future world: today it is modelling possible universes.

The ambition of artists who include their practice within the slipstream of historical modernity is to repeat neither its forms nor its claims, and even less assign to art the same functions as it. Their task is akin to the one that Jean-François Lyotard allocated to postmodern architecture, which *"is condemned to create a series of minor modifications in a space whose modernity it inherits, and abandon an overall reconstruction of the space inhabited by humankind"*.[1] What is more, Lyotard seems to half-bemoan this state of affairs: he defines it negatively, by using the term "condemned". And what, on the other hand, if this "condemnation" represented the historical chance whereby most of the art worlds known to us managed to spread their wings, over the past ten years or so? This "chance" can be summed up in just a few words: *learning to inhabit the world in a better way*, instead of trying to construct it based on a preconceived idea of historical evolution. Otherwise put, the role of artworks is no longer to form imaginary and utopian realties, but to actually be ways of living and models of action within the existing real, whatever the scale chosen by the artist. Althusser said that one always catches the world's train on the move; Deleuze, that "grass grows from the middle" and not from the bottom or the top. The artist dwells in the circumstances the present offers him, so as to turn the setting of his life (his links with the physical and conceptual world) into a lasting world. He catches the world on the move: he is a *tenant of culture*, to borrow Michel de Certeau's expression.[2] Nowadays, modernity extends into the practices of cultural do-it-yourself and recycling, into the invention of the everyday and the development of time lived, which are not objects less deserving of attention and examination than Messianistic utopias and the formal "novelties" that typified modernity yesterday. There is nothing more absurd either than the assertion that contemporary art does not involve any political project, or than the claim that its subversive aspects are not based on any theoretical terrain. Its plan, which has just as much to do with working conditions and the conditions in which cultural objects are produced, as with the changing forms of social life, may nevertheless seem dull to minds formed in the mould of cultural Darwinism. Here, then, is the time of the "dolce utopia", to use Maurizio Cattelan's phrase . . . .

Artwork as social interstice

The possibility of a *relational* art (an art taking as its theoretical horizon the realm of human interactions and its social context, rather than the assertion of an independent and *private* symbolic space), points to a radical upheaval of the aesthetic, cultural and political goals introduced by modern art. To sketch a sociology of this, this evolution stems essentially from the birth of a world-wide urban culture, and from the extension of this city model to more or less all cultural phenomena. The general growth of towns and cities, which took off at the end of the Second World War, gave rise not only to an extraordinary upsurge of social exchanges, but also to much greater individual mobility (through the development of networks and roads, and telecommunications, and the gradual freeing-up of isolated places going with the opening-up of attitudes). Because of the crampedness of dwelling spaces in this urban world, there was, in tandem, a scaling-down of furniture and objects, now emphasising a greater manoeuvrability. If, for a long period of time, the artwork has managed to come across as a luxury, lordly item in this urban setting (the dimensions of the work, as well as those of the apartment, helping to distinguish between their owner and the crowd), the development of the function of artworks and the way they are shown attest to a growing *urbanisation* of the artistic experiment. What is collapsing before our very eyes is nothing other than this falsely aristocratic conception of the arrangement of works of art, associated with the feeling of territorial acquisition. In other words, it is no longer possible to regard the contemporary work as a space to be walked through (the "owners tour" is akin to the collector's). It is henceforth presented as a period of time to be lived through, like an opening to unlimited discussion. The city has ushered in and spread the hands-on experience: it is the tangible symbol and historical setting of the state of society, that *"state of encounter imposed on people"*, to use Althusser's expression,[3] contrasting with that dense and "trouble-free" jungle which the *natural state* once was, according to Jean-Jacques Rousseau, a jungle hampering any lasting encounter. Once raised to the power of an absolute rule of civilisation, this system of intensive encounters has ended up producing linked artistic practices: an art form where the substrate is formed by inter subjectivity, and which takes being-together as a central theme, the "encounter" between beholder and picture, and the collective elaboration of meaning. Let us leave the matter of the historicity of this phenomenon on one side: art has always been relational in varying degrees, i.e. a factor of sociability and a founding principle of dialogue. One of the virtual properties of the image is its power of *linkage* (Fr. *reliance*), to borrow Michel Maffesoli's term: flags, logos, icons, signs, all produce empathy and sharing, and all generate *bond*.[4] Art (practices stemming from painting and sculpture which come across in the form of an exhibition) turns out to be particularly suitable when it comes to expressing this hands-on civilisation, because it *tightens the space of relations*, unlike TV and literature which refer each individual person to his or her space of private consumption, and also unlike theatre and cinema which bring small groups together before specific, unmistakable images. Actually, there is no live comment made about what is seen (the discussion time is put off until after the show). At an exhibition, on the other hand, even when inert forms are involved, there is the possibility of an immediate discussion, in both senses of the term. I see and perceive, I comment, and I evolve in a unique space and time. Art is the place that produces a specific sociability. It remains to be seen what the status of this is in the set of "states of encounter" proposed by the City. How is an art focused on the production of such forms of conviviality capable of re-launching the modern emancipation plan, by complementing it? How does it permit the development of new political and cultural designs?

Before giving concrete examples, it is well worth reconsidering the place of artworks in the overall economic system, be it symbolic or material, which governs contemporary society. Over and above its mercantile nature and its semantic value, the work of art represents a social *interstice*. This *interstice* term was used by Karl Marx to describe trading communities that elude the capitalist economic context by being removed from the law of profit: barter, merchandising, autarkic types of production, etc. The interstice is a space in human relations which fits more or less harmoniously and openly into the overall system, but suggests other trading possibilities than those in effect within this system. This is the precise nature of the contemporary art exhibition in the arena of representational commerce: it creates free areas, and time spans whose rhythm contrasts with those structuring everyday life, and it encourages an inter-human commerce that differs from the "communication zones" that are imposed upon us. The present-day social context restricts the possibilities of inter-human relations all the more because it creates spaces planned to this end. Automatic public toilets were invented to keep streets clean. The same spirit underpins the development of communication tools, while city streets are swept clean of all manners of relational dross, and neighbourhood relationships fizzle. The general mechanisation of social functions gradually reduces the relational space. Just a few years ago, the telephone wake-up call service employed human beings, but now we are woken up by a synthesised voice . . . The automatic cash machine has become the transit model for the most elementary of social functions, and professional behaviour patterns are modelled on the efficiency of the machines replacing them, these machines carrying out tasks which once represented so many opportunities for exchanges, pleasure and squabbling. Contemporary art is definitely developing a political project when it endeavours to move into the relational realm by turning it into an issue.

When Gabriel Orozco puts an orange on the stalls of a deserted Brazilian market (*Crazy Tourist*, 1991), or slings a hammock in the MoMA garden in New York (*Hamoc en la moma*, 1993), he is operating at the hub of "social infra-thinness" (l'inframince social), that minute space of daily gestures determined by the superstructure made up of "big" exchanges, and defined by it. Without any wording, Orozco's photographs are a documentary record of tiny revolutions in the common urban and semi-urban life (a sleeping bag on the grass, an empty shoebox, etc.). They record this silent, still life nowadays formed by relationships with the other. When Jens Haaning broadcasts funny stories in Turkish through a loudspeaker in a Copenhagen square (*Turkish Jokes*, 1994), he produces in that split second a micro-community, one made up of immigrants brought together by collective laughter which upsets their exile situation, formed in relation to the work and in it. The exhibition is the special place where such momentary groupings may occur, governed as they are by differing principles. And depending on the degree of participation required of the onlooker by the artist, along with the nature of the works and the models of sociability proposed and represented, an exhibition will give rise to a "specific arena of exchange". And this "arena of exchange" most be judged on the basis of aesthetic criteria, in other words, by analysing the coherence of its form, and then the symbolic value of the "world" it suggests to us, and of the image of human relations reflected by it. Within this social interstice, the artist must assume the symbolic models he shows. All representation (though contemporary art *models* more than it represents, and fits into the social fabric more than it draws inspiration therefrom) refers to values that can be transposed into society. As a human activity based on commerce, art is at once the object and the subject of an ethic. And this all the more so because, unlike other activities, *its sole function is to be exposed to this commerce.*

Art is a state of encounter.

Relational aesthetics and random materialism

Relational aesthetics is part of a materialistic tradition. Being "materialistic" does not mean sticking to the triteness of facts, nor does it imply that sort of narrow-mindedness that consists in reading works in purely economic terms. The philosophical tradition that underpins this *relational aesthetics* was defined in a noteworthy way by Louis Althusser, in one of his last writings, as a "materialism of encounter", or random materialism. This particular materialism takes as its point of departure the world contingency, which has no pre-existing origin or sense, nor Reason, which might allot it a purpose. So the essence of humankind is purely trans-individual, made up of bonds that link individuals together in social forms which are invariably historical (Marx: the human essence is the set of social relations). There is no such thing as any possible "end of history" or "end of art", because the game is being forever re-enacted, in relation to its function, in other words, in relation to the players and the system which they construct and criticise. Hubert Damisch saw in the "end of art" theories the outcome of an irksome muddle between the "end of the game" and the "end of play". A new game is announced as soon as the social setting radically changes, without the meaning of the game itself being challenged.[5] This *inter-human game* which forms our object (Duchamp: *"Art is a game between all people of all periods"*) nevertheless goes beyond the context of what is called "art" by commodity. So the "constructed situations" advocated by the Situationist International belong in their own right to this "game", in spite of Guy Debord who, in the final analysis, denied them any artistic character. For in them, quite to the contrary, he saw "art being exceeded" by a revolution in day-to-day life. Relational aesthetics does not represent a theory of art, this would imply time statement of an origin and a destination, but a theory of form.

What do we mean by *form*? A coherent unit, a structure (*independent entity of inner dependencies*) which shows the typical features of a world. The artwork does not have an exclusive hold on it, it is merely a subset in the overall series of existing forms. In the materialistic philosophical tradition ushered in by Epicurus and Lucretius, atoms fall in parallel formations into the void, following a slightly diagonal course. If one of these atoms swerves off course, it *"causes an encounter with the next atom and from encounter to encounter a pile-up, and the birth of the world"* . . . This is how forms come into being, from the "deviation" and random encounter between two hitherto parallel elements. In order to create a world, this encounter must be a *lasting* one: the elements forming it must be joined together in a form, in other words, there must have been *"a setting of elements on one another (the way ice 'sets')"*. "Form can be defined as a lasting encounter". Lasting encounters, lines and colours inscribed on the surface of a Delacroix painting, the scrap objects that litter Schwitters "Merz pictures", Chris Burden's performances: over and above the quality of the page layout or the spatial layout, they turn out to be *lasting* from the moment when the components form a whole whose sense "holds good" at the moment of their birth, stirring up new "possibilities of life". All works, down to the most critical and challenging of projects, passes through this viable world state, because they get elements held apart to *meet*: for example, death and the media in Andy Warhol. Deleuze and Guattari were not saying anything different when they defined the work of art as a "block of affects and percepts". Art *keeps together* moments of subjectivity associated with singular experiences, be it Cézanne's apples or Buren's striped structures. The composition of this *bonding agent*, whereby encountering atoms manage to form a word, is, needless to say, dependent on the historical context. What today's informed public understands by "keeping together" is not the same thing that this public imagined back in the 19th century. Today, the "glue" is less obvious, as our visual experience has become more complex, enriched by a century of photographic images, then cinematography (introduction of the sequence shot as a new dynamic unity), enabling us to recognise as a "world" a collection of disparate element (installation, for instance) that no unifying matter, no bronze, links. Other technologies may allow the human spirit to recognise other types of "world-forms" still unknown: for example, computer science put forward the notion of program, that inflect the approach of some artists' ways of working. An artist's artwork thus acquires the status of an ensemble of units to be reactivated by the beholder-manipulator. I want to insist on the instability and the diversity of the concept of "form", notion whose outspread can be witnessed in injunction by the founder of sociology, Emile Durckheim, considering the "social fact" as a "thing" . . . As the artistic "thing" sometime offers itself as a "fact" or an ensemble of facts that happens in the time or space, and whose unity (making it a form, a world) can not be questioned. The setting is widening; after the isolated object, it now can embrace the whole scene: the form of Gordon Matta-Clark or Dan Graham's work can not be reduced to the "things" those two artist "produce": it is not the simple secondary effects of a composition, as the formalistic aesthetic would like to advance, but the principle acting as a trajectory evolving through signs, objects, forms, gestures . . . The contemporary artwork's form is spreading out from its material form: it is a linking element, a principle of dynamic agglutination. An artwork is a dot on a line.

Form and others' gaze

If, as Serge Daney writes, "*all form is a face looking at us*", what does a form become when it is plunged into the dimension of dialogue? What is a form that is essentially *relational*? It seems worth while to discuss this question by taking Daney's formula as a point of reference, precisely because of its ambivalence: as forms are looking at us, how are we to look at them?

Form is most often defined as an outline contrasting with a content. But modernist aesthetics talks about "formal beauty" by referring to a sort of (con)fusion between style and content, and an inventive compatibility of the former with the latter. We judge a work through its plastic or visual form. The most common criticism to do with new artistic practices consists, moreover, in denying them any "formal effectiveness", or in singling out their shortcomings in the "formal resolution". In observing contemporary artistic practices, we ought to talk of "formations" rather than "forms". Unlike an object that is closed in on itself by the intervention of a style and a signature, present-day art shows that form only exists in the encounter and in the dynamic relationship enjoyed by an artistic proposition with other formations, artistic or otherwise.

There are no forms in nature, in the wild state, as it is our gaze that creates those, by cutting them out in the depth of the visible. Forms are *developed*, one from another. What was yesterday regarded as formless or "informal" is no longer these things today. When the aesthetic discussion evolves, the status of form evolves along with it, and through it.

In the novels of Polish writer Witold Gombrowicz, we see how each individual generates his own *form* through his behaviour, his way of coming across, and the way he addresses others. This form comes about in the borderline area where the individual struggles with the Other, so as to subject him to what he deems to be his "being". So, for Gombrowicz, our "form" is merely a relational property, linking us with those who reify us by the way they see us, to borrow a Sartrian terminology. When the individual thinks he is casting an objective eye upon himself, he is, in the final analysis, contemplating nothing other than the result of perpetual transactions with the subjectivity of others.

The artistic form, for some, sidesteps this inevitability, for it is publicised by a *work*. Our persuasion, conversely, is that form only assumes its texture (and only acquires a real existence) when it introduces human interactions. The form of an artwork issues from a negotiation with the intelligible, which is bequeathed to us. Through it, the artist embarks upon a dialogue. The artistic practice thus resides in the invention of relations between consciousness. Each particular artwork is a proposal to live in a shared world, and the work of every artist is a bundle of relations with the world, giving rise to other relations, and so on and so forth, ad infinitum. Here we are at the opposite end of this authoritarian version of art which we discover in the essays of Thierry de Duve,[6] for whom any work is nothing other than a "sum of judgements", both historical and aesthetic, stated by the artist in the act of its production. To paint is to become part of history through plastic and visual choices. We are in the presence of a prosecutor's aesthetics, here, for which the artist confronts the history of art in the autarky of his own persuasions. It is an aesthetics that reduces artistic practice to the level of a pettifogging historical criticism. Practical "judgement", thus aimed, is peremptory and final in each instance, hence the negation of dialogue, which, alone, grants form a productive status: the status of an "encounter". As part of a "relationist" theory of art, inter-subjectivity does not only represent the social setting for the reception of art, which is its "environment", its "field" (Bourdieu), but also becomes the quintessence of artistic practice.

As Daney suggested, form becomes "face" through the effect of this invention of relations. This formula, needless to add, calls to mind the one acting as the pedestal for Emmanuel Lévinas' thinking, for whom the face represents the sign of the ethical taboo. The face, Lévinas asserts, is *"what orders me to serve another"*, *"what forbids me to kill"*.[7] Any "inter-subjective relation" proceeds by way of the form of the face, which symbolises the responsibility we have towards others: *"the bond with others is only made as responsibility"*, he writes, but don't ethics have a horizon other than this humanism which reduces inter-subjectivity to a kind of inter-servility? Is the image, which, for Daney, is a metaphor of the face, only therefore suitable for producing taboos and proscriptions, through the burden of "responsibility"? When Daney explains that *"all form is a face looking at us"*, he does not merely mean that we are responsible for this. To be persuaded of as much, suffice it to revert to the profound significance of the image for Daney. For him, the image is not "immoral" when it puts us "in the place where we were not",[8] when it "takes the place of another". What is involved here, for Daney, is not solely a reference to the aesthetics of Bazin and Rossellini, claiming the "ontological realism" of the cinematographic art, which even if it does lie at the origin of Daney's thought, does not sum it up. He maintains that form, in an image, is nothing other than the representation of desire. Producing a form is to invent possible encounters; receiving a form is to create the conditions for an exchange, the way you return a service in a game of tennis. If we nudge Daney's reasoning a bit further, form is the *representative* of desire in the image. It is the horizon based on which the image may have a meaning, by pointing to a desired world, which the beholder thus becomes capable of discussing, and based on which his own desire can rebound. This exchange can be summed up by a binomial: someone shows something to someone who returns it as he sees fit. The work tries to catch my gaze, the way the newborn child "asks for" its mother's gaze. In *La Vie commune*, Tzvetan Todorov has shown how the essence of sociability is the need for acknowledgement, much more than competition and violence.[9] When an artist shows us something, he uses a transitive ethic which places his work between the "look-at-me" and the look-at-that". Daney's most recent writings lament the end of this "Show/See" pairing which represented the essence of a democracy of the image in favour of another pairing, this one TV-related and authoritarian, "Promote/receive", marking the advent of the "Visual". In Daney's thinking, *"all form is a face looking at me"*, because it is summoning me to dialogue with it. Form is a dynamic that is included both, or turn by turn, in time and space. Form can only come about from a meeting between two levels of reality. For homogeneity does not produce images: it produces the visual, otherwise put, "looped information".

Notes

1   Jean-François Lyotard: *The post modern explained to children*, London, Turnaround, 1992.
2   Michel de Certeau: *Manières de faire*, Editions Idées Gallimard.
3   Louis Althusser: *Ecrits philosophiques et politiques*, Editions Stock-IMEC, 1995, p. 557.
4   Michel Maffesoli: *La contemplation du monde*, Editions Grasset, 1993.
5   Hubert Damisch: *Fenêtre jaune cadmium*, Editions du Seuil.
6   Thierry de Duve: *Essais datés*, Editions de La Différence, 1987.
7   Emmanuel Lévinas: *Ethique et infini*, Poche-Biblio, p. 93.
8   Serge Daney: *Persévérance*, Editions P.O.L., 1992, p. 38.
9   Tzvetan Todorov: *La Vie commune*, Editions du Seuil, 1994.

CHAPTER 10

Gwen Robertson

An art encounter

Rethinking, renaming, redefining

> The history of performance art . . . is the history of a permissive, open-ended medium with endless variables, executed by artists impatient with the limitations of more established art forms, and determined to take their art directly to the public.
>
> —Rosalee Goldberg, *Performance Art*[1]

MY FRIEND PETRA SAYS, quite rightly, that it is an 'art historical disease' to want to name things. *As* an art historian, I am familiar with this affliction and see many reasons to resist such a compulsion. Like Petra, I am committed to open-ended, community-based art work, and I firmly believe in the power of the artist-practitioner to resist categorical clichés and stylistic imperatives in order to engage in more useful ideas and practices.

Community performance artists who today engage communities well beyond the traditional parameters of the art world – working in hospices, community centers, festivals, etc. – seemingly transcend the limitations of the old fashioned art world of style, 'isms', and objects. And, given the wealth of community-based arts practices emerging around the world, there is reason to argue that community performance art does not require art world validation. As the lines between the visual arts, the performing arts and community issues blur, it is folly to imagine that there should be absolute distinctions or vocabulary from any single field. The writings of, say, Paulo Freire can enrich and problematize our understanding of the work of visual artists, just as they have energized and complicated our readings and reception of theatre.

But at the same time, there are other issues at stake. I know a number of community performance artists who consistently struggle to explain what they do. One artist told me recently he had to put his community-based work on hold so he could produce enough 'traditional art objects' to get tenure at his American university. Another turned down a lucrative, long-term community performance commission in the UK because she feared it would typecast her as a 'community-practitioner' rather than an 'artist', and she couldn't risk losing exhibition opportunities.

Though anecdotal, I believe these experiences are not unusual. The question is, why are community-based practices so difficult to situate within the visual arts? At the beginning of the interdisciplinary, polyvalent, postmodern twenty-first century, why do such artists find recognition of their community-based practices so much more difficult to validate than more traditional artistic expressions?

My interest here is to investigate the parameters of community performance art from, for lack of a different term, an 'art historical' perspective. My interest is not to encapsulate or otherwise reify the practice in the name of 'style' or 'practice' (though I recognize this is always a threat) but instead to draw together the disparate voices interested in such practices so we might better understand how community performance fits into, and challenges, a contemporary 'art world' landscape with new content, new social aspirations and new practitioners.

My inspiration in this endeavor is the Encounters Group – a group of community-based artists whose work sits squarely between community development work and the realm of the 'high' or 'established' art world. Based in Sheffield, in the United Kingdom, this artistic team does *not* produce radical art forms that will somehow *save* their community, nor do they present themselves as visionaries who will reform how the community functions. Rather, they are devoted to the idea of *conversation* and believe that through the concept of 'art' they can cross boundaries and open doors traditional community, and artistic, practices cannot.

In their own words, the Encounters Group are dedicated to 'ongoing interactions with people and the places they live'. Their space is not the gallery or museum, but an empty shopfront in a dilapidated area of Sheffield. They lease the space for a short time (a month, a few weeks) and open the 'shop' to community members. Over the span of the project, the shops are filled with collections, stories, writings, photographs and 'found' objects. People are invited to come inside, to talk, to tell stories, to think about places, to reflect on the growth and the decay of their home town. Some shops had elaborate, orchestrated events, some had simple, open-ended practices.

It is the very mundane, real-world nature of their work (and the work of community-based artists like them) that is at the heart of the practice. The idea that an artistic work can literally be based in talking with people asks everyone to reconsider and to even 're-see' the expectations held about place, practices, art, neighborhood, etc. By gathering and developing ideas, rather than leading or creating them, and by respecting and learning from people rather than positioning them as a distant, removed audience, the artists of Encounters ask each person to think about their own ideas and their own expectations.

But such subtle revolutions are not always easy to see. Just taking myself as an illustration, it was hard to overcome long-held ideas about the parameters of artistic practice. Before encountering Encounters, for example, my idea of community performance art was a messy pastiche – a little Robert Morris, a dash of Daniel Buren, a splash of Yoko Ono, two parts Joseph Beuys, and a pinch of anti-institutional fervor. It is not surprising, perhaps, that it was difficult to imagine an art form that stepped away from these canonical conceptualists.

My first steps away from this (arguably dismissive) view were inspired by the early audience-interested work of Cedar Nordbye, especially his 2000 piece *The Mona Lisa Project*. In this piece, 'performed' at the Louvre, Nordbye stood outside the room where the Mona Lisa was hung and asked museum-goers *not* to see the famous painting, instead offering them an original watercolor he had painted as well as ten dollars. What he didn't specify was that he was also offering this interactive, museum-going audience a chance to do something they didn't often do: to stand and talk with someone about their expectations and assumptions about art. The results (many smiling portraits of people accepting or rejecting his offer) were printed in an artist's book documenting the project.

When I first saw the work, I enjoyed Nordbye's witty inversion of expectations and insightful questioning of how we value art, artists and place. What I realize now, however, is that I was missing the radical element of his approach. Nordbye was not simply playing with cultural assumptions about the Mona Lisa, but, by shifting the role of the artist away from an iconic 'master' and toward a present, very human, interlocutor, he also was (re)asserting the idea that the art might have a tangible (dare we say political?) involvement in contemporary life.[2]

Because Nordbye's early work was relatively easy to integrate into the language of art history and criticism, I framed it as 'Duchampian', formal (the book and photos are lovely) and conceptual. It seems that, lacking an alternative language, I failed to realize how limiting my own expectations and language about this art were.

With Encounters, neither the formal nor the Duchampian lens seemed to fit. It is hard to fetishize a shop, and a dry, Duchampian critique seems fundamentally at odds with Encounters' belief in community engagement. Their performance isn't obviously performative, they don't seem interested in shocking anyone, nor do they seem to worry about the scope or definition of artistic practice. Instead, they are interested in using the umbrella concept of 'art' to give voice to ideas, peoples, communities (however constituted), actions and artists so that assorted ideas might open and diverse dialogues might begin.

In an age where skepticism and ennui often seem the norm, this faith in the community collective surprised me. As an art historian, my questions were perhaps predictable: were they misplaced modernists, hopelessly whistling in dark shops and calling it art? Or were they instead *so* postmodern that they had transcended the term 'art', and forged some new identity or practice, begun some new vocabulary more complicated than the categories of my discipline led me to expect?

Talking with Encounters artists Ruth Ben-Tovin and Trish O'Shea confirmed my sense that this artistic practice was more complex than its 'real-world' context and interactive sensibility suggested. Neither misplaced utopians nor cynical postmodernists, they were instead pragmatic, self-conscious, knowledgeable artists dedicated to using their skills and arts training in their own community. They were bringing the realm of art directly into the realm of life, but they had no utopian motivations. They weren't obviously looking to solve anything universal, but they were nonetheless interested in solutions. They believed there was something for art and artists to do, but not in a vacuum. It was clear they believed in the possibility of positively working with/within the community and that this interaction could be artistic.

The performance that introduced me to Encounters was a retelling of the experiences they had in the first shop (two Sharrow-based shops followed). Ben-Tovim and O'Shea stood on stage and performed their work by reading statements written by community members who visited the 2003 shop during the month it was open. Readings from the audience (where the audience member took on the voice of one of the community members) punctuated the experience, thereby creating a more interactive environment. The performance was dramatic and simple, elegant yet also familiar. This was performance art as I knew it. The audience was full of 'art worlders', the stage was dramatically lit as the artists performed their readings in front of a projected video of the streets of Sharrow, and there was a discussion session following. We audience members all knew the basic rules of engagement. In standard performance-art-audience mode, I found myself wondering about duration ('How long will this take?'), about repetition ('Is this it?'), and about style ('Whose work does this look like?').

Yet despite this relatively traditional outlook, as the piece unfolded, the poignant, unvarnished words of the community members suggested an unfamiliar element. The work wasn't about the artists as much as it was the place. This 'performance' actually was *not* the heart of the work. The 'art' or the 'work' took place in the community. The art world performance was but its echo. The artists on stage were reading short passages that Encounters shop-going community members had written about their own memories of Sharrow. I had never heard of Sharrow (what I later learned to be an inner-city area of the larger post-industrial city of Sheffield) and I knew nothing of the demographics or history. Listening to the words read by Ben-Tovim and O'Shea, however, I got a sense of a town marked by waves of immigration, troubled by financial depression, and divided by class and racial issues; *but also* a place of community meetings, schools, parks, etc. People who wrote such simple things and short phrases communicated a depth of experience, emotion and history. Entries included brief elements such as: 'I like this area, the people, the school, we all went to Sharrow Infants and Juniors and we are all at Abbeydale Grange. We don't really like the flats, the drug dealing, the trouble' (S, age 12; S, age 15; A, age 14); or 'I miss Libya, my family, my work. I was a dental nurse . . . My husband came to study here and we will go back when he's finished. He is studying metallurgy engineering. I've got three children and we live on Hobart Street'; or 'There used to be gangs of youths around the stairwells but that doesn't happen so much now. Since moving to the estate I've been a victim of crime four times'.[3]

These short, informal notes about a distant city gave me a clear sense that this place was like many other places. It was, to these people at least, their home and they were attached to it because their lives happened there. People from all different ages, classes and ethnicities had come to Encounters to jot down their stories. In recounting them, there was no need to embellish.

This performative moment was flawed (there was a mixed reaction in the audience to conceits about storytelling, the presentation of object mementos, questions of class and access about the shops, etc.) and the artists were the first to acknowledge that it was a work in process. They were, they told me, still working on how to communicate to a larger audience the ideas and experiences so closely tied to a small community. Yet even in this mediated form, I found the Encounters Project a potentially liberating way to give art something *to do* that was not tied to the museum nor to a traditional 'art world' reliance on an art world audience. The performance from the stage that reached me, in the audience, was not it seemed the end result of the activity. It was not, that is, the *essence* of the art. It had happened without me, even in spite of me.

Additionally, the artists, deeply committed to defining themselves *as* artists, were not defined by the 'exhibition' of their work and, in fact, it was difficult to even say what the art product was. They saw themselves as a 'Sheffield-based arts initiative, using performance, film, photography, visual art and text to create art work in response to people and the urban environment'. Their projects, they explained, 'involve people of all ages, cultures and from all walks of life, enabling them to share ideas, stories and memories about everyday life'.[4] The performative experience of the shops unfolded over months and the things that happened in the shop were only loosely programmed (other artists and community programs were invited to share the shop space and even the space itself impacted on the process).

Ultimately, then, it is not simply that this work does not 'fit' into the definition of 'art work' or 'art world' as it has developed (for if nothing else, the twentieth century showed that those terms are infinitely malleable). Rather, it seems that Encounters ignores such traditional questions of 'fit' and instead charts its own territory that is undeniably 'artistic', but more complex to explain.

The people who visited the Encounters shops were not members of an art world audience. They did not seem to enter the Encounters shop because they sought elevation or some equivalent through art. Similarly, the artists created 'art', not by sculpting or molding material, but by creating a space of engagement, where people could talk about their lives. It isn't an especially earth shattering concept; people love to talk – but, as many have pointed out, there are ever fewer opportunities to stop and make human connections. It is arguably a different way to bring performance directly to the public than in the way art historian Rosalee Goldberg may have intended (there are no art 'stars' and the performance, such that there is, is less performed than it is simply experienced . . .), but that does not, I would argue, negate its performativity.

Goldberg theorized that when art reaches an impasse, 'artists have turned to performance as a way of breaking down categories and indicating new directions'.[5] In the past I had thought of this quote in a fairly traditional art world way (Joseph Beuys, Chris Burden, Carolee Schneeman, etc.). The Encounters Project, and community-based practice in general, break down so many categories and move in so many directions that it is difficult to isolate the performance from the concept. I could not, for example, decide whether it was actually a 'performance' to spend the day in a shop space waiting for people to come in and interact. And if a performance, was it performative on the part of the 'artist' or the 'audience/shop-goer'?

When asked about their most basic intentions in their artistic practice, O'Shea explained that, like most artists, they are interested in fairly basic things, such as getting 'people to ask something of themselves, to question, to look afresh, to be challenged, to be comforted, to be excited, to be made to laugh, to cry, to feel afraid, to feel a part of something and then to know what it is to be alone'.[6] The nature of Encounters, however, also includes a much more 'civic' component with imbedded, community-based concerns. Funding to support their project came from the Sharrow/ Nether Edge/Broomhill Area Panel so a project report was delivered to the council reporting on the achievements of the funded Encounters projects. The notes from the 8 January 2004 panel include Ruth Ben-Tovim's presentation, among a myriad of other local concerns (pedestrian access, firefighting capacities, housing services, etc.). In her report, Ben-Tovim explained that Encounters included an 'action research project, which would pilot ways to develop the audiences for art in Sharrow' as well as pilot 'effective methods for researching and involving local people in creative think-ing and activity, explore barriers to involvement, make proposals for how to deliver participatory arts activities . . . and to raise the agenda of arts and regeneration in the area'.[7] Even more significantly, the artists and the resulting shop were a part of the community and, as such, worked to build a picture of the issues and feelings of the people in the low-income area they were working in.

This more intimate, political, community-based project echoes what Lucy Lippard has for so long asked the art world to consider. Writing in her book *Lure of the Local*, Lippard calls for a fundamental shift in the way that the contemporary visual arts deal with issues of place and community. She writes: 'Too much art "about place", ... is more about art and the place of art than about the actual places where artists and viewers find themselves'. Clearly, as O'Shea identifies, the work of Encounters incorporates most of the expressive elements identified with the arts, and the integration of the work into community councils and community development projects suggests a movement away from themselves, away from 'the artist' and toward something much broader and inclusive. Lippard worries that in so much contemporary art, 'art is not set free within the place itself to work its wonders or to give voice to those forces that have formed the place'.[8] She hopes to 'see the discussion, go beyond this view of the margins from the center, to see the artists truly enter the realm of the decentered, or in a more positive light, the realm of the multicentered'.[9] From Lippard, then, we find a critical voice that is laying the groundwork for understanding the political and community potential in works such as those from the Encounters Project, which seek the polyvalent rather than the individually focused art work.

Encounters, as though in answer to Lippard's call to arms, is tied neither to a straight performance nor the production of an object (though there are both performative and tangible elements), and because the audience is participant, creator *and* viewer, the aspirations are more complicated than those for a normative art practice or even 'artist'. Even on the front page of their documenting website (www.sharrowencounters. org.uk), the artists of Encounters label themselves, 'artists and creative consultants' and explain that they have a 'proven track record of working with a wide variety of organizations, regeneration agencies and local communities to develop and deliver high quality arts projects, creative consultation, and community capacity building initiatives'.[10] It is not a question of them being *either* artists *or* community workers – but always a demonstration of both, of their projects being multivalent in an empowering way.

When asked if their work is, indeed 'Art', both Ben-Tovim and O'Shea are hesitant. O'Shea notes: 'creative practitioners who have experienced the work have said it is art ("real art"). A local person experiencing the work sees it more as documentation, a piece of where they live, an intrigue, a strange phenomenon . . . . It raises questions about what art is and who it is for.' Ben-Tovim adds to this the question of the distinction between 'art' and 'art world', noting that: 'we don't feel that we are particularly part of the art world locus. People from it, especially young, emerging artists tend to find us and get excited, which is great, but establishment-wise we are pretty invisible.' She even noted that, despite the fact that their shop was in the neighborhood of the local university and many students visited frequently, 'no lecturers ever have [visited] and despite our attempts to make contact we've not really had any participate'.[11]

Is this academic rejection, I've wondered, stemming from a disdain for community-based art? Or is it indifference? Or a specific dislike of the artists and their project? Though I don't know specifically why local academics didn't participate, there are reasons to be critical. Without the institutional 'seriousness' of an art world context, Encounters can appear more of a whimsical community pageant than a committed cultural engagement. For example, I recently read a posting where, in response to questions about property values in Sharrow, one writer (who identified himself as a community leader) extolled the virtues of the area by explaining that in the city, there are 'fantastic events that go on, like the Encounters art project, and the Sharrow festival, as well as . . . community parties, and trips out for the kiddies'.[12] Encounters here is equated to a festival, or an outing to the park. It is perceived not as social engagement, but as a kind of entertainment that might suggest increased property values. The social commitment of the artists is replaced by a sort of banal assumption that 'art' makes a community more desirable. The public, unfocused, partially-undefined nature of Encounters leaves it open to such assumptions – at both the community *and* the scholarly level.

By the same token, however, this also leads back to Lippard's frustration with the state of the visual arts. Lippard argues: 'a profoundly local public art has not caught on in the mainstream because in order to attract sufficient buyers in the current system of distribution, art must be relatively generalized, detachable from politics and pain (not to mention ugliness).' Both the impulse to see work like Encounters as a simplistic entertainment *and* the difficulty of arguing against this kind of critique come from this art world pressure to define art as apolitical, beautiful, uplifting. Without a sophisticated discourse to argue an alternative, such a discussion rarely even gets started. Lippard concludes her point by asserting that we 'need *some* artists to draw back from abstractions and consider shared experiences'.[13] It is this call (whether they know it or not) that community performance artists like Encounters are answering.

As noted above however, this call to action does not ensure access to the art world. Working in the community can be a complicated undertaking for artists. Ben-Tovim recognizes this: 'a lot of community based art work doesn't get noticed by the "art world". For us, even though it feels very easy to legitimize, fund and defend our work in political, governmental, and council circles in . . . art networks we feel pretty invisible.'[14]

Encounters, like other community performance art examples, is removed from the museum – separated by intention as well as logistics. Exacerbating the problem, in the visual arts, is the fact that there is not an especially lengthy tradition to draw upon. Lippard recognizes this, noting: 'theatre . . . more than visual arts, has inspired the most innovative developments in community culture.'[15]

Art history as a field has persistently framed the visual arts in terms of objects so that even the most iconoclastic turns (such as conceptualism, process and performance art) are defined specifically through their *lack* of an object. French curator Nicolas Bourriaud (a curator who has defined his career through his interest in community-based or relational practice) goes so far as to define traditional expressions of 'art' as 'a set of objects presented as part of narrative known as *art history*'.[16] Add to this the modernist tendency in the visual arts (*à la* Greenberg) to stridently defend and delimit (and therefore protect) the visual arts from other practices, and it is not so difficult to understand why Ben-Tovim reflected that they were 'told by a friend who taught some part-time hours at the local university that there was a very strong anti "community art" focus'.[17]

The challenge to those interested in understanding community performance art, then, is to expand upon art historical and critical underpinnings that already exist to support community-involved artists; not because community performance artists such as Encounters *need* the art world, but because the art world needs community performance art. It offers an intriguing answer to the clichéd postmodern crisis which has come from understanding that all action, aesthetic or otherwise, is politically loaded and in dialogue (if not complicit) with dominant cultural ideology, but does not know exactly how to move beyond this understanding. Community performance imagines that action and interaction is more important than absolute knowledge. As such, it positions the artist to interact with, and create within, a social structure rather than sitting outside, merely commenting.

In the context of the 'high art' world (large museums, galleries, etc.), Bourriaud has been especially concerned with this move from outside observation to a more direct, interactive form of artistic production. His work has sought to reach beyond traditional conceptions of art-as-object and to upset the expectation of an audience's traditionally static relationship to art. His term for art that engages in this way is 'relational aesthetics', which he defines as 'aesthetic theory consisting in judging artworks on the basis of inter-human relations which they represent, produce of prompt'.[18]

In the 1990s Bourriaud identified a trend toward artistic expressions stressing artist-to-audience dialogue. This creates an impulse to engage the audience through relational aesthetics or 'a set of artistic practices which take as their theoretical and practical point of departure the whole of human relations and their social context, rather than an independent and private space'.[19]

Drawing on diverse philosophical traditions, Bourriaud theorizes that the value of art in contemporary society comes from the ability of art to 'produce a specific sociability'. More pointedly, he believes that art represents Marx's idea of a social interstice, a place beyond the law of profit (dealing in barter, alternative production, etc.) that allows for, and even encourages, 'inter-human commerce that differs from the "communication zones" that are imposed upon us' by our late-capitalist life.[20]

For Bourriaud, these zones of inter-human communication take place in the museum (he is, after all, a curator) and the artists Bourriaud champions still fit nicely into the confines of the museum (Rirkrit Tirvanija, for example, may challenge the museum by serving food or creating a gathering space in a gallery, but the museum has shown itself suitably 'evolved' so as to accommodate this challenge gracefully). Bourriaud's ideas about the potential (even inevitability) of relational art to change the way we understand art, however, can be used as an interpretive tool beyond a museum context.

Bourriaud appropriately states that 'art is a state of encounter'[21] and that the value of this constant interaction is that it 'tightens the space of relations'[22] in an otherwise increasingly anonymous and automated urban environment. And, as I opened the discussion of Bourriaud, it provides a theoretical means for framing what makes work like the Encounters Project compelling. Working in the inner city, in a known but unused shop space, they provide a space outside the urban communication zone of the city, beyond the expectations of the market (art or otherwise), and dedicated solely to inter-human communication.

Ben-Tovim, who learned of Bourriaud's ideas only two years *after* beginning the work of Encounters explains: '[the] ideas of relational aesthetics have helped us to frame our work within an art context and also in some ways to understand our own work more. So it's been practice, theory, and now practice again which I feel will be more influenced perhaps by ideas of relational work.' On a very general level, she notes: 'it has given a legitimacy to the invisibility of the work and has helped us to understand the idea that the shops themselves were a whole relational project.'[23] Ben-Tovim concludes: 'the theoretical framework has also helped me re-find my artist role within the idea of the work as opposed to the community facilitator role. So it's a freedom thing.'[24]

The short remembrances, the found items brought to the shop and 'displayed', and all the other components that develop in the space of one of the shops, are tangible traces, but the art, as it exists, also happens through the human relationships and dialogues (the human encounters) that occur (and are noted, deposited, or otherwise recorded) through the work of the shop. The traces that remain (to be performed, or photographed, or blogged, etc.) document that exchange and serve as testament that this other kind of human relationship is/was possible, at least for the short time that the shop existed.

When asked about these remnants and whether they were the 'art product' of the Encounters work or something else, O'Shea explained: '[once we] placed the work in a gallery setting for a time (during the second shop) . . . it was quite remarkable how it changed the work. Placing found objects in well-lit glass cabinets made them profound, but forlorn, too. Naturally, the people who created the work, who found the work and donated stuff didn't access the gallery. Interesting, that Encounters can only exist if people participate – on the whole the work is from the people by the people.[25] Utopian and democratic overtones aside, this recognition that the work literally doesn't exist without a meaningful engagement with a larger community gives community performance work a double-edged responsibility for both the concept as well as the reception: two elements that are often hard to pull together successfully.

This challenging relationship between artist and constituency that the community-based artist explores is difficult and is not always perceived in celebratory terms. Some current critics and scholars who address contemporary performative work have touched on the issues inherent in community performance work and are critical of this tenuous relationship between aesthetics, concept and community responsibility. Scholars such as art critic Grant Kester and, to a lesser extent, art historian Miwon Kwon question the authenticity of such community-based engagements and express valid concerns about the move beyond the art institution. Kester, one of the most persistent American critics to deal with emergent performance and community-based art work, has concerns about the 'rhetoric of community artists who position themselves as the vehicle for an unmediated expressivity on the part of a given community'.[26] Kester, building upon Bourdieu's work on the creation of legitimacy of community delegates, worries about the potential for the artist to appropriate, or otherwise assume, the community for personal interests and career advancement.

Miwon Kwon, in her book *One Site After Another*, responds to this charge by pointing out that relationships between artists and community groups are not 'based on a direct, unmediated relationship' but are instead 'circumscribed within a more complex network of motivations, expectations and projects among all involved'.[27] For Kwon this is a negative recognition, for she charges the community-based artist with overlooking the complexities of such communal relations. Like Kester, she is skeptical about the ability of a supra-institutional artistic expression to move into successful community relations (though Kester ultimately hopes for such a relationship, while Kwon does not).

In his more recent writings, Kester explains that he is, in fact, 'particularly interested in a discursive aesthetic based on the possibility of a dialogical relationship that breaks down the conventional distinction between artist, art work and audience'.[28] What he terms a 'dialogic aesthetic' or 'littoral art' (building on the definition of 'littoral' as 'of or on the shore' to reflect the meeting point, or convergence site, of many different spaces/traditions[29]) is remarkably similar to Bourriaud's relational aesthetics, though their ideas grew out of very different backgrounds and contexts. Unlike Bourriaud, however, Kester is arguably more concerned with the dangers of this kind of practice (whether called dialogic or relational) than the products. First, he mistrusts the artist's tendency to imagine a 'highly individualized concept of personal autonomy' while at the same time perceiving themselves as able to 'transcend self through their mastery of a universal aesthetic knowledge'[30] for he believes this sets up status differentials that rarely benefit the community over the artist. Second, he is concerned about what he calls the 'problem of itineracy': the inability of an artist to commit to a sustained relationship with a given community. Ultimately, his complex, historically-grounded argument identifies the ways in which such community-based practices have gone astray in the past and he points out that today we have even less support for rethinking social situations than in previous times. He does, however, hold out hope that when these variables can be overcome, there is great transgressive potential in such work.

Thinking about Encounters through such a lens, I realize that, at least in part, the very definition of what 'transgressive' might mean is at stake. It seems that Kester is using it to mean an artistic practice that allows for the identification of assumptions (hegemonic ideals, etc.) and practices in order to alter (or at least decenter) them. But is this transgression a matter of degree? Which is to say, when the Encounters Project opens a shop in Sharrow with the intention of learning more, working with, and generally getting to know the diverse people and issues in their community, is that transgressive? If, as happened as a result of their first shop, the month-long shopfront project led to the commissioning of Encounters to lead several different community-based projects – such as the St Peter's Church Redevelopment Project (commissioned by St Peter's Parish Church Council and the Sheffield City Council, among others), or the Improvements Project for Mount Pleasant Park (funded by the Sheffield City Council), or the Sharrows Fathers Project (commissioned by the Family Service Unit and Sharrow Sure State) – is this transgressive? Is asking a group of artists, a group dedicated to helping their own community raise community participation and consciousness, to participate in local redevelopment projects transgressive?

If we think about Lippard's call for a multicentered artistic practice where the artist enters the realm of the decentered to push discussion to new depths, then perhaps Encounters, like so much community performance art, *is* transgressive. But in these multicentered practices, especially when they are as successful as Encounters, the thing most decentered is the artist (outside the institution, working with and funded by community interests, etc.). Working in their own community (and therefore inherently 'non-itinerant'), they frame their work around a dedication to place that borders on that of a 'community-worker' at least as much as it does that of an 'artist'. The danger of this, as Kester alludes to and Lippard seems to at least touch on, is that without the title or recognition (even maintenance) of the role of 'artist', the unique perception of the practitioners as being 'creative' or 'new' or 'innovative' would be lost.

The ability to define a cultural space for the community performance 'artist', then, is critically important. Looking at Encounters, for example, their 'artistic practice', as defined by the Sheffield City Council, included, 'walking "round the Lansdowne Estate, meeting and talking to people"' and that, through this, they had 'built up a picture of some of the issues and feelings from within the Estate'.[31] In itself, this is not obviously an 'artistic' process, nor does it provide some sort of scientific sampling data that might be said to comprehensively analyze the full breadth of community responses. And, to consider Kester's concerns about the artists' assumptions that they have access to some 'universal aesthetic' that allows them to parachute in and 'solve' community problems, we should at least question the community performance artist's assumptions – *can* Enounters contribute anything by such informal, artist-centered questions?

If we stop here, however, we miss a prime element that sets community performance art apart from, say, 'community-based' or 'site-specific' art. The most successful works by the most engaged artists only develop out of intense local involvement. Because the work worries less about the product and more about the development of ideas that will grow beyond the art moment or product, the emphasis is literally for creating a space within a community to think about changes (something that Kester identifies as especially lacking in our contemporary moment). Perhaps, in the end, it is exactly this space, one opened up literally by and for dialogue, that is the 'transgressive' element of community performance. It isn't gigantic, it isn't on the scale of early twentieth-century utopian aspirations, but that doesn't mean that it isn't a valuable contribution – to the community, to the art world – nonetheless.

When Encounters offered space within their shops to other groups interested in reaching out into the Sharrow community (such as the 'Sharrow Fathers: Father figures', which interviewed and sought to recognize community fathering; or the St Peter's Project, which started a community dialogue about the community use of a space created after the demolition of St Peter's Parish), they were making small, subtle interventions in the community fabric by developing non-traditional stakeholders and encouraging people to find ways to get involved in their communities. They cannot be a panacea to all that ails the Sharrow community. But they *are* interventions and they have demonstrated a persistent visibility in the community for often invisible issues such as race, class and gender access.

Encounters, I believe, does what Miwon Kwon argues for – a 'redefining [of] community-based art as a collective artistic praxis' in order to move beyond concerns (such as those raised by Kester) about the relationships between artists and community. This collective practice, in her view, is a 'projective enterprise' where the 'artist' is actually an artistic group created out of the individual elements of artist, arts or civic organization, local institution, etc., all locked in a constant collaboration. To her, this need to negotiate within and without helps to mediate the relationship between 'artist' and 'other/community'.

Looking at Encounters through such a lens, I am again struck by the way in which contemporary community performance artist/art collectives, such as Encounters, independently of these few but prominent writings and theories, have instinctively negotiated these ideas. Both as a collective, much in line with Kwon's call for artistic praxis, and constantly concerned about the differentials between artist-community member, the Encounters projects provoke more questions about the nature of community than they answer. O'Shea reflects on the more subtle findings of the Encounters work, noting that, for her, one of the most fascinating aspects of the shops has been, not how vast nor how global the results, but rather how subtle the experience of community is. She notes that: 'All three of our shops were within streets of each other . . . yet they were each distinct and reflected different aspects of the area – quite remarkable, really, when you think about how people talk of neighborhoods and communities – they might be a lot smaller than we imagine, or at least people associate themselves with relatively small areas.'[32]

In the end, the 'art' of Encounters is not about changing the world along some utopian or global vision provided by the artist, nor is it linked with a specific 'issue', or political cause, or art world revolution. Instead, it is about thinking about and reaching out into the places of daily life, and understanding not the global but the local, not the world community, but the local community.

For me, Encounters in particular, and the best of community performance practices in general, ask us to look for art both beyond and within the art world so that we let go of complacent intellectualism and learn to be more open to subtle innovation. Put it down as the relational/live art *Zeitgeist*, or attribute it to the open-ended potential for performative innovation, this ability to think of art as community-rich and intellectually polyvalent intrigues and heartens me. Encounters embody the richness of art historical tradition, but they also express the complexity of community tradition. Beyond Bourriaud's focus on the museum, more tangible than the aspirations of Kester and Kwon, beyond the indeterminacy of 'live art' and speaking to the plea of Lippard, Encounters offer an open-ended engagement with people that doesn't require the label of art, yet is enriched by it. It is this broader idea of and this greater potential for the possibility of a more open-ended idea of art that so intrigues me and which seems so promising.

The things that Encounters have accomplished do not, in themselves, represent major interventions in the community, nor are they obviously 'art works'. No, they will not substantively transform the lives of the working-class individuals living in the low-income housing, nor will they revolutionize the way that we understand the word 'art'. But they do challenge us to reconsider what it is we expect or want from an art-based activity. And, perhaps more importantly, they do so by foregrounding what it is we want from communities. The emphasis on community, on gatherings and groupings (as opposed to individual art production and reception), subtly both ignores and critiques some of the most fundamental relations at work in so-called traditional arts and art economies. In the face of such a critique, 'art' has either to reconsider itself or to stand by while its limitations are methodically, ritualistically spelled out by the emergence of community performance.

Notes

1   RoseLee Goldberg (1988) *Performance Art: From Futurism to the Present*, New York, Harry N. Abrams, p. 9.
2   Nordbye's later work, like the Empire Project and Hummer Project, are significantly more political and represent his more tangible contributions to the field.
3   These quotes are technically from the third Encounters shop (127 Club Garden Road) and not from the performance I saw, but the tone and scope are strikingly similar. Quotes can be found published in their entirety on the Encounters website, www.sharrowencounters.org.uk (accessed 20 April 2006).
4   Encounters website, home page, www.sharrowencounters.org.
5   Goldberg (1988), p. 7.
6   Unless otherwise stated, all quotes from Trish O'Shea come from a 3 November 2005 interview with the author.
7   See meeting minutes for further discussion and context at http://www.sheffield.gov. uk/your-city-council/council-meetings/area-panels/broomhill-central-netheredge/ agenda-8th-january-2004/minutes-8-january-2004 (accessed 30 April 2006).
8   Lucy Lippard (1997) *The Lure of the Local: Sense of Place in a Multicentered Society*, New York, The New Press, p. 278. In this chapter, entitled 'Places with a Present', Lippard is using a 1995 exhibition at the Art Institute of Chicago entitled 'About Place' as her point of departure for this discussion. She is juxtaposing her interest

in a more local, reflective and interactive art against the work of artists such as Brice Marden, Andrea Zittle and Anna Devere Smith who were included in this exhibition.

9   Lippard (1997), p. 277.

10 Encounters website, home page, www.sharrowencounters.org.uk.

11 Unless otherwise stated, all quotes from Ruth Ben-Tovim came from a 27 October 2005 interview with the author.

12 Plain Talker, 'Sharrow: A Good Place to Buy', online posting. Available at: http://www.sheffieldforum.co.uk/showthread.php?s=5c440c9083b9ecf51e9ac85a63af1400&threadid=27762 (accessed 20 April 2006).

13 Lippard (1997), p. 278.

14 Ben-Tovim in 27 October 2005 interview with the author.

15 Lippard (1997), p. 282.

16 Nicolas Bourriaud (2002) *Relational Aesthetics*, Paris, Les presses du reel, p. 107.

17 Ben-Tovim, 27 October 2005, interview with the author.

18 Bourriaud (2002), p. 112.

19 Bourriaud (2002), p. 113.

20 Bourriaud (2002), p. 16.

21 Bourriaud (2002), p. 18.

22 Bourriaud (2002), p. 16.

23 Ben-Tovim, 27 October 2005, interview with the author.

24 Ben-Tovim, 27 October 2005, interview with the author.

25 O'Shea, 3 November, 2005, interview with the author.

26 Grant Kester (1995) 'Aesthetic Evangelists: Conversion and Empowerment in Contemporary Community Art', *Afterimage* (January): 6, as quoted in Miwon Kwon (2004) *One Place After Another: Site-Specific Art and Locational Identity*, Cambridge, MA, and London: The MIT Press, p. 139.

27 Kwon (2004), p. 141.

28 Grant Kester (2006) 'Dialogical Aesthetics: A Critical Framework for Littoral Art', *Variant*, 9. Available at: www.variant.randomstate.org/9texts/KesterSupplement.html (accessed 30 March 2006).

29 See Introduction to *Variant*, 9 at their website (see note 28) for full discussion of term.

30 Kester (2006).

31 Minutes of meeting held 8 January 2004 at Sharrow Community Centre, Sharrow/Nether Edge/Broomhill Area Panel, http://www.sheffield.gov.uk/your-city-council/council-meetings/area-panels/broomhill-central-netheredge/agenda-8th-january-2004/minutes-8-january-2004 (accessed 20 April 2006).

32 O'Shea, 3 November 2005, interview with the author.

CHAPTER 11

Becky Shaw

'The Generosity Project'

'THE GENEROSITY PROJECT' is an art work in the form of a lecture. The lecture involves the projection of a series of slides, together with my verbal description of the making of 'The Generosity Project'. The slides contain photographs of eighteen people receiving a bunch of flowers from me. The photographs are taken in the apartments of the disabled people who live at the Amstelveen Centre, a privately funded care home in the Netherlands, for people unable to live independently due to physical disability. 'The Generosity Project' is given at art galleries and art conferences, but the work is also a box of slides and a set of instructions, in the art collection of the Municipality of Amstelveen, commissioned by the Kunstprijs Amstelveen. The work belongs to the gallery, who can do what they will with the set of slides. However, no one can actually *give* the work 'The Generosity Project' except me. The following text describes how and why 'The Generosity Project' was formed and asks how artists can work in communities at the same time as making a critical contribution.

I have been working in community and institutional contexts since 1993, often exploring the value of participation in visual and live art (such as in my 1998 thesis which explored whether making sculpture was a significant use of time for patients with life-threatening illnesses). At the same time I was also pursuing the communication of this work in the critical arena of visual and live arts (attending conferences, publishing in the critical literature, etc.). Pursuing these dual roles (one expected to deliver therapeutic outcomes, the other providing critical examination), I have become conscious of conflicting expectations in my work and in its reception. The more I've worked in community settings, the more I've become aware that it is not 'art' versus 'therapy' (where taking sides was expected), but rather a much more complex whole. It wasn't until I became involved in 'The Generosity Project', though, that I was able to recognize the importance of interrogating and critically questioning the values at

Figure 6 'The Generosity Project', Becky Shaw.
Photo: Wouter Stelwagen.

play in the community and artistic situation rather than interrogating the people or positions.

'The Generosity Project' arose from a strange series of events and it took me a long time to realize that the difficulties the situation continually presented were the most interesting and important keys to understanding an overlooked aspect of the contemporary social and political climate. In 2002, I was nominated by a UK selector to compete for (and was awarded) the Kunstprijs Amstelveen, or the Amstelveen Art Incentive Prize. The prize is awarded yearly to a young (under thirty-five) artist or designer, focusing on a different profession every year. The committee pitches Dutch talent against talent from another country. In 2002 the prize was for fine art, and Dutch graduates or students from the Sandberg Masters-level Academy were pitched against 'young British' artists.

In 2003, at the event held for the award of this prize, Sandberg Master Tineke Rejinders gave a lecture articulating her research on art she named 'generosity projects'. She collated a range of artists who undertake projects with, as she described, 'an almost unrealistic attitude of altruism and generosity'. The projects all involved the orchestration of acts to make life better, such as the work of Rirkrit Tirvanija, or Marisca Voskamp's project to make the sun shine in the night, or Otto Berchem's flower-laden shopping baskets, intended to aid romance in supermarkets. These acts, she argued, raise the possibility that life can be made better by the gift of art, and, at their most effective, offer a covert criticism of life as it is.

The practices Rejinders describes are part of a century-long artistic heritage that seeks to close the gap between art and life and to posit art as a tool for social change.

From the utopian aspirations at the beginning of the twentieth century to the 1960s radical critique of art as autonomous from society, art is posited as an alternative to a commercial art market, even a commercial society. Alongside the emergence of this historical critical directive was, of course, a much wider social movement engaged in the attempted dismantling of Western hegemony and authority.

In the UK in the 1990s and 2000s, this legacy became ossified in the governmental use of the arts to address issues of social exclusion and industrial decline. Well-meaning agencies sought to use the assumed beneficial effects of artists' work in the social realm to meet their own drive for inclusion, and to seek to recreate participation in a society suffering from a withdrawal from politics and a devastating fragmentation. A prime example of this is the UK's 'Creative Partnerships', an ongoing, country-wide programme to bring artists, schools and communities together, led by the Department for Culture Media and Sport and the Department for Education. While artistic thinking had shaped this critical directive, as a means to make art part of daily life, it became apparent that the reneging of critical autonomy on the part of the artist was a danger that had not been anticipated. Andrea Fraser recognized that artists were not victims but were complicit in this scenario:

> an invitation to produce specific work in response to a specific situation is a very direct demand, the motivating interests of which are barely concealed and difficult to ignore. I know that if I accept the invitation I will be serving those interests unless I work very hard to do otherwise.
> (Andrea Fraser (1994) 'How to Provide an Artistic Service: An Introduction', http://home.att.net/~archives/fraserservice.html)

With particular relevance to my own work, Fraser pinpoints the difficulty of taking on work and at the same time trying to find a critical space within it. By 2000, whatever the radicalism that the inclusion agenda and socially-engaged practice aspired to, it was made clear by Nicholas Bourriaud's 'relational aesthetics' and, more directly, his book *Postproduction* (2000, New York, Lukas & Steinberg) that the practices were part of the art status quo, offering a flexible made-to-measure, 'just-in-time' approach that reflected contemporary production. Motivations such as 'conviviality' and 'hospitality', once seen as means to critique art's autonomy, were easily used to enhance the public profile of museums and as useful image-building tools more generally. While, again, this is not necessarily a bad thing, it was not arguably the outcome radical practices had sought.

Kunstprijs Amstelveen emerges from a similar climate where culture is seen as the means to solve a multitude of social problems. Overshadowed by its close neighbour, Amsterdam, Amstelveen seems keen to find a sense of identity beyond that of a respectable and somewhat middle-aged suburb. The prize sought to create a cultural, cutting-edge identity for the town. The catalogue introduction describes the goals:

> The most important element, however, remains the stimulation of unfolding new talents, and the creation of opportunity for young artists. That goes well with the climate of a city like Amstelveen whose identity is partly determined by the 'Art and Culture' factor.

As the quote indicates, though, the prize has a double measure of atavism in seeking to give a gift to a young artist. As Jos Houweling describes in his text, 'Ten years of the Art Incentive Prize Amstelveen': 'what you give away isn't gone' as 'if the land of Amstelveen belonged to the artists you would get wonders in return'. The prize, he says, is 'a diamond with marvellous facets and an unexpected glitter'.

My work that won the prize was 'Killing Time'. I had spent four years working with palliative care patients, seeking methods of collaboration that involved the formation of a joint visual language. When awarded the prize, the work it seemed had managed to traverse some sort of gap between therapeutic potential and the exploration of critical and honest questions about whether art can be therapy. An art audience is often hostile to occupational crafts, but rather than simply saying 'this is not therapy', I sought to face the questions head on and articulate that the two worlds are not so easily separable; that therapeutic contexts and processes offer a space to think critically about therapy and art. Like most work which appears to 'do good', 'Killing Time' appears to be kind and generous to the 'dying people'. However, while the work is certainly not abusive or cruel, I wanted it to be assessed as a work of art rather than for its kindness. Unlike some work made in the community, I wanted it to be measured (as it was by the art masters who chose it for the prize) as a work in its own right that talked about, but did not take its authenticity from, the community who made it with me. Because of the circumstances in which the work was made, though, there was always the risk of it being perceived and measured solely as an act of generosity.

On the announcement of the Kunstprijs Amstelveen prize ceremony all of the participating artists were lined up and given flowers. The prize was 10,000 euros: I won the prize. In return I was to give the organization a new work, which, I understood, would be donated to a local collection. If, however, in return for the prize/money I had to give a new work, then the prize was actually a commission and sale, not a gift or prize. Commissions can be perceived as gifts, allowing artists the time and space to develop new work. However, it's vital to remember that however generous the intended gift to the artist, the benefit travels both ways.

As I make work that responds to context it was not of interest to me to make a work in the UK and send it to the Netherlands. I decided that if the organization were commissioning me then they must support me in finding a means to engage in some aspect of Amstelveen. I discussed this with the civic body and they said they would find a site for me. After many months Kunstprijs Amstelveen came back to me with one venue and had already secured the relationship. They decided that I would make a new work with the Amstelrade centre for physically disabled people, and that the resulting artwork would be shown in the forthcoming Disability Arts Festival in the Neuekirche. So by the nature of my community-based practice, they found themselves not commissioning an object but instead a gift of my time for Amstelrade. Yet the situation of this gift/commission meant that I had very little time to produce a work so I was not able to build relationships and negotiate a continued dialogue with participants. Instead, the commission was forcing me to do what I would usually consider unacceptable —to 'parachute in', make the work in a short space of time, then take it elsewhere. Given this unpalatable situation, I realized that instead of attempting to ameliorate this effect by seeing Amstelrade as the only context of the work, the prize itself was enabling me to think about the wider context of art work in social situations, and the values embedded in the use of art in social contexts. So rather than ignoring the difficulties, the imposed surface engagement would be a deliberate part of whatever work was made.

When I visited Amstelrade I was given a pink rose by the one of the centre directors. The centre coordinates a range of arts activities and was more than ready for the coming Disability Arts Festival, having prepared an excellent piece of contemporary theatre and a range of visual art works for exhibition. It appeared to me that they did not need a contemporary artist to make another work for the festival with them. I know of a number of disabled artists all fighting, as I am, for a degree of visibility for their work in a contemporary art context. None of these artists would ever consider showing in a disability art festival as they believe the content of their work is more important than their personal identity. If the people at Amstelrade wanted to put their work in a disability art festival then that was up to them, but I would not.

Amstelrade residents and staff made me welcome and the residents allowed me to join in activities and visit some apartments to view their record collections, etc. In response to some time spent at the centre, I devised an initial project that would be made at Amstelveen and would need the help of the staff. Following the receipt of my proposal, however, Amstelrade sent me back a breakdown of what the work would cost, including the charge for space hire and staff's time. The amount indicated was high but, more than that, it seemed there was a misunderstanding. I had seen the relationship as a collaboration, or at least me being given as a gift that the centre would gratefully use. It seemed, however, that Amstelveen saw me as an unwanted gift from the local council, a council, I learned, with whom they were often in disagreement. It appeared that taking money from me seemed one way to take money from the council, or at least a way to get recompense for giving their time and some kind of legitimacy to an artist and an art prize.

Amstelrade's reaction was distressing, undermining some of my own expectations that people would see working with an artist as beneficial. I considered forgoing the commission and the 'prize', but realized that in the unfolding situation were many issues that I had been negotiating as an artist for years and that this situation would provide the opportunity to tackle these head on. Rather than seeing the difficulties in commissions of this kind as 'normal' and to be simply smoothed away under the work, the context might enable me to confront contemporary expectations of artists, to question how and why we expect art to aid communities, and, in doing so, communicate something of importance.

While the 1960s image of the artist was bohemian and critical it now seems that the artist's image is one of a bringer of good, sometimes beauty, an addresser of social ills, a therapist, regenerator and social conscience. While these qualities are not, of course, negative, difficulties arise when the critical potential of art is forgotten and artists are seen as the remedy for political and social problems, or as gifts. It seemed that I sat within a patchwork of atavistic intentions – that the artist could enhance the value of Amstelveen, that a gift could be given to a young artist, and that a gift could be given to disabled people in the community. While it would be easy to criticize Kunstprijs Amstelveen for this, it was infinitely more interesting to me to think about these atavistic notions as a part of current thinking about culture, and the way we see artists and art. A range of questions then unfolded: how do artists maintain a degree of critical autonomy without valorizing (or underestimating) their role? Can you be critical without forming 'goodies' and 'baddies'? Rather than falling into utopianism and trying to cause small practical changes, or to 'empower,' etc., it seems to me that while exploring specific contexts artists must maintain a larger commitment to trying to understand the world better and to communicating this beyond particular circumstance.

I decided that I would grapple with this by bringing the most conventional motif possible to the situation, and one that had now been given to me on several separate occasions: a bunch of flowers. Flowers are used on numerous occasions as the most inoffensive gift possible – for example, for civic ceremonies or for visiting the sick and the weak. The people at Amstelrade were by no means sick or weak, nor were they requiring congratulations, but it was expected, by me and by the commissioners, that they should need or deserve the help of an able-bodied artist.

I decided to offer every one of the fifty or so residents at Amstelrade the opportunity of receiving a bunch of flowers from me. A bilingual activities coordinator translated into Dutch the text I had written asking for participants. The text explained that I would give them the flowers in a venue of their choice. A photographer would take a press-style photograph of the 'giving moment' in return for them taking the flowers. They could do whatever they wanted with the flowers. I explained that I wanted to ask what it meant for artists to do good or to bring beauty, and what it meant for an able-bodied person to give in this way to someone with a physical disability. I also said that through the work I wanted to examine what exactly 'giving' and 'taking' is. The photographic images would belong to me and I could show them publicly in a form I would describe to them once I knew. Seventeen residents agreed to participate.

We give to show love, we give to make the receiver feel appreciated, we give to thank, we give to force a deal, to humiliate a rival, to placate, to compromise and to assert power. Marcel Mauss in *The Gift* determines that gift-giving in traditional societies creates an economy not of altruism but of debt, whereby gifts must be returned and their value matched. Derrida, in *Given Time* reflects on the gift of a counterfeit coin and explores how the gift is actually an impossibility. Once we know something is a gift it demands something in return and starts a cycle of exchange. This description is perhaps an overdramatic and hysterical interpretation of a prosaic activity that we understand very well. We know that obligations and rewards come with gifts but this strange and unspoken indebtedness also bonds us to each other. It is a game we know and play well.

Another aspect of the gift is that you can only give if you have something to give. This reminds me of the position of the colonizer or employer who can afford to, and it is in their interests to, treat their subjects well. While it is true that giving emphasizes the giver's power, and could even create a position of moral superiority, there is a danger that in thinking this way I (or other artists) could then become overly critical about my/their individual position or even my/their individual behaviour. If artists self-flagellate themselves for their position as bounteous givers, this could result in self-indulgence and a kind of 'colonial guilt' that overemphasizes the significance of the artist, and helps nobody – making us see a situation as the *fault* of one individual, rather than seeing the artist's position as being created by a complex ideology.

My questioning about the role of artists continued as the project took place. The flower-giving happened over two days and while participants knowingly colluded in, and gave me, the representation of the 'giving moment', in reality all sorts of other human dynamics were at play. Firstly, communication was difficult due to their physical disabilities and my lack of Dutch. Some residents tried to explain where I should put the flowers, while some tried to explain that they did not want the flowers but wanted to give them to someone else. The photographer became a co-opted translator at times, but still I managed to knock over ornaments and place flowers on the wrong shelf. Many of the residents chose not to keep the flowers, but to give them away, enjoying giving more than receiving. One woman gave them to the man who fixed her wheelchair, in exchange for a new part, one woman, to my surprise, offered me sex, and many passed them on to staff.

One woman resident was, unlike the other residents, seriously ill and unconscious. As she had signed the consent form, staff insisted that I give her the flowers and take the photograph. The resulting photograph, along with many others, make me look ridiculous and uncomfortable. The other residents appear less uncomfortable about the eye of the camera; some of them seemed to enjoy spending time on their appearance; and others gave a stellar theatrical performance for the camera. One explanation for my own discomfort is that I fear the camera: I am more attuned to what artist Phil Collins calls 'the perils of representation'; I anticipate the image that the photograph is going to create or reveal, perhaps more than the residents did. But the other possibility is that I am overestimating the significance of the photograph and that I regard the residents' images as being of greater sensitivity than they do. For the residents, perhaps, it is simply not such a big deal. And maybe they are right. As in everyday life, the residents navigate the taking of a picture, knowingly navigate the scheme – and humour me, the outsider. I wonder who is made more exotic, them or me?

Adopting the internal logic of sociologist Pierre Bourdieu's 'Lecture on the Lecture', the final lecture format of 'The Generosity Project' is a work that describes the making of a work. More than a document of a process, it draws attention to two relationships – that between the artist and the subjects of the images used, and that between the artist and the audience. In the time I spent at Amstelrade I gave my time and the residents gave theirs. I took a photograph – one the subjects freely gave, putting on their 'best face'. But when I give the final lecture, I'm not sure who is giving their time, me or the listeners?

Recipients of 'The Generosity Project' (the lecture audience) often ask me what impact the work made on the subjects who appear in the work and the commissioners who can own it but not give it. As with most works of art, I have no idea what either thought, or for that matter what any subsequent audience thought. But I suspect that the content of the work may be irrelevant to the commissioners, the point being to give a prize, get it in the press and donate a work to the Municipality of Amselveen.

When I give the lecture I always get asked how Kunstprijs Amstelveen responded to the work, and it always seems that the audience wants to hear that 'they were really angry', as a demonstration that I had shown them the conceit of their ideology. I always explain to the audience that I never heard from Kunstprijs Amstelveen what they thought of the work and that this does not really surprise me. It seems to me that people rarely respond like this to art work, as usually any critical force is not necessarily read. I also would not want Amstelveen to feel I had aimed to punish them, when, after all, I had been given a prize – and my intentions are more about capturing how we feel about artists in the current climate. To some extent the work deliberately disappoints the audience who want to believe in a critical persona who antagonizes in an almost heroic way. The work thwarts the expectation that it should have any noticeable affect on any specific party, questioning the desire for a known measurable effect and refusing to be used as a tool to ameliorate social ills.

The second question I get asked is how did the Amstelrade residents feel about the project and what did they get out of it? Sometimes accompanying this is the criticism that the work does not conclude with the Amstelrade residents, but with the (generally) art lecture audience, so it does not actually serve the community. This observation is true: they posed, I submitted the images, I made the lecture: contract fulfilled. And, unlike many projects in the community, it was never my intention to give something to the residents, or to ameliorate or uplift them (although we can never be sure what people take from any experience). Rather, I engaged the residents in a clear experiment in their representation as recipients. Instead of thinking they needed me for their salvation, I asked them to knowingly negotiate a relationship with me, and for me. Through doing this I hoped to enable recognition of the problematic of such work for all parties, including the final lecture recipients.

Like Bourdieu's model of the lecture on the lecture, I sought to be in a situation and be critical of it the same time, seeking a means to fuse artistic action and critical discussion. Of course, the question of an artist's critical autonomy is by no means answered by this work. The further you look, the more problems you see, and new problems arise the further the practice develops and social situations change. Ultimately, rather than provide me with a moment to bring 'good' to the community, the prize presented an extraordinary situation where I could see political issues at play. These issues included the current belief that culture is an appropriate or effective solution to social problems, and the prevalent sense that the individual is fragile and in need of protection rather than intelligent and self-defining. In the particular situation of the prize and Amstelrade, I saw how these issues are experienced by artists, recipients, commissioners and audiences. I sought to grapple with questions that I consider to be of significance, including: whether art or culture can be used as an instrument to change social problems; what is the relationship between artist and 'subject' or 'participant'; and also how we can think critically and autonomously, without moralizing. I did not fulfil what can be assumed to be the needs of a community, but in not doing this it is possible that I gave something more.

CHAPTER 12

Cedar Nordbye

'Empire Project'

> Unlike the sale of a commodity, the giving of a gift tends to estab-
> lish a relationship between the parties involved. Furthermore, when
> gifts circulate within a group, their commerce leaves a series of
> interconnected relationships in its wake, and a kind of decentralized
> cohesiveness emerges.
>
> —Lewis Hyde, *The Gift: Imagination and the
> Erotic Life of Property*, xiv

DURING THE PAST SEVEN YEARS the center of my artistic practice has shifted from drawings in the studio to conversations with members of the public about social issues. To open the door to unconventional and uncomfortably topical discussions with strangers, I have employed the strategy of gift-giving. I have found that the ambiguity of the gift which is neither completely freely given nor a commodity item parallels the equally ambiguous topics at the heart of my work and functions as a tool in the initiation of social interactions. As an artist coming from the field of drawing, I take this constructional homonymity, this indeterminate and open relation to subject, common in the medium of drawing, and apply it to the medium of performance.

I use the gift to create a pause, a sort of eddy in the stream of daily business, a moment for people to stop and engage with an artist and an art work that they might otherwise avoid. The line between actual gift-giving and unusual forms of market exchange can be nebulous, but either an outright gift, or an unconventional market exchange, can be at once similar enough to our most comfortable way of interacting with strangers (commercial interactions) and enough out of the ordinary to allow people to examine or explore their circumstances. This ambiguous space that the gift or gift-like exchange opens up is a fertile ground for dialogues with members of the public.

In graduate school I was encouraged to venture into performance art when it was clear that I was more engaged in the ritual of the group-critique than my own studio practice. I resisted these suggestions because my impression of performance art was dominated by confrontational, shocking exhibitionist performances of the 1980s and I could not see myself engaged in such theatrics.

It was not until my 1999 experiment, 'The Mona Lisa Project', that I moved into the performative. For that 'action', I offered visitors to the Louvre $10 and a postcard of the Mona Lisa if they would agree to *not* see the Mona Lisa. I photographed participants and created a book documenting the exchanges. The conversational dimension of that project was inspiring and engaged my passion for human exchange in a way that traditional studio practice had not.

I had selected the Empire State Building as the site of my next project when flying back to the United States from Paris. The receptivity of the tourists at the Louvre, combined with the electric charge that the Louvre's unique location provided, had led me to search my mind for another lightning-rod location – one which, unlike the Louvre, had a connection to some of the issues central to my work. These consisted of an exploration of violence, an examination of Middle Eastern politics, and my investigations into my Jewish identity. Since 1997 I had been making images of the Empire State Building in reaction to an incident that occurred in February of that year, when a Palestinian man, Ali Abu Kamal, shot a number of tourists on the observation deck there. I began to consider a project for that site. In February 2000 I flew to New York with an unstructured plan to carry out a performative 'event' in which I would interact with people at the Empire State Building. I had made and distributed announcements, and I had a wooden ball that I planned on kicking around the observation deck on the 86th floor. I also carried in my bag a sheaf of silkscreen prints (depicting a gun) on sheets of tracing paper. The gun image and the wooden ball both arose out of investigations of violence that I had been carrying out in my two-dimensional work. Two days before my 'event' I had lunch with an artist friend, Anne Beffel, and we discussed my project. Her encouragement and ideas got my mind racing and the project took a tentative form, some parts of which were still in a state of flux the afternoon of the 'performance'.

This loose, 'drawing' approach to performance helped me to overcome resistances that I had to the staged and 'closed-circuit' of most performance art. It also allowed me to carry out a work, despite the discomfort and hesitancy that came from the fact that, in advance, I didn't feel like I knew exactly what I was doing. This indeterminacy has been central to my studio practice and allows me to engage with complex political topics while avoiding oversimplifying and flat-footed didactic statements. The indeterminacy also leaves an open space for the audience to feel that there is room for their ideas, thus a dialogue is possible.

I entered the Empire State Building at eight in the evening on the third anniversary of the shooting. I set the wooden ball down on the cement pavers and began kicking it along the observation deck. I then kicked it so that it rolled into the feet of a tourist looking out at the view. He turned around suddenly and was tense, confrontational. I said nothing and then gestured to the ball. At this point his body position softened and he smiled and kicked the ball back to me. I kicked it back to him and he laughed and walked away. I kicked the ball on and to another unsuspecting person. It took me about twenty-five minutes to circumnavigate the observation deck. During this time some people ignored me completely. A group of Italian tourists imitated soccer players and started passing the ball between them and doing little soccer tricks and shouting.

I was very interested in the fine line, the ambiguous border, that separates play from violence. When the ball hit a person's heel it was, at that moment, breaking consent and violent. But that person's decision to kick the ball back was a form of consent, and from the moment of that decision, they were playing. Did their decision somehow retroactively remove the violent nature of my action? When they laughed and kicked the ball back were they then accepting my gift, my invitation to play? The gentle bump that I delivered to random strangers was a benign echo of Kamal's bullets and brought up questions about philosophical differences between gun violence and boxing, between domestic abuse and sado-masochistic sexual play.

Once I returned to where I had started from, I took a handful of lottery tickets from my pocket and began offering them to people if they were willing to promise that they would give a third of the reward of a winning ticket (a third of ten million dollars) to the Israeli–Palestinian peace process. It surprised me that many people refused to take a ticket. Lewis Hyde reflected upon 'gift rejection' in his book *The Gift*: 'We often refuse relationship, either from the simple desire to remain un-entangled, or because we sense that the proffered connection is tainted, dangerous, or frankly evil. And when we refuse relationship we must refuse gift exchange as well' (Hyde, 1983: 73). While this phase of the event was the most uncomfortable and resulted in numerous awkward moments, it periodically resulted in a surprisingly deep level of engagement on the part of the members of the public with whom I was speaking.

At this point, after accepting the ticket, most people asked me why I was giving them away. I would tell them the story of Kamal and the shooting, of how police discovered on Kamal's body nearly a hundred, losing, scratch-off lottery tickets. I would tell them how he brought his life's savings from Palestine to New York, hoping to increase his family's finances enough to buy a piece of land (they had lost their land in 1948 when the state of Israel was created). I would tell them how he lost all of his money in a crooked investment scheme. Unable to return home to face his family, he traveled to Florida and purchased a handgun. He returned to New York on a Greyhound bus and rented a limousine, which he directed to the Empire State Building. He then took the elevator to the top and opened fire on random tourists on the observation deck, hitting eight of them. One of his bullets struck the head of a rock guitarist from New Jersey and left him severely brain-damaged, and another struck his band-mate, a Danish rocker, killing him. Kamal then turned the gun on himself and died there, with a treatise against the colonial powers of France, England, Israel and America in a pouch around his neck. Newspaper articles made sure to classify this incident as a personal psychological meltdown and not as a political event or an incident of terrorism.[1]

I then removed the silkscreen prints and pulled the top print off, and reached out through the fence and dropped the print. It didn't fall as I expected but kited out horizontally. As it drifted out it was caught in the spotlights that illuminate the building and lit up like a little movie screen. I dropped another and the same thing happened. Uninvolved tourists noticed and shouted, 'Ooh. Look at that!' I began handing prints to people around me and we all began to drop them, one at a time, watching them disperse widely over mid-town. In 2001, on the fourth anniversary of Kamal's attack, I returned to the Empire State Building and repeated the project.

In 2002 I assumed that the post-9/11 environment would be too tense for any kind of performance, but I was encouraged to proceed by an artist friend Bradley McCallum. He felt that there was something really important about the annual ritual of this kind of storytelling, this diligent yearly maintenance of this little history. He and I agreed that this repetition emphasized the air of determination about the project, that this story wasn't going away despite the eclipsing tendencies of the annual days of observation of the dominant culture, Independence Day, Pearl Harbor Day, Washington's Birthday, etc.

I invited friends to join me at eight o'clock on the observation deck for juice and cookies. I rode up to the top with juice, paper cups, cookies, lottery tickets and twenty gun prints ('Who knows?' I thought). I began giving away the lottery tickets. Later I dropped a ticket over the side and then a print. Minutes later I dropped another and then another. I was talking with a film-maker from Ireland when I felt a hand on my elbow. 'Come with us', a voice said and security guards took me to the basement. I was photographed and made to sign paperwork saying that if I ever set foot in the building again I would be subject to arrest. A guard walked me out of the building into the windy night.

Leaving the building, I felt shaken and a bit defeated. Riding back to Brooklyn on the subway I fingered the lottery tickets in my pocket. I had spent money on them and their entire value for me resided in their ability to initiate interactions. In my pocket they seemed wasted, so, after building up courage, I walked the length of the car handing out the lottery tickets. The people in the silent subway car didn't receive them well. A few people refused the tickets outright, more ignored me. When ignored, I just set the tickets down (on a book-bag or, in one case, on a man's knee) and kept walking.

When I returned to my seat I heard one person asking another about the tickets, then a woman across the aisle asked me why I was giving them away. I explained that I had been asking people if they would give a third of their winnings to the Middle Eastern Peace process. A man joined in, saying that he thought that religious fanatics had hijacked the process. Another man said that our country had big financial interests in the Middle East and that those drove our policies. One woman said that she didn't believe in gambling or the lottery and if she won, she'd give it all away. A teenaged girl laughed and said that would all change if she really did win. There were two other conversations that were too far away for me to hear.

The sense of community on this subway car was much more palpable than anything that I had felt on top of the Empire State Building. I believe that this sense of community existed because, unlike the gift-giving at the Empire State Building which had requirements for a form of reciprocation, these gifts on the subway were given freely. Subway passengers are used to gifts as part of a panhandling strategy, insubstantial gifts which are actually a pretext for the request of a more significant return gift. When it became clear that this gift had no direct expectation for reciprocation attached to it, the faith in the network of community was strengthened and a dialogue ensued. Riding under the East River amid the buzz of conversation in what had been a silent car minutes before, I was exhilarated and I began to plan the next year's event.

In January of 2003 I carved fifteen small wooden sculptures of the Empire State Building and painted them. In February I purchased fifteen lottery tickets and went to the Fifth Avenue entrance of the Empire State Building with a few of my friends. I approached visitors and offered them one of the carvings if they would give one of my lottery tickets to a stranger on the observation deck. The first people I approached avoided me, showing their street credentials by dodging what must have looked like a hustler of some sort.

Eventually I learned that if I handed a sculpture to a person before they had time to think, they would stop and be more likely to talk to me. Often, when I explained the arrangement, the tourists/participants would make me repeat the deal, trying to find the moment that I made my profit. When it became clear that I did not make a profit, they would ask me about my motivation. At that point I would explain that I had been making art about Kamal and the shooting and had decided to come to New York and memorialize the incident by speaking with strangers and giving away lottery tickets. Occasionally I was asked why I didn't just give away the tickets myself and I explained my lifelong ban.

In this way, my solution to being banned from the building enriched the exchange at the heart of my project by bringing into the process a second generation of giving. What had been an isolated event, an exchange between one member of the public and myself, expanded to include another exchange at a future time, one in which the audience members became the initiators. This allowed for the participant to have an increased ownership and internalization of the project. Also, the delay between the initial gift transfer and the second round (the giving of the lottery ticket), required that I trust the participant and that they move forward conscious of that trust. This extension of the project over time and the trust involved contain the ingredients for the creation of community. Hyde writes of the group-building tendency of this extension of the act of gift exchange:

> Reciprocal giving is a form of gift exchange, but it is the simplest. The gift moves in a circle, and two people do not make much of a circle. Two points establish a line, but a circle lies in a plane and needs at least three points . . . When the gift moves in a circle its motion is beyond the control of the personal ego, and so each bearer must be a part of the group and each donation is an act of social faith.
>
> (Hyde, 1983: 16)

By inviting others to become initiators of exchanges in this project I have blurred the line between artist and participant and introduced another layer of ambiguity into the project. This blurring also creates a relationship between the viewer and the art work that is less determined and unidirectional than the traditional discrete art object and moves the work of art into the realm of 'relational aesthetics'.

While the expansion of my project to include strangers is exciting to me and pushes my project further into the realm of the relational, it also raises complex ethical issues of responsibility, consent and agency. How responsible am I for the nature of the interaction that my 'collaborators' carry out on the observation deck? I have worked hard to treat the gravity of the story of the shooting with the respect and solemnity that it deserves, but I cannot guarantee that my 'proxies' will do so. What happens if someone that they approach flies into a rage about the Palestinian–Israeli conflict? Do these participating members of the public participate completely freely? Is it possible that they feel pressured to do so and have had some of their agency removed? These questions and other questions of consent, agency and responsibility have begun to interest me as much as the specifics of this work. The giving of a gift, and the initiation of a gift cycle, may give birth to a sort of quasi-community, but with community comes community ethics and, as an artist used to working solo in a studio, I am fairly unversed in these kinds of ethics. When presenting this project to an audience at the Community Performance Conference in 2004, a member of the audience, Canadian artist Devora Neumark, challenged me during the question-and-answer session to pay more attention to the ethical intricacies of my art-action. Later I discussed the ethics of social engagement in research with Claude Charpentier, a Professor of Psychology at Bishop's University in Quebec. She was surprised by the lack of a traditional ethical framework specific to artistic work that involves human subjects. In addition to needing to maintain an acute sensitivity to the ethics of this work I must work to be critical of the complex dynamic of this relational work, not merely banking on the bang that this somewhat new and novel approach to art carries with it.

> How the exchange of participation takes place must be carefully framed, so that the interaction itself brings about awareness not only of the pleasure or discomfort of social interchange but a consciousness of the workings of a larger political, economic or psychological framework as evidenced in these relations.
>
> (Morgan, 2003: 24)

I have begun to ask myself what it means for these tourists to enter into this gift-cycle, for them to initiate a conversation of their own. There are interesting questions nested in these questions, such as 'What is the role of the tourist in building culture?' and 'What does it mean to have tourists at the top of the Empire State Building discussing with other tourists a shooting of tourists that occurred there?' It is this process of questioning the symbolic and political dynamic of the interaction that has led me to examine the role of the gift-exchange.

The ambiguity of the gift-exchange was highlighted in the newer adaptation of my performance, for now I was giving a hand-carved gift to tourists, not a free gift, but one that contained a required re-gifting, a mandatory continuation of the act of giving.

Hyde suggests that for a gift to function as such it must not immediately return a gift to the initial giver, but must move through other channels: 'Now, it is true that something often comes back when a gift is given, but if this were made an explicit condition of the exchange, it wouldn't be a gift.' (Hyde, 1983: 9). In my project the required re-gifting was not reciprocal in a material sense, that is to say the tourist receiving the building didn't have to give any kind of object back to me, but rather they had to give something to another stranger. (It can, however, be argued that they did give something to me, they gave me their consenting participation in my project.) While this immaterial reciprocation was agreed to on their part, there was no enforcement should they have decided to ignore the terms of the gift. I don't know how many recipients of buildings got cold feet and neglected to approach a stranger at the top of the building, keeping the lottery ticket for themselves, but the trust that I had to have in them, and in their agency and ability to redefine the project, is important to me. Indeed, Bataille, in his book *The Accursed Share*, argued that this faith that a cycle will be continued is the crucial difference between a commodity culture of fierce individualism and a gift culture of trust in community. So it remains unclear whether the gift continues to be a gift, if it carries a non-enforced expectation for continued giving (as it could be argued that all gifts do) or whether it maintains the ability to challenge normal individualistic struggles for accumulation.

> A re-evaluation of the gift as a socially and morally charged exchange has been undertaken in recent years in an attempt, in part to escape the double bind of both Bataille and Derrida's interpretations – on the one hand the necessity for the drastically radical gesture as proposed by Bataille, and on the other Derrida's provocative claim that the gift is impossible since, from the moment that one even recognizes a transaction as a gift, it becomes weighted with obligations and therefore no longer qualifies as a full present.
>
> (Morgan, 2003: 23)

This re-evaluation allows for the exploitation of the gift's disorienting properties, and the utilization of that disorientation as a tool for initiating a complex social interaction. It is the very ambiguity of this exchange, somewhere between gift and commodity exchange, that the mysterious quality of the project exists, and it is this mystery that opens the door for the telling of this historically ambiguous event (should it be filed under terrorism or random shooting?).

Central to my interest in this project is the relocation of one of my favorite activities, that of discussing, even debating, difficult ethical or political issues, from the comfortable setting of my home and my friends or an academic setting to the normally prohibitive public realm. In doing so, the hegemonic space of the Empire State Building, which carries with it its own art-deco-clad narrative of the glory of industry and commerce, can be temporarily transformed into a site for the collective writing of local history. This local discussing of history has the potential to initiate a challenge to some of the macro-narratives disseminated in our mass media with a more democratic writing of history 'from the street'.

My choice of this particular story to discuss and maintain is in part motivated by its place in the larger narratives of Middle Eastern politics and the recent history of terrorism. The media as a whole was vehement in denying that Kamal's violent act was an act of terrorism, and in fact went to great lengths to emphasize his personal psychological meltdown, and to minimize his political motivations. So, while the personal and psychological nature of this incident prevented it from being assimilated into our larger narrative of terrorism and political struggles, the fact that authorities found a pouch containing a treatise against the colonial powers of Israel, England, France and America around Kamal's neck prevents his story from fitting neatly into the recent history of insanity-induced gun slayings. Bridging (and slipping between) these two narratives, Kamal's story is complex and confusing, and thus risks falling through the cracks of our history. It is just this kind of confusing story, one that resists the agendas of simplification and categorization, that can powerfully serve to open a discourse on issues of politics and history.

I am also very interested in what it takes to open the door to this type of conversation. People on the street in New York, particularly out-of-town tourists (as most of the participants in this project were), are often reluctant to enter into a discussion of a subject as intense as Middle Eastern politics or a shooting. The ambiguous act of gift-giving between strangers can serve as a tool to open such channels of communication.

Curiously, I have found in these projects that involve the trading of a 'gift' for participation in an action, that participation does not seem to hinge on the participant's appreciation of the gift. The 'gift' that is exchanged seems to exist on the periphery of the exchange and is often neither praised nor even acknowledged. During the Mona Lisa Project I even had one participant refuse the $10 that I had offered him not to see the painting (he skipped the painting in order to participate in the project and for no other reason). What role then does the quasi-gift play?

The first role of the gift is to break the ice and establish a connection. As a tourist myself in Barcelona in 2004, I occasionally went into shops to buy something like a bottle of water, not because I was particularly thirsty, but because it was a comfortable way to strike up a conversation with a local shopkeeper, to have a human connection and to add flavor to my day of wandering a foreign city. In the case of my work, the exchange of a commodity functions as a pretext for a human engagement. So many of our interactions with strangers revolve around the exchange of commodities that this trade I have established feels like a safe way to initiate a dialogue, to construct a collaboration with an otherwise wary passer-by. People often want to participate in a work of art, they just need the gift as a rationale for their participation.

While any gift might serve to initiate contact in these projects, the nature of the gift represents me to the audience and can demonstrate my commitment to them or communicate something else about my position. In the case of the Mona Lisa Project, my willingness to give them $10 demonstrated that I took what I was doing seriously. In the case of the Empire Martyr Transmission it is my hope that the handmade element of the carvings lend an aura of honesty or sincerity to the exchange, while at the same time setting this exchange apart from the normal peddling of cheap novelty tourist items. I had considered duplicating (through casting) the one wooden carving of the building that I had, but decided that it was important that the sculptures be handmade (in carving them I had even worked to avoid saw-marks and to create chisel-marks).

The third function of the gift is to serve as a souvenir, a marker of the event. The primary gift that the participant receives in these projects is the participation in a story. What they take away is an experience and a story that they feel they own. This is particularly effective in the Mona Lisa and Empire State Building interactions because the participants have all been tourists, and tourists are first and foremost gathering stories, building their personal histories.

This process of working in the public realm in a conversational mode with people out in the world serves to open up my creative process to the collaboration of strangers and exponentially increases the potential for my work to surprise me and lead in directions that I cannot anticipate. The experience of arguing with, and the act of becoming vulnerable enough, with strangers to have an argument and remain intact afterwards helps to build my sense of the benevolence of human beings. I have found that working within that sphere of public discourse I can effectively address issues of democracy and the oral maintenance of our histories. I have been very thrilled by the extent to which throwing myself into the unpredictability and improvisation of these public interventions has created poetic and revelatory results. Recently I have begun to ask some of the difficult questions that must be asked about the issues of ethical responsibility and consent that come with working with members of the public, and the interface between these delicate issues and the spontaneous and playful approach that I have brought with me from my drawing to my relational practices.

Today's threatening public spaces, where pedestrians are bombarded by commercial solicitations, attempted religious conversions and harassment by police, are not easy environments for enacting conversations and interactions with members of the public. The kinds of encounters that Joseph Beuys referred to as 'social sculpture' and Nicolas Bourriaud as 'relational aesthetics' do not unfold easily on sidewalks, and the gift is a useful tool for bypassing the defenses of the public and opening up doors to a dialogue. Rirkrit Tiravanija has cooked Thai food for strangers in the Spanish countryside, Anita Macke has handed out pies in Brooklyn, Charles Goldman has paid pedestrians a dollar to draw his portrait in Toronto, and Anne Beffel has given out bars of soap in the World Financial Center in Manhattan. These gifts vary dramatically in nature but all serve to create a pause, to open a door to an interactive space and ultimately build a sense of an extended community.

Note

1   When I first saw the headline that a Palestinian gunman had opened fire at the Empire State Building, I took it to be a terrorist action and I was amazed by the symbolism of the location. Reading further, I discovered that it was not exactly a terrorist attack, but something more ambiguous, something worth exploring in art work. Much later, when I planned an event at the Empire State Building, I knew that I didn't want to glorify Kamal, but I wanted to address the complexity and the lack of clarity of the event with a performance that would have to be open and indeterminate itself.

References

Hyde, Lewis (1983) *The Gift: Imagination and the Erotic Life of Property*, New York, Vintage Books, Random House.

Morgan, Jessica (ed.) (2003) *Commonwealth*, London, Tate Publishing.

CHAPTER 13

Devora Neumark

Home is Where the Walls Speak in Familiar Ways

Listening to the demands of ethics and witness in community performance[1]

> The ocean is perhaps only a grain of salt in distress
> that all the water in the world has answered.
> —Edmond Jabès, *The Book of Resemblances*

THE PROJECT *Décarie: A Community Based Exhibition Project*[2] is aptly named after the expressway that bisects Côte-des-Neiges and Notre-Dame-de-Grâce, the multicultural borough of Montreal immediately west of the Saidye Bronfman Centre, host to this mostly off-site series of artistic interventions. Initially built to accommodate the anticipated traffic of *Expo 67*, the Décarie expressway has now become one of Quebec's (if not Canada's) busiest thoroughfares. The challenge of understanding the highway's role in moving people through the core of the city is similar to the challenge of understanding the projects commissioned for this exhibition within the framework of community art.

In the modest publication printed for the occasion of this exhibition, John Zeppetelli, one of the exhibition's four curators and Project Director writes:

> *Décarie* is fundamentally a community-based exhibition project that grew out of the gallery's longstanding desire to develop and enlist new audiences form the surrounding neighbourhood. The exhibition is uniquely characterized by working relationships, brokered by the gallery, and forged between the invited artists and individuals, groups or institutions in the area.

Taken at face value this seems reasonable enough a premise. What is missing from this statement, and from perhaps the majority of the projects, similar to what was missing during the planning and construction of the Décarie expressway, is the taking into account of what the communities and their members wanted. For me, as a community organizer and artist committed to a practical and theoretical inquiry into and engagement with community and community art, beginning with such a structural relational imbalance opens the way to many questions.

Rather than explore these questions by way of a critical reflection of the exhibition in general, I will focus on *Home is Where the Walls Speak in Familiar Ways*, the work I co-developed with residents and staff of the Feldman Foster Home (and other participants). This self-reflective exercise is a deliberate – and I think necessary – element in the dialogic process, a process that I invite and welcome as a way of opening into what is still unknown and mysterious about home, its making and its undoing, as much as into what needs articulating about ethics and bearing witness in community performance.

With this work, the axis of intervention is (as it has been with many of my recent projects) predominantly listening. I have found that active listening framed as art work – a listening that isn't judgmental, prying or suggestion-prone – often creates the conditions for the one who speaks to begin hearing themselves. This listening however is not without risk for the teller nor for the one who bears witness.

I have approached this project as a means of exploring anxious questions around the home that we face in a world where increasingly people live without a sense of belonging and security, without, in many cases, even a physical dwelling. How do we make sense of the empty home when, as a civilization, we can barely extend the sense of humanness to those we label 'other' and 'enemy'?

On the opening night of *Décarie*, preparing for the moment when I would be asked to present the work, I looked over and saw one of the participants of *Home is Where the Walls Speak in Familiar Ways* listening with his entire body to himself singing a song he himself had written. Intuitively I knew that to speak in any way about the work at that moment would be to take power away from him and to claim authorship of the work inappropriately and even unethically – if, by ethical, I was to consider the nature of the relationship that he and I had established prior to his agreeing to participate, during the recording of his song, and in the intervening post-recording period. I was not willing to rupture that relationship in order to satisfy the needs of this gallery's opening ritual and yet felt torn because I had also established a relationship with *Décarie*'s project director who had expectations for my presentation.

Thinking about how I would present this work in the context of this chapter, I felt the anxiety of appropriateness once again. To tell the stories of this project could presume that I have the authority to frame the stories from my own perspective as the definitive experience of this project – which is not the case. And even if I were to take care to contextualize the stories as having emerged from my own personal experience, what you would take away is my version of the stories. In the absence of any other stories, as told by the participants for example, you might forget the subjective nature of my telling. And yet there are stories that want telling if only for the questions they raise – such as what happened with E.

Figure 7
Entre Nous (2001) was a year-long community art project (undertaken within the Quebec 1% Integration of Art and Architecture Program) facilitated by Devora Neumark. The stories told to her in response to the question 'What is the most significant object you have?' are manifest in the form of drawings and photographs that now hang in the agora of the long-term hospital facility housing the CHSLD St-Laurent and Les Cèdres in Ville St-Laurent, Quebec, Canada.

Photo: Devora Neumark.

As part of the process of creating this work, I had been going into the foster home every day for many weeks to be with S. (my aunt) and L., Y., J., E., M., J. and the others, for chunks of time each day. Taking time to 'hear' the voices in the wall that speak to my aunt, to be with her and the other residents, to dwell with their humanness, I found I was becoming more able to hear and accept my own.

E. is a young woman of seventeen who is in what is being called the terminal phase of renal failure. She has been on dialysis for all of her life and it is now no longer effective and no longer able to help her ailing body. She is wheelchair-bound, cannot speak, has very limited control over her facial expressions, and only the barest capacity to move her hands intentionally.

One day, having brought my guitar in to the house with me every day, playing and inviting anyone who wanted to play to enjoy making sounds with it . . . I was sitting around with at least five others besides E. in the living room, each one listening to the other on the guitar and waiting patiently for their turn to play. I thought to ask E. if she wanted to play and though she gave no apparent indication that she had heard me or responded, my intuition said that she had . . . so I gently and very slowly put the guitar on her tabletop tray that is attached to her chair, and she immediately arranged her hands as best she could so that her fingers were resting on the strings. Unable to strum the guitar, she tried sliding her fingernail along the string, making a really annoying screeching sound that made some of us laugh and others feel very disturbed. I showed her, as I had shown the others how to strum and continued to strum the strings with her continuing to slide her fingernail a quarter inch when she could for some minutes.

Others then took their turns and about half an hour later I asked her if she would like to play again. Placing the guitar on her tabletop, she was more able to arrange her hands and then, having assimilated something into her fingers, she began to actually strum the guitar strings up and down alone – and made a very few but absolutely gorgeous and clear sounds . . . everyone froze . . . some of the workers in the house, sensing that something was going on, silently came into the room from wherever they were (one with laundry unfolded in her hands, another with a medicine bottle in one hand and the cap in the other – mid-gesture of closing the bottle) and E. continued to strum for another few seconds – no one was breathing . . . but E. had the biggest smile on her face that you could imagine, her eyes focused for an instant. She then took her right hand shakily to her mouth, coming as close as she could and made the motion of kissing it with her lips before dropping it down on mine . . . there was absolute stillness in the room and then we all breathed in together.

That evening in the meditation at the closing of the yoga class, I felt all of the wonder and sadness, the celebration and strength, the dignity and joy of these moments that we shared and, unbidden, the tears began to fall, my entire body humming with the sounds that E. made.

None of what E. played was recorded. Can this experience or indeed anything of this nature be felt in the work?

Inspired by a passage from *The Social Figure in Art* as it appears in *Between Ethics and Aesthetics: Crossing the Boundaries* (see Ziarek 2002), I want to point out how the accent on the word 'work' (in 'art work') serves to express one aspect of why this listening functions as it does. This active sense of working that 'deemphasizes the static concepts of form and content, and draws attention to the temporality operating in art', refers not only to that which solicits the audience, but also – and perhaps foremost in the context of *Home is Where the Walls Speak in Familiar Ways* – that which works on the people who have created the work, in this case the residents and staff of the Feldman Home, other participants, and myself. And despite this level of participation and the ways in which this artwork has worked on the participants and me, I do not consider this work to be a community art project.

Definitions are necessary if we are to have a clear sense of what we mean when we speak of artist and community collaborations. Delineating the terms provides direction that is critical to setting intentions, contextualizing commitment, and understanding the ethical, affective and aesthetic processes and the results that emerge from such projects.

Whether we opt for categories such as community-based, community advocacy and community derived, or we choose to understand the practices of engagement based on a question of how collaborative specific projects are, we must address the issue of consensus. To speak of consensus (which, by definition, means agreement in opinion, testimony or belief), implies a decision-making process and an inherent power. Who gets to decide? Who is empowered to have an opinion, let alone make it be known and have it matter?

What beliefs are considered acceptable enough to be taken seriously, and by whom? What is being decided about and how real are the stakes?

I will come back to these questions about choice-making and power, but before I do I want to present some ideas that have emerged from years of direct experience and observation about what art, healing and conflict have in common. I have noticed, for example, that the central components of creativity often remain the same whether the creative process is being applied to artistic practice, lived as an integral component of wellness and the exercise of resilience, or emergent from within conflict negotiation processes.

And aside from adhering in some general ways to the creative process (often referred to in terms of a sequence of stages that sometimes defy sequential order), art, healing and conflict also require individual and social bodies to engage in some form of dialogue and enter into places of discovery and new learning – hence accept a certain level of risk. Though often the risk is symbolic within the realm of art, it is this very symbolism that can create the conditions to make something real enough to become possible. In other words, what can be experienced in the symbolic (but nonetheless real) realm of art often is transposed in non-linear ways to influence personal and social wellness and options in response to conflict.

In her book *The Way of Conflict: Elemental Wisdom for Resolving Disputes and Transcending Differences*, Deidre Combs proposes that conflict can be mapped as a four-phase process. She suggests that creativity is the key to offsetting the frustration and violence that often accompanies the refusal or incapacity to adapt to the disruption and chaos that are inherent in all shifting relational situations. (Disruption, according to this schema, being the first phase, it is followed by chaos. The cycle ends when, after passing through the fiery stage of creative evolution, social stability is re-established.)

According to Combs, if 'the stakes are high and much courage is demanded' the implementation of ideas found in the third stage of conflict (that would bring about a certain sense of stability and resolve the conflict), might involve a high degree of self-doubt: 'this struggle with insecurities and anxiety can be stifling. We may become controlling and "fix" everyone else instead of taking personal responsibility. Stuck, we will try to rescue instead of evolving.'

What I have found is that often it's just at the moment when one can really sense the possibility of change that it seems old beliefs scream loudest for attention, calling the individual or group back to what is familiar and therefore comfortable. Often it is at tense moments such as these that aggression becomes manifest as one acts out the disturbance in violent ways. Translating risk into symbolic language can help mitigate the doubt and the fear of what can sometimes feel like death as one lets go of old beliefs and restructures narrative.

I have often considered that artistic activities are referred to as artistic practice because they provide the artist(s) and participants/audience with the framework to practice dealing with issues that in real life may be too difficult to approach and handle directly. Given my own experience and observations, I suggest that not only is art itself inherently a process of conflict, engaging with art is a deliberate engagement with conflict. Such an engagement with the symbolic is a structured and relatively 'safe' means of dealing with challenging issues and inviting change.

In the case of individuals for whom the capacity for choice-making has been compromised (including myself) artistic practice can provide a symbolic (but nonetheless real) context for decisions of consequence to be taken. *Home is Where the Walls Speak in Familiar Ways* addresses this question of agency and choice-making to people (including myself) who have experienced the loss of home, and perhaps even more importantly the externally imposed loss of home.

Artistic practice, often through its inherent repetitive nature, invites the possibility for validation and integration as old stories are witnessed within a social holding ground. Artistic practice can also create the conditions in which new stories can be constructed and told. Art can teach us, with the use of symbolic language, to bring flexibility to our memories. And with the authority of memory being such an integral element in revealing (to ourselves and to others) who we are and what we value, this transformative element is powerfully healing. Translating risk into symbolic language – as becomes possible with creative practice – can serve to make the risk more approachable and the resolution more apparent.

As with anything unfamiliar, conscientious practice can hone skills and strengthen abilities as long as we are careful to not let practice become habit. *Home is Where the Walls Speak in Familiar Ways* has created a framework in which to hear what is at the nexus between life, trauma and home in both real and symbolically real ways. This framework however was not a priori consensual, nor can it be considered a 'community art' project, as the participants for the most part did not have control over the subject matter, process, aesthetics, production and diffusion of this work. This framework invites an active exploration of intersubjectivity, as it creates the possibility that just listening can sometimes make a difference . . . though how it works may not be immediately nor spectacularly apparent.

Understanding that creativity, violence, and the tendency to want to save others are intricately linked, means that we have to become conscious of our motives in creating art work that involves others as participants in the creative process. Given the conflict about home that has accompanied me since childhood, and that I have entered into symbolically with this project, I have to take response-ability for my own choices, choices that were not consensual. Having invited others who have in the past (and might be currently experiencing) conflict about home into this project, I've had to be aware of opening a fragile possibility for change in symbolically real and in really real ways.

The consequences of this listening project, like the project itself, might only be heard over time and cannot be predicted. The relationships that I have opened to with the participants and with the exhibitions organizers are not mutually exclusive. They do however have to be considered, each in their own right, especially as I locate myself as a member of the artistic community and as an extended member of the Feldman Home community – and have a commitment to both.

Notes

1   Some of the ideas presented in this chapter first began to take shape within the essay
'I am because we are . . . and in order to', a text jointly commissioned by the Inter-
Arts Office of the Canada Council for the Arts and the Modern Fuel Artist-Run
Centre (Kingston, Ontario).

2   *Décarie: A Community Based Exhibition Project* was curated by Gabriel Doucet-Donida,
Sylvie Gilbert, Isa Tousignant and John Zeppetelli for the Liane & Danny Taran
Gallery of the Saidye Bronfman Centre for the Arts (Montreal) and ran from 28
May through 5 June 2005 with commissioned works from Diane Borsato, Caroline
Hayeur, Devora Neumark, Farine Orpheline, William Pope.L, Althea Thauberger,
and d'bi.young.

For a critical overview of the *Décarie* exhibition see the French article 'Toucher
son but' written by Bernard Lamarche and appearing in Montreal's *Le Devoir*, 14
and 15 May 2005. Additionally, on 5 June 2005, CBC Radio ('Cinq à six') put on
a one-hour English language special highlighting: William Pope.L's *Bringing the Décarie
to the Mountain*; d'bi.young's *A Working Womban's Story: Domestic Labour in the Décarie*;
and my own *Home is Where the Walls Speak in Familiar Ways*.

References

Combs, D. (2004) *The Way of Conflict: Elemental Wisdom for Resolving Disputes and Transcending
Differences*, Novato, CA: New World Library.
Zeppetelli, J. (2005) 'Décarie: A Community Based Exhibition Project 04.28.05–06.05.05',
Liane & Danny Taran Gallery of the Saidye Bronfman Centre for the Arts (Montreal).
Ziarek, K. (2002) 'The Social Figure of Art: Heidegger and Adorno on the Paradoxical
Autonomy of Artworks', in D. Glowacka and S. Boos, *Between Ethics and Aesthetics:
Crossing the Boundaries*, New York: State University of New York Press, pp. 219–37.

PART THREE

Environments

Introduction to
Part Three

■ Petra Kuppers and Gwen Robertson

ENVIRONMENTAL EMBEDMENT SHAPES community performances: whether environmental concerns trigger the need for community performance interventions, or whether built or social environments shape the form that this intervention takes. Environmental work in its broadest sense, then, has been a concern for community performance practitioners for a long time, and in many different places – from ceremonial mediators working with and between different living beings, to political activists, such as Greenpeace, finding theatrical means to draw public attention to environmental damage. The 'environments' discussed in this section are human, more-than-human, other-than-human, and the art practices the authors profile show community performance as a force acting upon the wider world, and through the world. They see community performance as an outgrowth of an ethical *engagement* with the world: acknowledging the multiplicity of influences, effects and relationships.

The contributors in this section address environmental concerns in relation to ecology, to site-specificity, and to the social and cultural impact of environments for social groups. They show how art practice can be responsible and engaged, passionate and caring in its approach to the wider community. Each author, whether looking at the natural or cultural environment, critically examines and publicly engages the possibility of low-cost, high-yield dialogue to address complex problems in our world.

Theresa May and **Ubong Nda** use theatre as a way to increase dialogue and develop shared interest in natural environmental issues that threaten the lives and livelihoods of communities. May's work addresses the 2002 Kalamath fish-kill in the Pacific Northwest of the United States, and Nda's the challenge of environmental education in the environmentally degraded Nigerian state of Akwa Ibom. In both cases, they demonstrate the power of the arts to involve local communities successfully where other, 'traditional' methods have failed.

Marcia Blumberg and **Ana Flores** address different kinds of environments and crises, those of prison life and those of the challenges of respectful work surrounding HIV/AIDS. What they share is the belief that community performance has the ability to succeed in difficult environments where other forms of education fail. **Graham Pitts**'s piece also looks at how community performance can provide people in difficult environments with new tools to understand their experiences. Specifically, in opening up the complexity of an Australian public housing demolition and relocation project, he shows how community performance helps reclaim an otherwise rejected environment.

Together, these essays speak both of the integration of human performance work in wider structures and institutions, and the power of art practice to imagine new ways of seeing our places in our world.

CHAPTER 14

Theresa J. May

Toward communicative democracy

Developing *Salmon Is Everything*

IN SEPTEMBER 2002, during one of the largest salmon runs in recent years, upwards of 60,000 salmon died in a two-week period on the Klamath River in northern California.[1] Yurok, Karuk and Hupa fishermen left their nets to count the dead by 'hacking off their tails so they would not be counted twice'.[2] The event devastated local tribal fisheries, shocked biologists, made national headlines, and was symptomatic of a troubled watershed where science and politics have polarized stakeholders for generations. The fish-kill was an embarrassing demonstration of policy failures for state and federal officials. But for local tribal people it was apocalyptic. Many tribal elders characterized the event as a message, an interspecies communication, a scream. The salmon were angry, they claimed. In times past they had performed the 'Salmon Ceremony', a vital part of the reciprocity between people and salmon. But in the few generations since contact with white people the elements of the ceremony had been lost.[3] Now, the sustainer of their lives and way of life from 'time immemorial' was signaling a spiritual and ecological collapse. Others characterized the fish-kill as another buffalo-kill – one more act of aggression by the Anglo world intended to annihilate Indian peoples.

Both local and national news accounts framed the problem as farmers versus fish. I wondered, however, if agricultural water-users in the upper Klamath Basin were aware of the effects of low water on the river ecology and communities downriver, or if, as many tribal members believed, the farmers simply did not care. Believing that a community-based performance might help give voice to the Native communities that depended on the river for survival but had been marginalized in the highly political debate about water allocation, I worked with Native American faculty and staff and, together, we initiated the Klamath Theatre Project at Humboldt State University in autumn 2003. We brought together Native students with no theatre training, theatre students and community members to talk about the fish-kill and how theatre might be used to tell the stories surrounding the event. We envisioned a performance that advocated the position and experience of communities who were directly affected by the salmon crisis, especially Yurok, Karuk and Hupa tribal members. As the project proceeded, that purpose, and the concept of democracy it represented, would change.

Over the next two semesters, students and I interviewed individuals and groups in the Lower Klamath watershed. Native students interviewed parents, grandparents or boyfriends who worked as subsistence fishermen or for the tribal hatchery. Non-Native students interviewed commercial fishermen, white-water rafters and environmentalists. We went on field trips to the mouth of the Klamath River, and to ceremonial sites where the three tribes conduct annual bush dances. Students wrote personal narratives after each field trip. These, along with free-writes through which students reflected on, for example, the meanings of 'balance' or 'sacred', became some of the most compelling parts of the performance script, entitled *Salmon Is Everything*.

Before beginning the interviews, the students and I struggled to understand the scope and history of the issues (of which the 2002 fish-kill was but a symptom). Students researched the history of the watershed; read and discussed how the issue was presented in the local media, and shared with one another their own cultural knowledge and perspectives. Still new to the region, I learned that several dozen dams constructed in the early and mid-twentieth century, intended to provide irrigation for upper watershed farmers and ranchers as well as cheap public power, regulate the water flow of Klamath River. Consequently, Native subsistence fishermen downriver blame the farmers and ranchers upriver for using too much water and precipitating the fish-kill. In addition, Native communities and environmentalists argue, water quality has suffered over the years from agriculture's use of herbicides, pesticides and fertilizers. Feeling the press of Federal regulation under the Endangered Species Act (ESA), those farmers and ranchers in turn blame 'rabid environmentalists' for their own economic hardship. Meanwhile, official science has shown itself to be the stepchild of politics as agency biologists have been pressured by their superiors in the Federal government to skew their research in favor of agriculture. In turn, the tribes have hired their own biologists to conduct research that supports tribal lawsuits against agriculturalists. The resulting litigation and media firestorm has hardened feelings born not only of the current crisis but also of generations of embittered relations. Nevertheless, as if the salmon themselves had convened a watershed-wide town hall meeting, the economic and ecological relationship among upriver and downriver communities could no longer be ignored. Like it or not, Eastern Oregon farmers and ranchers, Trinity River loggers and miners, and the Yurok, Karuk and Hupa are all part of a shared watershed and its failed democratic process.

Grassroots activism is growing in both the Native communities and among the upriver ranchers and farmers. Both sides are sick and tired of top-down water- and land-use policies, particularly when those policies impinge upon their respective 'rights'. Such activism on the part of citizen groups, however, has merely entrenched and polarized watershed factions, adding resolve to lawsuits, and perpetuating demonizing characterizations of those 'others' up- or downriver. If the fish-kill is to function as

Figure 8 Salmon Is Everything, 2006. L to R: Josephine Johnson, Jason Tower, Mary Risling, Mack Owen, Ethan Frank, Robin Andrews, Darcie Black, Beth Weissbart, Mary Campbell, Bobbie Perez, Jason Reed.

Photo: Kellie Brown.

what Janelle Reinelt has described as a 'productive crisis', I thought, it must be understood as something more than another layer of bitter historical sediments, which already include Indian massacres by whites, land grabs, broken government promises, drought, Federal mandates, and the ESA.[4] If the Klamath watershed suddenly found itself in what Reinelt calls 'an enabling state of acute tension, opening a space of indeterminacy in conceptions, institutions, and practices formerly regarded as viable or at least entrenched', perhaps theatre could provide an alternative forum in which to open dialogue.[5] If the diverse people of the watershed could hear one another's stories, perhaps the compassion necessary to build consensus around the complex issues that plague our watershed might grow. At such a confluence of crisis and opportunity, Reinelt suggests theatre can 'intervene in the imaginative life of the society by providing meditations on its current balance of equality and liberty'.[6] Balance indeed is the challenge in the Klamath watershed: equity and liberty have been recurring themes in the numerous lawsuits surrounding the fish-kill. I felt committed to applying these theoretical ideas in the development of *Salmon Is Everything*.

Almost immediately, the project exposed my unexamined assumptions. My environmental studies background had allowed me to frame a watershed as a 'community' – not a frame shared by watershed residents. I entered into the project prepared to continually negotiate and acknowledge my status as an 'outsider' (i.e. non-Native), and I actively sought out the cultural authority of my students and Native colleagues with regard to the knowledge and experience I could not access from my own position.

But I was not prepared for a watershed fraught with such shaky stakeholder politics, entrenched positions, bureaucratic snarls, institutional rivalries and racism. My notions of community-based theatre as a tool for fostering dialogue soon shriveled in light of the dangers of appearing to advocate for one 'side' of the economic/ecological equation. In the process of allowing theatre to give voice to one segment of the watershed community, do we risk alienating others? Finally, I was confronted with the issue of access, and the depth of the grief and rage around the fish-kill. Tribal elders were reluctant to talk about it. Younger people were angry or mistrustful. Would the project aim to educate and foster dialogue, or would it be a lamentation?

Many of the challenges of the project, including authority, ownership of stories, creative license, interpretation, voice, inclusion and artistic agenda, are inherent to community-based theatre.[7] For example, initially, my own Anglo subject position conflated the North Coast tribes into a unified 'community'. But the students were rightly concerned about the balance of tribal representation in the play. Yuroks, they said, were over represented in our first draft; Karuk and Hupa tribal leadership might be offended. But, they warned, Yuroks were personally impacted by the fish-kill and might feel slighted if the Hupas received equal treatment in the script. This kind of discussion drove me nuts. Would we have a ten-hour play with cast of thousands? Why couldn't one fictional tribal family represent everyone? Theatre is symbolic, after all. But I held my tongue. Native peoples have long been universalized as if the thousands of distinct cultures and separate language groups that have inhabited North America are homogenous and interchangeable. The Native students felt strongly that they did not want any language or references in the play that would offend their own tribal elders, i.e. no swear words, no references to drugs or alcohol. Understandably, they didn't want their play to reinscribe stereotypes of Native people. Yet the people interviewed (as well as the students themselves) used harsh language liberally and spoke about their broken pasts. I felt as if my students wanted to represent a utopian Indian past, while avoiding the social issues fundamental to understanding the impact of the salmon crisis on their communities. The students were right, we needed to honor differences perceived by our community collaborators by being attentive to tribal differences. But I did convince them to allow the expletives.

More importantly, however, *Salmon Is Everything* constituted a collision for me between the idea of and the experience of community. I knew theoretically that when artists leap from theory to praxis we might find ourselves players in long-standing, embittered community dramas symptomatic of dysfunctional local democracies. Working from an assumption that our service is valued and needed, we may also assume that the particular group that we recognize as a 'community' also sees itself as such. In this paper I employ the clarifying gaze of twenty-twenty hindsight, not so much to share a methodology but to demonstrate that the efficacy of community-based theatre lies precisely where it is seldom measured – in process. While this may seem an obvious and overused cliché, it is an essential touchstone for artists whose energies are focused on results – results born of the expectations of those providing funding and the community with which they are working, the urgency of social issues, and the product-oriented craft of theatre itself. In the early stages of developing *Salmon Is Everything*, I wanted to prove to my colleagues and the watershed community that

theatre could make a difference; I wanted a *production* that mattered.[8] When I began
to understand the project as an aspect of what Iris Marion Young calls 'communicative
democracy', the subtle efficacies of the performance and its development *process* became
visible.

Theatre as a way-of-knowing

In 'Communication and the Other: Beyond Deliberative Democracy'[9] Iris Marion
Young provides a distinction that helped me recognize that, because I was accustomed
to 'deliberative democracy' (in which positions are laid out through debate and decisions
made by majority voices), I had envisioned the performance as part of the means
toward a solution of water-user conflicts. Under this deliberative model, difference
is something to be transcended, something to be worked through in order to find
so-called common ground. Deliberative democracy's quest for unity, Young argues,
may re-inscribe privilege by dismissing knowledge represented by the experience of
certain people or groups precisely because it is not commonly held (such as the Yurok
belief that the salmon are spirit beings and 'kin' as well as sustenance). Young notes:
'[the] problem with this conception of the unity of democratic discussion is that it
may harbor another mechanism of exclusion . . . where some groups have greater
symbolic or material privilege that others.' Such 'appeals to a "common good" are
likely to perpetuate . . . privilege.'[10] This has been the case in many of the mediations
and negotiations among water-users of the Klamath River where ranchers and farmers,
who are the contemporary counterparts of pioneer Americans, have a symbolic
privilege, as well as economic and political advantage.

The Klamath Watershed is typical of a pluralist body politic which 'face[s] serious
divergences in value premises, cultural practices and meanings, and these disparities
bring conflict, insensitivity, insult and misunderstanding'.[11] Indeed, I observed deeply
ingrained prejudice and long-standing rage when arranging interviews or attending
stakeholder meetings. Granting that the experience of some members of a community
may not be accessible to others, Young argues instead for a 'communicative democracy'
in which difference is valued and disagreement becomes a source of new knowledge.
Personal narrative, or story, is the mechanism by which this situated knowledge
(knowledge gained through lived experience or arising from particular historical/cultural
contexts), and allows the community access to its 'total social knowledge'.[12]

For the Native people I have worked with, story itself is a deeply respected
form of knowledge-generation, preservation and dissemination; it carries both feeling
(heart knowledge) and historical context. Young notes that 'deliberation can privilege the dispassionate, the educated, or those who feel they have a right to assert.
Because everyone has stories to tell, with different styles and meanings, and because
each can tell her story with equal authority, the stories have equal value in the
communicative situation'.[13] By representing alternative ways-of-knowing, community-
based theatre can restore some measure of equity in civic discourse. Story, memory,
ceremony, prayer, movement, image are all part of 'the situated knowledge available
. . . and the combination of narratives from different perspectives produces the

collective wisdom not available from any one position'.[14] Young's argument underscores the particular power of theatre to reveal difference, while not reducing and thus subsuming it. Thus, I was able to reframe *Salmon Is Everything* in terms of the democratic engagement of its development process. While the project aims to shift the balance of representation in civic discourse surrounding watershed issues, illuminating the marginalized experience of Native residents, the play does not advocate for one side of the debate or the other, nor does it lobby for a particular policy change. Instead, the project explores the cultural–economic–ecological implications of the salmon crisis through the unique way-of-knowing of theatre, giving rise to knowledge born of lived experience – knowledge that might make the kind of difference that more data, debate and deliberation could not.

Reciprocity

In developing *Salmon Is Everything*, the students and I have been committed to ongoing dialogue with community members – what Jan Cohen-Cruz has called 'reciprocity' – about the work, about the story being told, about the final product, and about its audience.[15] This dialogue has taken the form of post-play discussions we call 'listening sessions', as well as ongoing consultation with 'cultural experts'.[16] Listening sessions have not only helped shape the play, but also constitute a forum for communicative democracy.

The first reading (in spring 2004) attracted a diverse audience from the tribal communities, the environmental community and other local residents. Before the reading we asked the audience to pay special attention to the images that came to mind while they were listening, because we wanted to begin to find the visual/theatrical elements of the play. The reading lasted about one hour; the discussion following lasted two hours as the community expressed grief and anger around the fish-kill, but also as elders from the tribal communities responded to the reading by telling more stories. They gave us many suggestions: 'We need to have the smell of the dead fish!', 'I hear the sound of brush dancing', and 'We need images of the river, people fishing and dancing!' Then one elder said, 'We need the farmers' stories too; we need to invite them down for a salmon dinner after the play!' This comment began to shift the direction of the conversation and consequently of the project itself. Pressing us to reach the full breadth of the watershed, our next draft included voices from the *upper* Klamath communities. It is important to note here that the directive to reach out to hear the stories of farmers and ranchers (often called 'the enemy' by tribal members) came out of the community dialogue. As Jill Dolan observes: '[the] actor's willing vulnerability perhaps enables our own and prompts us toward compassion and greater understanding. Such sentiments can spur our emotion, and being moved emotionally is a necessary precursor to political movement.[17] When people hear their own story being told, they seem to be more open to hearing the stories of others. Had I initially suggested that the students listen to and consider the perspective of farmers and ranchers, who also love the land and have roots going back five generations, the idea would have been met with resistance. But after the first community listening session, when their own elders charged my students to include the voices of upper Klamath farmers and ranchers, the direction of the script began to change.

Lauren's story

My Native student collaborators came from families with long traditions in the Yurok, Karuk and Hupa communities. While I encouraged the students to research the history of the watershed since contact with whites, my Native students were very resistant to learning anything about the farmers and ranchers of the upper basin. Every region has its wounds, and my students' academic life literally runs atop very deep wounds – for example, the 1860 massacre of Indian women and children just a few miles from campus – a campus built on land that belong to Wiyot people.[18] I understood why my students referred to the 'greedy _____ farmers' or 'those selfish _____ Anglo ranchers who stole Indian land'. Their characterizations of upper basin farmers and ranchers grew out of their own knowledge of the history of Indian genocide.

In the second semester of work on the project, I suggested that, as part of her research for the play, a young Yurok woman named Lauren who was one of our group, should attend a Klamath River Stakeholder workshop, sponsored by the Klamath agriculturalists and held in the upper Klamath Basin.[19] These stakeholder meetings, many of which I had attended, had begun among ranchers and farmers concerned with just allocation of water, and I had been impressed by the sincerity of many of the upper basin people who wanted to hear the tribes' perspectives. Yet no tribal representatives had come to any of their meetings because the Indians did not believe the invitations were sincere. I told Lauren that the meeting needed her voice. She was the first Native person to attend one of these workshops. Meeting farmers and ranchers, Bureau of Reclamation officials, Fish and Wildlife agents, and commercial fishing families, exploded Lauren's stereotypes. Upon return she was on fire, saying 'I learned more than I thought possible!' The meeting was 'one of the best times I've had in a really long time.' And she discovered to her amazement that: 'these agencies and water users from up river who we have been directing our anger at, are actually just real people . . . people I genuinely like . . . We should be working together, instead of just being insulted that the tribes might have to consider the economic loss that our [needs] might cause for those upriver.'[20] Lauren was stunned to meet a Bureau of Reclamation official: '[who] offered to let me stay at her house . . . talk about getting in with the enemy! . . . I didn't expect to meet actual BOR people. She is awesome. I have so much hope now, after meeting all these people.'[21] Lauren's breakthrough enabled her to return with a clear vision of the possibility of theatre as a democratizing and healing force. 'Both sides [need to be] represented in our script. We have so much to learn from each other's perspectives . . . Our audience is us and them – the people who don't understand each other – the cowboys and the Indians!'[22] Lauren's presence at the stakeholders meeting created an opening for dialogue – the next stakeholders meeting was held in the Lower Klamath at the Yurok tribal headquarters. Tribal people and leaders came; the farmers and ranchers listened.[23]

Authority

Multivocal theatre needs to grapple with the notion of multivocal authorship. For Karuk, Yurok and Hupa people, stories are precious and contain the threads of continuity between past and present. Having had so many of their stories stolen, interpreted and published without permission, we needed to assure those we interviewed that their stories would not be used without their permission, that the university, for example, would not 'own' their stories, that they, the interviewees, would remain the owners of their own stories and their own words. As playwright and director I struggled with the ethics of shaping our gathered interview material into a play. Certainly there are examples to emulate: Moses Kaufman's *Laramie Project*, in which a company of actors took interviews and developed a docudrama about the beating to death of Mathew Shepard. Kaufman's work brought the issue of homophobic hate-crimes into the national spotlight. Nevertheless, I have concerns about a New York-based director who flew to a Wyoming town and struck professional pay dirt. A *Journal World* (24 April 2005) recently precipitated a heated email thread on the Native American Theatre List-serve about New York director Ping Chong's *Native Voices – Secret History*, a script based on interviews with Native citizens of Lawrence Kansas.[24] One conversant asks: 'What happens after the production ends? . . . who gets to be author? Will Chong take ownership of this piece because he co-wrote it by choosing and arranging the words of others?'[25] Indians know too well the ways their culture, stories, even their bodies, have been appropriated and commodified. The process of developing *Salmon Is Everything* has lead me to believe that ethics is *always* local and personal.

Dramatic structure

The dramatic structure of *Salmon Is Everything* has grown out of the challenges we faced in our process. Lauren's experience not only focused the purpose of the work, in the end it provided the narrative thread that would link the diverse interviews, monologues, characters and situations into a cohesive script. The narrative would follow the journey of a Yurok woman, modeled on Lauren, caught between her own family and community's rage and grief after the fish-kill, and her growing friendship with an upper Klamath rancher. Six fictitious composite characters (including a Yurok woman and her fisherman partner, a rancher and his ailing mother, a graduate student fish biologist and her partner) form a narrative core and function as a map that allows the audience to navigate the wide terrain of the diverse voices of the watershed. Community voices, drawn from interview material, became a chorus, form a container for the narrative, functioning like a Greek chorus by commenting on, providing depth, background and alternative points of view, or by taking issue with the dramatized experiences of the six main characters. This structure solved some other problems as well. It allowed for community members with no acting experience to become part of the performance, with little rehearsal, by being part of the chorus. The chorus voices can continue to change and evolve as the piece is performed and new material is added or revised. Chorus text could be memorized if the player's ability and time allowed, or read aloud without being memorized. Meanwhile, the six composite characters were played by actors with more experience.

The next community listening session took place during Earth Matters On Stage Ecodrama Playwrights Festival (EMOS), a national playwrights' contest hosted at Humboldt State University in Fall 2004.[26] Students who had worked on the script read their own work, joined by Native and Anglo faculty reading the roles of the elders and the farmers and ranchers. Primarily a non-Native community attended the reading: HSU faculty and students and theatre professionals attending the Eco-drama Festival. The listening session was facilitated by José Cruz González, the founder of the Hispanic Playwrights Festival at South Coast Repertory and the dramaturge for the festival. José and I wanted the project's emphasis on alternative ways-of-knowing to inform the community discussion following the performance. Rather than dramaturgical critique, we wanted to draw out feelings, images and stories. We came up with an idea that turned the 'talkback' into an 'art-back'. Immediately following the reading, we passed out drawing paper and colored markers, asking everyone to draw a picture. Then José began to ask people to talk about their pictures. We gleaned images and visceral feelings from what might have otherwise been a 'heady' group. As people told the stories of their drawings they shared in the vulnerability of the performers. This reading also showed those working on the project what the play might have to say to people outside the watershed.

When a performance occurred at a Klamath Watershed Stakeholder workshop (like the one Lauren had attended), the roles were played, Boal-style, by stakeholders from the watershed, including tribal representatives, ranchers, farmers, and federal and state agency personnel – the people and perspectives that were closely represented in the script. During this reading we realized that the script was beginning to be representative of all the groups sitting before us; that we were beginning to tell the multiple stories of this watershed community. Subsequent performances and listening sessions increasingly demonstrated that community-based theatre not only reflects community, but *forges* community, as if the play is a stone dropped in a lake generating circles of community that continue outward. A script that had begun as the marginalized voices from one side of a polarized argument was beginning to function as a bridge.

In 'Performance, Utopia, and the "Utopian Performative"', Jill Dolan reminds us that theatre's primary function is not to formulate the new organizational structures (laws, policies, etc.) of a more just and sustainable civic order, but to provide a forum in which people might taste one another's experiences, engaging the magical 'what if' of theatre: what if that was my grandmother, my child? What if I felt that humiliation, that fear, that rage? Theatre allows us to *feel* a new possible future, and feel it together.[27] Rather than advocate for a particular position in the water policy debate, the aim of *Salmon Is Everything* has been to express the diverse knowledge and plural ways of knowing of the Klamath watershed. When difference is understood as a resource, rather than an obstacle, Iris Marion Young argues, such knowledge enables community to move forward. 'The plural standpoints of the public enable each participant to understand more of what the society means or what the possible consequences of a policy will be by each situating his or her own experience and interest in a wider context of understanding something in other social locations.'[28] The goal of *Salmon Is*

Everything is neither agreement nor policy change, but a change of heart, a celebration of polyphony, a demonstration of the multiplicity of experience, and therefore of knowledge, within our watershed community. This then, as Young argues, composes the collective wisdom from which innovative and compassionate civic action arises.

Over the course of the project, some of the original students involved in the project have graduated; new students, Native and non-Native, theatre-trained and not, have joined the project. The script evolved as more interviews and additional research were added. As the project moved into production and I found comfort in the familiar process of theatrical rehearsal, I realized that, in the end, the set, lights and stage manager's crisp call for 'places please!' was only a small part of this project's democratic efficacy. In its development as well as its production, *Salmon Is Everything* provided a forum for acknowledging pluralism, for giving voice to stories that represented distinct discreet knowledge, which, while not shared by all members of a community, nonetheless enriched all members. In the imaginary world of the play that was eventually created, those groups and individuals who held so much ill-will toward one another spoke to each other through representation, as if in a dream. We were surprised and heartened by tribal members who came long distances to see the performance. Each night the theatre was full, and with many people who had never been to our campus before. In this way the concrete results of the process occured on stage, in the moment of performance, as well as in the discussions and interactions following the performances. Currently, tribal members are working with members of the cast to take the show on tour through the Klamath watershed. They have called it the 'Take It Home Tour' in honour of the elders who came to see the performance and said to us afterwards, 'This is a good thing that you have done. You have told the story. Now we have to take it home. We have to share with all the people in the watershed who are represented here.'[29] Community-based theatre is more than a preamble to social justice activism, it *is* civic action. Transcending the town hall, theatre functions as a site of collective dreaming where a seemingly impossible future might be envisioned.

Notes

1   The Klamath River is the third largest watershed in the western United States behind the Colorado and the Columbia rivers; it runs through two states, five tribal areas, and includes multiple counties, irrigation-districts, hydroelectric dams, incorporated towns, federally managed tracks of land, timber harvest areas, public recreation areas, national monuments and wildlife sanctuaries. The watershed includes 'wild and scenic rivers' such as the Salmon River, and ecologically at risk tributaries such as the Trinity River. The region also includes countless private mines, farms, ranches and homes.

2   From an interview with tribal fisheries personnel for the Klamath Theatre project, *Salmon Is Everything*.

3   The so-called California Mission Trail did not penetrate past the thick redwood-covered mountains of southern Humboldt Country, consequently contact with whites for north coast California tribes did not occur until approximately 1850.

4   Reinelt (1998) argues that 'live theatre enacts one of the last available forms of direct democracy, gathering an assembly of "citizens" in the tradition of . . . town meeting[s]', however it is not the issue being considered, but the ritual action of

coming together in order to consider which is akin to theatre (p. 286). Reinelt invokes Michael Oakeshott's 'practical definition of community' that begins neither with commonly held views nor even shared cultural identities, but with a willingness on the part of a group to concern itself with its own social relations and their political and economic outcomes: that is, 'a group of people who recognize that they are "attending" to their ongoing social arrangements, where the recognition makes them a community, not some particular bonds or common goals' (p. 288).

5   Ibid., p. 284.
6   Ibid., p. 283.
7   I build here on the analysis of Jan Cohen-Cruz, Sonja Kuftinec, Susan Haedicke, Tobin Nellhaus, and others, who have provided a diverse and substantial foundational discourse about the role of community-based theatre in local democratic processes as well as national democratic self-reflections. Their work has brought all of us – theorists and practitioners – a closer understanding of why and how the imagination is vital to a just and sustainable future, and how the collective process of community-based theatre can serve as a wellspring of social change.
8   Community-based theatre's roots in social activism tend to imply that its efficacy lies in social change 'results'. Artists and the communities they serve are then trapped into measuring their work by sociological standards that are embedded with unexamined notions of democracy and a narrow understanding of how art functions in society. Community-based theatre often finds itself theoretically caught along Richard Schechner's 'continuum', in which he locates qualities of efficacy on one pole and entertainment on the other. In *Local Acts*, Jan Cohen-Cruz traces the roots and contemporary emergence of community-based theatre arguing, in accord with Schechner, that this is 'art that is not only about something, but does something' (2005, p. 97). The emphasis on 'concrete social impact' rehearsed in much of the theory surrounding community-based performance betrays (in favor of the kind of simplistic call for 'measurable results' often required by grant applications) the complex and subtle workings of democracy as well as the role of the arts and imagination within a process of social change.
9   Iris Marion Young (1996) 'Communication and the Other: Beyond Deliberative Democracy', in Seyla Behhabib (ed.), *Democracy and Difference: Contesting the Boundaries of the Political*, Princeton, NJ, Princeton University Press, pp. 120–36.
10 Ibid., p. 126.
11 Ibid., p. 127.
12 Ibid., pp. 131–2.
13 Ibid., p. 132.
14 Ibid., p. 132.
15 Cohen-Cruz (2005), pp. 93–6.
16 The project acquired a grant to pay nominal honorariums to elders and other tribal community members who consulted, or gave interviews. Particularly because *Salmon Is Everything* is a project of the university, which is sometimes viewed as a privileged entity, this gesture of returning resources to the community was important.
17 Dolan (2001), p. 459.
18 On 26 February 1860, hundreds of women, children and men, indigenous to this area were brutally massacred by local settlers at Wiyot tribal village sites on Indian Island, at Eel River, and at the South Jetty, in Humboldt County California. The massacre at Indian Island occurred soon after the Native people had finished the Wiyot World Renewal Ceremony and Dance which had lasted for several days. This annual ceremony was held to give thanks for the previous year, and ask for good

fortune in the coming year. Members of the Wiyot, and other local tribes, including the Hupa, Yurok and Karuk, were killed while resting after performing this dance. About 200 people were murdered on the island, with one sole survivor, an infant child. Descendants of the survivors of the Wiyot genocide believe that the world has not been right since the Massacres of 1860.

19 Alice Kilham, former Clinton appointee to the Klamath Compact, has initiated a series of stakeholder workshops designed to get people to talk to one another. Although well intentioned, often moving encounters between stakeholders, these sessions nevertheless resolve *toward* a deliberation. Functioning as forums to find so-called common ground, some fear that these mediations may ultimately perpetuate and sustain the values that Native residents believe led to the fish-kill.

20 Taylor, personal email 19 November 2004.

21 Taylor, personal email 15 November 2004.

22 Taylor, personal email 3 December 2004.

23 By spring of 2006, six citizen-initiated Klamath Stakeholder workshops have been hosted by Alice Kilham, and facilitated by Bob Chadwick. Tribes and upper Klamath ranchers and agriculturists have begun to formulate grassroots agreements about water flows. Recently however, the National Marine Fisheries Service has warned that the returning salmon runs are so low that the 2006 fishing season may be canceled completely. See, Driscoll (2006).

24 The article by Mindie Paget appeared in the 25 April 2005 issue of *Journal World*, Lawrence, Kansas.

25 Personal email, Dianne Yeahquo Reyner, 30 April 2005.

26 For information about the EMOS Ecodrama Playwrights' Festival see www.humboldt.edu\emos.

27 Dolan (2001), pp. 455–60.

28 Young, p. 127.

29 Ron Reed (7 May 2006) Karak Cultural Resources Director.

References

Cohen-Cruz, Jan (2005) *Local Acts: Community-Based Performance in the United States*, London, Rutgers University Press.

Dolan, Jill (2001) 'Performance, Utopia, and the "Utopian Performative"', *Theatre Journal*, 53 (3), October: 455–79.

Driscoll, John (2006) 'Poor Prognosis for Salmon Season', *Times-Standard*, 10 March: A1.

Haedicke, Susan and Nellhaus, Tobin (eds) (2005) *Performing Democracy: International Perspectives on Urban Community-Based Performance*, Ann Arbor, MI, University of Michigan Press.

Klamath Theatre Project (2005) *Salmon Is Everything*, unpublished.

Kuftinec, Sonja (2003) *Staging America: Cornerstone and Community-Based Theatre*, Carbondale, IL: Southern Illinois University Press.

Reinelt, Janelle (1998) 'Notes for a Radical Democratic Theatre: Productive Crises and the Challenge of Indeterminacy', *Staging Resistance: Essays on Political Theatre*, Ann Arbor, MI, University of Michigan Press, pp. 283–300.

Schechner, Richard (1977) *Performance Theory*, London, Routledge.

Thompson, James (2003) *Applied Theatre: Bewilderment and Beyond*, Oxford, Peter Lang.

Young, Iris Marion (1996) 'Communication and the Other: Beyond Deliberative Democracy', *Democracy and Difference: Contesting the Boundaries of the Political*, in Seyla Behhabib (ed.), Princeton, NJ: Princeton University Press, pp. 120–36.

CHAPTER 15

Ubong S. Nda

Preferring a drama-based model for sustainable development advocacy

The Ikot Ayan Itam Theatre for Development experience

A S THE POOR STATE of the environment causes concern in various parts of the globe, the need has arisen for every profession, especially those concerned with the creation of outlets of information, to become stakeholders in the process of environmental education. The theatre, especially the participatory theatre for development, could be a credible methodology in the sensitization of people, especially the rural dwellers of developing nations, in sustainable development. With its provision for communal participation in play-creation, performance, after-performance discussions and decisions, the model is capable of ensuring considerations for local cultural sensitivities, and engendering communal ownership of the communication medium. This chapter reports on a practical experience in theatre and environmental sensitization, which took place in the village of Ikot Ayan Itam, in Itu Local Government Area of Nigeria's Akwa Ibom State.

Background to the project and methodology

I put forward the Theatre for Environment Sensitization Project to the Africa- America Institute as an entry for the 2002 Claude Ake Memorial Award. I proposed to use the village of Ikot Ayan Itam in Itu Local Government Area, in Akwa Ibom State, Nigeria as a case study.

Methodologically, this project entailed environmental survey/research, a practical theatrical presentation of the research findings and communal discussions on the situation and the way forward. The theatre for development approach (popularly known as community theatre) was employed with some modifications. The stages of consultation included: research, discussion/agreement on the play's story line and scenario, rehearsals through the usage of improvisational techniques, production/ discussions and follow-up.

Community research

I had first to undertake a study of the problems to be tackled and the background of the people in the area, including the major cause of the situation, what specific habits of the community enhance its escalation and how best it could be redressed in the short and long terms. I studied the background of the community in order to identify their beliefs, value systems, traditions, taboos, general world-view, relationship with neighbors, social, political, religious and economic activities, as well as the level of technological development. This was necessary because, for development to be socially and environmentally sustainable, 'it must take account and draw upon the values, traditions, and cultures of the people' (Davis and Ebbe, 1993). The specific taboos of the people had to be taken seriously into consideration as a wrong handling of such cultural sensitivities could create mistrust, alienation and even outright ejection of the team from the community.

Choice of sample community

Ikot Ayan Itam, the chosen area for the project, is a highly populous autonomous community in Itu Local Government Area (a local council area noted for its problematic topography) in Akwa Ibom State, Nigeria. It is a large village with about thirteen thousand people.

Ikot Ayan is a purely rural community. It has no electricity and no potable water supply system. It is almost surrounded by valleys and the roads are in a terrible state. Many years ago, the village lost its cherished status of lying along a government highway when the old Uyo–Itu road was abandoned for the new one. And, as is the case for many such situations in developing countries, the old Itu road that passed through Ikot Ayan has been allowed to fall into an unbelievable state of dilapidation. The bridge that once crossed 'idim efod' – a popular stream in Ikot Ayan – has collapsed completely because of erosion, and is now submerged in water. Beyond this stream, the so-called old road is a mere bush path.

In 1989, the government of Akwa Ibom State, in recognition of the environmental vulnerability of this area of the state, decided to hold the state launch of the tree planting campaign in Enen Atai, one of the villages adjoining Ikot Ayan Itam. It was an exercise that should have entailed the full mobilization of the villages around, comprising Enen Atai (the venue), Ikot Anie and Ikot Ayan. But the occasion, a mere government ceremony, just came and went without any inculcation of tree-planting awareness in the people. A few years after, in 1996, a visit by another governor to the erosion points in the area revealed that the exact spot where the tree planting ceremony of 1989 took place had become an impenetrable valley. It is this scenario of neglect and seeming helplessness, especially at the face of the serious environmental problems that beset the community, that informed the choice of Ikot Ayan Itam as the case study for this project.

Environmental problems of Ikot Ayan Itam

One of the serious environmental problems plaguing this community is erosion. As a result of the undulating nature of the Itu topography, the soil is easily susceptible to erosion and landslides. There are more than twenty erosion-prone sites, and about ten full-blown cases. The worst of them, the 'aba ekpe' ravine, almost cuts off the village from the rest of the Itam clan villages. The road that links Ikot Ayan with Ikot Anie, and through which the people gain access to the Uyo–Itu–Calabar major road, is almost taken over by the 'aba ekpe' ravine. The topsoil of this community has been exhausted by overcultivation, rendering it helpless in the face of raging water and other forces of denudation. The problem of erosion has also affected the supply of water in the village. Ikot Ayan has no piped water facility, it therefore depends on the local streams for its water supply. The hilly pathways to most of these streams are becoming impassable, blocking the people's access to the available sources of water.

Another very serious environmental problem of Ikot Ayan is the pollution of water resources through the dumping of waste materials. The village is lucky to have been endowed with streams almost all round its boundaries (one can easily count about twelve streams at different points in the village). Unfortunately, these streams have been polluted with effluent from further upstream and from the Ikot Ayan community itself and water hyacinth has almost taken over the 'idim efod', one of the surviving streams, and a major source of water supply for a greater part of the village.

The poor environmental habits of the community

Although some environmental problems are due to natural causes, especially where issues like topography are involved, research and general observations have shown that a great deal of them are man-induced. After all, even where an area has a difficult terrain or topography, a careful planning of the land use could offer a buffer against any unpleasant situation. The land use in Ikot Ayan, just like in any typical rural community in Africa, has not been well planned. The human omission or poor planning in land utilization has continued to be a problem for environmental control, even in the urban centers of developing countries. For the Ikot Ayan villagers, this issue is considered to be beyond them, as activities of such scope, they believe, could only be handled by government.

The problem of erosion in the community has been seriously abetted by farming activities in erosion-prone areas. The 'aba ekpe' ravine, for instance, has been escalated through cultivation by the villagers. Almost the entire space of the ravine has been cultivated repeatedly, rendering the topsoil vulnerable to the forces of erosion.

Another activity that has seriously contributed to the degradation of the Ikot Ayan community is sand and gravel excavation. The slopes of the village streams are rich in gravel and red earth. Some of the young men are busy excavating these resources for sale in order to make ends meet. The slopes of the popular 'idim efod' are already suffering from this activity.

The silting of the water sources in the village also stems from waste dispersed into these streams, for example, weeds and other residues of cultivation are thrown into them. Some of the streams do not take their sources from Ikot Ayan, but rather flow into it and in some cases, flow out of it. Thus, the waste disposal activities upstream, and at Ikot Ayan itself, have created heavy deposits that have settled over the years, polluting the water and causing the blockage of their flow.

At the bottom of most of these problems are reckless procreation and poverty, the major endemic features of rural Africa. The family planning campaigns have not yet reached this village, as such programs are still principally urban-centered. Neither has the AIDS campaign. Even if they did reach the people of Ikot Ayan, the emphasis on the use of condoms, for example, would seriously clash with the villagers' cultural sensibilities, causing their alienation. As is the case in most rural areas in Nigeria, young girls of school age are giving birth to babies without definite homes. This reckless procreative situation has given rise to the type of scenario described by Dr Babs Sagoe, a one-time United Nations Population Fund official in Nigeria:

> Suppose a farmer owns ten acres of land. If he has ten children and divides the land equally among them, each child will have an acre. If each of these children has ten children and divides the land similarly, each of their children will have one tenth of an acre. Clearly these children will not be as well off as their grandfather, who had ten acres of land.

Here lies the cause of the land fragmentation in Ikot Ayan and the rest of rural Nigeria, especially in the southern states. This situation has led to overstretching of natural resources through overcropping, cultivation on any and all available land spaces, even on erosion-prone areas, and the use of chemicals in fishing, which have coalesced to inflict on the Ikot Ayan Itam community an environmental situation that does not portend a meaningful future for inhabitation.

The project

Consultations and meetings

The reception of this project by the leadership and people of Ikot Ayan village was overwhelming and encouraging. The initial contacts I made with the village were facilitated by Mr James Edet – a versatile theatre artist and drama producer in the television service of the Akwa Ibom Broadcasting Corporation, Uyo. Mr Edet himself had received the idea with encouraging enthusiasm. The Eteidung (the official title of village heads in the Ibibio ethnic nationality – the predominant group in Nigeria's Akwa Ibom State) received the project with warmth. A stable, intelligent, but humble, leader of his people, Eteidung Anieting Akpan Mboko, is about 62 years old. He is well respected by the community because of his high sense of responsibility. He remarked that he and his people were ready to cooperate with any person, persons and organizations that would wish to contribute positively to the development of the community. He referred to the past when the village had been deceived by persons who promised to attract development projects to it but never returned after they were granted full cooperation.

Constitution of a core team

I put together a core team to assist in the execution of the project. This team was comprised of myself, an environmental consultant named Mr Effiong Ntukidem, and an artistic director, Mr James Edet. Mr Ntukidem is an indigene of Ikot Ayan Itam and is a staff member of the Akwa Ibom State Ministry of Lands and Housing. He holds a BSc degree in Geography and is a Master of the University of Uyo Science program in Urban and Regional Planning. His good grasp of environmental issues and his thorough understanding of his village were great assets to this project.

Mr James Edet, also an indigene of Ikot Ayan Itam, is a staff member of the television arm of the Akwa Ibom Broadcasting Corporation, Uyo. He holds a BA in Theatre Arts from the University of Calabar. A good organizer of people, his vast knowledge of the history of Ikot Ayan Itam and the good public relations he has had with the villagers over the years aided the smooth execution of this project.

Meeting with the community

The meeting with the village community was held on a market day, which was convenient for most of the people. The large markets in the area are convened on specific days, and any event held on any such days would not be attended well. This consideration guided subsequent meetings with the members of this community.

The meeting introducing the project was well attended. Questions were asked and clarifications made, especially as the program was outside the partisan political and governmental programs that the people have been inundated with for some time. From their comments, it was possible to deduce that these are people fed up with government developmental declarations and political pronouncements, which ultimately earn them no real dividends. They embraced this project wholeheartedly in the belief that it would not only help them in realizing themselves, but also open their community to outside assistance, especially in the combat of environmental problems and infrastructural deficiencies. They expressed deep appreciation for the inclusion of their members in the core team of the project.

Formation of a volunteer performance group

A date was fixed for those interested in participating in the theatre performance to meet with the members of the project team. Again, the attendance at that meeting was encouraging and I again ran through the objectives and methodology of the project. I told the gathering that there was no prepared script for the production, but a suggestive improvisational framework, which was open to their acceptance or rejection. The group contributed ideas to the building of the story line and the different scenes.

Script / scenario

The agreed story line was as follows. While the Eteidung and the members of the village council are meeting in the Eteidung's palace, a woman rushes in wailing. She tells the bewildered council how she and her husband were cultivating the slopes of 'aba ekpe' (the big ravine in the village that is almost claiming the village access road), and there was a landslide, which has almost buried her husband. The Eteidung calls on the village youth leader and two other young men to go and extricate the man from the disaster. An argument ensues between the council members on the likely cause of the problem. One of them suggests that the gods are angry and must be appeased. Others oppose him. Another is of the opinion that either the man or his wife could be products of twin birth, who, according to their mythological sources, are not supposed to enter the bushes of 'aba ekpe'. Another scene involves two women, one returning from the farm who meets the other still weeding in hers. They discuss the water situation in the village where streams are thinning-out and the routes to the streams are becoming impassable because of erosion. And in another scene, someone complains to the village council that he had given another villager a goat to take care of only to find out that the goat had fallen into the woman's pit latrine. While that issue is being handled by the village council, the son of the Eteidung, who had been studying away from home for a long while, returns home. It is he who unravels the riddles of the environmental problems plaguing the community. The entire village is shocked at his explanations and they collectively decide to take remedial and preventive measures on their situation.

Scripting

The choice of an unscripted public participatory creation of the play is deliberate. I adopted the democratic model of the community theatre process where the project team plays the role of guide and not of imposer. Development processes that emanate from the top-bottom approach have failed in various parts of the world, but the bottom-top approach has been accepted as capable of engendering communal ownership. Besides, in the process of crafting the play, the problems of the village and their suggested solutions were being entrenched in the minds of the actors / actresses, who were not mere entertainers but participatory recipients of the lessons of the production.

This project was a total improvisational experience though some dialogic situations, too important to be left to a free improvisational effort, had to be given to the actors. The improvisation allowed for greater individual treatment of the subject matter and solidified the spirit of local involvement. It also provided for the accentuation of major symbols through subtly prescribed dialogues.

The production strove to be dramatically convincing. It presented the people with the problem they know, and went on to expose or reveal the environmental habits that have caused problems, a scenario where a personal norm had 'to be accompanied by a high awareness of the consequences' (Hopper and Nelson, 1991:195–200). The production also had to present suggestions on how to resolve the problems. These were well embedded within the play and presented convincingly. A warning by Carlton (as cited by Epskamp, 1989) was found vital in this regard:

> Rural people are not sheep who can be led blindly. They generally do not respond well to preaching and propaganda that fail to give them convincing reasons and new insights into why they should change their customary behaviour and practices.

Cast

Another important issue that required careful consideration was the casting of the production. Initially I had been inclined to provide some of the actors and also to invite local volunteers from the community to fill some of the roles. A performance that fails to make an impact on the great majority in the community because of the unseriousness of the cast is not suitable for educative and enlightenment purposes. The performance should be accorded the once-and-for-all attention and seriousness it deserves. But my experience in the field showed that the local volunteers were capable of giving visual expression to the message of the play without the employment of professionals. In the end, all the roles in the play were performed by the villagers.

Rehearsals

As an improvisational dramatic experience, the actors/actresses were allowed to develop their roles and externalize them within their capabilities with the director acting as a guide.

The rehearsals for this production lasted for five weeks, not because the actors/actresses were not ready, but because the social and economic programs of the local community made it impossible to stage the production as early as intended.

Technical needs

In a community theatre project of this nature, it had always been thought inappropriate to employ all the elements of the *mise en scène*. Lighting has always been derived from the natural sunlight. There is no fabricated scenery. The director has only the body of the actor, his voice, his gestures, to communicate his message. The director therefore pays serious attention to the delivery of the actors/actresses. Appropriate costumes and make-up are hardly utilized.

But the need arose to tread a different and innovative pathway. We decided to jettison the less formalistic presentation method associated with the community theatre experience. This decision was based on certain considerations.

The use of the open-air arena staging is strongly suggested for theatre projects of this nature because it is a more informal, intimate theatre environment (Wilson, 1991:

310). But where favorable weather could not be assured, an open school hall might be used, as was the case in this project. Ikot Ayan Itam is within the rain belt of the Nigerian climatic environment and, until the morning of the production, the area was still experiencing rainfall. It therefore became expedient to adopt the hall of St John's primary school in the village.

The theatre for environmental sensitization project is essentially a theatre for development activity. Development entails a change of state, behavior or methodology and change is a response to stimuli – new information or awareness that must be more credible than an existing knowledge or position. The medium through which this new information is presented must be attractive and possess the capacity of being taken seriously. Many Nigerian communities are used to cultural performances in their village squares. They are also used to various ceremonies associated with marriages, births, deaths, etc. These performances and ceremonies are masterpieces of color and spectacle. For a new concept, such as our project, to attract and influence, it must show a greater level of seriousness in spectacle. The medium of any communicative process has a profound effect on the perception and reception of the message. That is why I went out for a full formalistic theatrical production with lighting, fully constructed scenery, appropriate costume and make-up.

Based on the decision to adopt a formalistic theatre approach, the provision of the technical/*mise en scène* elements of theatrical productions became imperative. First, there was the need to provide a stage. St John's primary school has a long hall designed to meet the classroom needs of the school, and it was this hall that was employed in our production. The proscenium staging method was adopted: with a stage, two feet above the ground, at one end of the hall. The lighting equipment used was provided by Mr Charles Nwadigwe. Although the performance took place in the afternoon, there was the need to provide proper illumination for the dramatic action.

Most of the costumes for this production were provided by the actors/actresses themselves, through the prescription of and under the supervision of Mrs Justina Nkanga, a Lecturer in Costume and Make-up in the Department of Theatre Arts, University of Uyo. Some of the necessary materials like the regalia for the traditional chief were provided by the project leader and the artistic director. Mrs Nkanga also handled the make-up of the actors/actresses on the day of performance.

Date/publicity

Continued rains in the area forced postponements from the initial dates for production. Market days and the community's social diary (for example, funerals, marriages, church ceremonies, etc.) had to be taken into serious consideration. The total dependence on the community's internal negotiation for a convenient date was meant to ensure that no other activities requiring important communal participation were fixed for our performance day. The early rescheduling of the date of performance was also meant to create enough time for publicity to be spread among the individual elements and groups in the community. The use of the village town crier, a means of publicity controlled by the traditional government, as well as announcements in churches and group meetings, were employed.

A few invitation letters were issued to persons outside Ikot Ayan and its environs. Those invited were the State Commissioner for Environment, the Head of Department, lecturers and students of the Department of Theatre Arts, University of Uyo, as well as members of the press. The utmost care in the issuing of invitation letters was based on two major considerations. Primarily this project, though based on general global environmental problems, was essentially directed at the people of Ikot Ayan Itam and the environs. There was, therefore, the need to ensure that there was enough space for the people of Ikot Ayan. The second consideration was based on the political climate in the country. As Nigeria gets deeper into electioneering processes, politicians are angling for fora to sell themselves to the electorate, especially in densely-populated areas such as Ikot Ayan. A theatre for an environmental sensitization project, and indeed, any theatre for a development program should be insulated from partisan politics if it is to accepted by and believed in by the people. A careless spread of invitation letters would have exposed the occasion to political campaigners and this would have dented the credibility of the entire project.

Public presentation

The public presentation of this production took the form of a matinée, beginning at 3.00 pm. The village council had ensured adequate publicity for the event and on the day of production the town crier was out at about 1.00 pm to remind people to go over to the primary school premises. The preparatory processes also served as last minute publicity activities. The stage construction and intensive rehearsals of the last few days before production helped in creating anxiety and expectancy for the production.

The performance was well attended by both the village community and people from its environs. It began with my introductory remarks as the project leader. I invited the community to participate in the performance and the discussion segment that would follow.

The first segment was the choral performance by the pupils of St John's primary school. The group adapted some of the folk songs popular in the community into environmental messages, urging the people to abstain from the blockage of drainages, from cultivation on erosion-prone sites, from sand and gravel excavation on slopes, from the dumping of waste in water sources, and from poor care of their family habitations.

In the second segment of the production, the students of the Department of Theatre Arts, University of Uyo, performed a dance drama entitled 'Flood'. In it the students represented, through dance communication, situations where people farm, build and construct roads on water routes. An allegorical character, Flood, demonstrated the devastation he unleashed when people refused to allow water the right of passage. This lasted about ten minutes.

The main performance was that of 'Mfina Idung Nyin' ('The Problems of Our Community'), a drama for which the story line had earlier been provided. This performance lasted for about forty minutes. All the segments were well received by the audience, who watched and listened with rapt attention as the actions in each segment unfolded.

Discussion session

The discussion session that followed was a very important aspect of the project. The community members engaged in the revelations from the entire production. From the various comments made by old and young, males and females, educated and uneducated, it was obvious that the community saw and appreciated the need to effect changes in their environmental habits. It was interesting that an issue like selling of firewood, which had not been treated in the production, was mentioned by one of the women, discussed by the community and accepted as one of the acts that must be refrained from if the environment is to be saved. The community resolved to take actions that would forestall the environmental drift of Ikot Ayan Itam.

Post-performance, evaluation and follow-up

The end of the performance was not the end of the project, but actually the beginning of another phase – the follow-up and monitoring. This process entailed observation of the situation through individual and group contacts. The monitoring and evaluation of this project was based on the agreed action plan of the community. The community had agreed on the need to refrain from all forms of sand and gravel excavation on the slopes of 'idim efod' and other streams, restrain the destruction of vegetation on erosion sites and to stop reckless deforestation. The resolutions also empowered the community to embark on remedial measures such as planting of trees, shrubs and grass at the 'aba ekpe', and the creation of routes for water channeling within the village community.

The community also called for assistance from the local, state and federal governments, as well as public-spirited individuals, groups, non-governmental organizations, individuals and corporate members of the international community. The village reasoned that the well-developed erosion sites in the village, especially at 'aba ekpe' (which is on the verge of claiming the village road link to other villages) would need permanent erosion-control measures, the cost of which was beyond their means. The people of Ikot Ayan also made a passionate appeal to organizations in any part of the world to assist them with the provision of piped water and electricity. With the present state of water pollution in the community, the village risks a serious epidemic if the people continue to depend on the contaminated and drying-up streams for their sources of water. The provision of electricity in the area would economically empower some of the people in the community to venture into money-earning occupations and trades (for example, welding, barbing, etc.) that would take the pressure from the overused land resources.

Submissions

The good reception of this project by the people of Ikot Ayan Itam is an indication of the acceptability of the drama method of message presentation. The community was thrilled by the introduction of an alternative to the 'talk shop' methods which they had found boring, and considered a 'talk-down'.

Based on the foregoing, I would wish to strongly submit that there is an urgent need for the sincere sensitization of local populations, especially the rural dwellers, who form the great percentage of the nation's population on environmental issues. Even though the amount of information on the environment available to urban dwellers is still scanty and inadequate, at least some efforts made in the creation of environmental awareness has been to their advantage. Yet urban dwellers only constitute about 30 percent of the nation's population, and if the rural constituents of this population continue to be left out of the environmental drive, then the pace of environmental change in behavior will continue to be slow. In contrast, the proper sensitization of the majority will signify a major breakthrough in the bid to save the local and global environment.

Drama could be principally employed in the process of rural sensitization on environmental issues. The model as described in this project has shown the plausibility of using drama in this way. Neither seminars nor workshops with talk presentations can effectively draw the rural audience's attention to technically based, but naturally truthful, issues such as environmental damage. But drama, with its attractive and didactic attributes, can conveniently and satisfactorily be used.

In the employment of the theatre/drama medium, the organizers should not rigidly follow the already set patterns of community theatre, but should rather study the community and the circumstances of the project at hand to enable the preparation of a model that would best suit the situation to be devised.

Theatre- and drama-based organizations should rouse themselves to the important social responsibility of maximizing the beneficial characteristics of their medium in environmental sensitization. Cultural center boards, university theatres, etc., could reach out to the rural communities in this regard. Governmental and non-governmental organizations could (in recognition of the place of the environment as the base for the sustenance of life) sponsor such activities, as the finances of theatre organizations may not stretch to funding the logistics for these projects.

Communities such as Ikot Ayan Itam that have fully realized the damage caused by the poor environmental habits of both the past and present generations and are ready to embrace sustainable development methods should be assisted and encouraged.

Conclusion

This project has established the plausibility and possibility of employing theatre/drama as a good medium for the dissemination of environmental information, especially in the rural areas. The sustained enthusiasm and acceptance, which prevailed throughout the course of this project, and the active participation of the rural people, are vital indications of a success that could be replicated elsewhere, if the process is carefully planned and executed, with a strong awareness of the particular requirements of the local community.

References

Abah, Oga Steve (1997) *Performing Life: Case Studies in the Practice of Theatre for Development*, Zaria, Bright Printing Press.

Davis, S.H. and Ebbe, K. (eds) (1993) *Traditional Knowledge and Sustainable Development*, Washington, DC, The World Bank.

Epskamp, Kees (1989) *Theatre in Search of Social Change: The Relative Significance of Different Theatrical Approaches*, The Hague, Centre for the Study of Education in Developing Counties (CESO).

Hawthorne, Maria and Alabaster, Tony (1998) *Citizen 2000: The Development of a Model of Environmental Citizenship*, Zurich, Elsevier Science.

Hediger, Hubert C. *et al.* (1973) *Modern Theatre Practice*, New York, Meredith Corporation.

Hopper, J.R. and Nelson, J.M. (1991) 'Recycling as Altruistic Behaviour: Normative and Behavioural Strategies to Expand Participation in a Community Recycling Programme', *Environment and Behaviour*, 25.

Nda, Ubong S. (1992) 'Strategies for Broadcasting to Further Rural Development in Nigeria', Unpublished Press Fellowship Project, Cambridge, Wolfson College, University of Cambridge.

Oko, Mathias (2000) 'Conflicts of Policies', in *Newswatch*, 16 October, Lagos, Newswatch Communications.

Open File (1994), International Planned Parenthood Federation of Nigeria (IPPF), London.

Peters, Sunday W. (1994) 'Environmental Problems', in Sunday Peters, Edet R. Iwok and Okon E. Uya, *Akwa Ibom State: The Land of Promise*, Lagos, Gabumo Publishing Company.

Timothy-Asobele, Jide (1984) 'Development of Children Theatre and Books in Nigeria', in Nigeria, No. 151, Lagos, Federal Department of Culture.

Toakley, A.R. and Aroni, S. (1998) *FORUM: The Challenge of Sustainable Development and the Role of Universities*, Zurich, Elsevier Science.

Vargas, Claudia Maria (2000) *Sustainable Development Education: Averting or Mitigating Cultural Collision*, Zurich, Elsevier Science.

Wilkins, Elizabeth (1976) *An Introduction to Sociology*, London, Macdonald & Evans.

Wilson, Edwin (1991) *The Theatre Experience*, New York, McGraw-Hill.

Witherspoon, S. and Martin, J. (1992) 'What Do We Mean by Green?', in R. Jowell *et al.* (eds), *British Social Attitudes. The Ninth Report*, Cambridge, Cambridge University Press.

World Commission on Environment and Development (1987) *Brundtland Commission – Our Commission Future*, Oxford, Oxford University Press.

CHAPTER 16

Marcia Blumberg*

Puppets doing time in the age of AIDS

OVER THE CENTURIES puppetry has developed into a multifaceted art form that includes ritual, folk art, plays, and a popular entertainment especially geared for children in the interrelated genres of theater, the movies, and television. In pre- and postelection South Africa puppets have played an important role in breaking new ground.[1] Peter Larlham's 1991 essay about theater in transition documents various events, including Gary Friedman's Puppets against AIDS, and lists some defining features of South African theater:

> a theatre that addresses issues of immediate relevance to South African society with a de-emphasis on producing Western works; play making rather than working from preexistent scripts—the actor is regarded as a role-maker rather than an interpreter of roles; a theatre that assists in re-education after the long period of enforced censorship and disinformation.[2]

In an unusual mode puppetry is fulfilling these criteria and making a radical contribution toward theater as a transformative force in South Africa at a significant time when, in the opinion of a local AIDS expert, Dr. Clive Evian, "the South African epidemic is one of the most explosive in the world . . . and will have devastating consequences for the country."[3] As the brainchild of puppeteer Gary Friedman, a pilot project developed out of ten years of work with puppets to promote HIV/AIDS awareness. Puppets in Prison utilizes the stark locale of a prison environment to intervene through the medium of puppetry in the harsh reality of oppressive structures, brutal practices, and the ever-growing AIDS pandemic.

My essay situates this puppet project in its specific national and sociopolitical coordinates at the nexus of theater as an interventionary force in the prison milieu and the AIDS pandemic. In historicizing the context for these complex issues, it is valuable to analyze the role of one South African prison in the history of the nation. Although the criminal and the political grounds for incarceration were often deliberately blurred and regarded by some as equivalent in the apartheid discourse. Robben Island, a political prison from 1667, has since 1961 assumed a unique position as the bastion of the liberation struggle, signifying courage, survival, and the dream of freedom. Leaders of then-banned political organizations kept faith with their ideals despite the harsh conditions and physical demands. Nelson Mandela articulated the dilemma: "The great challenge is how to resist, how not to adjust, to keep intact the knowledge of society outside and to live by its rules."[4] Strategies to enact this challenge involved the often surreptitious circulation of reading materials, a determined effort among prisoners to share their knowledge, whether teaching rudimentary reading and writing, upgrading skills, or keeping one another apprised of the latest political developments, and participation in weekly performances of poetry, story-telling and dramatic material.

Robben Island also provides a context for theater in prison as a vehicle of intervention, *The Island*, devised in 1973 by Athol Fugard, John Kani, and Winston Nshona, gives spectators a window on a world that, John Kani reminds us, "we never talk about, no one can write about, the press cannot talk about, not even white South Africans, free as they are can talk about."[5] Yet this collaborative work evokes salient aspects: the opening scene, which includes a sequence of "back-breaking and grotesquely futile labour"[6] (which can take an interminable stage time of ten minutes or longer); the complex bonding communicated by the two actors and prison inmates, John and Winston; the power of theater to voice protest, here in the form of the play-within-the-play, *The Trial of Antigone*, derived from Sophocles's tragedy. Since the playlet is performed at the prison concert, *The Island's* spectators watching the action on the bare stage are cast in the added role of prison audience; unlike the prison inmates, they are free to leave the theater and necessarily occupy spectatorial positions synonymous with the prison warders (guards). In the moments of enforced complicity spectators hear Winston's Antigone refuse to remain silent in the face of injustice and voice his resistance to Creon and other authority figures. Theater within this prison setting focuses upon rights and rituals of ancient Greece and at the same time speaks to the oppressive structures that expose problems of race, class, and gender roles as well as restricted liberty for the vast majority of South Africans until 1994.

Robben Island in the mid-nineteenth century also served as a hospital for the mentally ill and from the last decade of that century until 1930 functioned as a leper colony. A book on Robben Island addressed to high school teachers and students sets tasks in each section; one proposed debate, titled "Are AIDS Victims the 'Lepers' of the 1900s?"[7] refers to a reprinted 1994 local newspaper report suggesting that children in Swaziland infected with HIV/AIDS should be barred from school, since they have no future and are damned by divine punishment. Notwithstanding the highly contested word *victim* so reviled by people living with HIV/AIDS, many of whom courageously face daily hurdles and prize their empowerment, however much illness may create challenges, the analogy between AIDS and leprosy raises Paula Treichler's concern that "AIDS is simultaneously an epidemic of a transmissible lethal disease and an epidemic of meanings or signification."[8] While ignorance, bigotry, and discrimination spawn fear and stigmatization of people infected with HIV/AIDS, the distrust of official policy bred during the apartheid years exacerbates the complexity of the issues.

The AIDS pandemic in South Africa constitutes different demographics from that of North America or Britain in that those infected with HIV or living with AIDS are mainly black men and women; statistics also show that approximately one in four black babies is born seropositive.[9] In fact, the term *child-headed household* is now used when both parents have died from AIDS-related causes. Mary Crewe explains how apartheid structures have affected the AIDS crisis:

> There is little doubt that AIDS has generated a good deal of angst in South Africa. Although it is a new disease, it is laying bare and exacerbating the social prejudices, the economic inequalities, discriminatory practices and political injustices that have been the cornerstones of apartheid.[10]

Here Crewe insists on an awareness of differentials of marginalization and their effect on the situations of people living with HIV/AIDS. In her 1992 report on an "AIDS and Lifestyle Education Project Undertaken in Rural Zululand," Lynn Dalrymple provides extensive analyses of the methodology and rationale for drama education rather than conventional teaching around the issues of HIV/AIDS. Among many aspects she highlights the work of Paulo Freire, whose *Pedagogy of the Oppressed* challenges what he calls "the banking concept of education," which supposedly deposits information into putatively empty vessels and calls instead for "learning through doing"[11] and an understanding of how society functions. This DramAidE project provides for participants' active involvement and has made such an impact that related programs have started in Grahamstown and Johannesburg.[12]

Gary Friedman has also made a marked contribution to this field of AIDS awareness; his work particularly epitomizes the transformative potential of puppet theater. Returning to his homeland in 1987 after training in Paris with the Muppet master, Jim Henson, Friedman founded the African Research and Educational Puppetry Programme (AREPP), which is a community-based educational trust. The group's first project, "Puppets Against AIDS," is periodically updated and takes life-size puppets onto the streets to perform for adults outside health clinics, at the mines, taxi ranks, and other street venues; transportable theatrical projects such as the group's consciousness-raising version of Punch and Judy also visit factories and offices. Different shows geared for audiences at primary, junior high, and secondary schools approach HIV/AIDS issues from various perspectives and employ a range of puppets and media to entertain and involve spectators and concomitantly engage pressing issues.

In 1994 Friedman left AREPP[13] to tackle new challenges, including a pilot project, "Puppets in Prison." This peer group educational theater program developed for prisoners directly confronts the nexus of apparently unrelated but vital issues in a postelection South Africa: violent crime on an unparalleled scale and the rapidly increasing AIDS pandemic. Gary Friedman acted upon his belief that "without the element of risk— in life, in theatre—things are not worth doing."[14] For this innovative project, undertaken in 1996, twelve[15] long-term prisoners were selected to participate in an eight-week workshop from a section of Diepkloof Prison, Johannesburg, that houses inmates from the ages of eighteen to twenty-four years and offers no recreational facilities. His modest proposal should be compared with another approach to theater as a supposedly interventionary vehicle: Mbongeni Ngema's lavish 1995 Musical, *Sarafina 2*, purported to be an entertaining as well as educational production about AIDS and issues of safe sex. Scandalous budgetary demands (over 14 million Rand, approximately 3–5 million dollars) funneled into salaries and promotional excesses resulted in the discrediting of officials, including the Minister of Health and the return of funds to the European Union; the closure of the production within a few months hinged on these factors as well as inflated ticket prices and the musical's poor reception. Most significantly, the lack of advice from activists, health professionals, and people from the Communities who are most affected not only demonstrated arrogance but resulted in poor and irresponsible communication about salient issues within the framework of the production. Adele Baleta discloses that "Dr. Evian, a public health physician, saw *Sarafina 2* and described it as a 'slap in the face to AIDS health care workers struggling with meagre resources.'"[16] The gross wastage is easily assessed when calculations demonstrate that the *Sarafina 2* budget would have funded over 150 Puppets in Prison workshop series (at a cost of approximately ninety thousand Rand each).

Unlike the *Sarafina 2* situation, health professionals initiated the prison project with sessions on AIDS awareness and its impact on the prison community, in particular. Friedman and Nyanga Tshabalala provided training in puppet making, acting, and rudimentary set design. Most important, they created a safe space and engendered a collaborative process based on a growing trust in which prisoners/puppeteers utilized the opportunity to share personal experiences and fears about HIV infection, AIDS, rape, prostitution, gangsterism, and other related scenarios that eventually constituted the narratives of the puppet playlets. Friedman emphasizes that "puppets can do and say things that real live actors wouldn't dare do."[17] Ventriloquizing their stories through the mouths of the puppet characters has a liberating effect, since the actors can communicate their concerns in a narrative that engages sensitive and even dangerous issues, yet there is no direct line of retaliation, since it is the puppet character and not the actor performing his own story. These "created performers,"[18] a term coined by Eileen Blumenthal, although manipulated and spoken by the actors, mediate between the embarrassment or shame of personal revelation and the necessity to impart educational material in dramatizations that entertain the audience and empower the actors who know that their performances are relevant to the prisoners' lives, Adele Baleta explains the process: "The workshop is presented to up to 50 inmates a day and is constantly revised and reworked."[19] These sessions culminated in performances for high-profile officials from the Department of Correctional Services (DCS), other prisoners, and warders; the latter frequently occupy contradictory positions as agents for forced prostitution and other coercive situations and are totally ineffectual in imparting information on AIDS awareness to inmates, who regard them with distrust.

A detailed evaluation of the process and the final performance product of Puppets in Prison by Renee Bub and Dr. Clive Evian demonstrates an overwhelmingly positive reception by the various audiences. The few negative comments from prisoner/spectators were content related and spoke particularly about absences—issues they regarded as especially pertinent but which the narratives had failed to include. Bob and Evian cite the opinions of some inmates: "There was no depiction of warders. If you did it would make it more real to our day-to-day lives and problems"; and "Yes it is realistic to prison life, some of the time. But the warders selling juvenile prisoners to older prisoners was not revealed."[20] Hazel Friedman assesses the warders' absence from a different perspective: "Their exclusion is perhaps one of the loudest statements prisoners can make about temporarily reclaiming power through theatre in a place where they have been stripped of it completely."[21] Despite her view of their envisaged empowerment to enact the scenario within the inmate hierarchy, the prisoners' comments insist on greater complexity within the narratives and representations that conform more closely to the reality of their prison world.

For the project the group chose to work with two kinds of puppets. Glove or hand puppets in the format of a Punch and Judy show were situated in a puppet booth fashioned from a tent. In addition, large rod (body) puppets were played in front of the booth in full view of the audience. Puppeteers used their arms as the puppet's arm and showed the manipulation of the rod puppet. Small microphones worn by the actors/manipulators amplified their voices during the performance. The twelve prisoners each created a character, developed a narrative, and made an appropriate puppet in one of three playlets. These constitute rudimentary scripts that fall within the general rubric so apt for prison life: "love has no bars." In analyzing these scenarios, all of which revolve around networks of power and sexual relationships, the performed narratives are examined in conjunction with a video of workshop sessions and remarks by the puppeteers, newspaper reviews, and a thirty-eight-page evaluative report of the project to assess it as a vehicle of transformation and rehabilitation, albeit on a small scale.

The first scenario centers on a male prostitute dubbed Sharon Stone whose relationships with two inmate "bosses" demonstrate a sexual and material economy that also involves the transmission of HIV. Cas St. Leger identifies the complex relationship between actor/creator and character:

> Sharon Stone would never have recognized herself. . . . Anonymous in drab prison garb and hidden behind the puppet stand, which is light years away from seaside Punch and Judy shows, 20-year-old Johannes Mmusi from Alexandra [township] was at Sharon Stone's Controls. . . . The dread locked Sharon Stone represents a gay prisoner in drag. The words "she" speaks in a hodge-podge of South Africa's official languages are the proud creation of Mmusi.[22]

These observations also expose displacements of race, gender, and sexual orientation in the embodiment of the particular construction, which takes into the heart of a restrictive locale identity issues only recently addressed in South Africa by anti-discrimination laws. Since eleven of the twelve prisoners in the group were black, these shifts constituted a sense of realism for the creators and prison audience alike, all of whom seemed to value that aspect of the scenarios as a basic necessity for peer identification and awareness raising.

The playlet's plot line is simple and direct. When the rich boss, Tshepo, falls ill, the doctor's diagnosis of AIDS takes them all by surprise. This reaction is quite understandable on an individual level but also represents a different form of denial: an initial widespread disbelief in the existence of AIDS that stems from the apartheid years, when distrust and misinformation were engendered and manipulated by the dominant power structures. Tshepo's death, while accelerated and far-fetched in terms of a lived reality, nevertheless foregrounds the effects of risky sexual practices and negligence about health care and testing. This condensed time sequence equates AIDS with death and provides a simplistic and terrible certainty that elides the possibility of years of living with HIV, especially at a time when antiviral cocktails have shown promising results. Yet perhaps this situation more accurately exposes the reality of the AIDS pandemic in South Africa and other parts of the continent, where exorbitantly priced medication is just not a viable option, since poverty and deplorable conditions often prevail. Since Tshepo and the poor boss, Spiwe, have had sex with Sharon Stone, they are both fearful and engage in mutual blame. Sharon's cough necessitates a doctor's visit, which includes an HIV test; the importance of retaining "her" role as prostitute in the prison hierarchy prompts a decision to remain silent about the test results: "'I am only responsible for me and nobody else,' growled Ms. Stone, 'girlfriend' of prison 'bosses' Spiwe and Tshepo." St. Leger further clarifies the situation: "Johannes and his fellow prisoner-puppeteers . . . believe they have a responsibility to each other."[23] This exposure of Stone's bravado, or perhaps what she considers a necessary lack of knowledge in order to survive the prison locale, emphasizes the antithesis. The actors, whose serostatus was unknown to Friedman, displayed concern about HIV; from the beginning of the workshops they developed a sense of motivation particularly within their roles as peer educators, who in the final analysis could feel responsible for saving lives.

The second playlet focuses upon rape, a practice prevalent in prison but here performed as a sexual initiation rite into the dynamics of gangsterism. When Bra Biza, the knife-wielding boss of a prison gang, who is also HIV-positive, hears about a new inmate, he sends his "guard" Roger to procure the young prisoner for himself and promises the newcomer material comforts: "clean bedding, soap, cigarettes." Biza's act of rape accompanied by the youngster's screams for mercy loses none of the horrific violence when enacted by puppets. The lack of physical and emotional inhibitions of puppets adds to the potential for increasing the severity of the violence, yet the human involvement is never forgotten, as the actors manipulating the puppets are fully visible; this linkage emphasizes egregious modes of behavior in and out of prison. When Roger takes his turn to repeat the violent act, the intervention of the former guerilla fighter, Sporo, who has lost a friend to AIDS, provokes a fight in which Bra Biza stabs Sporo and Roger and triumphantly declares to the audience, "I am boss." Daryl Accone reports Gary Friedman's assessment of this moment: "To watch the delicacy of a huge guy manipulating a glove puppet, a character that has been stabbed to death with a pair of scissors, is amazing."[24] The exchange of commodities and sexual favors in an oppressive hierarchy of machismo and territorial claims raises questions of danger within prison culture that places the transmission of AIDS in juxtaposition with other, more familiar concerns. The message is always one of fear and spells out the equation, AIDS = death. This scenario uses the viral threat as subtext while showing a trajectory of violence that begins with the circulation of power within a gang and enacts rape as an extreme form of sexual violence that can result in death.

The third scenario dramatizes what the first playlet debates. Boss "owns" the cell and protects his "girlfriend," Maria Podesta, in exchange for loyalty and sexual availability. Sexual relationships are demonstrated in an unusually graphic way by the construction of a "Mdiya-diya." This tentlike structure of sheets around a bed offers privacy of a sort so that other inmates know and hear what takes place without seeing it. What may seem a creative solution to an expected event is in the context of this prison performance a daring act, since the authorities deny that sexual relationships occur in prison and therefore forbid the distribution of condoms. Other characters bring AIDS awareness to the fore: the puppet, Special, knows about AIDS from life on the outside, and the doctor discusses sexually transmitted diseases and advises Maria, who is wracked by pain, to abstain from sex. While this decision enrages the boss and disrupts his life, the dialogue provides an opportunity for discussion and information on many issues, including the benefits of monogamous relationships and the necessity for condom use. Rafiq Rohan reports Gary Friedman's dilemma: "We may teach the prisoners about HIV and AIDS and the use of condoms but we cannot distribute condoms. This dichotomy . . . creates difficulty and is cause for great frustration."[25] Describing the situation as a "health time bomb," an editorial in the same newspaper argues:

> It appears that everyone except the Minister [of Correctional Services] is aware of the looming threat. . . . It would be highly irresponsible for the department to take the position that because it is not permitted, sex among prisoners is not happening. Equally dangerous is the rather puritanical view that to provide prisoners with condoms, as they should be, would encourage sexual relations behind bars.[26]

This scenario also proves reductive of the many complex nuances of the issues it raises, but, unlike the two preceding playlets, it moves from violence and harshness to an insistence on the necessity of dialogue and understanding other perspectives.

Baleta suggests the anticipated trajectory of Puppets in Prison: "Friedman had submitted a one-year budget of less than one million Rand. . . . The plan was to train eleven groups of prisoners, who through the medium of puppetry, would educate their peers in jails in all provinces."[27] The significant projected continuance of puppeteers to train other prisoners and impart skills and vital aspects of AIDS awareness was aborted due to lack of funds despite high praise from the DCS, an African National Congress (ANC) cabinet minister's statement on video that this program should be implemented in every prison in South Africa, and the known statistics that approximately 20 percent of the Diepkloof prisoners were diagnosed with HIV/AIDS. Internal government political feuding has proved an immense obstacle to the project. Gaye

Davis argues that the "chief casualties of the conflict between the correctional services minister [Dr. Sipo Mzimela], and then ANC Member of Parliament, Carl Niehaus [now an ambassador in Europe], are the prisoners, prison staff and prison reform."[28] Mzimela has been criticized for hasty decisions, lack of consultation with parliamentary committees, and morale problems at a time when violent crime continues to escalate. Moreover, dire overcrowding in prisons has led the authorities to consider and reject the proposed conversion of disused mine shafts into prison cells in favor of prison ships anchored in naval dockyards. While these suggestions elicited outrage in certain quarters, a report from the *Herald Sun* reminds us that "South Africa has one of the world's highest crime rates, and has already granted amnesty to some prisoners to relieve a growing burden on the prison system."[29] In an address on penal reform Jody Kollapen notes the untenable conditions, which he attributes to gross overcrowding, militarism within the correctional system, and the lack of effective educational and vocational opportunities:

> Within the prison system hundreds of thousands of abuses of human rights took place [under apartheid] and still continue. . . . [W]e need to transform our system not because others expect us to do it but rather because we as South Africans believe that the system is wrong, that it negates the very ideals we fought for and that it negates the important features of a democratic society.[30]

Although conditions at many of the correctional facilities are deficient and even dangerous, recidivism is high. Nyanaga Shabalala explains that for many young black South Africans the lack of education, skills, jobs, and opportunities combined with the high cost of basic necessities for living often translates into a desire to be caught and sent back, since life may be easier to handle in the structured environment of the prison.[31]

The Diepkloof project was not reinstated, and each time I hear the participants' views on the video or read the evaluation report I feel a combination of anger, a sense of their betrayal and wasted opportunities, and a fear for their futures. John Sloop considers rehabilitation of prisoners an outmoded process yet at the same time offers Edgardo Rotman's deeply felt argument for "rehabilitation not as something granted to the criminal but as a human right. . . . [I]t is the task of society to provide all outlets for the cultivation of human independence and self-determination."[32] The rehabilitative function of Puppets in Prison is clearly articulated by the puppeteers involved. They reiterated how the program served as a turning point in their lives when, for the first time, they formed long-term goals and future visions. Most notable was their increased confidence and sense of self-worth; their newly learned skills and significant roles as peer educators translated for them into the potential for a viable future, especially when AIDS education addresses life and death issues and the other interconnected problems of violence that form a cycle that impacts on life both in and outside prison.

During the workshop the puppeteers also developed a commitment to the project and to its participants, learned a self-activated discipline, and practiced physical training and meditation; the creative and performance aspects offered them a special opportunity in an otherwise harsh prison routine that allowed no recreational outlet. Their understanding of stigmatization came through clearly in the workshop and discussion process but is less prominent in the scenarios than the ramifications of the existence of the virus and the prevention of its transmission. Nevertheless, the process as a whole is markedly different from the situation outlined by Philippa Garson in a 1994 report:

> One of the HIV-positive inmates in a Johannesburg Prison describes the level of stigmatization: he no longer has a name, no longer has rights. "My name is HIV or AIDS kaffir." Most of them receive no counseling and the news of their status is often given in public as they wait in line with other prisoners. Even their food is labelled HIV.[33]

These intolerable acts of discrimination and harshness are even more oppressive by virtue of their containment within a prison environment and exacerbate the stress and vulnerability of people already coping with the virus.

The demise of the Diepkloof project occurred despite many initiatives on the part of Gary Friedman and others as well as critical appraisals such as the one from Daryl Accone: that this project "may well provide the blueprint for HIV and AIDS education in our jails."[34] The comprehensive evaluation report, which analyzes many aspects, concludes with overall praise for the project as "an excellent AIDS initiative that gave audiences important information about AIDS and also served to stimulate further interest in and discussion about the disease." Yet it was also threatening on other counts, "Certain of the prison staff felt that 'Puppets in Prison' was giving a negative message to the outside world. Furthermore they were shocked by some of the feedback they received pertaining to the programme. As a result they were not comfortable with the programme."[35] Nevertheless, a second workshop was held in January 1997 at the Ekuseni Youth Development Centre in Natal involving a new group of prisoners and scenarios. An invitation for another workshop in 1998 and the reported benefits of the first, like that of the Diepkloof project, mark this puppet theater as a transformative vehicle but remind us that these initiatives are tenuous unless funding is available for support. Reporting on a South African theater festival at Lincoln Center, New York, during August 1997, Donald G. McNeil Jr. warns that

> South African theater is in some danger of dying, not for lack of topics to write about, but because crime is choking off audiences. Theatregoers are nervous about driving downtown at night to venues like the world-famous Market Theater. Theater in black townships is "literally dead" because of crime, [Duma] Ndlovu said.[36]

How fitting that this vital theater project within prison should have gained support and gathered momentum, yet its limited deployment relates directly to paucity of funds and governmental inaction. Puppets in Prison fulfilled an opportunity to confront violence on all levels and procure greater well-being in this time of AIDS.[37] Now more than ever, its demise should be countered by renewed efforts and an urgent realization: in the postelection transition period doing time can be synonymous with a productive use of time.[38]

Notes

I acknowledge sincere appreciation to Gary Friedman and Nyanga Tshabalala, who inspired me with their commitment and who generously provided me with interviews, e-mail correspondence, video, scripts and evaluation repots that brought to life a process that I couldn't witness. A warm debt of gratitude also to Stephen Barber for his inspiration and ongoing engagement with my work. Special thanks to the Social Sciences and Humanities Council of Canada for a postdoctoral fellowship supporting my work.

* Marcia Blumberg is a Research Fellow at the Open University, England. Her involvement with the Puppets in Prison project stems from her conviction of the relevance of theater to productive societal change. Puppets in Prison forms part of a cross-cultural study, "Staging AIDS: Theatre as/and Activism," now in progress. She coedited *South African Theatre as/and Intervention* with Dennis Walder and is completing *Engendering Intervention in Contemporary South African Theatre*.

1   Highly innovative puppeteers are Handspring Puppet Company's Basil Jones and Adrian Kohler, who have collaborated with artist and filmmaker William Kentridge on three internationally acclaimed productions: *Woyzeck on the Highveld* (1993), *Faustus in Africa* (1995), and *Ubu and the Truth Commission* (1997). Their multimedia cross-cultural revisionings of canonical texts transform conventional readings and dazzle spectators with brilliant theatrical values that utilize the collaborative efforts of actors, puppeteers, animated drawings, magnificently carved puppets, and haunting music. The latest production is the most pared down but superbly explores the complex nexus of representations of the controversial Truth and Reconciliation Commission, historical process and artistic licence, the impossible dilemma of amnesty and the bartering of justice for truth and reconciliation, and various Ubu figures in revisioned forums that satirize national and cultural stereotypes. Notwithstanding tremendous critical success in Europe and mostly favorable reviews in South Africa the response of local spectators is revealing: some gave a standing ovation, others sat stony faced without applauding, while a few walked out to refuse engagement with the disturbing scenarios.

2   Peter Larlham, "Theatre in Transition: The Cultural Struggle in South Africa," *Drama Review* 35, no. 1 (Spring 1991): 211.

3   Clive Evian, "Latest AIDS Epidemic Update," *AIDS Management and Support* (May 1997).

4   Penny Nyren, ed., *Dreaming of Freedom: The Story of Robben Island* (Johannesburg: Sached Books, 1994), 60.

5   W. B. Worthen, "Convicted Reading: *The Island*, Hybridity, Performance," *Crucibles of Crisis: Performing Social Change* (Ann Arbor: University of Michigan Press, 1996), 174.

6   Athol Fugard, John Kani, and Winston Nshona, *The Island, Statements* (Oxford: Oxford University Press, 1974), 47.

7   Nyren, *Dreaming of Freedom*, 37.

8   Paula A. Treichler, "AIDS, Homophobia and Biomedical Discourse: An Epidemic of Signification," in *AIDS: Cultural Analysis/Cultural Activism*, ed. Douglas Crimp (Cambridge, Mass.: MIT Press, 1988), 32.

9   In a report by R. W. Johnson in the *Times of London* that appeared in Johannesburg on 26 April 1997, South Africa's health minister, Dr. Nkosana Zuma, unveiled new figures showing that the number of people infected by HIV rose in a year by 33 percent. In 1996 about 2.4 million people, or 6 percent of the population, were HIV-positive, a rise of one-third over 1995. These statistics should be read with the knowledge that there is underreporting in the wake of social stigma and medical confusion about the syndrome in a country where tuberculosis is rife and other diseases also take a huge toll. Inexplicitness about sexual practices and modes of transmission of the virus, to avoid offending conservative African social mores, exacerbates the problem when misinformation results from understatement and veiled allusions. While the average time for conversion from an HIV-positive status to full-blown AIDS seems to be twice the length (about ten years) of that occurring in the rest of Africa, probably in light of relatively better health care and food, it also means that more people are able to transmit the virus for a longer period, especially in a situation where initiatives in AIDS awareness are inadequate.

10 Mary Crew, *AIDS in South Africa: The Myth and the Reality* (London: Penguin, 1992), 54.

11 Paulo Freire, *Pedagogy of the Oppressed*, trans. Charles A. and Maria-Odilia Leal McBride (New York: Continuum, 1989), 58, 59.

12 Michael Carklin's detailed description and analysis of methodology used in the Grahamstown DramAidE project form part of his article "Rainbows and Spiderwebs: New Challenges for Theatre in a Transformed System of Education in South Africa," in *South African Theatre as/and Intervention*, eds Marcia Blumberg and Dennis Walder (Amsterdam: Rodopi, 1999).

13 Gordon Billbrough his now at the helm of AREPP; it has continued to develop the initial programs and is also offering new material.

14 Daryl Accone, "Master Puppeteer Gary Friedman Pulls Strings, Not Punches, as He Unmasks Us," *Sunday Independent*, 21 April 1996, 4.

15 In a discussion on 7 July in Grahamstown Gary Friedman explained that there were initially fifteen members in the group. One dropped out of the project; two others tried to escape by jumping off the roof. One broke his neck and died; the other was caught and put into chains.

16 Adele Baleta, "AIDS 'Made Real' for Inmates," *Weekend Argus*, 21–22 June 1996, n.p.

17 Fiona Chisholm, "It's Soweto II—The Puppet Show," *Cape Times*, 22 March 1996, 13.

18 Eileen Blumenthal, "Life and Death of Puppets," *American Theatre* (January 1997): 17.

19 Baleta, "AIDS 'Made Real' for Inmates," n.p.

20 Renee Bub and Clive Evian, "A Qualitative Evaluation of the 'Puppets in Prison' Programme Conducted in Jahannesburg Prison," June 1996, 17.

21 Hazel Friedman, "Puppets Get Behind Bars," *Weekly Mail and Guardian* 12, no. 15 (12–18 April 1996): 25.

22 Cas St. Leger, "No Stone Unturned," *Sunday Times*, 7 April 1996, 3.

23 Ibid., 3.

24 Accone, "Master Puppeteer," 4.

25 Rafiq Rohan, "MPs Hear about Sex in Prison," *Sowetan*, 20 March 1996.

26 "Sowetan Comment," *Sowetan*, 20 March 1996.

27 Baleta, "AIDS 'Made Real,'" n.p.

28 Gaye Davis, "Mandela Steps in to Cure Bad Blood in Prisons," *Weekly Mail and Guardian* 12, no. 12 (22–28 March 1996): 13.

29 "Outrage over Mine Jail Plan," *Herald Sun*, 6 March 1997, 26.

30 Jody Kollapen, "Transformation and the Challenges Facing Corrections in South Africa," address delivered at a Penal Reform International Seminar, London, 19 May 1995, *Penal Lexicon*, 3 November 1997, 1–5.

31 At a meeting in London on 14 September 1997 Gary Friedman and Nyanga Tshabalala, Tshabalala explained why Ekuseni offered a more promising environment for the project. At Diepkloof, where prisoners were often moved around, gansterism was rife and participants left their separate enclaves to work together for four hours each weekend and virtually occupy another world from their usual prison routine. On their return to the cell the boss and gang members often berated and effectively punished them for their participation in a project that gave these individuals "unearned" prominence. In contrast, Ekuseni is a rehabilitation center for youth with ongoing educational and vocational programs to equip inmates for reintegration into society. The Ekuseni Workshop, held 7–23 December 1998, marks the final stage of "Puppets in Prison."

32 John M. Sloop, *The Cultural Prison: Discourse, Prisons and Punishment* (Tuscaloosa: University of Alabama Press, 1996), 199.

33 Philippa Garson, "The 'AIDS Kaffirs' of Johannesburg Prison," *Weekly Mail and Guardian* 10, no. 30, 29 July–4 August 1994, 4. *Kaffir* is an offensive, abusive term for a black person in South Africa.

34 Accone, "Master Puppeteer," 4.

35 Bub and Evian, "Qualitative Evaluation," 36.

36 Donald G. McNeil Jr., "A New Stage for South Africa," *New York Times*, 6 July 1997, 2:5.

37 In "The Deadly Gender Gap," an article in the *Village Voice*, 30 December 1998–5 January 1999, Mark Schoofs reports: "Just last week a South African activist, Gugu Dlamini, was stoned and beaten to death by her neighbours, furious that she had spoken out about her life with HIV." When stigmatization combines with violence to enact such brutality in the world outside prison, how much more complex is the experience of HIV/AIDS within the prison community. This incident occurred at the same time that the final Puppets in Prison workshop was completed in Ekuseni.

38 I would like to honor the memory of the South African activist Simon Mkoli, who died of AIDS-related causes on 30 November 1998. His warmth, vitality, gentleness, and resolute commitment touched me, as did his life and legacy of activism, which will continue to make a difference in international venues and throughout South Africa, particularly in Johannesburg and Soweto, where he founded GLOW (Gay and Lesbian Organization of the Witwatersrand), TAP (Township AIDS Project), and PAMP (Positive African Men Project).

CHAPTER 17

Graham Pitts

reLOCATED

Project: A tribute to tenants

Location: Kensington Housing Estate

What happens to such lives, to such memories, if people are "relocated"?

WHEN WE FIRST ARRIVED on the estate, around April 2001, we met first with cranes, scaffolding and padlocked fencing. A sizeable section of walkup flats (four storey buildings without lifts) were reduced to rubble, while another sizeable section of the estate felt like a ghost town as flats were emptied and boarded up for stage two demolition. The simultaneous process of relocating, demolishing and renovating meant no easy access to people and communities. They were in the throes of moving beyond their community borders, moving from balconies to courtyards, moving from rooftop views to grassy borders, moving furniture, pets, babies . . . into new suburban landscapes with varying degrees of emotion, from deep anxiety to high euphoria, from **I can't wait to leave this place** to **I want to come back!**

The stories, photographs, opinions and feelings were gathered through a varied process of interviews, Polaroid, drama and writing workshops, informal discussions, on-site displays and Outreach connections . . . Several thick notebooks and hundreds of images and stills later, we wanted to creatively present our work in a way that reflected the structural demise and reinvention, and the complexity of feeling evoked through prescribed living and sudden change. Further, we wanted to acknowledge the estate as a pivotal piece of contemporary Australian history, so it was imperative that our final presentations be based at the estate.

Angela Bailey, Angela Costi, artsworkers, Kensington housing estate

Jane Crawley consulted with the nucleus of a reference group of residents and community development workers at the estate. Funds were supplied for photographer Angela Bailey to immediately commence documenting what was happening to the site and its people. Before long she was joined by writer Angela Costi. No-one knew what might eventuate. The imperative was to capture the time.

The success of long-term community cultural development (though no one at the early stage knew *reLOCATED* would ultimately be a two-year organic process) often depends on stage-by-stage activities. These usually result in artworks which have been developed in collaboration with the members of a community. They are presented to the broader community and invite responses which in turn feed into the next activity. Guided by the reference group of agency representatives and residents, the artsworkers of *reLOCATED* began producing postcards and exhibitions in the flats.

In 2001, two types of postcards depicting the estate were dropped in letterboxes, posted to relocated tenants and distributed to the wider community. A series of photographs with text were produced as stickers and pasted around the estate, inviting public response.

> FLAT EXHIBITION. Apart from a small wardrobe and a large poster of an Essendon football player, Flat 1/36 Derby Street was empty, stripped and ready for demolition. This three bedroom flat was turned into an exhibition space by keeping the flat's internal structures intact and highlighting life on the estate through:
>
> * large scale photographs
> * found items left behind
> * portrait gallery of photos and dialogue
> * mapping the estate
> * origami crane curtain with photos and story
> * poetry, stories and text on the estate's history.
>
> Excerpt from book *reLOCATED*

Photographer Angela Bailey had studied in Brisbane before moving to Melbourne to study fine art and photography at the Victorian College of Arts. Writer Angela Costi came to the project with ten plays already written and produced. A lawyer who turned to writing in 1993, she says she found herself relatively poor but incredibly enriched by experiences such as Kensington.

By 2002 a large amount of material had been gathered through the exhibitions, work-shops, sound recordings, performances and many other contributions of residents. It was decided to publish a book with free copies given to all tenants. But much of the same material could be used beforehand in a final performance, a true on-site culmination, a ritual event, Barry Laing joined the team as a theatrical director and dramaturg (script adviser). He worked with Angela Costi on the script, both of them believing that the work should not be a piece of naturalistic theatre with a single narrative plot: there were instead many individual stories to be shared.

The performance/installation entitled **reLOCATED** was produced in April 2002. The stage was a large grassy area between two walk-ups, with the audience sitting at banquet tables. Familiar sounds, such as those of demolition and pigeons in flight, were amplified through the space. Images of the estate were projected through windows or blown up and projected onto buildings. Professional actors and tenants performed together or, in many cases, the tenants performed alone.

The event continued, scene by scene, before an audience of hundreds. The stories were familiar to some, unknown to others, but always provided a strong sense of both communal grieving and shared proud celebration.

At one stage, all the balconies of the flats suddenly blazed into light. On every balcony was at least one woman banging a pot. They were re-enacting their welcome of the New Year, banging away at the pots.

> There was no thought initially of it turning into a long-term residency. But Angela Costi came aboard, we were given a room to work out of, next to the Tenants Union, we visited people who had already moved out . . . and everything just grew organically as we spent more and more time with a mix of Anglos, some of whom had been there for thirty years, and Greeks, Italians, Vietnamese, people from Somalia and the Horn of Africa. A varied, extraordinary, invigorating mix . . .
>
> It wasn't a sealed-off enclave but you didn't see a lot of people just walking through, it did have a stigma attached because it had been ear-marked for demolition. The people who still lived there actually had a good range of services nearby in terms of health services, the recreation centre, the adventure playground, bus, transport, shops . . . and the actual environment of the estate, in terms of what had been planted and allowed to grow, was amazing. There were all these simply wonderful pockets. Like a garden which had been planted by boys long ago as a part of an employment program and the older people were very proud of the luscious environment.
>
> I realised that people had formed a close relationship not just with their neighbours but with the place itself. Hardly your stereotyped ugly housing estate? Some wanted to move out, of course, couldn't wait to go. But for many it was loaded with recollections, memories and beauty.
>
> **Angela Bailey**, *interview*

We are at 504, 100 Altona Street: that's me, my 2 sons, 5 cats, 1 dog and my Oscars – they're the large black and orange fish in my aquarium.

My neighbour at 504 was Evelyn MacMillan, 502 was the Vietnamese
family with three girls, 505 was the Kosminskis, 506 was Pierre, 507 was
Dot and her sons Michael and Jimmy (Michael's now dead), 508, that lady
died, 404 were the Coffeys, Edith, Bill, Keith and Andrew, 401 were
the Dosleys, 307 was her grandson Tony, 206 were Mr. and Mrs. Kemp,
306 the Cedelands family . . . on Derby Street, at 20, were the Cattons,
at 24 were the Swanstons and the Shells, in flat 1 of block 2, there was
Shirley and in the same block was Donald, Robby, Gary, Mark and Dianne,
at 44 Derby Street were the Gottingers at 72 Derby Street were Sandra
Lawrence and Tommy, the Spanish couple, Mr. and Mrs. Cung were at
100 Altona, 30 Derby Street Ruby, Guy and Margaret Campbell, the Lucas'
lived in 72 Altona, the Reirdons in 74. Oh, and Lucy Winkworth at 303,
100 Altona Street – she's passed on.

Sandra Joy, tenant, performing in *reLOCATED*

WOMAN CHORUS:
Happy New Year!
It's gonna be bigger and better
It's gonna be louder than ever
Gonna give up the smokes, I am
Sweet biscuits an' soapies, pokies
An bingo – give 'em all up, I am.
Happy New Year!
It's gonna be bigger and better
It's gonna be louder than ever
Watching our boys playing footy
Watching our girls wearing lippy
Watching our boys . . .

Suddenly, unexpectedly, a male streaker comes running through the crowd.

Go slower, go slower
Is that your son, Bev?
Nah, it's Trev, Pam's boy.
Little Trevor Watson?
My God he's grown.
He's a big boy.
Sure is.
Not now Elaine . . .
Aw what's the harm.
Happy New Year!

Then another male streaker comes running through. The women continue to bang
and bravo him on but now more as a background experience: as Wendy's vivid memory
is evoked.

WENDY: *(To the streaker.)* **Ronnie, I know it's you.**
The streaker looks up at one of the balconies as he's running by.
STREAKER: *(Sheepishly.)* **Hello sweetness . . . I mean Mrs. T.**
WENDY: Sweetness – that was my nickname. Jim's name for me.
           Sweetness, can you get me a packet of cigarettes? When he
           knew I was going up the shops. Whenever you walked up Macauley
           Road you'd be there for a couple of hours, you'd bump into someone
           you know. I'd see Beryl, or someone. We had 3 banks, 3 butchers, 2
           supermarkets including Johnsons. Now no banks, 1 butcher and Safeways
           is now up at Racecourse Road. **But as long as your nails are clean,
           your hair is done, and your shoes are clean, you can go
           anywhere.** Jim lived by that – God rest his soul.

SCENE SEVEN. *Banging Our Pots and Pans. reLOCATED*

During the early stages of the project, Angela Costi and Angela Bailey had found tiny
paper cranes in the window of an empty boarded-up flat. The thoughts the discovery
inspired became the poetic Scene 13, The Crane's Story in the *reLOCATED*
performance. The earlier exhibitions in the empty flats had also led to the identification
of the person who made the paper cranes.

The *reLOCATED* project in all its various forms and manifestations captured a time
of great change in the lives of thousands of public housing residents. Many of them
went to live in the outer suburbs of Melbourne and set about rebuilding the social
connections vital to a sense of belonging. But as Melbourne Lord Mayor John So said
in his introduction to the book *reLOCATED*, the project ensured the individual and
collective memories associated with the estate were not erased with its physical
demolition.

> Hundreds of little, colourful origami cranes hung together by string and
> wire as curtains. We also came across a photo of a little girl standing
> proudly in front of these origami curtains. The tradition of shenbazuru
> states that once you've made your thousandth crane, you can make a wish
> for such things as health, peace, a happy home . . . what did the little girl
> wish for? Unfortunately the girl and her family couldn't be traced. **They're
> somewhere in Yarraville,** someone said. But the little girl, Marilyn
> Ngo, was eventually found. Through serendipity her Grandfather, Mr.
> Tran, attended the exhibition at the Estate and saw the cranes. He was so
> overjoyed that he promptly left to fetch her. Marilyn Ngo said she had
> made every crane herself but her wish will always remain a secret.
> **Angela Costi: Angela Bailey,** from the book *reLOCATED*

Hundreds and hundreds of paper birds
The wishes cranes carry
Almost in flight

Make a wish
Why did the little girl leave them behind?
Maybe they were too fragile for her to take with her
Maybe she wanted them to stay
Her wish had come true?
After her very last bird
She would have sat down before
all of them
Looked up and wished for . . . for?
Good health? A great birthday?
A party dress?
A happy home in Yarraville
A happy home
What would you wish for?
To leave and be happy
To stay and be happy
To return and be happy
Make a wish
A wish . . .

SCENE THIRTEEN. *The Crane's Story, reLOCATED*

The group was united in its desire to work against stereotyping and
objectification and to avoid becoming too controlling. This meant, among
other things, that no specific outcome was envisaged or expected and no
time frame firmly set. It meant the artists could spend a significant time
on the Estate without pressure to achieve predetermined results. This was
crucial to allow connections with tenants whose trust of photographers and
writers was not too strong given the way in which their homes and lives
had been depicted by media in the past. People could control the degree
to which they became involved and could in a real sense determine what
happened in the project. The **reLOCATED** project ensured the individual
and collective memories associated with the estate were not erased with
its physical demolition. It invited the public onto the estate to share these
memories and it provided opportunities for change to happen with dignity
and pride. It also made great art.

The Lord Mayor of Melbourne, **John So,** in the preface
to the book *reLOCATED*

CHAPTER 18

Ana Flores

AIDS narrative murals*

THE VISUAL CONCEPTS for most of my community art projects are inspired by world mythology and folk art traditions: traditions that arise out of the people's collective imagination and voices. Through the use of art I also try to create a bridge between ancient belief and some of our contemporary concerns. In the fall of 2002, these concepts and my understanding of community were uniquely tested when I was invited to do an artist residency at the York Correctional Institution for Women, a maximum security prison in Niantic, Connecticut. Joe Lea, an educator, library media specialist and self-proclaimed arts administrator at the school for the prison wanted me to propose an idea for a collaborative HIV/AIDS mural project.

As I prepared for the project and read more about HIV/AIDS, I felt that this issue had such tragic and heroic proportions that a visual form was needed that forcefully conveyed the drama and urgency of the epidemic. The words 'tragic', 'heroic', and 'drama', words that come to us from Ancient Greek, provided the initial inspiration and key to the visual form. I turned to the tradition of Greek vases from the fourth to sixth centuries: these vases were not only functional objects, they served a larger role of providing a space for the culture's visual narratives. For a largely illiterate society without the flood of imagery we take for granted today, the stylized, visual narratives illustrated on these surfaces in the limited palettes of black on red clay, red on black or black on white clay carried the equivalent impact a billboard has today on a deserted stretch of road. The contemporary vases I would design with the York women would not be sculptural, they would be painted at life size – like a billboard – on wooden panels.

Before the project began it was required that I attend an introductory session on the unique social factors and restrictions of prison life. I was met by Mary, a small, middle-aged woman, a veteran volunteer, who guided me through a series of six security stations, each with a set of massive metal doors opening and closing behind us. The last doors opened into a large well-lit corridor permeated with the smell of cut onions. Mary told me this was the entrance to the school and prison kitchen. Women dressed in baggy blue prison uniforms, wearing clear shower caps on their hair were pushing trollies loaded high with potatoes, and paper products. Several of the younger ones criss-crossed dangerously close to us, giggling as they played a restrained game of bumper cars. To the left doors opened into the kitchen, busy with the lunchtime meal being prepared by more women with plastic caps on their heads.

Mary said little but I could see she was closely observing my response to the inner workings of the institution. She led me to her office, unlocked her metal door and we walked into a space the size of a large closet brimming with crocheted handiwork: crocheted picture frames, tea cozies, baby blankets, hats of all sizes, afghans. The soft, delicate colored objects were strewn on every available surface, hanging from book edges, dangling from a lamp, stuffed into boxes pushed into corners, softening the hard contours of the cement block construction. With little emotion she told me 'This is what I do with the women', and proceeded to clear a space on her desk and pull up a chair for me to sit. I smiled and looked closely at the baby booties and hat that were on the edge of her desk. Upon inspection, I could see the unevenness of the weave but I deeply appreciated the slow, meditative, functional process that Mary shared with these women: these mothers and grandmothers.

We did not linger over the handiwork. Mary wanted to make sure I understood the history and regulations of the prison, with its strict set of rules of what not to wear, or say, or bring, and a list of objects and art materials that were forbidden: scissors and knives could be used as weapons, clay could be used to jam a lock. She told me I had been invited in to serve as a teacher and as a positive role model but warned me that prisoners were very quick at 'sizing me up', finding my weak points and figuring out how they could manipulate me, to ask me to bring illegal things in for them.

After my experience with Mary, I went down the hall to meet with Joe Lea. His office was full of light – maps, original artwork of Buddhist themes and photographs of modern dancers. He told me this was his growing, private collection of art which he displayed here for his enjoyment and for that of the women. In his office, he had also gathered a small group of teachers who would be exploring the interdisciplinary aspects of my project and how they could work it into their writing curriculum. They were already excited about the narrative aspects of the murals, the history of the vases and the discussing the etymology of words in the English language derived from Ancient Greek. During our brainstorming session, a number of writing prompts were developed to encourage the AIDS narratives from the students:

- Imagine you are the HIV/AIDS virus, what would you want to say?
- Explain to a family member of loved one that you have HIV/AIDS.
- Write a letter to a friend who has passed away as a result of AIDS.
- Share a memory or story with someone who has HIV/AIDS.

Excited by the compassionate and creative educators I had met, I began the project with a core group of women, members of an AIDS/HIV support group, and other students interested in participating. There were twelve in this small group. I showed slides of the Greek vases and discussed some of the myths and battles illustrated on them. We also spoke about the often invisible battle being waged against HIV/AIDS by themselves and loved ones. They began to see the parallels between themselves, and the stylized warriors, the gods and goddesses depicted on these ancient clay surfaces. Our studio was the back half of a large classroom used to teach a Health Aide Certificate Program, during 'open studio' sessions other inmates could come in and help or just observe. I also did short workshops around this theme with other groups of women.

The AIDS narrative writing theme inspired many personal essays and poems. From these we chose compeling anecdotes to act out. Using the hallway as a small theatre area, a small group acted out scenes of professional and emotional support, living with the disease and mourning the loss of loved ones. The actors would freeze in different positions which captured the essence of these situations. Students who were not acting would draw the actors at full scale by tracing their bodies and shadows directly onto large brown paper. These life size figures on brown paper were then composed into monumental vases shapes outlined on wooden panels. I had chosen to work with two traditional shapes found in Greek vases: the 'Kraters' – expansive, bold-shaped urns with florid handles used to commemorate victories in battle; and 'Lekythos' – tall slim vessels with minimal handles that held oil for libations to the dead.

During the six weeks of the project, students were involved with all the phases of the work: preparing the panels, composing scenes, finding faces in magazines, drawing and painting. The communal working process created a place where personal stories could be told, expressed and woven into a larger whole. Slowly they each discovered an artist inside of themselves, a way to express their voices, to transfigure their pain and loss into something of beauty. One student, Annie, who claimed on the first day not be to be able to draw evolved into one of the master artists on the mural. On the first day I helped her as she struggled to draw a dove – a dove to symbolize hope. After a few attempts and coaxing from me, she drew a very beautiful small bird that brought out a great smile in her. As the mural panels evolved, her small dove was enlarged and became the central motif on the panel entitled 'AIDS is a part of us all'. As her confidence grew she began to guide other women and protected the aesthetic evolution of each panel. In the end there were four panels: two were 8′ × 8′, two were 4′ × 8′.

The mural project was made possible by the support from two excellent funding groups, the Concerned Citizens for Humanity (CCfH) and Community Partners in Action, both experienced with promoting and collaborating on arts projects in Connecticut prisons. These groups not only celebrate creativity as a way of healing and personal growth, they also believe that these incarcerated voices have much to tell us. They encouraged and engineered the dissemination of the visuals from the AIDS narrative as graphics for numerous health brochures, posters and calendars that were distributed statewide. The photographs of the process of making the panels became part of a traveling exhibition of prison art and the murals were permanently

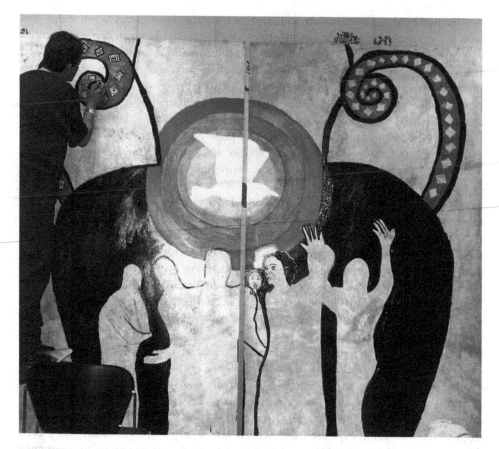

Figure 9 HIV/AIDS mural project in a women's prison in Connecticut, USA.
Photo: Ana Flores.

installed in the corridors of the York school. The compilation of writing that came out of the project was published in a booklet that was distributed for World AIDS day, 1 December 2002, the writing exercise was also the impetus for a 'One Vision, Many Voices' poetry jam, structured as an artist residency, with a visiting poet who helped the women write and perform poems about their experiences with AIDS. This project culminated in a CD, using an image from the AIDS narratives mural, which was distributed statewide on World AIDS day 2003. In the end, the dove that Annie drew flew free and high outside of the prison walls, and the women had shown us that the power of their collective imagination can never be caged.

Note

* A collaborative art project orchestrated by visual artist Ana Flores and the women in the school of York Correctional Institute, Niantic, Connecticut, USA. Funded by the Concerned Citizens for Humanity.

Rituals, embodiment, challenge

Introduction to
Part Four

■ Petra Kuppers and Gwen Robertson

THIS SECTION PRESENTS WRITINGS that put community performances within
the realm of embodied experience. Bodily being – located in specific sites, institutions,
ways of thinking and ways of knowing – is the material out of which community performance
shapes itself. The practices discussed in these sections acknowledge this material ground
of performance work, the political embeddedness of specific bodies, the daily practices of
embodiment, and spin their processes out of these embodied specifics.

Anna Halprin's work in California, as analyzed by **Libby Worth** and **Helen Poynor**,
provides a perspective on alternative forms of politics in shared ritual, and shows folk-forms
and healing practices as aspects of community performance work. UK-based dance artist
Christine Lomas models ways of thinking about non-exclusionary dance politics in her
discussion of work that values the aesthetic contribution of dancers with developmental or
cognitive disabilities (and the problems of naming 'conditions' already points to the problems
of finding respectful and meaningful ways of engaging and creating a community). Similarly,
Petra Kuppers discusses the challenges and opportunities of non-exclusionary practices
in her work in a mental health setting. **Terry Galloway**, **Donna Nudd** and **Carrie Sandahl**
address an aesthetic of accommodation and inclusion by discussing the working methods
and assumptions of the 'Actual Lives' projects in Austin, Texas and Tallahassee, Florida.

Two texts that do not specifically draw from community performance, but intersect with
it, complement this section: **Deborah Hay** shares choreographic processes and the alchemy
of creation in her instructions for a four-month 'Playing Awake' workshop. **Cynthia Novak**'s
discussion of contact improvisation as an art, folk and community practice shows how new
ways of thinking about performance aesthetic can open up avenues to challenge and expand
mainstream aesthetics.

Together, the texts in this section provide touchstones for thinking about embodiment
in community performance practice.

CHAPTER 19

Libby Worth and Helen Poynor

The mountain performances, *Circle the Earth* and *The Planetary Dance*

Background and evolution

IN 1981 HALPRIN EMBARKED on a project which would sow the seeds for a major strand of her work for the next 20 years, work which is still evolving in the early years of the twenty-first century. Initiated with her husband Lawrence, as a local community project, entitled 'A Search for living Myths and Rituals through Dance and the Environment', it unexpectedly evolved into a five-year cycle of performances and community events inspired by Mount Tamalpais, where the Halprins live and work, in 1985 this transformed into *Circle the Earth*, a large-scale ritual performance which was recreated and performed in several countries until 1991. *The Planetary Dance*, a global participatory dance ritual, grew out of *Circle of the Earth* and developed alongside it from 1987 onwards. *The Planetary Dance* continues to be performed, in spring each year, by communities and groups across the globe.

Through this ongoing process Halprin has developed her practice and thinking concerning performance and ritual and working with communities. In the course of its evolution she has explored the relevance of myth and ritual in the contemporary world, pushing the boundaries of dance as a transforming medium for individuals and communities, a means of healing on a personal, community and global scale, and an effective tool for social action. Halprin refers to it as a dance which 'has been many years in the making, as many years as I have lived. It is the largest manifestation of my own search for a dance of meaning, content and spirit' (Halprin with Kaplan 1995: 1).

The mountain performances

'A Search for Living Myths and Rituals' began as a series of workshops with members of the Halprins' local community in Marin, California. The series was envisaged as 'a search for a myth with a community vision', an opportunity for the Halprins to explore 'the mythology of the collective' (Halprin with Kaplan 1995: 8) using collective creativity. For Anna Halprin it marked a broadening of her work with students at the San Francisco Dancers' Workshop and the Tamalpa Institute in personal and creative process, to a community-orientated approach. Lawrence Halprin's contribution was crucial since he had been 'working with groups of people around issues of community development in relationship to the environment' (Halprin with Kaplan 1995: 8). The project and its subsequent developments also signalled a return for Anna Halprin to public performance. The mountain performances were performed by Tamalpa dancers in a local theatre and were followed by a community event. *Circle the Earth* involved a minimum of 100 performers and an audience of witnesses. With *The Planetary Dance* the performance element, together with any notion of audience, dropped away as the event became a participatory ritual.

In the 'Living Myths and Rituals' workshops the Halprins used art, movement and the environment to draw the community participants together, creating a context and shared language to facilitate the emergence of a group myth. They had no pre-conceived idea about what would evolve. Early in the workshops the image of a mountain kept recurring; more than an archetypal image this theme had poignant local significance. The community was located at the base of Mount Tamalpais, a beautiful natural reserve usually widely enjoyed by the public, steeped in legend and seen by Anna Halprin as 'the spiritual center of our area' (Halprin with Kaplan 1995: 8). At that time the trails on the mountain had been closed because several women had been murdered by a serial killer who was still at large. Through the workshops the mountain emerged as a 'living myth' central to the community, with a clear connection to the participants' lives. 'We discovered our need to reclaim the mountain in order to reclaim our sense of community and vision' (Halprin with Kaplan 1995: 9). The project culminated in *In the Mountain, On the Mountain*, a two-day event created in response to this need. *In the Mountain* was a ritual theatre performance by dancers from the Tamalpa Institute (including Halprin) with a chorus of participants from the 'Living Myths and Rituals' project. The performance ritual was divided into three parts, Initiation, Offerings and Regeneration, imagined to be taking place in the heart of the mountain. It was dedicated to the spirit of the mountain, the Miwaks, the indigenous people who lived beneath her including those among them who had lost their lives, and the women who were killed on the trails. The purpose of the performance is clearly stated:

> It is our intention to evoke the spirit of the mountain through our performance and to feel a unified sense of community. . . . We hope this performance will inspire you to become your own performers, and to find your own personal and collective myths tomorrow 'On the Mountain'

as we do a ritualized walk down its trails. The walk will symbolize the re-investment of hope and the rebirth of Spring.

(Tamalpa Institute 1981)

This was a performance in which the life of a community in crisis was clearly interwoven. Community participation had furnished the central theme of the performance, which included ritual re-enactments of the violence. Friends and relations of the victims were in the audience. There was tension as people wondered if the murderer might attend the performance.

During the night of the performance in *Passage*, a preparation for the community ritual the next day, participants were encouraged to create their own rituals and ceremonies culminating in a sunrise ceremony. On the second day, *On the Mountain*, 80 members of the community of all ages, invited to wear white, travelled up the mountain by bus. As a group they walked to the summit to view the four directions which had been invoked in the performance. Participants were asked to consider what they wanted to restore in their lives. There was a silent ritualized walk down the trails; offerings, including poetry, meditations, music, song and a tree planting, were made at the sites of the murders 'as a way of marking these tragedies, and affirming the community's need to reclaim the mountain' (Halprin with Kaplan 1995: 9). The procession was completed carrying bamboo poles and a panel from the *Running Fence* by the well-known artist Christo, objects that had been invested with symbolic significance during the performance, and culminated in a sunset ceremony.

Two days later the police were alerted by an anonymous telephone call. Three weeks later the killer, who had been active for two years, was captured. While not claiming direct causality between the ritual and the killer's arrest, Halprin is clear that the two events are related: 'In one sense we performed a prayer and our prayer was answered' (Halprin 1995: 230). What is clear is that a ritual had been created and enacted, which effectively reclaimed a site of significance to local people, a site that had been desecrated by violence and had become unsafe for them. The Halprins' search for an authentic living myth and ritual empowered a community paralysed by fear, by a combination of expression and action through an interaction of the arts and the environment. The outcome was more far reaching than the Halprins had anticipated.

The next year (1982) a dance of thanksgiving was created to commemorate the end of the murders and the renewal of the mountain. Perhaps this would have been the end of the sequence if it had not been for Don Jose Mitsuwa, an indigenous Huichol shaman who came to the Tamalpa Institute to present a deer dance ceremony. He commended what had taken place on the mountain, describing it as 'one of the most sacred places on earth' (Halprin with Kaplan 1995: 9) but commented that it would be necessary to dance there for five years in order for the purification to be successful. Halprin followed this advice and created mountain dances for the following three years. The synchronicity that marked the first event continued, as it took five years to convict the murderer.

While the essential theme of the dances remained the struggle of life against death, each year the performances had a different emphasis. *Return to the Mountain* (1983) was the first one to be described as a peace dance. It included a dance inspired by animal imagery and a ceremony for peace between people and the environment. Don Jose was invited to participate in the ceremony on the summit of the mountain. *Run to the Mountain* (1984) was a dance for peace among all the peoples of the world. Running was the central motif 'because running is common to all people and helps communicate the urgency for peace within ourselves, with each other, with our communities, our nations and throughout the world (Tamalpa Institute 1984). In the lead up to the performance the company of Tamalpa Dancers ran with brightly coloured banners across Golden Gate Bridge. The audience were gradually becoming more involved in the performance, participating in communal running dances. At the beginning of the mountain ceremony on the day after, the performance runners, including members of the audience, ran up the mountain from the four directions. The spiritual leaders invited to participate alongside Don Jose now included a representative from the American Indian Council of Marin and a Presbyterian minister.

Circle the Mountain, a Dance in the Spirit of Peace (1985) completed the five-year cycle and marked a radical change in structure that prefigured its transformation into *Circle the Earth*. The dance embodied a vision of world peace, 'the underlying objective is to make a vivid statement for mutual understanding and peace – one that can be taken from its performance here and shared with many people in many places' (Tamalpa Institute 1985).

Halprin felt that a small performance company was no longer a potent enough vehicle for such a vision. She aimed to create a dance with 100 participants, so that the scale of the vision would be matched by the scale of the performance:

> Making a peace dance, like making peace is not a small task. It takes the harmony of many to stop a war that only a few might begin. So our peace dance needs the commitment of more than two, or ten, or twenty, or even fifty performers. I am seeking 100 performers. One hundred performers to create a circle large enough for clear images at peace to come through. One hundred performers to create a spirit voice, strong enough so that our peaceful song is heard and our peaceful steps felt.
>
> The weapons of war have a critical mass. So too do the hopes of peace. We need 100 performers, 200 feet, to dance upon the planet for its life and its healing – to find a dance that inspires us to keep the earth alive.
>
> (Tamalpa Institute 1985)

Halprin offered a nine-day workshop to prepare the participants who were no longer all Tamalpa trained. The second day (Easter Sunday, Buddha's birthday and the day after Passover) was spent in a ritual celebration on the mountain, Lawrence Halprin was actively involved in the group's preparation for the mountain celebration, as he had been in 'Living Myths and Rituals'. Bill Wahpehpeh from the Kickapoo and Sac and Fox tribe in Oklahoma, head of the international Indian Treaty Council, participated in the ceremony on the mountain, continuing the involvement of Native Americans. During the workshop Halprin collaborated with composer Terry Riley who created a new composition for voices for the performance. On the eighth day *Circle the Mountain* was performed to an audience of invited witnesses. The intention had broadened from restoring peace on the mountain to peace on the planet. The dance renamed itself *Circle the Earth* and began to travel. In 1985 it was recreated in sites across America including the United Nations Plaza and Central Park, New York.

'Circle the Earth'

A contemporary peace dance ritual for 100 performers, *Circle the Earth* was recreated in Marin, California, at Easter in 1986, 1987 and 1988. The format continued to be a nine-day workshop, with the second day spent in ceremonies on Mount Tamalpais, culminating in the performance. By 1987 the scores which formed the basic structure of *Circle the Earth* were clearly articulated although they continued to evolve. Many of the scores developed elements from the earlier mountain performances including running, honouring the four directions and the theme of restoration. Each year had a different emphasis. In 1987 participants were given the choice of working with Halprin or with vocalist Susan Osborn on a new musical score. In 1988, inspired partly by the events in Chernobyl, the whole event was held on the Marin headlands and the focus was on our connection with the natural environment. Every year the story of the original dance on the mountain and the capture of the killer was reiterated. This repetition served to re-enforce the event as a contemporary myth. From 1986 onwards *Circle the Earth* travelled not only across America, including being performed at the American Dance Festival and Esalen, but to Europe including Germany (Freiburg and Essen), Switzerland (outside Zurich 1989), Italy (Mont Blanc) and to Australia (Melbourne 1987) and Bali. Its growth was unprecedented. In 1987, in order to respond to the interest worldwide and to allow communities in different countries to participate in their own way, Halprin created *The Planetary Dance*, based on the 'Earth Run' score in *Circle the Earth*, which is still being performed in 2003.

Circle the Earth continued to be performed and in 1989 there was another major shift in emphasis. *Circle the Earth, Dancing with Life on the Line* confronted AIDS, a crisis which was threatening the community around San Francisco and in which Halprin had become involved through her work in the healing arts. 'From the killer on the mountain, to the killer in the world, we now journey inside to confront the potential killer within ourselves' (Tamalpa Institute 1989). Participants included members of two groups Halprin had been working with: STEPS Theatre Company for People Challenging AIDS and Women with Wings for Women Challenging AIDS through Dance and Ritual. AIDS was still seen as a frightening taboo surrounded by ignorance and prejudice. Halprin confronted this taboo head-on:

> Among the dancers this year will be men and women in various states of
> wellness after exposure to the HIV virus. Their healing journey will be
> the focus of the 1989 performance of *Circle the Earth*. But *Circle the Earth*
> is not just for people who are HIV+; it is for all of us. We need to dance
> together.

AIDS is a crisis of the body, and in this crisis it is important the body speak in its own language movement. AIDS touches not only those who face it, but also those who do not. This year we ask YOU to dance with those among us who are fighting for life, to support the commitment and honor the courage of our brothers and sisters who are challenging AIDS.

(Tamalpa Institute 1989)

This version of *Circle the Earth* was the culmination of the work of all the previous years. For Halprin it was 'the first time where our goal was not at a distance from the ritual itself (Tamalpa Institute 1989). The personal and collective crises addressed were totally interconnected. Like the first performance of *In the Mountain, On the Mountain, Dancing with Life on the Line* was addressing an immediate and specific issue. The intensity of both the process and the performance reflected the immediacy of the crisis for all concerned, participants and witnesses alike. It closely paralleled Halprin's own experiences dealing with cancer and she led the participants with passion in the performance. In this performance her long-term concern with healing was fully integrated in the artistic process. The effects of *Dancing with Life on the Line* were so far reaching that this version of *Circle the Earth* was recreated in 1991. This was the last time that *Circle the Earth* was performed in its entirety, although Halprin continued to work with elements of it in *The Planetary Dance* and in workshops.

'The Planetary Dance'

With the increase of requests for *Circle the Earth* to be run in different parts of America and the world, it became clear that Halprin would not be able to facilitate them all. Although other facilitators had been trained by Halprin to run *Circle the Earth*, if the dance was to grow into a global form as she had envisaged, '100 communities world-wide performing this dance simultaneously via satellite' (Tamalpa Institute 1986b), it would be necessary to create a simpler form. The new dance ritual, called *The Planetary Dance*, was based on the 'Earth Run' section from *Circle the Earth* since this was a dance that 'would be accessible to many people, no matter where they lived' (Halprin with Kaplan 1995: 11). The flyer that went out to friends, colleagues and former students in 1987 explained that the intention was to create a worldwide performance in the spirit of peace with all those who had touched *Circle the Earth*.

It was never Halprin's intention that the Marin format for the dance should be slavishly adhered to across the world and one reason for selecting the 'Earth Run' from *Circle the Earth* was that, as a closed score, it was the easiest to facilitate and follow. As a ritual it was self-contained. More significantly the activity itself acted as a metaphor for the intention of achieving 'harmony and peace in our lives' through its demand for group awareness 'as people run together – accommodating each others' physical capabilities and speeds' in a 'moving act of Peace' (Planetary Dance Board 1988). Although the instructions for the score were precise, offering a unity of purpose and activity, there was emphasis in the invitation to participating groups on two ways that the dance could be made to resonate with the local community's needs/character as well as the global intention. Groups were invited to 'frame the score (preparation and closure) in different ways a ceremony, ritual, blessing, or dance pertaining to something special in your community or culture . . .' (Halprin 1987) or to change some of the resources in the 'Earth Run' score, particularly the spoken text. If, even with these suggestions, it was not possible to organize a run, then there were other ways that individuals or families could participate through, for instance, doing the 'Peace Dance Meditation' (part of the first preparatory score for *Circle the Earth*).

While from 1987 to 1991 *The Planetary Dance* in Marin ran alongside *Circle the Earth*, from 1992 onwards it settled into a regular day-long format that varied slightly each year in response to the chosen issue and altering community involvement. Each spring the event began with a group of all ages greeting the sunrise with ceremonies and songs, many having run to the summit of Mount Tamalpais. The men's and women's rituals that took place simultaneously on local beaches became regular features of the day. All groups met at a site on the mountain to share readings, stories and interdenominational prayers before rehearsing for the 'Earth Run'. At this point greetings from other groups taking part in the dance from many parts of the world were read out, reaffirming the global nature of the dance ritual. Halprin then led everyone in a long snake into a carefully prepared site to form a square of kneeling people within a circle (defined by flour and banked straw in *The Planetary Dance* 2002). With drummers and musicians playing to keep a regular pulse and help the runners maintain energy and focus the 'Earth Run' was performed in a series of concentric circles.

While extra runs might be included for the children or 'in memory of loved ones who have died' (Halprin and friends 1995), the essence of the dance remained the same. This included each dancer voicing a dedication for their run, and a unified intention to dance '[a] prayer for peace among people and peace with the Earth' (Halprin and Planetary Dance Community 2002). The day concluded with thanksgiving, music and a feast.

Since this was a global dance ritual, it was important to set up lines of communication that would allow groups to grasp the size and impact of the whole event. Halprin had requested feedback from all those who had participated in the first *Planetary Dance* (1987) and due to time differences across the world this began to arrive by phone, first from Amanda Levy in New Zealand before the dance had even begun in Marin. Over the next few months Halprin 'received word from groups in Switzerland, Australia, Germany, Spain, Mexico, Israel, England, Egypt, New Zealand, Indonesia, India and many places in the United States' (Halprin 1987). By 1996, as Halprin had envisaged, *The Planetary Dance* had been performed by over 2000 people in 37 countries. The dance continues to be performed each spring across the world but by 2002 Halprin no longer knew how many people from how many countries take part as it had become too large to track.

The 'living myth'

Despite the radical changes that took place during the creation of the mountain dances, *Circle the Earth* and *The Planetary Dance*, there are continuous threads that link them, as emphasized by the recent publicity that states 2002 will be the '22nd annual world-wide Planetary Dance' (Halprin and Planetary Dance Community 2002). Although there have not been 22 years of *The Planetary Dance*, the connections between the different forms are seen to be sufficiently strong and significant to be acknowledged in this way. Some of the major contributory elements that have supported the longevity and expansion of the dance, from its early performance structure through to its current participatory form, are considered below.

In 1987 Halprin described the score for *The Planetary Dance* as 'open-ended and self-renewing', adding that: 'It could be the recycling score to all future *Planetary Dances*' (Planetary Dance Board 1988). Judging by the version held on Mount Tamalpais (2002) and in many locations around the world, this has remained the case. The essential 'ingredients' pinpointed in 1988 were all apparent, yet it was not a tired repetition of the same material, but an invigorating, heartfelt, community response to new challenges that had arisen through the year. In the wake of the attacks on America on 11 September 2001, the escalation of violence between Israelis and Palestinians and the fear of nuclear war between India and Pakistan, tension was evident amongst the participants of the spring 2002 *Planetary Dance*. Although much of the structure remained the same, changes were made in the choice of text and in the way the four directions were marked in the walk around the peak of Mount Tamalpais. These reflected a sense of urgency in the need to look beyond America to forge greater links and understandings across nations. Individual dedications for the 'Earth Run' were highly charged as news arrived of the dance rituals being held in New York's Central Park and in different countries around the world. Making room for the individual statement of commitment to act for 'peace among people and peace with the earth' (Halprin and Planetary Dance Community 2002) was just one of the means by which *The Planetary Dance* shifted and stayed vibrant year after year.

From the original exploration that the Halprins undertook in their 1980–1 workshops 'A Search for Living Myths and Rituals through Dance and the Environment', the idea of the 'living myth' has remained crucial, it was described as:

> a narrative pattern giving significance to our existence, whether we invent or discover its meaning. A myth is not a fantasy or an untruth. It is a true story we discover in our bodies, and it is both unique and common to us all.
>
> (Halprin and Kaplan 1995: 4)

Every year the original 'myth' of the killings on Mount Tamalpais was retold as a reminder of both the history of the event and the purpose of this particular style of dance ritual. While the retelling of the 'myth', along with other actions and ceremonies directly echoed previous dances, repetitions alone would not keep the dance alive. There were more fundamental issues facing contemporary society that needed to be addressed: 'We live in a society fractured by differences and a series of dishonored tribal and cultural affiliations. The absence of a solid community base creates a spiritual and social vacuum that needs to be filled' (Halprin with Kaplan 1995: 4).

From the start in 1981, it was clear that the performance must address the community's shared cause and desire for action. In shaping this first dance and the subsequent performance rituals, Halprin used terms such as myth, ritual, ceremony and prayer in conjunction with dance and performance. This opened out the original community need to a broader perspective, suggesting that a higher power be engaged or contacted. The issue of spirituality and belief systems that this approach raised is a vexed one, since a premise of the work was to engage with a society fractured by differences who do not share religious beliefs or indeed see religion as relevant to their lives. How then is it possible to call upon a 'higher power'? Whose symbols and rituals are they?

Halprin refers to the centrality of the 'living myth' throughout the performance series because she values individual input bound by a common intention. In taking part in the dances it is necessary to recognize both the importance of creating a community with shared tasks reflective of a joint intention, combined with an acknowledgement of the differences each person brings from their own community. The individual's contribution and story is essential to the growth of the collective myth and is one of the reasons for Halprin's insistence that contemporary ritual making should not import wholesale, established rituals from a particular religion or culture. Halprin's close contact with Native Americans and particularly with the people of the Pomo Tribe, into which she was initiated, has had a profound and lasting influence on her beliefs. However, she is adamant that the way to find and develop 'living myths' is not through the appropriation of ancient or indigenous peoples' myths and rituals:

> The history of Western culture is largely one of the exploitation and destruction of indigenous cultures. We must return to the resources that are really our own – our bodies and our experiences – to forge a new way of honoring peace and human dignity.
>
> (Halprin with Kaplan 1995: 5)

From 1981 onwards the history of the performance has been enriched year by year through the 'gifts' of those who participated in it. This enabled the piece to renew itself in kaleidoscopic fashion as fragments gifted by a particular year, individual or group shifted into central focus and others moved to the periphery. For instance elements in the ceremonies that connect with Native American practices were present through Native American participation in the dance. In another country entirely other symbols and activities would emerge in response to the needs of the local community.

There is no doubt that the project the Halprins assigned themselves – the search for 'living myths' – was ambitious. It involved the community in answering some 'fundamental questions' about individual and group identity combined with how these might connect with the environment, 'attitudes about life and death' and what spiritual values the group embraced (Halprin 1995: 5). If the 'myth' in Halprin's terminology is uncovering the stories around those basic questions then the term 'ritual' refers to the enactment or performance of the myth through whole group participation.

Encapsulated in the idea of the 'living myth' is a sense of fluidity of content that can adapt to political, community or circumstantial changes. In her evaluation of the 1994 *Planetary Dance* Halprin notes the importance of finding a balance within the relationship between tradition and experimentation in order to achieve this: 'In order to make rituals that create change, we need to remain in an experimental mode, while holding fast to the elements of our rituals that are weighted in time' (Halprin 1995: 236). This balance has been supported consistently through the contribution of many artists of different disciplines. Some have stayed involved over many years, while for others it has been a passing connection, but their role in collaborating on the projects has been essential to its growth and vitality. For example *The Planetary Dance* (2002) was coloured by contributions of giant painted puppets at the entrance to Santos Meadows, oral poetry, drumming, singing and violin playing at the centre of the 'Earth Run' and, at its close, classical melodies by a virtuoso whistler. Many of those who contributed through their art form or in other ways have been engaged from the start of the mountain dances. While just as welcome have been newcomers, such as the teenage group from two local schools who had worked together to offer short songs or poems and to begin the 'Earth Run' (2002).

The variety and creativity of the dances performed around the world were shown in the photographs and documentation that arrived in Marin after each *Planetary Dance*. They testified to the success of another type of collaborative process that could operate across distance and over time. Halprin's vision for a global peace dance entailed those who had taken part in *The Planetary Dance* initiating new forms in their own countries or communities. This would 'keep the material truly alive and creative' (Halprin 1987) in a process best illustrated through recounting her reaction to the growth of a sweet pea in her garden. While preparing for *The Planetary Dance* (2002) she spoke with pride of the sweet peas she had cultivated, but noted with a combination of curiosity and pique that one single plant dwarfed the others with its rich blossom, stature and luxuriant growth. She had not planted this one, it had self-seeded in the best possible spot, watered by a drip from the tap, in semi-shade protected from harsh sun and wind. The innocuous comment on the resilient self-seeder became a running metaphor for the way that participants in *The Planetary Dance* could begin the dance in their own community, finding just the right conditions and context for it to thrive (Halprin 2002a).

References

Halprin, A. (1987) Letter to Friends of Circle the Earth.

Halprin, A. (1995) *Moving Towards Life: Five Decades of Transformational Dance*, edited by R. Kaplan, Hanover and London: Wesleyan University Press.

Halprin, A. (2002a). Interview with Libby Worth, Kentfield, California, 31 April to 2 May.

Halprin and friends (1995) The Planetary Dance Flyer, Kentfield, California.

Halprin, Anna with Kaplan, R. (1995) 'Circle the Earth. A Search for Living Myths and Rituals through Dance'. Unpublished. Kenfield, California.

Halprin and Planetary Dance Community (2002) The Planetary Dance Flyer, Kentfield, California.

Planetary Dance Board (1988) Letter to Circle the Earth/Planetary Dance network.

Tamalpa Institute (1981) In the Mountain, On the Mountain program, Kentfield, California.

Tamalpa Institute (1984) Run to the Mountain program, Kentfield, California.

Tamalpa Institute (1985) Circle the Mountain, a Dance in the Spirit of Peace with Anna Halprin, promotional leaflet, Kentfield, California.

Tamalpa Institute (1986b) Circle the Earth – A Dance in the Spirit of Peace, promotional leaflet, Kentfield, California.

Tamalpa Institute (1989) Circle the Earth, Dancing with Life on the Line. Promotional Leaflet, Kentfield, Calfornia.

CHAPTER 20

Christine Lomas

Cultural constructs, community, and celebration

To MANY PEOPLE art and therapy are mutually exclusive categories, but surely this is a distinction without a natural difference, just as the work/leisure distinction is a cultural construct. This is a matter of emphasis. The "Being Ourselves" company was involved with the creation of dance; the therapeutic experience was a by-product. What predominated in our work was celebration. The core was authenticity. Surely art, by virtue of attempting to reconcile nature (birth and death) and culture (life), is inherently therapeutic. The function of art within the traditional aesthetic is to reconcile nature and culture; because it emphasizes content and form, it fails to embrace the authentic behavior of celebration. The vast majority of our potentially celebratory experiences have become ceremonial for the individual and the community, adapted rather than authentic experience, an embracing of that which is imposed and accepted unthinkingly. The ceremonial is experienced as artifice, requiring obligatory interaction by the individual; however, obligation rarely makes available or strengthens a sense of ownership or belonging. This disempowerment of the individual, a loss of self-intimacy, of significance, clearly negatively affects community experience and interaction.

MacIver, in his major work on community written almost 70 years ago, offers sentiment as a starting point for the reinstatement of the concept of community (1924, 209). By "sentiment" he means an understanding and a recognition by others of the significance of the individual, which, in turn, affords a sense of community solidarity. Although significance may be wide-ranging and disparate in relation to others, the acknowledgment and embracing of individuality support a community of solidarity and facilitate identification of sentiment. We are born into a community and are intimately dependent on community for life. In 1934, a decade after MacIver, Simpson writes,

> Community is no circumscribed sphere of social life, but rather the very life-blood of social life. Community is not simply economic, nor simply political, nor simply territorial, nor simply visceral. Nor is it all these special elements added together. Ultimately, it is a complex of conditioned emotions which the individual feels towards the surrounding world and his fellows.
>
> (quoted in Clarke 1973, 34)

As Simpson implies, communities do not empower communities; individuals empower communities. Community dance does not empower communities; individual empowerment, self-intimacy, interaction with one's authentic self, a sense of fulfillment, a feeling of achievement all contribute to the larger whole, the community of solidarity, the "we" and the "ours"; this affords a sense of security to individuals and communities of individuals.

For the individual human being, although drawing upon the limited category distinctions shared by all animals (e.g., recognition of our own species, recognition of what is edible), individual survival within the human environment is not sufficient. In our capacity to create and communicate metaphor we can see a shift from animality to humanity, which is a combination of our determination to reconcile nature and culture. If art is viewed as mediator in relation to nature and culture, then we may also view it as mediator of the authentic (nature) and the adaptive (culture) behaviors. In this sense, it becomes clear that viewing art from the traditional aesthetic is a consequence of adaptive rather than authentic behavior. Proposing an emphasis on celebration —behavior that is least inherently conservative and certainly least dependent upon prescribed behavior—implies a possible aesthetic that is inclusive rather than exclusive, optimistic rather than pessimistic. In such an aesthetic meaning results from intent and context rather than from form and content alone.

My involvement in Jabadao's work with people with special needs led to my search for understanding how these people are able, via dance, to share themselves, to interact in deeply moving and energizing ways, to perform in the traditional aesthetic and at the same time bring to the performance an empowering experience for themselves and for the audience. Jabadao works with groups of people who do not belong to the community as defined by locality, economics, institution, and geography. Instead, Jabadao works with "threshold people" (Turner, 1969), "liminal" people, on the margins; those who elude, I would suggest in some cases by necessity, the generally imposed classifications of kinship, economy, and so forth. Via dance, Jabadao involves these people in social bonding over and above any that occurs as a result of regulated social relations and organized social groups. This social bonding is a condition referred to by Turner (1969) as *communitas*: bonding people over and above socially imposed units or formal ties.

On this basis, the work of the animateur movement (whose predominant concern is community dance) can be identified as largely responding to regulated, organized social groups and being required by funding bodies to work with dance in an "appropriate" way. These funding bodies support the teaching of dance via technique, emphasizing content and form and supporting adaptive behavior, rather than exploring

Figure 10
From left to right, Suzy Mitchell, Linda McCarthy and Alison Lapham performing *Reflections*. Choreographed by Linda McCarthy. Magpie is an inclusive community dance company for adults with and without learning disabilities and has been based in Bromley, UK, for over ten years.

Photo: Phil Polglaze.

the potential of dance to capitalize on the authentic experience via celebration and concomitant communitas that community dance should offer. I am not advocating for the dismissal of form and content per se as aesthetic criteria, but I do wish to see the inclusion of intent and context as meaningful criteria. Likewise, I do not advocate the dismissal of organized social structures, but the recognition that being on the margins of society may be a condition experienced by us all and that the positive elements of communitas can inform our culture and cultural change. All of us, by virtue of our age and experience, know what it means to be on or at the margins. The people with whom Jabadao is concerned are in perpetual liminality; therefore, we must seize the by-product of liminality, communitas, and exploit it.

The recent experience of a final year undergraduate at University College Bretton Hall serves to amplify the nature and response of individuals to the physical and social engineering of communitas in relation to the elderly. The building of residential homes is society's recognition of and response to the "preliminal" in the aging process and offers a constructed communitas—the home for the elderly. During her first visit to such a "home" the student discovered that its members did not know each other's names, did not know who was living in the room next to them, that they were isolated from one another. Some individuals chose not to speak at all; others spoke only of their sadness at being taken away from their own homes and being put in a "home." The student introduced dance to the elderly residents and used it as a mediator with an emphasis on the individual, and the experience of communitas for these isolated elderly people began to emerge as they started to bond with one another.

References

References unavailable.

CHAPTER 21

Petra Kuppers

Straitjackets of representation

WITHIN OUR CULTURE, people with severe mental health problems are excluded from self-representation. The cultural histories of hysteria, depression, and schizophrenia are histories of silencing, muting the 'other'. The artwork of people institutionalized within mental health systems has often been perceived within the framework of 'therapy'. This therapeutic frame has meant that this work may be read as a way 'into the patient' as a way to understand her experiences, often as a more or less transparent tool in the diagnostic process. A representation of self outside the clinical categories is made impossible by the discourses that govern the idea of the 'free self'. Instead, the theme of madness subsumes self-expression, or governs it. Moreover, just as forms of therapy have become subjects of art discourse, many artists themselves have become case studies for different forms of treatment of 'mad' people. Antonin Artaud and Sylvia Plath, for example, have become associated with different forms of electroshock therapy. Mary Barnes has become the 'hypersane' pet-artist whom R.D. Laing claimed as recovering through her work, even while he used her as a romanticized lens for perceiving the malaise of the 'normal' world.[1]

At the same time, performance work with people diagnosed with mental health problems has to deal with a history of bodily stagings, of recognized and (potentially rehearsed) performances. The readability of 'hysteria and fits' fascinated the psycho-analysts Charcot, Freud, and Breuer. As Elaine Showalter notes, they photographed or analyzed hysteric women in turn-of-the-century French 'madhouses' and found that the strange physical contortions and paralyses of these women's bodies could be read and labeled as stage symptoms of mental states and brought back to normality by the talking cure.[2] More contemporary performances of 'madness' include Hannibal Lecter's animalistic sniffing in *The Silence of the Lambs* (1990), and the sudden and explosive destructive fits of other film madmen in *The Shining* (1980) and *Session 9*

(2001). The demented homicidal maniac has become a recognizable set piece in horror and thriller films.

By working with people in mental health settings, I soon realized the existence of a connection between the physical and the representational, their deep implication in each other. Many of my performers' physical experiences seemed to mirror their representational silencing or distortion in the media. Some were people who found no space for themselves, their bodies, their movements in their social and physical environments. They were excluded from living alone, getting an apartment, leading a life free from constant contact with medical practitioners or rigorous timetables of pills and injections. Their bodies could be invaded, as the law allows them to be drugged against their will. Many had been temporarily hospitalized. This lack of physical and mental privacy had undermined many people's ability to be confident in their use of space. The representational and social aspects of madness had affected the sense of embodiment of people diagnosed with mental health difficulties.

My experience in these settings showed that potentially, as a result of these exclusions, 'centering exercises' as every performance class knows them – could be difficult. I came to see that it is not just drug-induced spasticity and rigid body-tensions that prevented the performers from claiming the space – that is, owning the portion of a room inhabited by their bodies. Some had fundamental difficulties asserting their physical space: standing still, breathing deeply, or allowing their voices to resonate. With this inability to take space, simple actions such as reaching and touching became problematic.

As a result, validating our spatial experience became an important aspect of our work. We had to rethink spatial and temporal aspects of embodiment, and politicize them. In other words, we had to find ways to assert the simple acts of breathing and being as interventions into the social sphere. By working on the sense of embodiment at its most fundamental levels, we were at the same time working on the images and practices that limited our experience in the first place. Breathing exercises, creating an awareness of the body's inner space through visualization, feeling our muscles relax, reacting to the influx of breath: these acts became not warm-ups but the actual core event. When later during our sessions we physically walked through the room while imagining ourselves clad in exquisite clothes or waltzing through shimmering halls, this theatrical experience was designed to lead us back into our inner space experience, to strengthen our focus on the perception of movement rather than providing training to be channeled into a performance event.

Based upon these realizations, we began to use the following process in our sessions. They started and ended with meditative exercises in which we explored movement in stillness. Thus, I might lead the group through a relaxation sequence, asking them to count their breaths or see their breath run through their bodies, into their feet and hands. By slowly working their way through their bodies, always connecting the exploration back to the filling of breath and relaxing of limbs, the group members could experience themselves as taking space – able to be filled by breath, able to 'see' and 'feel' their bodies as spatial forms. While they were in a state of deep relaxation, I ran them through a visualization. These visualizations did not aim to explore psychological issues: there were no portals, doors, or other mechanisms to get the

Figure 11
The Olimpias. Video still
from *Traces*.

Photo: Margaret Sharrow.

participants to explore some inner 'truths' about themselves. Instead, all of my visualizations were aimed at sensory and movement experiences. These experiences included sailing among clouds, in outer space, through oceans, over deserts, or floating in streams and meadows. I tried to create a sensation of being corporeally engaged in an experience by using strongly kinesthetic vocabulary such as 'gliding', 'rushing', 'hovering' I also carefully avoided giving a lot of visual information (I hardly ever mentioned the colors of landscapes) but, rather, placed more importance on sensations such as 'you can feel the sun on your hands' or 'smell the fresh air'. This was important in order to ensure that participants could feel safe – they were never left alone to cope with new situations in their dream world (a device often used in conventional visualization). This relatively continuous input was seen as particularly helpful by those performers who were voice-hearers (a condition often cited as a symptom of schizophrenia); they felt they needed the continual connection to my voice, with concrete instructions, in order to combat the competing commands or emotional pleas they often heard.[3]

This facilitation of different corporeal experiences and intense focus on the sensation of corporeality in space were designed to foster what I want to call 'body-ownership': an awareness of one's own body in space, and the pleasures and possibilities of this embodiment. Thus, after the dream journeys, we briefly exchanged information about the experience – not in order to 'probe deeper' but in order to share how everybody saw different colors or encounters different 'movement partners' such as fish or weaving plants. Everybody owned a unique corporeal memory of the visited spaces. In the more conventional movement work that we created together, we also found ways of maintaining individual input. This was highly valued by the participants. (One member said in an evaluation session, 'I am proud because we are not copying each other, we do our own movement.') We often used storytelling devices to create new physical experiences and open up our movement imagination. In these sessions, we sat in a circle and started up a story, with everybody adding to it, either by witnessing others' contributions or adding a word or a longer passage, depending on people's vocality and willingness to participate. After the story was created, we explored it physically: first mimetically, then more freely. The impetus for the story was shared but the execution was individual. We echoed other people's a movement through our own physicality, but made each movement our own.

It is important to stress that the experience of the dream spaces was whole; just as a dream can regulate body temperature and accelerate a person's heart rate, these dream journeys were experienced by the participants as whole sensory experiences, not merely as 'films' of purely visual information or as 'radio plays' in which my voice provided the sole sensory input. I found that some participants became so proficient in the use of meditative techniques that they could sometimes use them to control their voices in everyday situations and overcome restlessness.[4]

In these movement sessions, the political impetus consisted not of claiming roles in traditional theatrical formats but rather of claiming inner space. Work that happens at this initial level can eventually change the participants' sense of themselves and, through this, power relations and representations in the larger social sphere. This appropriation and habitation of inner space is a way toward being wholly in the shared, social space.

Placing emphasis on this interior work for its own sake does not, however, preclude public sharing. Our work in this group involved a journey that culminated in the public sharing of our video installation, *Traces*. This journey also helped the development of a theory that, in conjunction with the practice, suggests a method for moving from private group work toward public sharing, as well as for understanding the transformative effect such sharing can have on an audience.

Notes

1   This chapter does not chart the challenges associated with working as an artist in medically defined areas. For everything that did work, many things didn't. One group in Swansea eventually folded since it proved impossible to impress upon the daily workers that the sessions needed concentration opportunities; we were very often disrupted by tea wagons and care workers coming in and going out. A mental health nurse forebade one of his clients to attend the sessions because of the dream journeys involved; his argument focused on the client's need to distinguish reality from fantasy. The individual involved wanted to come; once I made clear to the nurse that the content of the journeys were specifically movement-based and that the sessions involved a safe rehearsal space for these borderline experiences and their negotiation, the client eventually rejoined the group. Ultimately, the distinction between therapy and artwork cannot really be maintained (and is only included here in the sense of distinguishing our work from that initiated by the 'medical establish-ment'). The work remains open for people to take many things away from it – self-esteem, safe places for self-expression, etc. The group members report on many different positive outcomes of our work together. 'We've all been there together in the mental health hospital ward, etc.'; 'We get our frustrations and anger out in some movement, and can be free to relax and listen to other movements'; 'I feel alive when I get home on Tuesdays'; 'When we create something, I am talking to the family about it, and it gets me out of myself'; 'I don't feel so empty now.'

(These comments were made in an evaluation session in which I asked members whether there was anything they would like to tell people who read this chapter.)

2   This romantic image of the mad artist is problematic. At the 1977 premiere of David Edgar's play about her experiences, *Mary Barnes*, Barnes told reporters that she still experienced depression and periods of withdrawal (Showalter, 1987: 286). Today, the depiction of the drug Prozac as a lifestyle accessory has initiated new discussions about the relationship between art, consumerism, and health. In the public health service of an economically depressed part of the UK, the main form of treatment available to the people I work with is drugs and a variety of activities offered to them through day-care services (walking, yoga, writing, card playing, crafts, etc.). Given the differences in medical treatment of mental conditions throughout the last two centuries, the images of 'mad' people in the mainstream remain relatively constant. The hysterical woman and the homicidal man are still with us.

3   My dream-journey calling and the preceding relaxation sequences were informed by my training in autogenic (self-hypnosis) methods and Gerda Alexander's eutony-two techniques that involve biofeedback. Both are healing methods that allow people to live more fully and aware. Here, again, we are on the borderline between therapy and art. These healing forms were used in our artmaking; they were not specifically aimed at the symptoms of the people with whom I was working.

4   As time went by, it was possible to offer more and more 'free space' – longer periods where people could explore their physicality in the dream spaces created. Participants reported that the work in the sessions was able to give them ownership of thoughts as well. Some felt better able to acknowledge the presence of voices in their heads, and thereby to continue with whatever they were doing when the voices started up, without putting all of their energy into either listening to or shutting out the voices. It is important to stress, though, that the work was quite clearly focused on physical experience and sensory perception, and not on feelings or sharing oneself through language. The group respected privacy and the 'unknown' condition of the other.

Reference

Showalter, Elaine (1987) *The Female Malady: Women, Madness and English Culture 1830–1980.* London: Virago.

CHAPTER 22

Deborah Hay

My body trusts the unknown

> Because I have taken my body, by my will, to so many unknown,
> strange, demanding and frightening places, it is no longer afraid.
>
> —*Linda Montana*, artist

THE I CHING, an ancient Chinese book consisting of sixty-four oracles, was
the single source of guidance to which I referred for choreographic direction
before the start of my four-month workshop, Playing Awake, 1995. To consult a
hexagram, three coins are tossed in the air six times. The combination of heads and
tails determines which of sixty-four oracular messages one consults. How I have
interpreted the hexagrams has profoundly changed the course of my life. In this instance,
the tossed coins fell to the hexagram *Following*, changing to *Gathering Together*. *Following*
contains these messages: "The thought of obtaining a following through adaptation to
the demands of the time is a great and significant idea . . ." and "No situation can
become favorable until one is able to adapt to it and does not wear himself out with
mistaken resistance."

The word "adaptation" had never crossed the threshold of what I believed was
my vastly inclusive artist's consciousness. I could even say that, until that moment,
my dances had been choreographed and staged according to stringent principles of
nonadaptation.

The first day of Playing Awake 1995 I asked everyone to perform a short solo
with the following guidelines:

1.   the dance could be performed anywhere in the studio,
2.   no preparation was necessary,
3.   there was no need to be creative.

I took notes. Each solo contained moments of eccentric and moving material. A few days later, I asked everyone to prepare and perform a monologue about something that aroused their passion. They had three days to write and practice before presenting their monologues in the workshop. My reasoning was that, given these two assignments early on, everyone would confront their worst fears about performing right off the bat, and, hopefully, they would recognize the value of the performance tools I would then be offering them in the course of the workshop.

It was not my intention to manufacture the rich supply of resources from the solos and monologues that inevitably became the structural continuity of *my heart*. Nonetheless, I selected from and adapted the material, which, in turn, sped up and eased the choreographic process. *my heart*, the name I gave the dance to help me remember mine, was frightfully simple to paste and put together choreographically.

The implementation of "adaptation" was not without its cost. I knew was using the students' work for my own ends, and I suffered recurrent bouts of guilt.

Six weeks into the same workshop, I had the following dream: A man dressed in medieval hunting clothes grabs a small bird by its tail feathers. He presses the tip of its tail firmly onto a table. As the bird frees itself, some of its feathers remain on the table and scatter. The man turns to me and says, "This means looting." The message I interpreted from the dream was that holding onto anything, for example my students' creative bounty, was looting.

The structure, imagery, and clarity of the dream was so haunting that I included it, as text, in *my heart*. Two different performers told the story at different intervals. Not being skilled in dramatic arts, they found it difficult to pronounce "looting" without over-articulating it. It being the last word in the story further compounded its troubling pronunciation: "looting" became the focus of the story. I listened to my dream repeated twice a day for over three months. It wasn't exactly like being hit over the head.

In a letter to my brother, I described what was happening. He sent back a T. S. Eliot quote: "Immature poets imitate; mature poets steal . . . The good poet welds his theft into a whole feeling which is utterly different from that from which, it was torn." Reading this, I felt much better, although the guilt did not disappear entirely.

Five months later, while choreographing *Violà*, the solo form of *my heart*, I discussed the dream with my dream group, seven women and a Jungian-oriented psychotherapist. I read aloud from my dream journal, and then described what was happening in my life at the time of the dream. I spoke about the hexagram *Following* and my struggle with the concept of adaptation as far it concerned my art. The group leaned inward. I was asked to describe the man in greater detail. I said he was large and gentle and wore heavy, richly textured clothes. His face was courteous beneath his pointed hat. He may have been an alchemist. When he said "This means looting," he lowered his voice and opened his arm toward the scattering feathers. As I made this motion with my arm, this, referring to the feathers, replaced looting as the subject of the story for the first time.

This is adaptation, transformation, integration, art, and life.

CHAPTER 23

Cynthia Novak

Contact improvisation

An introduction

CONTACT IMPROVISATION IS MOST frequently performed as a duet, in silence, with dancers supporting each others' weight while in motion. Unlike wrestlers, who exert their strength to control a partner, contact improvisers use momentum to move in concert with a partner's weight, rolling, suspending, lurching together. They often yield rather than resist, using their arms to assist and support but seldom to manipulate. Interest lies in the ongoing flow of energy rather than on producing still pictures, as in ballet; consequently, dancers doing contact improvisation would just as soon fall as balance. Although many contact improvisers demonstrate gymnastic ability, their movement, unlike that of most gymnastic routines, does not emphasize the body's line or shape. Even more important, they improvise their movement, inventing or choosing it at the moment of performance.

The participants in contact improvisation have characterized the dance as an "art-sport," a dance form which simultaneously provides a communal movement experience for the participants and an example of movement behavior for the audience. The dancers in contact improvisation focus on the physical sensations of touching, leaning, supporting, counterbalancing, and falling with other people, thus carrying on a physical dialogue.

One contact improviser has described the dance form as "a cross between jitterbugging, wrestling, and making love." This phase captures some of the influences combined in contact improvisation: it drew in its formation from social dance, sport and martial arts, and intimate, personal interaction. It also constitutes a part of the development of modern dance in America, that oppositional artistic and social movement which emerged at the beginning of the twentieth century.

Modern dancer Steve Paxton "invented" contact improvisation in 1972, giving a name to movement ideas that he had been investigating with colleagues and students. The naming both described the formal experiment and acknowledged the formation of a group of people who practiced the dance socially and performed it publicly. When the original dancers dispersed and taught contact improvisation elsewhere, larger numbers of people began to participate in cities throughout the United States, Canada, and Europe (although until the mid-'80s, most of the teachers and leaders of contact improvisation were Americans).

The people creating contact improvisation during the '70s were for the most part young, college-educated, white, middle-class Americans living in transient, communal settings. While the experiments with the movement developed, participants and viewers began to see the dancing as an expression of a way of life with certain values. The body, the primary focus of contact improvisation, became imbued with specific meaning. Contact improvisers have seen the body as a sensuous, intelligent natural part of each person, requiring acknowledgement and promising insight.

Traditional modern dance concerns with the choreographic shaping of movement materials or with the explicit expression of ideas or emotions have often been absent from contact improvisation; emphasis has been placed instead on the physical dialogue of two dancers, the action which results from the sensations of touch and weight. Many contact improvisers have trained in modern dance; however, they frequently have looked for inspiration and ideas to physical techniques such as Tai Chi Chuan or aikido, both Asian martial arts, or to movement techniques based on kinesiology, rather than to traditional modern dance techniques based on expressive vocabularies.

Contact improvisers have often stressed the social nature of their activity as much as its formal, physical properties. Unlike other American theater dance forms, contact improvisation was and is often practiced by groups of people in informal, open social settings ("jams"). Contact improvisers, particularly during the first ten years of the form, have sometimes claimed their dancing is a kind of folk dance, something that anyone can participate in and learn.

Many of the early participants, audience members, and critics felt that the movement structure of contact improvisation literally embodied the social ideologies of the early '70s which rejected traditional gender roles and social hierarchies. They viewed the experience of touching and sharing weight with a partner of either sex and any size as a way of constructing a new experience of the self interacting with another person. The lack of conscious compositional focus in the form represented spontaneity in life, a literal "going with the flow" of events, just as the dancers followed the flow of their physical contact. The group with no director symbolized an egalitarian community in which everyone cooperated and no one dominated. Finally, the mode of practicing and performing contact improvisation resembled a social dance, an informal gathering in which anyone could participate who wished to do so; distinctions between amateur and professional dancers were consciously ignored initially.

At the same time, the values which dancers have attributed to contact improvisation have been open in practice to flexible and/or ambivalent interpretation.[1] Individuals in different circumstances have taken the initiative of using contact improvisation to fit their personal scenarios, and contradictions inherent in the clash of certain values have been worked out (or not worked out) in various ways. How does someone exert leadership within a movement which denies it? How do people take action when the prevailing ideology is to let whatever happens, happen? How is egalitarianism maintained within an individualistic community? What happens when contact improvisers incorporate as a company and enter the dance marketplace?

In fact, by the late '70s, distinctions between amateurs and professionals began to emerge as the technique of contact improvisation became extended and refined and as performance opportunities increased. Contact improvisation companies (not-for-profit corporations) were formed around the country. The growth of the contact improvisation movement was also part of a much larger trend in American theater dance—a proliferation of choreographers and dancers in the '60s and '70s.

By the early '80s, change in contact improvisation and in American culture was evident. The dance style, which in the early years had been extremely intense, risky, uncontrolled, and inwardly focused, had become more facile, fluid, controlled, and outwardly focused. Its former mixture of participation and presentation had given way in large part to a more clearly presentational manner; yet at the same time, contact improvisation companies seldom lasted longer than four or five years. In the late 1980s many dancers continued to practice and teach the form, usually performing on an occasional, ad hoc basis, but many others studied the form as a technique to be used in other kinds of dancing. Also, groups developed which organized social dance activities featuring contact improvisation; for these groups, the emphasis was on social interaction.

Apprehending these historical changes raises larger questions about the interplay of artistic techniques with the lives of participants and audiences in artistic events. It also raises questions about the relationship of cultural ideas to social institutions and movements. Contact improvisation embodies issues which must be negotiated in American culture, concepts and practices of physical skill, art, mind, body, touch, movement, play, sexuality, freedom, and difference. As a social movement, contact improvisation documents changes in these concepts that occurred during the upheavals of the 1960s.[2] Looking at how ideas central to a historical period can surface powerfully in an aesthetic environment gives insight into what "the '60s" were in the daily behavior and thoughts of some Americans. Furthermore, people doing contact improvisation maintained a countercultural image long after the '60s as a political phenomenon had ended.[3] Contact improvisation thus provides an example of the possibilities and problems of maintaining cultural ideas and practices in the face of social change.

Notes

1   See Robert Murphy (1971) for a cogent discussion of the usefulness of distinguishing values, norms, and actions while seeking to understand their refractory and oblique interrelationships.

2   In trying to understand a countercultural movement, I have benefited from Hervé Varenne's (1986) suggestion that American culture be viewed not as a set of concrete traits but as a series of constraints.

3   Fredric Jameson (1984) discusses the widespread economic and political conditions which might define or "periodize" the '60s as lasting from about 1960 until 1972–74.

CHAPTER 24

Terry Galloway, Donna Marie Nudd and Carrie Sandahl

'Actual Lives' and the Ethic of Accommodation

I N THE EARLY 1990S when Terry Galloway was touring with the PS 122 Field Trips in Manchester, United Kingdom, she was asked to conduct a theatre workshop for disabled people. As Terry puts it: 'I blithely assumed that being deaf somehow uniquely qualified me for this task.' The workshop was held at a cinder block community center in a room that doubled as a chapel. She went in thinking that she would draw on her theatre background and do something easy and fun, perhaps some stretching exercises and some standard theatre games, such as mirroring or body shadowing.

Twenty-five people waited for her. Among them were: a 55-year-old man who had recently suffered a stroke and had lost all feeling in the left half of his body, a 30-year-old former dancer whose lower spine had been snapped in two when she had been hit by a drunk driver, an 18-year-old woman who had literally gone blind overnight, a 24-year-old man who had lost half his brain in a car accident, and two small-stature adults with Down Syndrome who were twins, brother and sister. The twins, like Terry, were curious about the long black curtain that obscured the back wall of the room. When Terry opened the curtain to reveal a pulpit and a cross, the twins fell to their knees, crossed themselves and began to pray. Terry did not realize the theatrical potential of that group until many years later. What she did realize was that all her standard theatre games and practices had been rendered instantly obsolete.

Traditional workshop and presentation methods could not capture the rich material this group had to contribute: interesting bodies with idiosyncratic ways of moving, life stories that shatter disability stereotypes and narrative, and unique ways of perceiving the world. Terry recognized that disability experiences need not be considered deficits to be hidden or exploited – but, rather, these experiences are far more interesting than any theatrical gloss of them. To this day, she is not sure the group got anything of value from the workshop she ended up doing, but she got from it two things that have remained invaluable: a name and an idea. The name is 'Actual Lives'. And the idea is simple: if standard theatre material is inappropriate to uncover the richness of disabled people's lives, she would create writing and performance workshops geared toward uncovering and representing their *actual lives*. These workshops would have to revise traditional theatre ideals and practices from the ground up. The practice of these revisions would become what she called the 'Ethic of Accommodation'. This ethic is a particular practice of inclusion that does not simply issue an invitation to everyone to participate in theatre-making. Equal treatment does not always translate into equal opportunity. Genuine inclusiveness requires a willingness to make changes to core beliefs, practices and aesthetics. In some cases, practicing this ethic requires willingness to spend time and money to change the fundamental structures of an organization. In this essay, the three of us (Terry Galloway, Donna Marie Nudd and Carrie Sandahl) delineate and explore key aspects of the Ethic of Accommodation in practice as we have experienced it in various incarnations of the 'Actual Lives' project.

The Ethic of Accommodation

The three of us have collaborated on various artistic and academic projects over the years. Out of discussions about our work, we began to articulate a manifesto of sorts in the Ethic of Accommodation. This ethic is not abstract to us, but integral to our work and lives. We have all been affected by traditional practices of theatre that still ensure that the disabled, queer, female, non-white bodies remain a rarity on stage, except in roles that reinforce the most demeaning stereotypes. We feel the exclusion personally because of our own bodies (Terry is deaf and Carrie has an orthopedic disability), because of our queer and radical politics (Donna and Terry are lesbians), and because of our families (Carrie has a trans-racial family formed through adoption). We three share a commitment to social justice and in the spheres we can influence, we attempt to make structural changes toward flexibility and openness. The Ethic of Accommodation, as we have come to understand it, is intimately tied to disability politics, which seeks to accommodate difference rather than 'tolerate' it or smooth out our rough edges.

In US disability legal parlance (developed for civil rights laws such as the Rehabilitation Act of 1973 or the Americans with Disabilities Act of 1990), an accommodation is an adjustment made to an environment, an attitude or requirement so that a disabled person is able to participate as fully as possible in public life. Disability activists have long argued that disability is not the result of individual medical pathology, but the result of a disjuncture between bodies and environments. Accommodation is rooted in a concept of justice and means more than passive non-discrimination; it is a concept that implies action, a requirement to make significant change to both attitudes and architecture.

Most theatrical organizations we have encountered tend to consider accommodations a thorn in the side: costly renovations made for 'those' people and foisted upon them by unfunded government mandates. When theatres do make accommodations, they tend to make minimal changes to the theatre house, box office and bathrooms. While many theatres make their audience spaces minimally accessible, little thought is given to disabled performers. The Ethic of Accommodation is different in that we change theatrical structures, processes and performances for maximum participation of both performers and audiences. We can break down the ethic into four key components:

1   At its core, an Ethic of Accommodation means that the majority does not rule. Instead, accommodation means including everyone wanting to participate, often necessitating that the majority make difficult changes in its practices and environment. These changes are not made begrudgingly, but with goodwill, creativity, and a strong dose of humor, elements that often find expression in the performances themselves.
2   The ethic includes the politics of listening as well as the politics of speaking. Whereas most minority groups maintain they have been 'silenced' by the majority and thus place speaking at a premium, disability communities often place listening on the same plane. People with disabilities often feel they have not been listened to or even addressed. In this context, listening does not have to happen with the ears. Listening, here, means being taken into consideration, being attended to.
3   The Ethic of Accommodation means making room for difference possible, letting go of preconceived notions of perfectibility, and negotiating complex sets of needs. Often these needs 'compete' with one another. Accommodating disability or other forms of difference often does not seem practical or marketable, since doing so often raises costs or necessitates work that seemingly benefits only a few. Marketability is not our concern.
4   The Ethic of Accommodation inspires creative aesthetic choices from casting, choreography and costuming, and also the use of space for the creation of new material. Practicing the ethic enhances theatrical practice.

The Ethic of Accommodation in action

The first incarnation of the 'Actual Lives' writing and performance workshop exclusively for disabled people took place in Austin, Texas, in 1999. Terry teamed up with one of her former graduate students, Chris Strickling – an occupational therapist, who was writing a dissertation on disability autobiography at the time. They were joined by Celia Hughes, Executive Director of VSA Arts of Austin, Texas.

Terry modeled 'Actual Lives' on the other writing and performance workshops she had been doing at theatres, universities and conferences over the years, but armed with the knowledge of her experiences with the Manchester group. The group members resembled the Manchester group in that they had various kinds of disabilities, including traumatic brain injury, visual impairment, cerebral palsy, multiple sclerosis and spinal cord injury. But the problems inherent in creating theatre with a community of people who have varying physical abilities, little or no background in theatre, and few or no performance skills were both more difficult and far easier than she had first supposed.

She began the workshop by saying, 'Take out your pencils and write down your most powerful and compelling memory' – a simple assignment – but not if half the people in the workshop do not have the strength or dexterity to hold a pencil or perhaps the cognitive skills to write at all. Simply put, the group pooled its resources to use whatever ways it could think of to translate a memory into a script. Those among them who could hold a pen and write took dictation from the ones who could not hold a pen or could not write. They verbally cued those who had trouble holding a thought. They lent computers to the people who could not write in cursive but could type. Any means to get the stories out and put on paper.

Once the stories were written down, she was faced by another unforeseen issue: how to convince people who are generally under- or unvalued by society that their own stories, their own lives, constitute the very stuff of drama. Terry thought that that particular insecurity would resolve itself the way it had usually resolved itself. Past experience taught her that the minute people share what they have written with other members of a group, they see, hear and feel the responses – the laughter, gasps and tears – and know they have contributed something of value. They're hooked. Simple. But sharing what they have written is not so simple if some of the people are hearing impaired. Or if they cannot speak above a whisper because they lack muscular control or have breathing problems. Or if they become confused and lose track of their own thoughts mid-story. Or if they cannot read, or cannot commit to memory what they cannot read. Again, she practiced the Ethic of Accommodation – trying to figure out any and every way people could 'voice' their own stories.

When they could afford the technology, they miked people, used open captioning, audio description and American Sign Language so that people whose voices were impaired or who were deaf or blind could understand and be understood. Often these accommodations were jerry-rigged when the technology was not available. They simply let people tell their stories however they could. People with cerebral palsy, for instance, were encouraged to take as much time as they needed to articulate as clearly as they could, even if sometimes they had to have someone else repeat the story a few lines at a time.

And they used humor to make it all seem less labored, less a test of everyone's patience. They allowed themselves to find it hilarious when the man with a traumatic brain injury was translating the speech of a woman with severe cerebral palsy for the woman who was profoundly hard of hearing, and all three of them found themselves in a time warp of painstakingly slow repetition.

All of those things – technology, inventiveness, humor and patience – lifted that burdensome expectation of perfection off everyone's shoulders and emboldened them to take risks when they went on to the next step: performing these stories for an audience.

It is never a simple matter to put people who are new to theatre on stage. Some people have no idea how to project, where to stand, how to hold for a moment or for a laugh. What about people new to the process who *cannot* project, *cannot* stand, *do not* perceive the moment or hear the laugh? Too often, theatres that include disabled people do not bother teaching them these skills and instead hold lower expectations of them. But the Ethic of Accommodation encourages curiosity and inventiveness, insisting that a way can be found to communicate everyone's story in a theatrically compelling way. What could the group members in actuality do? Could the guy with multiple sclerosis steer his power chair at breakneck speed without hurtling over the lip of the stage? What would it take for the blind woman to make her way quickly to center stage and find her spot? How high could the woman with cerebral palsy lift her arm so the 'fuck you' would be visible? How easy or difficult would it be for the guy in the manual chair to throw himself out of it and crawl up the stairs to an inaccessible stage? After they began asking themselves questions, they started playing with their differences and finally became captivated by them. They started making them part of the script, part of the performance itself. For example, the slow motion walk of a 23-year-old woman with advanced juvenile rheumatoid arthritis became the focus of a dance piece featuring her particular Pina Bausch-like dreamscape gait. Or the particular segregation in communication felt by the deaf became the focal point of a group piece about the hierarchy of disability.

And then they put the results on stage for all to see: a series of autobiographical monologues, music, and movement pieces, performed in a small, quirky black box space with an accessible stage.

The show's first audiences seemed to soak up the Ethic of Accommodation by osmosis, practicing the ethic in their willingness to let go of preconceived notions of perfection and just enjoy the experimentation. If the first audiences had been more exacting and unforgiving, 'Actual Lives' might never have continued. The audience was a great mix of family members, other disabled people, health care professionals, theatre professionals, university professors and students, and some truly edgy representatives of the avant-garde. This was the ideal audience for an experimental and risky step forward that would fail almost as often as it would succeed. They were willing, appreciative, intellectually and emotionally curious people who could be trusted to recognize that something wonderful was happening on that stage and trusted to envision how – with more hard work and continuing inventiveness – even more wonderful it could eventually become.

From 1999 to 2004, the Austin incarnation of 'Actual Lives' created and performed numerous different local and regional productions. The performances would expand to include multimedia and multi-character scenes. Terry, Chris and Celia produced most of these productions, with Donna Nudd and other creative artists contributing their efforts when they could.[1] During this time, the producers and seven of the original performers in Austin provided a stable center to a larger more movable group of fifteen. The members continued to hone their writing and performance skills in workshops held – formally and informally – throughout the year. 'Actual Lives' has continued to evolve both practically and theoretically. Two recent incarnations of 'Actual Lives' – a version produced and performed in Tallahassee, Florida, and a

version produced in Austin and performed in Washington, DC – are worth mentioning
in some detail for the ways in which they stretched the Ethic of Accommodation in
new, exciting, and challenging directions.

Because Donna and Terry live in Tallahassee, travel to Austin became increasingly
difficult both financially and logistically. So they decided to create an 'Actual Lives'
project in the community in which they lived. They decided to apply for a local arts
grant to run a different type of 'Actual Lives' in Tallahassee through the Mickee Faust
Club, the cabaret troupe which they co-founded in 1996. This time they would include
two groups which are often often-marginalized – African-American college students
and the elderly population – along with people with disabilities.[2] Carrie participated
in several of these workshops as an advisor and assistant director. Participants were
recruited initially from the various targeted groups through organizations or institutions
with which they might be affiliated. The diversity of participants created opportunities
to make surprising and intense connections across identity groups that would normally
rarely, if ever, find commonality with one another. In one example, a writing exercise
when the participants were asked to describe their obsessions, the 18-year-old African-
American male was surprised to find himself sharing the same fixation with cleaning
filthy bathroom fixtures as the 60-year-old white female.

This Tallahassee-based 'Actual Lives' project culminated in a staged performance
called *A Happy Life, If You Can Stand It*. Like the early shows of 'Actual Lives' in Austin,
A Happy Life primarily featured monologues, written and performed by the workshop
participants. The final performance took place in one of Tallahassee's funky coffee
shops, Java Heads. The place was packed with people from walks of life as diverse as
the participants. Before the show, the audience and performers shared coffee, laughed
and just enjoyed being together. In performance, powerful examples of how connections
were made across ability and generation became apparent. A series of three separate
monologues that concluded the performance began with an 89-year-old woman,
telling a haunting autobiographical tale about being kidnapped against her will. She
was trapped in a car driven erratically at breakneck speeds on the Interstate as
she desperately tried to make eye contact with the other drivers, hoping they would
save her. She cried with relief when the state police finally stopped their car. In the
monologue that followed, the next performer, with much chagrin, told of taking her
mother on a wild midnight drive in retaliation for a snide comment her mother made
about one of her friends. In the final monologue, a second middle-aged woman told
of getting a call in the small hours of the morning from the state police, informing
her that her elderly mother was stranded in Georgia and her mentally ill sister was
in jail. The Ethic of Accommodation allowed these stories of illness, disability,
generational conflict and aging to be told in ways that transcended the personal and
entered the realm of both art and community.

Practicing the Ethic of Accommodation's commitment to including everyone is
not easy, especially when extraordinary financial and logistical efforts are involved. In
June 2004, the 'Actual Lives' company in Austin performed at the International VSA
Arts Festival in Washington, DC. While traveling is difficult for any theatre company,
for 'Actual Lives' it was an exceptionally challenging feat. Since the majority of company
members were unemployed or underemployed, fundraising was necessary to cover as

many expenses as possible for the disabled performers, personal care assistants, American Sign Language interpreters and members of the artistic or production crews. Fundraising efforts by the 'Actual Lives' company and VSA Arts of Texas netted nearly $12,000 to offset the company's airplane, hotel and transportation costs, with most of the money being cobbled together from small donations from family, friends and disability organizations.

The complexity of travel logistics for the company cannot be overstated. But once again, company members aided each other. Chris spent ungodly hours at the hotel registration desk righting their snafus so that all company members and their personal assistants had the requisite room accommodation for their specific needs. More financially privileged company members contributed for the expected huge tip to the porters for the group's collective luggage, which included not only everyday clothes, but also specialized wheelchairs and shower seats, as well as all the costumes and props for the show itself. And there were major mishaps, most notably, for example, when power wheelchairs were broken during transport both to and from Washington, DC. These challenges were doubled by the challenges that any on-the-road theatre company experiences, but again, inventiveness, patience and humor were the order of the day. Meeting these challenges while pulling off an epiphanic performance proved to be a culminating experience for the group.

The future for 'Actual Lives'

The work continues, albeit in two different locations. Austinites Chris and Celia continue working with the 'Actual Lives', Austin company. They are looking to conduct the workshops for recently disabled soldiers returning from Iraq.[3] Donna, Terry and Carrie are working with the Mickee Faust Club to create other 'Actual Lives' workshops in North Florida's rural communities. We plan to use DVD compilations of these workshops and their resulting performances to further expand the Ethic of Accommodation by making the work more widely available to audiences in both rural US communities and internationally. Those of us who participate in the many incarnations of 'Actual Lives' are finding ways to tell our own stories and convince an indifferent society that our actual lives do matter.[4]

Notes

1 Over the years, 'Actual Lives', Austin has worked with professional artists and scholars to hone their performance skills, including Kathleen Juhl, Olivia Whitmer, Tommy Schoffler, Elizabeth Barber, Cheryl Green, Holly Rutherford, Joni Lee Jones, Jill Dolan and Stacy Wolf.

2 Terry and Donna co-founded the Mickee Faust Club in 1987, in Tallahassee, Florida. For further information about this company, see Nudd et al. (2001), 'Is This Theatre Queer'.

3 In a personal email, Chris Strickling provided us with the details about 'Actual Lives'' travel and fundraising for the Washington, DC tour and her current and future work for 'Actual Lives' in Austin.

4   A monograph on how to create other 'Actual Lives' workshops has been published
      and distributed internationally by the VSA arts in Washington, DC. And the recent
      issue of *Theater Topics* featured a lengthy article by Strickling discussing both the
      theories of body and the practice of 'Actual Lives'.

Works cited

Galloway, Terry and Strickling, Chris, *Actual Lives Performance Project*, VSA Arts, Monograph
      funded by US Dept of Education.
Nudd, Donna Marie, Schriver, Kristina and Galloway, Terry (2001) 'Is This Theatre
      Queer: Mickee Faust and the Performance of Community', in Susan C. Haedicke
      and Tobin Nellhaus (eds), *Performing Community, Performing Democracy: International
      Perspectives on Urban Community-based Performance*. University of Michigan Press, pp.
      104–16.
Strickling, Chris Anne (2002) 'Actual Lives: Cripples in the House', *Theatre Topics*, 12
      (2): 143–62.
Strickling, Chris Anne (2005) 'Follow up to phone conversation', email to Donna Marie
      Nudd, 28 October.

Practices

Introduction to
Part Five

■ Petra Kuppers and Gwen Robertson

I N T H I S S E C T I O N, five very different community performance practices emerge in detail, and in the languages and formats appropriate to their settings, audiences or professional frameworks. The examples include the set-up of an intergenerational dance project in the United Kingdom (**Diane Amans**), the complex use of text and movement by the Liz Lerman Dance Exchange in the US (**Jan Cohen-Cruz**), the hip-hop work of Morganics in a music/improvisation project in Australia (**Rebecca Caines**), 'Eel Catching', a project that documented the lives of the African-American Christian Avenue community in Setauket, Long Island, USA (**Glenda Dickerson**) and the challenges and methods of a community theatre project in the Philippines (**Eugene van Erven**).

The authors in this section use very different voices to present the material, and to frame the intentions and approaches of different practitioners and community members. In all of these writings, the power of performance becomes the object of analysis: what addresses people, what enables oral history, how can forms of self-expression emerge and be shared, how do politics evolve out of shared experience? What makes the work powerful, to whom, and how can the power be transmitted in writings *about* the process?

This section concludes the Reader, leaving the emphasis not on policy, overview or roots, but on the local, the specific, the dignity of the expressive work, and the trickster work of 'making do'. We hope that you can see connections to your local worlds, and see themes and inspirations for shaping strong, rich and rewarding community work that values individual voices.

CHAPTER 25

Diane Amans

At My Age

An intergenerational dance project

'It was fun dancing with Grandma'

IN SPRING 2004 Freedom in Dance, a UK-based community dance company, completed a video project called *At My Age*. Over thirty children, young people and older adults worked with choreographers and a film artist to create a short video which explored intergenerational relationships and perceptions of youth and ageing.

The participants ranged in age from 2 years to 83 years and many came with members of their family. Mothers, daughters, fathers, sons, grandparents, grandchildren, cousins, brothers and sisters all created dances together. The project ended with a celebration event for participants as well as their families and friends. An invited audience viewed a large screen showing the finished film and short sections of the dance performed live. They then shared a meal and danced together to music performed by a ceilidh band.

> – I liked dancing with my mummy.
>
> – I was really surprised when my husband joined in – he only went to drop the children off.
>
> – Loved being able to dance with my child *all* day.

How the project was set up

The project was funded with a lottery award and a local council voluntary arts grant. The aims of the project were:

- To promote better mutual understanding between people of different generations.
- To challenge stereotypes of youth and ageing.
- To increase skills and creativity of participants.
- To extend access and participation in community dance.

Participants were recruited from local families and community groups in the Stockport area of northwest England. Some participants had previously taken part in community dance, others were new to the activity. The proposed project was advertised with posters in local shops, listings in the newspaper and fliers sent to people on existing dance projects. Most of the participants came as a result of hearing about it from a relative who was already involved in community dance classes.

Project structure

There was a one-day introductory workshop for all participants to dance together and meet the artists. This first workshop ran from 10 am till 4 pm and included a range of ice-breaker games and creative dance activities. Some of the very young children went home at lunchtime and other participants joined in at their own pace. Following this introductory day there were three further phases and dancers could choose to take part in as much or as little as they wanted:

Phase 1   Three Saturday workshops with choreographer Paula Hampson. Participants used dance activities to explore relationships between different aged dancers.
Phase 2   This was an intensive workshop held over a weekend, led by break-dancer Terry Kvasnik and choreographer Diane Amans. Participants devised a dance piece that challenged stereotypes of youth and age with a focus on break-dancing.
Phase 3   This one-day site-specific workshop offered an opportunity for an inter-generational group to create and perform dance in an outdoor park location.

Inclusive approaches to leading intergenerational workshops

Intergenerational projects present interesting challenges for the dance practitioner who facilitates them – particularly when all ages are together in the same session. In a workshop which includes toddlers, schoolchildren, teenagers, young adults, older adults and elders, there are contrasting energy levels, diverse interests, varying tastes in music and different physical and emotional needs. In the *At My Age* project we developed an inclusive approach, which managed to engage everyone's interest and meet the needs of participants who wanted to be very physical and those who enjoyed a more leisurely pace and time to chat.

In the early stages of the project there were frequent changes of activity, and the very small children remained engaged as they had an opportunity to take the lead.

Figure 12 Workshop during *At My Age* project (director Diane Amans) an intergenerational dance project exploring stereotypes of youth and ageing.

Photo: Jackie Mellor.

For example, in a warm-up activity a 3-year-old was the leader. She called out 'Stop', 'Go' and the rest of the group moved in response to her directions. She chuckled with delight as she realized she was in charge.

Later on three children created a sound score with a drum, triangle and tambourine. We performed shaky movements to the tambourine, made strong shapes to the beat of the drum and melted to the sound of the triangle.

> I loved it when the children made the music. The look of being 'in control' on their faces was brilliant – getting us to 'dance to their tune' . . . . Changing the power balance is what dance across the generations is all about for me.

As the project leader I felt it was crucial that all participants felt that their contribution was important and that all ideas and suggestions would have equal value. Once the children realized this they showed remarkable patience and commitment to the project. From time to time they found it more interesting to play with their toys than to listen to the grown-ups talking, but they soon responded when we started moving again.

Props such as large balloons, parachutes, scarves and a giant elastic band all helped to create a 'failure-free' culture where there was no wrong way of doing things. Most of the choreography was based on structured improvisation and all participants were involved in artistic decisions.

The break-dance routine – performed in 'hoodies' so the audience could not tell the age of the performer – captured the energy and essence of the form but incorporated choreography which allowed all the participants to perform sections which suited their skills and physical abilities. Small children crawled into the performance space, lay on their backs and made scissor actions with their legs. The break-dancer and other young people mirrored these moves whilst doing handstands. Older members of the group made a series of tableau shapes. One 73-year-old looked at the floor-based routine and said – 'Hmm – You're not getting me on the floor! I'll just stand here and look mean.'

This was the only part of the project where dancers spent part of the workshop sessions in groups with people of similar age. The teenagers practised their handstands together, older adults devised tableaux, and the small children worked with the choreographer finding playful ways to enter and leave the dance space.

Positive role models

The 26-year-old break-dance artist showed considerable ingenuity and patience in devising sequences for everyone to join in. He was an excellent role model for the other young people on the project – some of whom had only joined in because Terry was going to be involved. To them he is a local celebrity, as he has left the region to follow a career in break-dancing and often appears on UK television. His mother attends a community dance class and he was happy to be part of the *At My Age* project. His easy communication style and willingness to engage with all participants as equals helped to break down barriers between generations.

A lively 60-year-old was very popular as his humour and a sense of fun was much appreciated by the children and young people. He had a constant group of admirers waiting for his next joke and project photographs are full of images showing laughter and delight.

Documenting the project

The project was filmed during each of the phases and the impact of the project was documented using a range of methods:

- Project log for participants' comments and drawings. People contributed to a large book whenever they had something to say (or draw). Parents and grandparents encouraged children to talk about their dancing after the sessions and brought drawings and comments for the project log.
- Photographs.
- Questionnaires.
- Discussions at the end of workshops.
- Informal discussions with small groups and individuals.
- Comments book for audience responses.

The video film and project log were presented at an intergenerational conference in Canada where some delegates expressed surprise at the diversity of this group who chose to dance with people from different generations.

Impact of the project: challenging stereotypes

In the UK we do not usually dance with our grannies (or anyone else in our families for that matter) except for special occasions like weddings. Even these social occasions are usually dominated by noisy discos which drive generations apart. This can often reinforce stereotypes of youth and age and we miss out on a wonderful opportunity to celebrate diversity and promote better understanding between people of different generations.

Participants in the *At My Age* project commented on the fact that it challenged their perceptions of themselves and members of different age groups. Dancing together created relationships which helped them break down barriers.

> I would never have thought old people could dance like that . . . at first it was a bit embarrassing but then you realize – they're just like us really. Just older.

> Seeing myself within an age continuum reinforced the awareness that my external appearance is at odds with my internal self – a useful reminder that 'the elderly' and 'young people' are not ring fenced.

> Working with a wide range of people of different ages challenged my own concepts.

> I would never have expected to do 'break-dancing' at my age.

> The adolescents were a revelation. I had expected them to be much more self-conscious and less willing to participate. They were a joy to work with.

> I liked dancing with the old people. It was fun.

Engaging with each other on equal terms

The project brought generations together to take part in new activities on equal terms. As the dance activities were unfamiliar to all participants they worked collaboratively and shared their skills.

> I was surprised how things flowed naturally . . . between generations. It amazed and delighted me . . . He took it so seriously . . . (Sylvia talking about dancing with her 12-year-old-grandson).

It's very much a oneness dancing with people of different ages . . . there haven't been any boundaries.

We come together and we work in a way which uses everybody's abilities and physicalities. Each of us is different – we just accept that and move together.

We've been making dances we can all do together – whether we're young or old.

Conclusion

Following the project there is an ongoing community dance class attended by a mixed age group. Some of the group have since performed together at a number of community dance showcase events. Freedom in Dance has plans to create an intergenerational dance programme to tour in the UK. It will include new choreography and training for community dance artists who wish to develop skills in leading intergenerational dance workshops.

We can all be a dancer in our heads – whatever age we are.

For further information about any aspect of the company's work: Freedom in Dance +44 (0)161 427 5093; or email freedom@amans.fsnet.co.uk.

CHAPTER 26

Jan Cohen-Cruz

Compositions

The Liz Lerman Dance Exchange

L IZ LERMAN DANCE EXCHANGE is one of many companies that uses its own aesthetic approaches to compose work with community participation. Company founder and artistic director Liz Lerman has been inspired by a range of artists and experiences. Dada is one of her biggest influences, particularly Marcel Duchamp. She revels in surprising combinations, so characteristic of the avant-garde, and critiques prevailing notions of professionalism that she finds overcompartmentalized: "You are a dancer if you take two technique classes a day, wait tables, behave and dress a certain way, perform once a year. You are not a dancer if you teach dance in a senior center. You are a social worker. You are not a dancer if once a month you work with the rabbi at the synagogue. You are a liturgical something." In other words, the narrow definition of dance as art has led to a narrow practice. Lerman critiques professionalism that devalues art in community context, indeed devalues any performance with a larger frame than a proscenium stage. She wryly points out that working as a waitress is considered more the mark of a "real dancer" than making dances with nonprofessionals.

In the early 1970s, Lerman studied Graham technique in Washington and did guerrilla theatre in Boston. In 1974, she spent a requisite season living in New York City, struggling to make it as a "pro," earning her living as a go-go dancer. Finally fed up, she returned to Washington, DC, to pursue the integration of her various passions: "I had the idea that dance could belong in a community and that there would be a mutual change in both the dancer and the community if it were there." She applied political organizing principles to dance—"meet people on their own turf, affirm what they already know, bring them together"—as a way to build community.

One of Lerman's major contributions to the dance world has been the broadening of the basis for who is included. In 1976, to help work through her mother's death,

Lerman choreographed a piece incorporating women in their seventies and eighties. She was already aware that dance is not all about technique, that technique can obscure as well as clarify. That same year she founded the Dance Exchange, composed not of a group of perfect human specimens in their twenties, such as typifies dance ensembles, but rather of moving movers of various shapes and ages. (At first she had a younger and an older dance company, which she eventually merged.) She became smitten with the older dancers' "impact on an audience, their incredible openness to learning, the beauty of their movements, and what they had to teach me about dancing." Incorporating older people into her work, where the thrill, as she puts it, cannot possibly be seeing how high someone's leg is going to go, has had the salutary effect of weaning audiences from the habit of overvaluing technique. Contrary to the stereotypic conception of community-based art as an oxymoron, Lerman's criteria for artistic merit—how committed and connected a person is to the movement—expands art itself: "And if I don't see *that* on stage I'm bereft." Thus for Lerman, a deepening of the artistic, experience—the emphasis on an aesthetic of commitment as well as technical prowess— takes place concomitant to a focus on communal representation.

Continuing the avant-garde practice of marvellous and surprising assemblages, Lerman integrates forms, ideas, and people that are usually kept apart. Take *Shehechianu*, a Lerman dance/theater piece that explores a century of interactions, overlaps, and frictions among various ethnic, racial, religious, and sexual legacies in the United States. It is an example of an avant-garde aesthetic in terms of its unlikely range of sources. They include a speech by Teddy Roosevelt, a film of vaudeville performers and exotica that appeared in the 1904 World's Fair, excerpts of company members' family history, a contemporary score with influences from ragtime, and various levels of characterization—a mosquito, Teddy Roosevelt, company members playing themselves—some of which are fantastical, some representational, some real. The tone of the piece shifts between dreamlike, real, surreal, and disconnected, creating a dynamic sense of the century through the mix.[1]

Lerman grounds the piece in her favourite Jewish prayer, "Shehechianu," Hebrew for sustenance. It is usually translated as "Blessed art thou, Lord our God. Ruler of the Universe, for keeping us alive, sustaining us, and permitting us to behold this day." She ties a meaningful personal source, Jewish identity, to the history of other peoples by retranslating the prayer thusly: "Isn't it amazing that, given all our different histories, we've gathered together at this moment?" The company examined the theme of sustenance through a series of questions, such as, "What is the meaning of prayer in relationship to your own cultural history? What has sustained you in the face of the wounds you have suffered? Are you to remember and be burdened by those memories or forget and move on? Do you see other choices?" These were explored through movement and storytelling in three contexts: within her company, in short workshops (a half day to two weeks) with interested people around the country, and at an extended residency in Portsmouth, New Hampshire. Portsmouth became a source for *Shehechianu* because in 1995–96, the company was also working on *The Shipyard Project* there, so ideas and materials from the two inevitably overlapped.

One of the Dance Exchange's core approaches is the combining of text and movement. Company members create aesthetically exciting dances from anybody's story using a series of techniques that Lerman and the company have developed. She elaborates: "One of the ways in which movement and stories go together is when you listen inside a story for the movement metaphor. That's a movement image taken from the story, standing for something in the story. Then what the dancers do is explore. They forget the story for a few minutes. We explore in as many ways as we can the beauty, the excitement, the thrill of the image, maybe being a little wacky even. So we stop the meaning, and we do the movement. We look at all the movements we've gathered, and we begin to work with the movements that are the most striking. Then when we go back to the story, we look for possible relationships" (Borstel 2003b, 9).

The company started work on *Shehechianu* with the prayer itself, both the shape of its Hebrew letters and its meaning. They talked with Hebrew scholars about the root meanings of the words. Different translations offered different movement ideas; for example, the word *vihichianu* can mean "caused us to reach" or "caused us to endure." In a 1997 company newsletter, dancer Rome Quezada expressed the energy that struck him about the letters themselves as swirling and pulsating movements, also communicating his experience of his own life at that time, which required him both to reach and to endure. In the same newsletter, company member Jeffrey Gunshol said that he "was drawn to the letter that represents Adonai, which means 'Lord' . . . [and] has two hooks near the top. So I am jumping into the air while hooking my finger and knees."

Images may be developed via detailing, a technique that "draws movement ideas from concrete physical evidence by observing the immediate environment and by conjuring details of a scene from memory and imagination" (Borstel 2003b).[2] Lerman gives an example of detailing from *The Shipyard Project*, using this line: "I stood on the bridge and looked at the shipyard":

> The details are the unstated imagery in the sentence. The details are in what I didn't say. So, the details might be: What is the ironwork on the bridge? What are the patterns of the ironwork? . . . Which way was the wind blowing my hair? . . . What happens choreographically is, I might take the patterns of the ironwork, which is like a crisscrossing pattern, and I might take the cranes, which are at very disjointed angles to each other. I might take my arms and form a criss-crossing pattern and then take my arms and form a disjointed, angular pattern. So now I would have two movements.

She would do those two movements while she said the line. Where she places her arms vis-à-vis her body adds more layers of communication, an underlying feeling about the bridge she has discovered (Moyer 1996, 10–11). Lerman avows that emotion is often embedded in the details, suggesting that one model of her artmaking is to tell the story and dance the details. This is a widely accessible exercise suitable for the wide range of people with whom Lerman makes dances.

Shehechianu evolved into a tritych zooming in first on the 1904 St. Louis World's Fair, then on critical midcentury moments in two American cities, and finally on the time period that the Dance Exchange was performing it, at the edge of the millennium. Part 1, "Faith and Science on the Midway," opens with an evocative sense of beginnings. The characters appear all in white. It is the opening of the piece, the start of the century. As "Faith and Science" unfolds, the company represents the fair's attractions, within which are imbedded stereotypes of cultural "others" displayed for their entertainment value, that continue to (mis)shape perceptions of different groups to this day. These images also bespeak the personal histories of the dancers. Rome Quezada does the dance of a Filipino on the midway, naked except for a white cloth covering his genitals. Judith Jourdin, as an exoticized Palestinian Jewess with a large fake nose, tells the audience about the letters in *Shehechianu* as her two assistants dance a hoochie-coochie. Peter Dimuro plays a congenial white anthropologist, measuring the head of the pygmy Otabenga, a particularly painful display. Andy Torres, a dark-skinned Latino, plays a carnival barker selling cure-all potions but moving in the physical step-and-fetch-it language of nineteenth-century minstrelsy, which has plagued the representation of African Americans since before the Civil War.

Juxaposed against these large racial and cultural representations are small, detailed movements and the text. "The essence of life is in smallness." We are thus brought into the uniqueness of the individual dancers, beyond their cultural markers. Is this also a clue to the bizarre mosquito character, bearer of malaria, the first in a series of plagues including cancer and AIDS that scourged the century? Why is this bearer of bad news so cute, too cute, so round and lyrical? The piece contains a certain amount of mystery. The company thus resists the equation that accessibility to broad audiences means aesthetic simplification. But Lerman does include a guide for looking at art in the program when they perform for audiences new to dance.

Part 2, "Bench Marks," evidences moments in which two core elements of human sustenance, namely love and work, are in social crisis. The section starts in the shipbuilding town of Portsmouth, New Hampshire, after World War II and focuses on the collective history of workers and their families. Indeed, fourteen minutes of *Shehechianu* is accompanied by an audiotape culled from Portsmouth stories. Images, too, are drawn from former shipyard workers. In one segment, the dancers are lying on the floor doing work gestures they learned from shipbuilders as, on tape, a Portsmouthian recounts a story about twelve generations of her family who worked there. Peter DiMuro confirms, "Portsmouth feeds our art. We are pushed to explore new metaphors. You don't put it together in the same way because you have different ingredients" (Whitney 1996, 20).

The second part of "Bench Marks" takes place in Washington, D.C., the Dance Exchange's home turf. It depicts the 1950s, when gays and lesbians in the U.S. government were hunted out and ejected from their jobs. It also suggests the complicated relationship between work and love. One section danced to the tune of "Young at Heart" is unabashedly romantic with pleasurable couplings of various sex, race, and age combinations. There's a woman in love with babies, and another in love with her vacuum cleaner. Gay love is complicated with spies lurking in bushes, shifting the mood from nostalgic romance and satire to paranoid intolerance and ruined careers.

Part 3, "The Skin Soliloquies," evidences how our different histories affect the way we relate to each other in the present. Characters from earlier in the piece arrive at the edge of the millennium and consider holding onto their historical scars or forgetting their pasts. One carries a box, one a sphere, one the branch of a tree. The dancers, friends and fellow travelers, comfort each other. A hand reaches down, lifts someone up, and their heads rest on each other's shoulders. One kisses another's cheek. Others take hands, balance, twirl, leap, and give more kisses. They pass the sphere, one to another. Sometimes they appear to be carrying the weight of the world on their shoulders; other times, the sphere is a playful, oversized beach ball. And another kiss. Torres sings: "Don't know why, there's no sun up in the sky, stormy weather." Evoking the emotional geography of loss of the sustenance of love. The space is empty but for an enormous panorama with tree, sky, and Hebrew letters floating on a scrim. *Baruch, atah aonai. . . .*

African American dancer Gisel Mason ponders: "Wouldn't it be amazing to be seen without my scars? Scars on my knees from bending, picking. On my chest from Otabenga's chest. Can't forget, your water fountain is over there. I'm trapped by my own skin." Picking up Torre's minstrel shuffle from part 1, she mutters, "I'm going as fast as I can." Mason then asks for us all: "Is my worth always to be measured by the weight of my burden? Do I diminish my ancestors if I move forward? Do I diminish myself if I look back? In part 3 we have arrived at the edge of the century as in a vast wilderness. Is this where Moses saw the burning bush? Both are evoked by *shin*, the first letter of *Shehechianu*—looking like three flames reaching upward or Moses with his two arms stretched upward. Indeed, throughout the piece the dancers raise their arms up to the sky or, more often, out to each other. Or is this that famous landscape, barren except for a single tree, from *Waiting for Godot*? For these characters are also trying to figure out how to go on.

Lerman describes her choreographic role as "creating an environment in which people can do their best work," in contrast to her "own rotten experiences in other people's dance"—that is, being told exactly what to do. As a choreographer she observes that creation improves when the dancers participate in the process of making it. To that end, Lerman typically shares the big picture with the dancers. She describes getting a group of teenagers to edit their section of *Hallelujah*, a five-year, multi-city project celebrating what people praise. The teens were very attached to their choreography, but Lerman explained her perspective on it: "I tell them the whole story; of how I liked the movements when I first saw it earlier in the day, and of how I had come to see that it would have to be trimmed. I ask them to go away in small groups and edit out all of the material that they think will not work when set against the Whitman poem. In spite of their attachment to their choreography, they are inspired and interested in the problem. They work efficiently and return with their edits." By framing the issue as larger than them and their dance, Lerman observes "that they can really think beyond their own needs when they are asked to confront the larger questions of the work, including what the audience will actually experience" (2002a, 24).

Lerman takes what people offer up and shapes it into art. For example, she was collaborating on a *Hallelujah* piece with Rudy Hawkins and his gospel choir. She wanted Hawkins to write a song in which Adam and Eve fight over what to take in their suitcases when they are banished from the Garden. Lerman recounts, "At that suggestion, several of the singers looked at me in dismayed exasperation and said, 'What suitcases? What argument? They messed up and they have to leave. Period.'" Moreover, Hawkins explained, "I can't write an argument in gospel. Gospel is only for good news." He thought for a moment, then grinned and said, "I can write it in the blues, though. But they may not sing it . . . most of the singers have left the blues behind for gospel" (Lerman 2002b, 29–30).

Lerman later asked Hawkins to take something he had written for one dance and play it elsewhere. When he balked, she observed, "Our greatest difference is that I always take things apart and try to put them back together in new ways, and you always try to keep things whole and connected." She also noted "how close faith values and aesthetic values can be" (2002b, 30). This suggests that Hawkins is a religious and aesthetic purist, whereas Lerman is eclectic, finding sources and inspirations for both her spirituality and art in multiple traditions. Lerman's ability to articulate difference without rancor is a skill that has surely been as necessary to her work as have pliés and relevés.

Lerman's methodology includes educating her audience so they can *see* the company's aesthetic choices. In program notes, she suggests to audiences that they pay attention to the following: gestures, from small to how amplified and expanded; repetition, how and why; sequence: why; numbers of dancers changing, why and when; geometric shapes the dancers make and their approach and recoil vis-à-vis audience; variations on a theme re: levels and body parts; where dancers facing; unison (and how many), individual, variational dancing; relation between music and dancing, music and space; stories and their relation to each other, the movements; explicit/implicit content and effect on spectator; what a given spectator likes (2002a, 26). This is a concrete way to facilitate audience engagement in company performances.

Lerman's deep connection to art that flows out of everyone's life exists comfortably alongside that which is created by professionals. One of her inspirations is "the passion play at Oberammergau, where who gets to play Jesus is an issue in that community and the person who is chosen brings himself to that. And the knowledge you have about him filters into what you see." For Lerman, that does not take away from the performance but enriches it. At the same time, she revels in the intensity of long technical rehearsals, insisting, "I think I'm the better for having both. I don't see why we can't practice the art of dance and have those things and many more. That seems much more what the role of an artist should be."

The myriad ways in which Lerman shapes what people offer up, be it company or community participants, bespeaks an effort known in Hebrew as *lishlam*, to make whole, the noun form of which is *shalom*, translated as peace. But wholeness, the literal translation, is a more complex and apt word. It means bringing everything in, with all the discomfort that suggests. Community-based artists develop ways of working through conflicts that arise as a result of the plurality of voices. Lerman describes this as "colliding truth," accidental insensitivities to each other as a result of different perspectives (1993b, 16). Lerman is committed to not leaving in the face of conflict but rather working through the discomfort. Her writing is sprinkled with variations of lishlam. She writes of feeling fragmented, of recognizing fragmentation as the state of most people in these times, and of art as a way of bringing all the parts together.

Lerman imagines that dance played a popular role in ancient cultures, that everyone knew the dances, and that dance was not an experience for specialists apart from everyday life. She states, "What we've really been about is trying to take these incredible functions of dance and reintegrate them into art" (17).

Notes

1   I am grateful to Dance Exchange Humanities Director John Borsted for conversations about *Shehechianu* that informed this analysis.
2   The Dance Exchange as an entity uses and refines all of the techniques, but the source of the initial impulse varies. Detailing, for example, originated with choreographer Celeste Miller before she was part of the Dance Exchange. Lerman has evolved it to the point that she and Miller now practice it in distinctly different versions.

References

Borstel, John (ed). (2003b) *Liz Lerman Dance Exchange Basic Toolbox*. Takoma Park: MD, Author.
Moyer, Judith (1996) 'A Most Excellent Conversation.' *The Music Hall's Shipyard Project Book*, 7–16. Portmouth, NH: Author.
Lerman, Liz (1993b) 'Are Miracles Enough?' *Dance/USA Journal* (spring): 16–20.
Lerman, Liz (2002a) 'Framing it Bigger: Meaning, Morale and the Question of Quality' and 'How to Watch a Hallelujah.' In: *Hallelujah: The Extraordinary Essence in Everyday Life*, 29–30. College Park: Clarice Smith Performing Arts Center, University of Maryland.
Lerman, Liz (2002b) 'Walking the Thin Border: A Parting Thought on Art and Faith.' In: *Hallelujah: The Extraordinary Essence in Everyday Life*, 29–30. College Park: Clarice Smith Performing Arts Center, University of Maryland.
Whitney, D. Quincey (1996) 'Week of Dance Fetes Portsmouth's Past.' *Boston Globe*, September 15, 20.

Figure 13 Scene from *The Age Exchange*, an original play devised by residents of Silvercrest Senior Residency Center and students of Arcata High School, conducted and directed by Helga Rosenfeldt-Olsen, Andrew Phoenix and Tara Cariaso, MFA degree students of The Dell'Arte International School of Physical Theatre, Eureka, California, 2006.

Photo: Petra Kuppers.

CHAPTER 27

Rebecca Caines

Haunted voices in everyday spaces

The community-based hip-hop of Australian 'guerrilla' artist Morganics

Down River
When it's really hot, we go to the river and swim
When we go fishing, we catch some bream
When the river's high, we jump off the bridge
When we get home, we play some didg[1]

They call me Wally this is where I'm at
I wear on my head a baseball cap,
Parramatta[2] is my team if you know what I mean,
To be the captain, that's my dream . . .

When Colroy's here, have no fear
All you wild pigs better watch out for my spear
I'm with the gang and I'm almost ten
I wanna be an actor like Jackie Chan

Lendell's my name and I like to do backflips
Listen to the words that come from Wally
Jump off the bridge and I play the didg
When I catch a fish, I put it in the fridge . . .

My name is Buddy and I can't stand still
Wilcannia to Dubbo to Broken Hill[3]

I've been moved around
From town to town
And this is how
I get down

> (Excerpts from *Down River*, by the Wilcannia Mob
> facilitated by, produced and performed with
> hip-hop artist Morganics, 2001)

IN MY OWN WORK as a community arts practitioner working with young people, and in the practices of those I study, I have become most interested in what could be called community based 'guerrilla' performance – community performance which is both *site*-specific and involved with challenging power relations. Such community-based guerrilla artists are combining community dialogue, new performance forms *and* a politics of multivocalism, contact and self-expression, while creating place-based guerrilla actions in an increasingly conservative, de-localized Australian arts climate.

I will concentrate here on the work of Morgan Lewis, a.k.a. Morganics, a hip-hop artist who politically challenges the space and practice of the 'everyday' through the performance of a pluralistic sense of community. This chapter examines Morganics' community hip-hop by looking at his body of practice and then concentrating on two pieces he facilitated and produced. It concludes with some questions about the responsibilities and problems inherent in the reception and response to this powerful and at times disturbing art work.

Morganics' guerrilla practice: background and aims

Rediscovering the term 'guerrilla art', appropriated from didactic political actions popular in the 1960s and 1970s to analyse contemporary performance forms,[4] it is possible to see how combining site-specific practices with community work creates interesting political potential for artists. The contemporary guerrilla artist aims to challenge notions of authorship, genre and control. They work with and mobilize space, and engage with radical politics where it intersects with the street, with the home and with everyday life. In Morganics' community-based guerrilla practice there is also a blurring of community and performance with artistic identity, and the constant creation of spaces for the performance of difference.

Morganics is an MC/rapper, beat-boxer,[5] Bboy (break-dancer), music producer and dance and physical theatre teacher. He also has an established career as a solo contemporary performance artist and as an actor, as well as director of multimedia theatre events. He has several solo hip-hop albums on major labels to his name and also is responsible for producing two CDs, *All You Mob* and *All You Mob 2*, which are compilations made with participants from the community workshops he has conducted, working for multiple different community employers all over Australia. This chapter focuses on this latter community work, with new and young artists in Australian jails, regional areas, social welfare centres and isolated Aboriginal communities.

Shifting authorship, genre and control

Morganics utilizes all of the elements of his diverse performing career when working in dialogue with community workshop participants. On his community tours and performance projects, he has taught break-dance, beat-boxing, rapping/MC-ing and physical and multimedia theatre. At times he has also worked with other artists to teach elements of hip-hop, graffiti DJ-ing and sampling, as well as R 'n' B and other dance forms, visual arts and film-making. He has worked in collaboration with social welfare groups, theatre companies, other professional artists, community elders and leaders, and participants of all ages. As a facilitator, not only does he teach technique and share his wealth of training, knowledge and experience, he also devises and bounces ideas around, learns the oral histories of the places and people he visits, provides moral support, and performs with and creates music and beat-box backings for his workshop participants. The experiences of constant travel, engagement with large numbers of local people, immersion in their daily lives, hopes and tragedies, also deeply affect the way his practice develops.[6] Hip-hop has in its make-up the elements of showing-off, of performing to each other, challenging, jamming. It is a form with dialogue at its heart, and in a Morganics workshop it is often difficult to see who is the teacher, and who the student.

Morganics' hip-hop thus continually unsettles what it means to be an 'artist' creating 'site-specific' work with 'communities'. In his performance events, he performs *with*, *to* and *parallel to* his (mostly young) workshop participants. He is thus *simultaneously* facilitator/producer, peer, co-actor/performer, collaborator and audience member for the performance work he coordinates. The communities he works with are *both* pre-established groups, geographically, ethnically or disadvantage-bound (like the young Aboriginal Wilcannia boys performing in *Down River*) *and* new communities created through the involvement with Morganics and the creation of new work based on radical difference, pluralism and mobility. His hip-hop disrupts ideas of place, space and politics through both evoking the everyday places of the participants (both regional and urban), and allowing them to challenge, recreate and subvert the spaces of their lives through the creation of hip-hop performance events.

It is perhaps the difficulty in separating artist from art work and community that actually defines much contemporary community practice. The contemporary community performance-maker works with the community participants to articulate, challenge and disrupt community narratives, understanding that theirs is just another voice in the finished 'product', both vital to the art work and at times invisible inside it. Neither author nor manager, the guerrilla artist, tied to space and to politics, works with and is changed by the specifics of community.

Examining two of his pieces next to each other rather than in isolation allows us to see how this transient, mobile artist creates spaces where he can work side-by-side with his community participants in creating a place-specific politics of multiplicity and everyday life.

Creating and mobilizing site-specificity

Morganics' work is site-specific in that it re-combines what Henri Lefebvre calls *perceived spaces* (the way physical space defines and shapes us), *conceived space* (the way spaces are mapped and represented) and *lived space* (the way place is practised into being).[7] Lefebvre saw these different dimensions of space as integrated and inseparable; and it is through examining artists such as Morganics that it is possible to see how the contemporary guerrilla artist works fluidly between the three. Lefebvre's ideas of a spatiality, not tied just to physical location, are played out in the practice of site-specific artists, who are increasingly recognizing the power of articulating and challenging community through foregrounding different ideas of spatiality and place. Site-specificity, as US-based public art theorist Miwon Kwon reminds us, is thus no longer just tied to traditional ideas of geography for artists. 'Dispersed across much broader cultural, social, and discursive fields, and organized intertextually through the nomadic movement of the artist – operating more like an itinerary than a map – the site can now be as various as a billboard, an artistic genre, a disenfranchised community, an institutional framework, a magazine page, a social cause or a political debate. It can be literal, like a street corner, or virtual, like a theoretical concept.'[8] Morganics' work is always heavily based in space and place, and it is often in beginning to describe their homes and daily activities that participants start to engage in with their communities and the areas which interest and concern them. Working from the everyday urban streets, parks, rivers and living rooms of the participants, as well as simultaneously from the realities of the power relations in these spaces, and the dreams and visions of the participants for change, Morganics creates room for a re-creation, re-mapping and re-living of these spaces, simultaneously evoking place and challenging it.

I've heard and seen raps in Morganics' workshops about going to school, about smoking 'pot' (marijuana), about bringing up kids in Australia as a single mother, about the ugliness of a building, and the beauty of a evening sky. There are raps about dating Pamela Anderson, just as there are raps on the *All You Mob* CD about towns, high schools, inner states of mind, different languages, babies' voices, political tensions and the state of the Australian music industry. These voices fight stereotyping through multiple representations from massively different perspectives. There are, importantly, contradictory raps about the same place, and raps that constantly shift between the multiple voices all – coexisting in the same performances. This is a place where voices that rarely get to speak publicly are heard, and the performance of hip-hop, in all of its guises, is a performance of group dynamics involving intimacy and contact, with the performers and their environments, and with each other. The initial performance events are almost always intimate, rowdy, interactive affairs, in dialogue with the spaces and communities they shape and work in.

What follows is an analysis of two pieces developed by young people working with Morganics. Through understanding the range of Morganics' practice, one can see the performance of a pluralized community, the challenging of space and the localization of the politics of everyday life which works across Morganics' body of guerrilla art work.

Guerilla art facilitated by Morganics

Down River

Down River was made as part of an outer Sydney-based Shopfront Theatre hip-hop workshop tour. Morganics was employed by Shopfront to teach hip-hop and produce performances with these isolated young people. The piece was made in the tiny, remote rural town of Wilcannia, almost a thousand kilometres northwest of Sydney and 195 km east of Broken Hill, population 750, climate 'hot, slow and dry'.[9] The following are members of the *Wilcannia Mob* hip-hop group, formed during a Morganics workshop: Keith Dutton, 13; Buddy Blair, 12; Colroy Johnson, 10; Wally Ebsworth, 13; and Lendal King, 10. This group has since gone on to achieve considerable fame in Australia, including a debut as a group at Sydney's youth music festival 'Homebake' to audiences of over ten thousand, and going on to win Best Single at the 'Deadlies', the nation's most prestigious Aboriginal sport and culture awards. Recently they have been involved in performances at the Opera House (2004–5), and in documentaries and features on ABC TV (Australian Broadcasting Authority – the government sponsored national TV and Radio Agency) and SBS (multicultural TV broadcaster) 2003–5, as well as considerable air play across public and commercial radio and TV. The CD their work was produced on has, however, remained signed with the non-commercial ABC Music and any funds from commercial air play and CD sales go into a trust fund managed jointly by Shopfront Youth Theatre and the families of the participants. Involvement with Morganics has deeply affected these young people, from their life experience, career prospects and financial situations through to the way they identify themselves to their community and Australia. The full impact of this guerrilla activity may not be properly understood for many years.

The Morganics workshop in beat-boxing and rapping, from which the piece *Down River* and the group the Wilcannia Mob sprang, included: a discussion of the art form of hip-hop and its elements, a practical demonstration of techniques, the playing of tracks developed by other young people in Morganics' workshops and shows, the breakdown and teaching of the techniques and finally the writing, performing and laying down of tracks. Morganics performed for the young people and 'jammed' with them. Participants were directly encouraged to speak in their own voices/accents and sometimes their own languages. They were encouraged both to create fiction and to describe their lives and things that were important to them. Morganics specifically encouraged them not to imitate or copy famous American hip-hop artists, or use American accents, but instead to articulate whatever they wanted to say through the medium of hip-hop and to hear it back. This is not to erase the vital place of sampling, sarcasm or parody in hip-hop, or to erase the powerful connection some disempowered people in Australia feel with the history of resistant African-American hip-hop, but rather to encourage participants to start from a place that is open with the world they daily engage with.[10] The 'site'-specificity of Morganics' community hip-hop thus also relates to the specificities of the histories, languages and voices which make up site/space/place.

In *Down River* (excerpted at the beginning of this article) the Australian accent is strong, as is the specific sense of place, the Darling River where the boys play. Kerry King, Lendell's mother, described the experience in an interview as 'another big burst of pride and honour and self-esteem'. 'The song gives a positive image back to Wilcannia,' Ms King said. 'The simple things they sing about indicate our lifestyle; how we can live in a remote area in a harmonistic way. There are not a lot of material things out there, but it's about using what's there in the river and being part of our life."[11] Through Morganics, these boys learnt to engage with their own visions of Wilcannia, but also with the Wilcannia of their families and peers.

Down River, however, is also a narrative previously unheard in mainstream Australia, a fresh story of everyday life, an insertion into a national understanding of what it might be like to be a particular Australian young person. Morganics' work makes room for the expression of a geographical community, 'Wilcannia', a diaspora 'Aboriginal young people', an imagined community 'the hip-hop community' and a resistant link to African-American culture, 'the global political hip-hop artist'. All of these images simultaneously then feed and disrupt how these boys articulate their home and dreams. At the time, the political climate in Australia was producing far-right politicians such as popular Queensland Independent Pauline Hansen (1997–2003) who forwarded a radical anti-immigration and anti-Aboriginal rights platform. Additionally, Australia had a right-wing Coalition conservative national government in power which arguably destabilized Australian multiculturalism through refugee mistreatment and anti-terrorism policies. Against this background, his piece, played repeatedly on national, government-sponsored youth-radio station Triple J and then given so much national commercial media attention, ensured that a singular media portrait of Australian youth was not possible. Additionally, the reduction of Aboriginal and non-white people to simplistic stereotypes was made much more difficult. The guerrilla practice of Morganics and these Wilcannia boys together thus challenged the power relations that shaped all of their/our lives.

Despite the strong *evocation* of place and personality in this piece, there is, of course, also the *creation* of place. The Darling River in 2001, for instance, was in severe drought and almost completely dry. Memory and desire (of swimming and fishing in this river), imagination (of dreams of football captaincy or being a movie star) and lived practice (playing didgeridoo, spearing wild pigs, doing backflips, swimming, travelling) all combine. There is no mention of other social realities of Wilcannia such as isolation, lack of resources, boredom, and extreme poverty. This is not just a naive practice of attempted 'identity representation', this is a created place of idealism and humour. The community and place here are being simultaneously lived and dreamt into being. Here the site-specificity encouraged by all of Morganics' practices resurfaces, as his community hip-hop encourages the participants to name these physical, conceived and lived places into being, and to reconnect the dreams of the future with the activities of daily life. Perhaps as these pieces are played and replayed in Wilcannia, and throughout Australia, the contradictions and omissions inside the piece, the contrasting economic/spatial realities and desires brought to light can be further understood and challenged.

The Block

The second piece, *The Block*, has a very different history, even though it was made in the same year and features on the same non-commercial CD, *All You Mob*. This piece was initially made with Morganics as part of a multimedia performance event, *Stand Your Ground*, directed by Caitlin Newton-Broad. It was performed with students from a variety of inner-city high schools at the PACT Theatre in Erskineville, Sydney in 2001, and then later released on the compilation CD. This was also a piece about everyday lives and the performance of community, made by three high-school boys in consultation with their families and friends. There were two accompanying video clips made, showing the boys on the streets and gyms of Redfern, which were projected behind the performance of the piece in the show. The segment featured the three boys and Morganics rapping and breaking in front of the video screens to a packed house comprised of friends, families and theatre audiences.

The Block

Stand your ground, black people from the block
We are not moving on so rack off cops[12]
With the Redfern housing company[13]
Gonna manifest our own destiny
Junkies from the block
If you've had a bad shot
You get your final bed
Triple 0, call the Ambos[14]
He's not dead
Junkies better throw their needles away
Or they'll never see the light of another day
Just walk away, just walk away
Doing bag snatching, coppas coming this way
Running out of puff trying to get rid of the hot stuff
Dealers, junkies, gamblers all bringing the coppas around
Making a bad rap for our part of town
We've had about enough
They better move on
We're comin at ya rough from the microphone
This is where we live, what we call home . . .
Standing in the street in the park in the dark
No shoes on with needles around
The playground
Pemulway[15] Park is the place to play
It's not just young 'uns I'm here to say
People running around with needles in their arm
Falling on the ground doing themselves harm
The government took my people away and now I'm never ever going to
    see them again[16]

It's a pain when I'm waiting in the rain
A guy asks for a pie
Not again
I feel sorry for the poor buggar
But no one else seems to bother
He must be a gubba,[17] a gubbariginal
And here comes the rain, just another day . . .

(Excerpts from *The Block*, Jesse Close and the Clevo St Boys
(Cleveland St High School), facilitated and mixed by, and
performed with, hip-hop artist Morganics, 2001)

The piece talks about 'The Block', a residential area in Redfern, situated near to the prime real-estate central business district of inner Sydney.[18] 'The Block' is the area in West Redfern bound by Eveleigh Street, Vine Street, Louis Street and Caroline Street. Redfern was the first successful Aboriginal urban land rights claim in Australian history and this part of Redfern has a long and troubled history. This prime inner-city real-estate would be worth tens of millions to potential property developers who are prevented from moving in by the land rights claims and resistant community. Most of the houses on 'The Block' are nearly one hundred years old and are 'well past their use by date'. Many, if not all the houses, 'are derelict or close to derelict and are far from suitable for human habitation', and there are continual, controversial plans for redevelopment of the area and the construction of new homes for the Aboriginal residents, as well as an equally controversial programme of relocation, moving Aboriginal families away from Redfern. The area has 'a notorious drug trade, a high record of crime and arrests and constant tension between police and residents'.[19]

The Block, like many of the pieces developed with Morganics, unsettles the idea that community hip-hop could somehow be just a vehicle for the transparent reproduction of everyday life, as it is obviously both a description of everyday activities of walking, playing, catching trains at the same time as it is an articulation of desires, for police to leave them be, for the drug trade in Redfern to move on, for self-actualized destiny manifested through involvement with strong community organizations, for resistant, celebratory identities. It is embedded in the places and communities of Redfern, even as it challenges them. When performed by 15–16-year-old Redfern residents, in a mostly non-commercial performance venue and medium, it unsettles 'popular' ideas of the area as simply apathetically mired in crime, or teenage rap music as inherently tied to commercial profit. It was written by the boys, Morganics and an uncle of one of the boys, himself a member of the Redfern Housing Company. It is both a constructed Redfern and one lived and embodied by these boys every day, just as it is both a celebration of difference and a strategy for producing it. This multi-authored guerrilla work is thus on the one hand community-based, site-specific and involved in the contestation of relations of power, while on the other hand it remains embedded in the daily lives of the authors and performers.

Morganics was present at the *Stand Your Ground* performance event at the PACT Youth Theatre in Sydney, where Jesse and his friends sang along to their pre-recorded words played over the sound system, rediscovering them, re-emphasizing them, making them anew. That was the first public showing of this work. Morganics facilitated with co-writing and producing the initial recording, working in production on the night (clearing stages, setting up equipment), in solo performance in drumming and beat-boxing and in co-performance and moral support, breaking and rapping on-stage with the boys during the performance of *The Block*, even at times in friendly competition. Once again the line between artist and community blurs despite the fact that Morganics, as a white middle-class professional artist, does not presume to understand or be part of the reality these boys live with.[20] This powerful work was a product of the guerrilla activity and performance of both Morganics and these boys.

Obviously linked to the type of resistant, often oppositional, hip-hop of African-American rap performers, with echoes, for example, of NWA's classic 'Fuck the Police', at times equally angry, anti-authority and simplistic, this work in performance is specific, contemporary and controversial. Through engagement with the work of Morganics, an art work was created which foregrounds a district many non-Aboriginal Australians would prefer to ignore, one associated with crime, drugs and slums, yet one which, in performance, also produces laughs in the audience as the boys impersonate mean 'bad-boy' poses with smiles, improvise around the lyrics and make black-humoured jokes about white Australian beggars as honorary Aboriginals, 'gubbaroginals'. *The Block*, like Morganics, often slips away from attempts to categorize it. Perhaps because of the smaller population, the lower scale of commercialization and relatively new 'scene' of Australian hip-hop, this work does not run the risk of merging into a mass-produced rap music genre, but remains a refreshing new voice in young people's music – a shocking insertion into stereotypes of apathetic, drugged-out young people, somehow unaware of their own situation. Instead it showcases teenagers involved in analysing and resisting complex social situations as part of a shifting community. The performance by this community in *The Block* is a palimpsest, a text written and rewritten over so many times that it's impossible to see where the art work begins and the community ends.

This song, despite also being recorded on the *All You Mob* CD, has had very little media attention or radio air play. It is not surprising really, that the cute voices of the country kids talking about their lives in *Down River* is given huge media attention, while the didactic, aggressive description of teenage inner-city living in 'The Block' is not. They are both, however, performances of place and of community, working from daily life.

Haunted voices

Australian theorist Linnell Secomb in her paper 'Haunted Communities', analyses Jacques Derrida's idea of 'impossible mourning',[21] a type of mourning which doesn't reduce memories of one deceased to some sort of containment inside the self, but instead continually projects their presence, voice and desires into the future.[22] Secomb suggests that the actively remembered 'spectres' of people no longer physically present can still 'haunt' society, forming 'haunted communities' where the re-remembered bodies/voices of the past interact with the physical present, their presence constantly demanding responses. This is especially true, Secomb asserts, where massive injustices of the past form a lineage that can never ethically be 'laid to rest',[23] as is the case for indigenous Australian history. I would argue that these are the haunted spaces of community hip-hop.

I would add to this argument by saying that the lived space where this 'haunting' occurs is not an empty space. In this 'performing palimpsest', the traces/writing we identify are living and re-remembered complex bodies, interacting with each other in intimate social networks. Histories, identities, memories, injustices, the desires of past and present people, voices and 'hauntings' all begin to have equal weight and become almost impossible to separate. This is a palimpsest of 'liveness', of bodies and ghostlike memories, invigorated through bodies. Thus, everyday spaces are never empty and, under this analysis, performance is ethically and politically both a space for haunted voices to be heard and a continual call for action to be taken to right the injustices of the past. It is in community performance that these voices can be heard.

I heard the track *The Block* in 2001, just after it was recorded on the original home-produced *All You Mob* CD, and was blown away by its aggressive political 'everydayness'. But watching this performance again in 2005 on video, I have been haunted by my own spectres. I cannot watch videos of this performance, for all its resistant celebratory joy, without thinking of another performance that happened years later in Redfern, one I know hardly anything about, bar the images in my head from sensationalist commercial media.[24] The images I am haunted by are the bricks, glass bottles and flaming bottles filled with petrol, thrown by indistinct shapes illuminated by the light of fires, and the wall of 250 riot shields advancing down Eveleigh Street in Redfern on the evening of Sunday, 15 February 2005 – the so-called 'Redfern riots'. I am haunted by the spectres of those one hundred or so, mostly young, bodies engaged in violent, destructive resistance to police presence following the death of a local teenage boy, T.J. Hickey (a relative of one of the performers in this piece), who died the day before these riots because of his involvement in a controversial police chase. I can't help but think that the notion of allowing subjugated voices to articulate their communities and their engagement with the space of everyday life is one thing, but I have to wonder, what happens when these subjugated voices of daily life, brought to light by the work of guerrilla artists such as Morganics, speak loudly and clearly but are not listened to. Surely a sustained social response by Australian society is needed to continue this powerful community political action? What happens, we have to ask, when these haunted voices, so vibrantly articulated in the everyday spaces of our lives, meet no community of response?

Notes

1   The didgeridoo is a musical instrument traditional to the Australian Aboriginal peoples of Arnhem Land, far Northern Territory, now more widely used.
2   Parramatta Rugby League football team (based in Sydney).
3   This is a round trip distance of about 3,000 km.

4   For examples of this work see Henry Lesnick, *Guerrilla Street Theater* (New York, Avon, 1973). Also John Weisman, *Guerrilla Theater, Scenarios for Revolution* (Garden City, NY, Anchor Press, 1973).

5   Beat-boxing is the artistic practice of creating melody and rhythm through the creation of sounds and sound effects made with the mouth on the microphone.

6   In his autobiographical theatre piece *Crouching Bboy Hidden Dreadlocks (Sydney 2000)*, Morganics discusses how the poverty and hardship of some of his participants made him re-evaluate how he debated the role of hip-hop in his workshops.

7   Henri Lefebvre, *The Production of Space* (Oxford; Cambridge, MA, Blackwell, 1991).

8   Miwon Kwon, *One Place After Another: Site-Specific Art and Locational Identity* (Cambridge, MA, MIT Press, 2002), p. 4.

9   Peter Munro (30 November 2002) 'Mob Rules', *Sydney Morning Herald*.

10 Morganics, Morganics interviewed by R. Caines (11 January 2004).

11 Steve Munro, 'The Wilcannia Mob', *Sydney Morning Herald*, 20 November 2002.

12 The lyrics were 'Piss Off' in the original, but were edited for school performances.

13 The (Redfern) Aboriginal Housing Company mentioned in the song is a private non-profit charity and the first affordable housing provider for Aboriginal and Torres Strait Islander people in Australia. Incorporated in 1973, the Company's formation was in direct response to the widespread discrimination Aborigines experienced, at the time in the private rental market. Working off an initial grant, the Company bought and still manages properties in Redfern for the exclusive use of indigenous families. The Company also helped kick-start grassroots indigenous civil rights in conjunction with other organizations such as the Aboriginal Medical and Legal Services.

14 Dial 000 for an Australian emergency phone call.

15 Pemulway was an Aboriginal military leader in the resistance against colonial invasion. The local park is named after him.

16 This refers to the policy of forcibly removing Aboriginal children from their parents and placing them in institutions, forced domestic service and government 'care', which continued in Australia until around 1970, resulting in what has become known as the 'Stolen Generations'.

17 Aboriginal language colloquial term for a 'white person'.

18 All references to the history, culture and problems of 'The Block' are sourced from the Aboriginal Housing Company website of the Aboriginal Housing Company, home page, 2004. Available: http://www.ahc.org.au, accessed 1 May 2004.

19 The Aboriginal Housing Company, home page, 2004.

20 In interview Morganics stated: 'I mean, what do I have in common with a 16-year-old Aboriginal girl, nothing, and I wouldn't try to,' Morganics interview with R. Caines.

21 Jacques Derrida quoted in Linnell Secomb, 'Haunted Community', in Michael Strysick and ebrary Inc. (eds), *The Politics of Community* (Aurora, CO, Davies Group Publishers, 2002), p. 138.

22 Ibid., p. 138.

23 Ibid., p. 138.

24 Brad Cramer and Ben Emery, 'Redfern Riots: A Seven News Report', *Seven News* (Australia, Seven Network, 2004).

CHAPTER 28

Glenda Dickerson

Festivities and jubilations on the graves of the dead

Sanctifying sullied space

Eel catching in Setauket

A living portrait of the Christian Avenue community

> Alexanduh, the old root doctor, wuz stil libin when I wuz a boy. Dey say
> duh boat leab fuh Savannah and Alexanduh he yuh. He say goodbye frum
> yuh and tell em tuh go on widout im but he say he see em deah and wen
> duh boat git tuh Savannah, Alexanduh he in Savannah on duh dock tuh
> ketch duh line.
>
> (*Drums and Shadows*, p. 184)

A LEXANDER, THE ROOT DOCTOR, is a folk son of John Henry and Aunt
Hagar. He lives eternally in Georgia Sea Island lore. He has a blood brother
living in the village of Setauket on Long Island, who can perform the same miraculous
feats.

When Pete Tucker felt like dancing, he walked all the way from his home in
Setauket to the county seat in Riverhead. He walked slow and easy, not in a hurry.
Carriages filled with lustrous ebony, sepia, butterscotch, and tea-rose party-goers
passed him on the way; but when they arrived, he was always there ahead of them
lounging insolently against a gnarled post in the barn which served as their dancing
space. The villagers of Setauket speculated, but they did not know how he accomplished
this feat. Most of them thought he was "nothin' but the devil." Ted Green told me
that he could make the hoes work by themselves or lay down in the field, according
to his mood.

One thing they knew for sure, Pete Tucker was a "bad nigger" who fought white men, but could not be kept in jail. Pete Tucker lives in the collective memories of the Christian Avenue folk.

Setauket's Christian Avenue community is one of the oldest African American communities on Long Island. Pete Tucker revolves in their minds along with visions of pipe-smoking great-grandmothers and babies stolen by gypsies. His tale symbolizes for us the magic power of oral history. The folk whisper and glance around when they say his name. They drop their eyes, reluctant to tell his story. They remember his icy, grey eyes and they make of that memory an incantatory protection, a repository of fear, taking a sly pride in his arrogance.

One day not too long ago, I was looking out the window of my lonesome house in Setauket. I was trying to think of something to do since New York City was farther than the posted sixty miles, Africa was across the water and Heaven only comes to those who wait. The toothless trees outside my window soughed and sighed and prepared to blabber their delicious secret. My hair stood on end as they whispered invitingly, "Want to have some oldtime fun? When you take your sunset walk today, keep on going till you come to the Mill Pond. Seek out the spot where the Setacott Indians first camped and called it 'land on the mouth of the creek.' You'll know when you come to it because you'll be standing on holy ground. From there it's an easy step to Christian Avenue."

Well, that's exactly what I did. When I got to Christian Avenue and walked past the cemetery, past Bethel African Methodist Episcopal Church, past the houses, sitting there warm and solid like my grandmother's fresh-baked monkey bread, I tell you Shango danced on my spine. It was a moment of whirring wings and glad awakening.

I ran home willy-nilly, pummelled by purpose, and did not forget to thank the blabbering trees. I had heard how old this community was (some say it predates the revolutionary war) and that its important history was in danger of being lost. The folk have been there as long as the Village, but the university folk weren't aware they existed. They were invisible. That very day, I took as my goal the task of documenting and preserving the history of the people who lived in those houses, along with the histories of their ancestors and descendants, by collecting their stories in their own words.

Collecting the stories and devising the means to tell them took two years. A performance and exhibit was presented 22–25 June 1988 in a huge black box in the Theater Arts Department at the State University of New York at Stony Brook where I was on the faculty. The event was called "a living library" and included a walking tour, an exhibit of artifacts produced by the community – arranged to felicitous impact by Tyrone Mitchell, a visual artist imported from New York to create the environment – and dramatic vignettes woven from the collected stories which were performed amidst the artifacts.

The title of the project is taken from a painting by William Sidney Mount, an American painter born in Setauket in 1807. His 1845 painting, "Eel Spearing at Setauket," depicts Rachel Holland Hart spearing for eels in a canoe navigated by a young caucasian. Rachel Holland Hart is the foremother of the Hart/Sells clan. Her descendants are the premier families of Christian Avenue.

The Harts and Sells live where their ancestors were born. They are surrounded by historic sites and landmarks. The ancestors sleep at either end of the community, enclosing the residents in a magic circle, with Bethel A.M.E. Church at its center. Near one end of Christian Avenue, a haphazard array of tombstones rambles over Laurel Hill. Wildflowers cozy up to the tombstones. At the other end, enclosed by an old picket fence, Bethel Cemetery sits upon her dignity. The burying ground is dotted with jaunty little American flags, placed by veteran Theodore Green, memorializing veterans of the world wars.

Mr. Green, descended from both the Harts and Sells, was my guide on the two-year journey deep into the community.

> "Now those families in the old cemetery, other people don't know about like we do. Those Stones is, ah, almost 167 years old, those stones up there . . . if they ever move the stone, I wrote it down myself . . . because if I ever go there and the monument is gone I can put another one there . . . I can put another monument up there."[1]

For two years "Eel Catching" was centered at Bethel African Methodist Episcopal Church. The Black church, born in slavery, was the sole source of personal identity and sense of community for a people peremptorily stripped of the comforts of home. It became the home base for revolution. For these reasons, I wanted to make Bethel the home base for "Eel Catching."

For two years I, along with consultant Fai Walker and student interns, visited in the homes of the community, looking at old photographs and other artifacts, marking them down, wooing them away from the folks for the coming exhibit at Stony Brook. When completed, the exhibit would include photographs, paintings, family Bibles, cooking utensils, clothing, hair ornaments, sports equipment, furniture, pot-bellied stoves, and many other artifacts. The photographs and artifacts told their own stories, themselves as eloquent as the stories we heard from women and men who have walked this ground for nearly 100 years.

The stories are sepia-toned. They are ebony, butterscotch, and tea-rose like those long-ago party-goers. They are delicate like the white lace handkerchiefs the church ladies wear on missionary Sunday. They are strong, like the hands of community resident Alfred Hobbs, New York State's only Black farmer. They are vital, like Harry Hart's shovel, which hollows out the community graves. They are legendary, like Pete Tuckers's mandolin which made the hoes fall down in the field. "I sho heahd em talk bout grat doins an Ise headh Onkle Israel say duh hoe could wuk by itsef ef yuh know wut tuh say tuh it" (the speaker is Ben Sullivan, St. Simons Island. *Drums and Shadows*, p. 182).

For two years, I sho heard 'em talk their lives and listened closely, spinning a drama in my head all the while.

Lucy Agnes (Hart) Keyes, Mother of Bethel Church, was born in 1900. She was one of twelve children of Jacob and Hannah Hart. She is a great-great-great grandmother.

Many evenings as the sun went down, I sat in Mrs. Keyes's front room or garden and listened enraptured to her talkstory.

> I'm known as Lucy . . . I love that name . . . Lucy. And my mind is so clear how as clear about back then as it is about now. What happened a month ago I have to stop and think, but it is clear as a crystal all the way back when I was 4 or 5 years old.

Mrs. Keyes told me the story, told to her by her mother, of a minister finding her grandmother.

> I wish I could remember the name of that minister. He came to Setauket to preach and mama was telling him . . . she never knew after her mother (she was) sold from her. This minister got in touch with different people and he found mama's mother and mama was married then, had several children. Papa got enough money together and she went down to Richmond to her mother. She stayed down with her, I guess, a whole month.

I heard 'em talk of a neighborhood changed forever.

> "The water is bad." This is what they said. That was the reason why they decided to move the people out . . . They tried to use the whole area for development . . . no homes at all, just stores, office buildings. After they decided that! . . . they had to get out and go find homes all over. That was a big human saying for awhile, "We don't know where to go! Where are we going to go?" . . . A whole street full of people out – could be put out with no place for them to go.
>
> (Ethel Lewis, community resident)

I sho heahd 'em talk about ties with the Shinnecock Nation which have woven patterns through the Hart/Sells lineages. On Labor Day, I rode with them on a rented bus up to the Shinnecock Pow Wow. It was wonderful to see the faces of women who looked like my daughter, dressed in traditional garb, celebrating their native heritage. I heard 'em talk their heritage.

> There were a lot of nationalities. I think we were the only Indians in there . . . One time, one time in our class we were the only Americans in the class the rest of the kids were Irish, Polish, Lithuanians, all from Europe and the Blacks were the only true citizens.
>
> (Nellie Edwards, community resident)

Student interns, under the tutelage of Fai Walker, oral historian, assisted in the recording of existing history and in the interviewing process. In May 1987, the students presented oral reports at Bethel Church. These reports drew sketches of community dwellers the students had interviewed, such as Hazel Lewis and Nellie Edwards, and served as a prelude to the living library event which would follow the next year. I heard 'em talk.

> I can see now why they say 50 is the golden age. Before conducting my interview, I'm ashamed to say that I had preconceived notions of what it would be like to be 50. Nellie Edwards changed my mind.
>
> (Karen Thomas, student)

The year leading up to the Eel Catching living library was one of shifting, reading, researching, arranging, plotting, planning, checking, cross-checking, and re-checking. The volume of collected material was tremendous and the list of donated artifacts long. The effort it took to weave them into a unified whole was a challenge the blabbering trees had not warned me of.

Beverly C. Tyler, president of the Three Village Historic Society, provided invaluable aid and assistance in my research. He provided me with space, in an upstairs room of the historic house which served as the society's headquarters, to house the volumes of tapes, notes, and paper artifacts I was collecting and contributed tidbits of local history. Bev devoted the entire May 1988 issue of the *Journal of the Three Village Historical Society* to "Eel Catching," a beautiful souvenir journal containing photographs and quotes to document my project. The middle section of the journal served as the program for the actual event. Together, we stewed and typed and argued over the layout.

In May 1988, the professional actors came to town. Lynda Gravatt, Lee Dobson, Kenshaka Ali, and Gwendolen Hardwick, together with Stony Brook student performers Jo-Ann Jones, Gerald Latham, Rhonda Lewis, and Michael Manel, and stage manager Anitra Dickerson, spent weeks steeping themselves in the community lore, witnessing the tone and mannerisms of the people we would portray and rehearsing deep into the night, often crashing at my rented house.

Saturday night, before we were all to go to Bethel for Father's Day services Sunday morning, we visited Mrs. Regina Morrison, widow of the former pastor. She told us how God had delivered her from a vast illness. She served us cake and lemonade, lent us a stylish hat (which she modeled) and would not let us escape until we fell to our knees so she could pray over us. We formed a circle, joined hands and went back to Sunday School as she sang

> Spirit of the Living God
> Fall afresh on me.

Jo-Ann Johnson and Gerald Latham, two angelic-voiced students, sang this old spiritual during the performance as other actors read aloud the names from each stained-glass window and pew in Bethel, along with the year of dedication by the family which had purchased it. Mrs. Morrison saw herself portrayed to a saucy turn by Lynda Gravatt, but died soon after I left Stony Brook. My daughter represented me at her funeral, a magnificent homegoing put on by the congregation of Bethel A.M.E. Church.

From all the Sisters of Bethel who were to be represented in the drama, I had the actors coax church hats and missionary white lace handkerchiefs to wear from scene to scene.

Finally 22 June 1988 arrived and all was ready. Before being bussed to the black box to witness the drama, the audience took a guided stroll through the community with Bev Tyler and me. At the beginning of the tour, I read from the souvenir journal inviting them to become "eel catchers":

> An Eel Catcher is a person who loves people and old pictures and history and characters and folklore and drama and textures and art and fun and laughter and doesn't mind experiencing them all at one time.

Each evening during the walking tour, I picked flowers from Lucy Keyes's garden. When we returned to the black box to see the performance, I presented the flowers to Linda Gravatt who stood in a canoe holding a real eel spear – borrowed from Bev Tyler's brother-in-law – frozen in a tableau which conjured up Mount's painting. At that moment the painting came to life and addressed the audience. At that moment, the Christian Avenue community dwellers, past and present, sprang into visibility.

> Now step this way and I will learn you how to see and catch eels. Steady there at the stern and move the boat according to the direction of my spear. Slow now, we are coming on the ground. On sandy and gravelly bottoms are found the best fish![2]

And we were off! From there the audience, who never sat down, followed a swirling travel of vignettes spoken out in the midst of community artifacts which documented that particular story. Both actors and audience rested for only moments on their journey through time. Periodically the actors would freeze in tableaux of other William Sidney Mount paintings on display such as "The Banjo Player" and "Farmer's Nooning." Great huge slides hung in the air in an ever-changing tapestry.

We enacted the history of the African Methodist Episcopal Church from Richard Allen down through all the pastors of Bethel, ending with Reverend Raynor's Fathers' Day sermon which he had just preached the previous Sunday. Lee Dobson portrayed each of the pastors in turn. Reverend Raynor was just dumbfounded and the audience could not believe their eyes when Lee Dobson put on a pair of shades and mimicked exactly the rakish pose revealed in the big slide of Reverend Raynor which hung over his head. One former pastor, Reverend McKenzie, who had left Bethel under a cloud and required much persuading to attend the event, buried his face in a big white handkerchief when he heard his words (I had salvaged them from an old souvenir program), and wept aloud for the duration of the speech.

> This is a crowning experience for a beautiful dream come true. It is a moment of great joy and pride, yet filled with deep humility.
>
> (Reverend Albert McKenzie)

GUIDE TO EXPERIENCING THE EXHIBIT

This is an invitation to become an Eel Catcher. An Eel Catcher is a person who loves people and old pictures and history and characters and folklore and drama and textures and art and fun and laughter and doesn't mind experiencing them all at one time.

From June 22–25, 1988, Eel Catchers will be able to enter into the magic circle of Christian Avenue.

6:00–6:30	Eel Catchers will gather at SUNY/Stony Brook and be driven by bus to Christian Avenue for an introduction to and brief history of the community.
6:30–8:00	Eel Catchers will walk along Christian Avenue to see the major sites such as Bethel A.M.E. Church (which has worshipped on the same site for 114 years) and say a prayer with Rev. Melvin Rayner: the Irving Hart Legion Post to sample a traditional dish and meet Post commander, Theodore Green and other Christian Avenuers like 88-year-old Lucy Keyes; and Bethel and Laurel cemeteries where the ancestors of Harts and Sells and other early family names are buried.
8:00	Bus back to Theatre Arts Department.
8:30–10:00	Eel catchers will visit the living exhibition which illuminates and dramatizes the Christian Avenue community. The living exhibit will feature community artifacts such as hairdressing utensils, church hats, old crystal, sepia-toned photographs, and church pews; here also Eel Catchers will hear the stories of Christian Avenuers they just met as well as the stories of Rachel Holland Hart, the foremother of Christian Avenue, "bad nigger" Pete Tucker and root doctor Levi Phllips.

WON'T YOU COME AND BE AN EEL CATCHER TOO?

Figure 14 "Eel Catching in Setauket," from the souvenir issue of the *Journal of the Three Village Historical Society* (May 1988).

Lee Dobson's eyes rolled in his head and big beads of sweat stood on his forehead as the old preacher wept, but he did not break character. Mysterious chills and shivers ran through the crowd. The old people intoned in an undercurrent, "just hold to his hand, to God's unchanging hand" and murmered – in benediction – "amen."

Lucy Keyes, with the other elders, sat on church pews in the middle of the performance space. When time came for her story to be told, Kenshaka Ali, in the persona of Levi Phillips the Root Doctor, escorted her to an arrangement of her own Queen Anne dining-room table and crystal inherited from her grandmother. Gwendolen Hardwick sat at one end of the table and Mrs. Keyes at the other. When Gwendolen quoted Mrs. Keyes, punctuating her lines with Lucy's famous refrain – and I'm 88 –

she would turn to Mrs. Keyes and Lucy would smile and say "that's right," blessing and sanctifying the story. By the second night, Lucy Keyes didn't wait for her escort. She walked to her space by herself, to relish again the Richmond reunion she had only heard of before. As Lynda and Gwendolen, the actors portraying her mother and grandmother, embraced, our eyes filled with rears. We were all returned to our mothers' bosoms. We were children again. The frozen tableau took on biblical dimensions.

In the magical space created by concrete birdbaths, crystal, sepia photographs, church hats and lace handkerchiefs, old furniture, baseball gloves, and grave-digging shovels, Lucy Agnes Hart Keyes sat in a place of honor, witness to the grandeur of her life.

In my vision, today's residents of Christian Avenue are one with the eelers and other workers who first came to Setauket, not voluntarily, and stayed to make history. In my vision, the autumnal elders will live in eternal Indian summer, safe in the magic circle. In my vision, Rachel Hart rests easy as she spears her eels and tosses them into my basket.

Wishes

> The poem the song the picture
> Are only water taken from the well of the people
> And should be given back to them in a cup of beauty
> That they may drink and in drinking come to understand themselves.
> ——Frederico Garcia Lorca

I worked for a time in Newark, New Jersey, called by Mayor Sharpe James the Renaissance City. I worked for a time on an ambitious project, "Wellwater: Wishes and Words," an oral history project which would create a living portrait of Newark and her people. The portrait was to be drawn from stories told by Newark community dwellers and focus on their dreams, wishes, and aspirations.

Part of the community outreach program of the Department of Theater Arts and Speech at Rutgers University Campus at Newark, where I was chair, the project began in 1989, collecting videotaped oral histories at such sites as North Ward Center, the Northern State Prison and the Straight and Narrow Drug Rehabilitation Center for Kids. My wish was to illuminate Newark's rich history and culture, exploring her diversity and discovering how she fell so low from her rich beginnings.

I began researching the old steamboats, the old trains. I read about the fiery frustration that torched the city. About the invisible people who tried to burn her at the stake. But she refused to die. Now she lies about like a slattern, sleeping until noon, trying to regrow her singed hair and graft new skin to cover her scars. Like Maria Hanson, she hawks self-protection devices for a living. And the Renaissance City is stubborn as Sapphire. My prying fingers could not force her mouth open. She holds her secrets close and is close-mouthed about her checkered past. She would not yield her talkstory to me.

I wound up with a work-in-progress at the Newark Public Library on Monday, 28 October 1991. The excerpt was performed by a combination of student and professional actors, two of whom had spent their youth in Newark. The evening's program began with a documentary made from the videotaped interviews at the above-named sites. The play scrap, augmented by slides of familiar Newark sites, including epitaphs from the stones and markers in the Mount Pleasant Cemetery, featured dramatized stories from three sources: memories of the two actors who grew up in Newark; a book edited by Rutgers professor Audrey Faulknes, Wendell Holbrook *et al.*, entitled *When I Was Comin' Up, An Oral History of Aged Blacks* (1982, Hamden, CT, Archon Books); and oral histories gathered through the New Jersey Historical Society, donated by Dr. Giles Wright, curator.

With the excerpt from "Wellwater," we wellwishers helped the Renaissance City celebrate her 325th Anniversary. Then I walked away from Newark forever.

> I've traveled a lot, so I've roamed all over. Ain't many places that I haven't been. I've traveled there – down in the Islands – the West Indies Islands and I've been to the Hawaiian Islands . . . like I can't stop.
>
> (Lucy Keyes)

> Road, road, road, O!
> On that no'thern road.

I walked away from my Renaissance Sister to train women warriors at Spelman College to dance with swords in their hands. To a city where Native Americans protest a development complex being built on their burial ground:

> The commission was asked to curtail plans for a 372 home subdivision on 187 acres in Dacula because on the parcel are some 200 ancient Indian burial mounds. The rest of the land could be used for housing but each mound must be protected by a six foot chain link fence, before building permits would be issued.

> This is our cemetery. If this was Arlington Cemetery . . . They're not going to pin a fence around Jackie Kennedy's grave now and start building subdivisions . . . It's like allowing a soccer game in a cemetery.[3]

I imagine the red ghosts of the First people, hovering about the chain link fence, wondering among themselves if the grave-robbing contractor, who protests (in Wiechard's article) that he always does things by the rules, follows the letter of the law, ever heard of the interior tribes of the West Coast of Africa who say that however great a thief a man may be, he will not steal from a grave. "The covered mirror will lie there and waste in the rain, and the valuable garment will flap itself to rags in the wind, but human hands will not touch them."[4]

To a city where Mammy stands glowering in regal splendor next to Scarlett O'Hara, ready to march through America like Sherman through Georgia.

To the city where the marta (moving Africans rapidly through Atlanta) is my transportation of choice. On a train going to Lenox Mall, a huge crowd of beer-soaked white guys coming from a game at the Georgia Dome, loaded into my car. I am the only Black person in the car. A picked pocket is discovered. I feel right. I cannot wait for the suspicious eye to turn my way so I can launch into a sermon about the space race in America.

Blue moon over Ibo Landing

> "Alexanduh say he could fly. He say all his family in Africa could fly."
> —Floyd White, *Drums and Shadows*, p. 177

It is October and November on Ibo Landing. The blue moon hangs in anticipation as the shadow of the earth approaches shyly, hungrily, to nibble her into darkness. The great wide pointed belly of Gaia rises in a taut mound out of her primeval lap. She is etched in bas-relief against the crystal night sky. Her thighs fall open in ecstasy. Her arms stretch back beyond the horizon, calling her soul to come see. And on her navel sits a Black woman, firmly held in place by her umbilicus, looking everywhere, seeing everything, gobbling greedy gulps of out/her space.

The stories of the painter, the eel catcher, and the wellwishers are haphazardly documented. Some with audio, some with video, some with handwritten note cards. I am the documentation. Within my body I hold the voices, sights, sounds, songs, that constitute the lives of these invisible people as they were told to me. Like Christian Avenue's Theodore Green I can remember if they move the monument.

Some Black women I know, such as Anabelle (Lee) Washington, Rachel Holland Hart, Lucy Hart Keyes, never have to get out of the way again. They can walk anywhere they want to. They have a space for their own Blackreality. The sassy, sacred space created when I put their talkstories up for the world to see and for they themselves to witness. It is like the moment in a *vodun* ceremony when the Mambo raises her skirt above her head and hollers, "If you would look upon life, it is here to see!" in creating drama from oral history I pay homage to my ancestors while praising my living kin.

"The reception of the soul of the deceased in spiritland and his final prestige are altogether dependent on the grandeur and liberality of the human entertainment" (Leonard, *Lower Niger*, pp. 157–8). Gravesites of all the wandering ghosts, wherever they may be, call to me to honor their dead, to remind and to re/member. To celebrate their lives and the lives of their descendants with grandeur and liberality. And to sanctify the space so sullied by the obscene festivities enacted over their heads. So, like the griots of old, I dress up in my finery, silk, and spun gold, and prepare myself with meditation and prayer for Toh-fo (one lost),[5] a ceremony held when a person has met with death, for instance by drowning, and the body cannot he recovered. I dance with my sword in my hand as the sanctified spirits gather from all the places of invisibility, staring at each other with deep drinks of recognition. I fight to sing their praises, to keep alive their voices, to make them visible. I jubilate as I pour libation on the sacred graves of the dead.

I continue on the northbound road.

Notes

1   From "Bound No'th Blues," in *Selected Poems* by Langston Hughes, copyright 1927 by Alfred A. Knopf and renewed 1955 by Langston Hughes. Reprinted by permission of the publisher.

2   The quote is from a poem, "Golgotha Is a Mountain" by Arna Bontemps, in *The Poetry of the Negro, 1746–1949*, ed. Langston Hughes and Arna Bontemps (Garden City, New York: Doubleday & Co., 1949).

3   Georgia Writers' Project (1986, c.1940) *Drums and Shadows, Survival Studies Among the Georgia Coastal Negroes*, Athens, GA: The University of Georgia Press, p. 185.

4   See Buddy Sullivan, *Early Days on the Georgia Tidewater* (McIntosh County, GA,: Board of Commissioners, 1990), p. 16.

5   The words of the painter quoted in this section are from tape-recorded interviews with Annabelle (Lee) Washington on separate occasions over a four-day period in August 1992 on St. Simons Island.

CHAPTER 29

Eugene van Erven

Philippine community theatre in the 1990s*

DAY THREE: EXPOSURE

On Wednesday morning the group leaves at 7.30 a.m. to visit two inland riverside communities, Sitio Ogbac and Binunga, which have been devastated by the mining disaster. The two PRRM participants in the PETA workshop have secured permission for the visit from the village leaders. The trip, by borrowed bus, takes about an hour, partly over badly damaged dirt roads. The participants are divided into two groups and before they embark on their exploration, Ernie gives them some final instructions on how to conduct their interviews. He tells them to be sensitive and not just record people's stories but also smells, sounds, and visuals. In addition, he asks them to bring back an object from the site: a stone, a broken plate, or an old can; anything that might carry some symbolic meaning. The participants work in pairs, one conducting the interview and the other taking notes. Ernie finally reminds them that they are collecting raw materials for a theatre performance that should benefit Marinduque. They should, therefore, not forget to invite the people they interview to come to the show on Saturday.

THE FIELD TRIP TURNS OUT to be a rewarding experience with the villagers more than willing to talk. As they eat their lunch in the bus on the way back to the primary school, the participants enthusiastically exchange stories they heard. Back in the workshop venue, Dessa first takes them through a movement exercise called 'Follow the Leader', for which she uses a tape recording of 'Bathala', a popular environmental awareness song by Joey Ayala. Divided into groups of four and spatially

Figure 15 Cast of the play *Ginto sa Ilan, Putik sa Karamihan* ('Gold for the Few, Mud for the Many'), which was developed by youngsters from Marinduque island under guidance of professional artists from Manila, Boac, the Philippines, May 1997.

Photo: Eugene van Erven.

arranged in the shape of a diamond, one person in each group invents movements to the music, which the other three are supposed to follow. Rotating to the top of the diamond, each participants gets a chance to choreograph a dance.

AFTER THE EXPOSURE

The rest of the afternoon is devoted to creatively processing impressions from the exposure trip. Each participant makes a visual arts collage on a large sheet of paper, using newspaper clippings, colouring pencils, and the symbolic objects they have brought back from the exposure site. It gives them a chance to reflect on the experience. They each take turns explaining their art work to the rest of the group and then get half an hour to compose collective collages in four groups. As they present these, the germs of some stories emerge. They get another half hour to work out the story line of these embryonic plots and then present them, with a beginning, middle and end, to the others in the form of dramatic improvisations. One of these features an old man, Luis, who talks about how many fish he used to catch in the Boac River and how sorry he is for his grandchildren, who will now no longer be able to experience this. Another story is about Mang Roger, a Marcopper employee who remembers how one day his supervisor, engineer Cruz, warned him way before the disaster happened never to drink from the local pump nor to build his house near the low-lying areas, because the soil and the water there were already contaminated.

Day four

Feeling the time pressure, the group has agreed to start an hour earlier. They begin their warm-up at 8 a.m. The creative work of that day begins with a brainstorming session about the theatrical form they want to use for their production. Since they have to perform in the open air and will not have money for a good sound system, realism, which works best in intimate indoor settings, may not be so appropriate. The group decides to compromise and to alternate realistic scenes with some music and dance numbers to cater to the Filipino hunger for theatrical spectacle. They each sign up for a writers pool, a music pool, a movement pool, and a design pool to divide the artistic responsibilities for the show. They proceed to discuss a possible script outline and soon agree that the play should start with the opening of the mine back in the 1960s and the recruitment of local workers, followed by the disaster and the effects on the inland communities. The performance should end, they feel, with some kind of people's protest. They want to use Joey Avala's song 'Bathala' to weave together the different components, but, Dessa explains, 'We insisted that they also put in something local. That's how they came up with the idea to put in three different versions of the *putong*, the traditional Marinduque welcoming song, to accentuate the three different moods of the play: peace, lament, and defiance.'

The group covers a lot of ground that Thursday morning, sketching the contours of what will become the eventual scenario. They determine that Mang Roger, two village children, and a clairvoyant, Lydia, will become their main characters. Their research had revealed that a child had been hospitalized after eating fish from the contaminated river and Lydia, they explain to the PETA team, is an actual person living in the bush near the Malindig volcano. She roams around the island warning everyone about a mythical Golden Calf that lies buried in the mountains and which, when greedy people who dig for it reach its horns, will cause Marinduque to disappear. 'This story fascinated me,' Ernie told me later in Manila, 'for it gave the story of the mine – digging for a golden calf – a metaphysical quality with biblical overtones, while still remaining true to the stories of the people that we had interviewed. We did use the actual works of Mang Roger and the children.'

Once the entire group has agreed on the order of the episodes, they begin to flesh them out, working in four separate groups. By lunch time, the dance prologue and the opening vignettes are already done. The rest of the day they improvise the remaining scenes, selecting the best bits for consolidation in a preliminary script. There is now intensive activity all over the school compound: outside some participants are writing a poem for the chorus under a picnic shelter, while others rehearse scenes inside or in some vacant corner at the back of the main venue. At nightfall, the group performs all the scenes they have created that day. While most of the actors go home, the writers continue working on the script until the early hours of the morning.

Day five

As usual, the day begins with a full body and voice warm-up followed by a recapitulation of the previous day and the assignment of a new 'O-A-O team', Edwin, the stage manager, then chairs a production meeting, expertly talking the entire cast through the blocking and the set and prop requirements for each of the episodes. The rest of the morning is spent on improving and mounting the scenes they had been unable to complete the previous day. After lunch, the group splits up to work in separate groups again. Ernie and Dessa now emphatically take charge as co-directors, coaching the actors on line delivery, reacting to cues, and timing entrance and exits.

At 3 p.m., the group travels by public transportation to downtown Boac to do a complete run-through on the stage of the covered basketball court, which doubles as the town's main square. However, an official basketball tournament, complete with whistle-blowing referees and amplified play-by-play commentators, makes rehearsing practically impossible. Ernie is not easily flustered: in the Marcos days he pulled off countless performances during black-outs, improvising stage lighting with car headlights, oil lamps, or even by burning dried waterbuffalo turds. So, while the basketball match goes on he and the group explore the stage, adjust the blocking, try out the opening dance with the fabric they have brought along, and walk through all the episodes. Afterwards, they sit down to listen to Ernie's director's notes, in which he hammers mostly on insufficient voice projection and concentration. 'You have a good message to give to your people, but if they can't hear you what's the point?'

Day six

About half the group has stayed overnight at Eli's house to continue preparing props and costumes. Over breakfast, before the video camera, Ernie looks ahead at what is still to come:

> Yesterday we did the blocking on the stage where we will perform, and even though they know the order of the play, they missed their lines and cues and their voices were too soft. So, today we have to really work hard on voice projection and scene polishing, plus of course production: we still don't have all the props we need. We will have a costume parade to see if what they have is appropriate for their characters. It may seem that the facilitators come out as always critiquing what they are doing, but we have to do that so that they will raise their aesthetics. We feel that they have the capacity. That's why yesterday we gave them an exercise,

'*Ako ay magaling*' ('I am god'), to give them more confidence, because there are at least four or five who are still quite inhibited.

Dessa opens the morning session with a thorough work-out consisting of a full body stretch followed by an elaborate series of vocal exercises specifically geared to improve voice projection and concentration. Then they rehearse the new scenes, try on the costumes, and do one more complete run-through before going to the basketball court. After trying to attach the backdrops, Eli realizes that the electric cables are not long enough to connect the PA system and the lone follow spot (which constitute the only available lighting) to the power point. With less than an hour to go, they are forced to move the acting area down to the basketball floor. By 7 p.m. about two hundred people have gathered to watch the show, including a handful from the two *barrios* the workshop participants had visited for exposure.

The performance

The play, now entitled *Ginto sa lilan, Putik sa Karamihan* ('Gold for the Few, Mud for the Many'), opens with a striking movement piece to express the Marcopper spill. Harold Miciano pulls a long yellow cloth, representing the tailings, through a tunnel of white material held open by two other actors with their hands and feet, after which the cast presents brief snap shots of what is to come. First we see a family packing up in a panic to flee from the flood, then two children who get sick from the river, the clairvoyant who announces further disasters, and a farmer whose crop no longer grows. The entire cast then dance to 'Barthala' to conclude the prologue.

The first full scene takes us back to the past: Canadian Marcopper officials are being welcomed to the island as saviours with a traditional *putong* ritual. A chorus, which accompanies all the scene transitions, then imitates the sound of bulldozers and drills before reciting a stanza about local people being kept in the dark about the environmental damage caused by the mine. The next scene, about Roger being warned by engineer Cruz not to build on low-lying land, is taken almost verbatim from the exposure trip. It is again followed by the chorus, which now exhorts the audience not to believe Marcopper's promises to clean up and recompense. The chorus makes way for a strong solo by a priest figure, acted by Rommel Doria, whose pro-environment speech is rudely interrupted by angry Marcopper workers who urge him to stop his militant talk because they fear it will cost them their jobs. They gang up on the priest and freeze as the chorus comes back on to recite another stanza about a child who has lost his natural playground, which is immediately followed by a scene of two children playing on the contaminated river bank.

Thus, the Balangaw actors continue to string together realistic scenes interspersed with verses form their collectively composed choral poem. Many of the scenes feature disaster victims being fooled by medical doctors, mine officials, or local politicians. The clairvoyant, impressively performed by Jeanet Legaspi, provides the play's turning point by singing a lamentful *putong* about disease and suffering, while other members of the cast place candles around the stage.

The next three scenes are long solos, all based on verbatim material from the exposure trip. The first one, acted confidently by Laurence Sadiwa, features a fisherman named Luis who talks about how easy it used to be to fish in the river but that now he cannot catch anything any more. He can no longer pay the school fees nor indeed buy medication to treat his young son's fever. The second solo is for a visibly nervous Dennis Majaba, one of the PRRM participants. He plays a farmer named Cardo, who talks about his little daughter who died. In the third solo Rayleen Rey plays 'Lena', whose husband, a fisherman, died in a factory accident in Manila after he had to leave the island to find work.

Although content-wise the solos are moving, they are overly long and, with the exception of the first, not really acted strongly enough to hold up in the large basketball court. But the chorus manages to pick up the energy with a militantly sung *putong*, while individual actors step forward to tell the audience their personal resolutions to make a better future for Marinduque: one wants to become a human rights lawyer, another a social worker, and a third a doctor. Finally, the entire cast, holding pro-environment placards and singing the national anthem, exhort the audience to unite and fight.

Evaluation

After the show, Ernie takes the microphone to tell the audience that the play they have seen is the result of a five-day workshop with members of Teatro Balangaw and artist-teachers from PETA and that they dedicate the performance to all the people of Marinduque. Melo Miciano, Harold's and Hajun's father, tells me he is proud of his sons and expresses the hope that they will perform the play in other Marinduque communities as well. Several unidentified local environmental activists comment that they equally enjoyed it and that they noticed that a lot of the factual information in the play was new to the audience:

> Many people from Boac town have never been up to the *barrio*. They know about it, generally, but don't seem to care. Looking around me I also noticed how people tuned in to the entertainment elements in the show, but tuned off during the more serious parts. But this kind of theatre is good; it will draw people's attention, like fish to a bait.

While some audience members continue the discussion, the cast and facilitators sit down in a circle to evaluate the week's work. Each participant gets a chance to speak, but most of their comments do not go beyond expressing thanks and sadness that the workshop is over. Ernie and Dessa reaffirm their commitment to return to the island. Trina Malaga, the Marinduque PRRM coordinator, is clearly impressed with the effects of PETA's methods on the participants: 'I notice that their faces are bright and that the experience has built up their confidence, that it has challenged them to go further.' Eli Obligacion is equally pleased: 'Teachers had already told me that the young people in Teatro Balangaw had become more disciplined and responsible through our theatre. But it's incredible what the PETA team has managed to create here in only one week.'

Back in Manila, both Dessa and Ernie regret there was too much performance pressure on the participants. It would have been better, they agree, to create a simpler production for a low-key performance in the workshop venue or in the sites they had visited for the exposure. This would have allowed them to spend more time on genuinely empowering the participants, some of whom continued to be nervous or inhibited until the end. Dessa had noticed that before PETA's intervention Teatro Balangaw's artistic process had been quite top-down:

> Experience in improvisation and awareness of the creative process will give the actors the basis for evolving from here. Quite a number of them, especially those in the writers' pool, now look ready to take on larger responsibilities. They are the ones that would qualify for trainer's training in a Level Three Workshop, which will teach them how to create their own plays and start other youth groups here.

But the initiative for advanced training should come from the participants themselves and, unfortunately to date no Balangaw members have applied. The group did, however, perform their Marcopper play in several other Marinduque communities and Ernie has returned to the island once for further consultations. In December 1998, Teatro Balangaw participated once again in PETA's annual festival, but the group continues to be overtly reliant on Eli Obligacion's energy and resources.

Judging by the Marinduque workshop, then, PETA's BITAW method is a transparent and effective way to create community plays with youth groups in the rural Philippines. I have also seen it work well with different age groups in the big cities and, outside the Philippines, with Philippine migrants as well as with art academy and university students. Still, the BITAW is not some magic formula that will automatically yield positive results wherever it is implemented. Its success relies heavily on the personalities of the artist-teachers guiding the creative process. Their interventions are more likely to be effective when they possess extensive prior knowledge of the circumstances they are going to work in, when they have sufficient pedagogical expertise to design workshop syllabi and the didactic skills to implement them. But most helpful of all are flexibility, charm, and energy, qualities that are well-nigh impossible to learn.

Note

* Community theatre workshop with the Teatro Balangaw, Boac, Marinduque, Philippines, an area that has to deal with toxic contamination from open-pit copper mining. PETA refers to the Philippines Educational Theater Association, PRRM to the Philippines Rural Reconstruction Movement.

Internet connection

PETA e-mail: peta@drama.com.ph

Index

Disability and Contemporary Performance: Bodies on Edge

Petra Kuppers

Disability and Contemporary Performance presents a remarkable challenge to existing assumptions about disability and artistic practice. In particular, it explores where cultural knowledge about disability leaves off, and the lived experience of difference begins. Petra Kuppers, herself an award-winning artist and theorist, investigates the ways in which disabled performers challenge, change and work with current stereotypes through their work. She explores freak show fantasies and 'medical theatre' as well as live art, webwork, theatre, dance, photography and installations, to cast an entirely new light on contemporary identity politics and aesthetics.

This is an outstanding exploration of some of the most pressing issues in performance, cultural and disability studies today, written by a leading practitioner and critic.

ISBN13: 978–0–415–30238–8 (hbk)
ISBN13: 978–0–415–30239–5 (pbk)